THE TRANSFER AND DIFFUSION OF INFORMATION TECHNOLOGY FOR ORGANIZATIONAL RESILIENCE

T0189253

IFIP – The International Federation for Information Processing

IFIP was founded in 1960 under the auspices of UNESCO, following the First World Computer Congress held in Paris the previous year. An umbrella organization for societies working in information processing, IFIP's aim is two-fold: to support information processing within its member countries and to encourage technology transfer to developing nations. As its mission statement clearly states,

> *IFIP's mission is to be the leading, truly international, apolitical organization which encourages and assists in the development, exploitation and application of information technology for the benefit of all people.*

IFIP is a non-profitmaking organization, run almost solely by 2500 volunteers. It operates through a number of technical committees, which organize events and publications. IFIP's events range from an international congress to local seminars, but the most important are:

• The IFIP World Computer Congress, held every second year;
• Open conferences;
• Working conferences.

The flagship event is the IFIP World Computer Congress, at which both invited and contributed papers are presented. Contributed papers are rigorously refereed and the rejection rate is high.

As with the Congress, participation in the open conferences is open to all and papers may be invited or submitted. Again, submitted papers are stringently refereed.

The working conferences are structured differently. They are usually run by a working group and attendance is small and by invitation only. Their purpose is to create an atmosphere conducive to innovation and development. Refereeing is less rigorous and papers are subjected to extensive group discussion.

Publications arising from IFIP events vary. The papers presented at the IFIP World Computer Congress and at open conferences are published as conference proceedings, while the results of the working conferences are often published as collections of selected and edited papers.

Any national society whose primary activity is in information may apply to become a full member of IFIP, although full membership is restricted to one society per country. Full members are entitled to vote at the annual General Assembly, National societies preferring a less committed involvement may apply for associate or corresponding membership. Associate members enjoy the same benefits as full members, but without voting rights. Corresponding members are not represented in IFIP bodies. Affiliated membership is open to non-national societies, and individual and honorary membership schemes are also offered.

THE TRANSFER AND DIFFUSION OF INFORMATION TECHNOLOGY FOR ORGANIZATIONAL RESILIENCE

IFIP TC8 WG 8.6 International Working Conference, June 7-10, 2006, Galway, Ireland

Edited by

Brian Donnellan
National University of Ireland, Galway
Galway, Ireland

Tor J. Larsen
Norwegian School of Management
Oslo, Norway

Linda Levine
Software Engineering Institute, Carnegie Mellon University
Pittsburgh, PA USA

Janice I. DeGross
University of Minnesota
Minneapolis, MN USA

 Springer

The Transfer and Diffusion of Information Technology for Organizational Resilience
Edited by B. Donnellan, T. Larsen, L. Levine, and J. DeGross

p. cm. (IFIP International Federation for Information Processing, a Springer Series in Computer Science)

ISSN: 1571-5736 / 1861-2288 (Internet)

ISBN: 13: 978-1-4419-4176-3

Printed on acid-free paper

eISBN: 10: 0-387-34410-1

eISBN: 13: 978-0-387-34410-2

9 8 7 6 5 4 3 2 1
springer.com

Contents

Part 7: Organizational Impact of IS

Part 8: Innovation Cases

Part 9: Keynotes

PREFACE

In a turbulent world where companies are trying to realign their resources faster than the competition, resilience is defined as the capability to absorb strain and recover from untoward events through continuous reconstruction. Resilience implies a capacity to be robust under conditions of stress and change (Coutu 2002). It can be achieved by creating and maintaining cognitive, emotional, relational, or structural capabilities sufficiently convertible and malleable to cope with a dynamic environment. In the competitive marketplace, many countries are making the transition from technology-importing, efficiency-based development to innovation-based development. Organizations located in so-called "first world" economies are increasingly concerned with making local enterprises more resilient in their current geographical location and firms in "third world" economies are keen to establish and retain knowledge-based economic activities.

The focus of this conference is on how IT innovation can contribute to making organizations more resilient. Commercial organizations are trying to make sense of the competitive environment and quickly generate new strategic options. Public organizations are struggling to meet societal needs for innovative information services. IT staff have spent much of their energy improving transactional efficiency. IT now needs to be seen as a positive force for making business innovation resilient. Issues such as IT organizational design, social networking, diversity, improvisation, and rich media are likely to advance our understanding of resilience in this context, and account for an organization's need to sustain innovation. Where firms fail to achieve resilience, the financial and social costs of organizational failure can be high. Many large, reputable firms linger in a coma for years before dying (Meyer and Zucker 1989). Both the United States and Europe are strewn with once-thriving industrial cities severely impacted by the inability of large local enterprises to quickly adapt to new technologies, globalization, or competition.

The path to organizational resilience is a difficult one and can require some fundamental changes in culture and strategy (Välikangas 2004). Managing a resilient corporation requires a willingness to access information from multiple sources for richer content, and to carefully question guidance from those with a vested interest in the status quo. Resilient companies don't simply develop a portfolio of product innovations; they employ experimental strategies, mining ideas from all parts of the company. For example, Nokia refocused the entire company on mobile phones, realizing it had a technology advantage due to its home market in the Nordic countries. Nokia also considered itself a fashion house (rather than a producer of gadgets), which helped to open up a younger market. IBM, today, is an IT powerhouse together with a newly acquired consulting services arm. IBM acknowledges that it is services—not IT—that its clients wish to buy.

Most companies create budgets based on the legacy principle; a resilient solution uses market-based mechanisms to manage resources so that funding of known opportunities is balanced by an appetite for new ventures. Effective organizational governance can be used to provide safeguards against wrongdoing and improve leadership. Directors, feeling the heat from shareholder activists, litigators, and regulators, have to make sure that management has a plan for the future—a plan that doesn't just relive the past.

Sheffi (2005) points out that modern organizations are struggling to build resilience in the face of many turbulent forces. There are disruptions to the means of production. Hazard vulnerabilities include both random disruptions and malicious disruptions such as international terrorism and product tampering. Financial vulnerabilities include a wide range of macro-economic and internal financial troubles from currency exchange fluctuations to credit rating downgrades to irregularities in financial statements. Strategic vulnerabilities include everything from new overseas competitors to public boycotts to ethics violations.

In this turbulent environment, the transfer and diffusion of IT is a critical issue. Enterprise systems are being looked to for assistance in overcoming forecasting problems that are particularly problematic in a rapidly changing economic landscape. Globalization is exerting an influence because supply chains are getting longer, resulting in longer lead times, a need to forecast in advance of sales, and greater communication challenges. Increases in product variety and decreases in product life cycle are resulting in many new products that have no "history." In addition, the sheer volume of new products and increasing variety of existing products mean that each is sold to an ever smaller market segment, which is more sensitive to random variations. Increasing homogeneity of demand is also having an effect: when markets act in unison, the amplitudes of their uncertain fluctuations are larger. Moreover, this trend makes it hard to dump obsolete inventory into secondary markets.

These challenging operating conditions are forcing users of enterprise systems to adopt forecasting methods that address the uncertainties described above. There is greater emphasis on data aggregation. Aggregate forecasts are more accurate than disaggregate forecasts because errors tend to cancel each other out. Time horizons are shortening as the longer a time horizon, the less accurate the forecast. Where possible, there is greater reliance on historical data because forecasting methods rely on history and experience, although when companies enter new markets, data are scarce, making it hard to forecast. There is a growing reliance on trading partners who may have information that can aid forecasting. For instance, retailers can provide data on sales patterns so that suppliers can base their forecasts on actual consumer patterns.

Organizations are also developing behavioral norms that support resilience (Mallik 1998). These organizations are adopting positive adaptive behaviors, rather than programmed responses. They are trying to ensure a steady supply of external resources (e.g., advice, information, finance, and practical help) and are expanding their decision-making boundaries—in terms of ability and authority. Bricolage is being embraced because the ability to fashion a solution on the spot differentiates organizations that are similar on price and quality parameters. There is also a growing tolerance for uncertainty because resilient organizations have the capacity to make good decisions under conditions where the amount of information they have is less than what is desired. IT architects are building virtual systems because a virtual system can provide a work environment where the team can continue in the absence of one or more members.

These researchers all assert the criticality of resilience while emphasizing different issues and views. We ask, is there a common platform or common underpinnings for understanding the need for change and agility, and the dynamics of the change process—including its outcomes, stakeholders, and decision makers? Based on their analysis of 25 innovation efforts, Van de Ven et al. (1999) suggest that complex innovation processes include six major and interacting issues: ideas, people, transaction, context, outcomes, and process. Indeed, these are high level notions, but at present they are the best argued set of change-related issues. We hope that this conference can open a dialogue and move our understanding one step further to identify the major constructs and dynamics in creating and using "resilient" information systems.

This conference will examine some of the critical issues underpinning the current debate on resilience. Themes that will be explored include the role of IT in nurturing resilience, the impact of knowledge exchange on resilience, and how improvisation relates to resilience. The keynote speakers will also focus on three themes that are central to the topic: agility (Bob Galliers), innovation (Liam Bannon), and business resilience in a global economy (Rory OConnor).

Brian Donnellan
Tor J. Larsen
Linda Levine
Janice I. DeGross

References

Coutu, D. "How Resilience Works," *Harvard Business Review* (80:5), May 2002, pp. 46-50.

Hamel, G., and Valikangas, L. "The Quest for Resilience," *Harvard Business Review* (81:9), September 2003, pp. 52-63.

Mallik L. "Putting Organizational Resilience to Work," *Industrial Management*, November-December 1998, pp. 8-13.

Meyer, M. W., and Zucker, L. G. *Permanently Failing Organizations*, Newbury Park, CA: Sage Publications, 1989.

Sheffi, Y. *The Resilient Enterprise: Overcoming Vulnerability for Competitive Advantage*, Cambridge, MA: MIT Press, 2005

Välikangas, L. "Four Steps to Corporate Resilience," *Strategy + Business*, May 24, 2004 (available online at http://www.strategy-business.com/)

Van de Ven, A. H., Polley, D. E., Garud, R., and Venkataraman, S. *The Innovation Journey*, New York: Oxford University Press, 1999.

CONFERENCE CHAIRS

General Chair
Linda Levine
Carnegie Mellon University
Pittsburg, PA U.S.A.

Program Chairs
Brian Donnellan
National University of Ireland
Galway, Ireland

Tor J. Larsen
Norwegian School of Management
Oslo, Norway

Organizing Chair
Willie Golden
National University of Ireland
Galway, Ireland

PROGRAM COMMITTEE

Tom Acton, National University of Ireland, Galway
Par Ågerfalk, University of Limerick, Ireland
Liam Bannon, University of Limerick, Ireland
Frank Bannister, Trinity College, Dublin, Ireland
Chris Barry, National University of Ireland, Galway
Richard Baskerville, Georgia State University, U.S.A.
Deborah Bunker, University of New South Wales, Australia
Tom Butler, University College Cork, Ireland
Michael Cavanagh, Balmoral Consulting, U.K.
Kieran Conboy, National University of Ireland, Galway
Jan Damsgaard, Copenhagen Business School, Denmark
Amany Elbana, London School of Economics, UK
Joe Feller, University College Cork, Ireland
Brian Fitzgerald, University of Limerick
Pat Finnegan, University College Cork, Ireland
Marcus Helfert, Dublin City University, Ireland
Martin Hughes, National University of Ireland, Galway
Helle Zinner Henriksen, Copenhagen Business School
Séamus Hill, National University of Ireland, Galway
Martin Hughes, National University of Ireland, Galway
Karl Kautz, Copenhagen Business School, Denmark
Séamas Kelly, University College Dublin, Ireland
Michael Lang, National University of Ireland, Galway
Moez Limayem, Lausanne University, Switzerland
Jo Lee Loveland Link, Volvox, Inc., U.S.A.
Björn Lundell, University of Skövde, Sweden
Lars Mathiassen, Georgia State University, U.S.A.
Tom McMaster, Salford University, U.K.
Fred Niederman, St. Louis University, U.S.A.
Peter Axel Nielsen, Aalborg University, Denmark
Steve Sawyer, Pennsylvania State University, U.S.A.
Murray Scott, National University of Ireland, Galway
Carsten Sorensen, London School of Economics, U.K.
Richard Veryard, Veryard Projects, U.K.
Richard Vidgen, University of Bath, U.K.
David Wainwright, University of Northumbria, U.K.
David Wastell, Salford University, UK
Edgar Whitley, London School of Economics, U.K.
Bob Zmud, University of Oklahoma, U.S.A.

Part 1

Networks

1 COMPLEX NETWORK-BASED INFORMATION SYSTEMS (CNIS) STANDARDS: Toward an Adoption Model

David Kelly
Joseph Feller
Patrick Finnegan
University College Cork
Cork, Ireland

Abstract   *This paper proposes an adoption model for complex network-based information systems (CNIS) standards which extends current diffusion of innovation theory within a specific technological context, that of ambient intelligence (AmI). The issue of open and closed standards is especially important for networked information systems; however, a range of factors impact the adoption decision and challenge existing models of adoption. Such models are based on DOI theories that have their roots in more simplistic technological innovations. In order to extend the current view on adoption, the adoption context must be closely considered. Agile organizations must constantly survey the external environment to determine the potential of emerging technology. Open standards may make organizations less vulnerable to environmental flux due to uncertainties caused by the lack of transparency of proprietary standards. Accordingly, the proposed model moves toward providing a means to assess factors impacting the adoption of open and proprietary standards.*

Keywords   Emerging IS/IT, diffusion of innovation, standards adoption

1 INTRODUCTION

Organizational agility is based on two attributes: the prompt response to change in appropriate ways, and the ability to capitalize on the opportunities presented by change

Please use the following format when citing this chapter:

Kelly, David, Feller, Joseph, Finnegan, Patrick, 2006, in International Federation for Information Processing (IFIP), Volume 206, The Transfer and Diffusion of Information Technology for Organizational Resilience, eds. B. Donnellan, Larsen T., Levine L., DeGross J. (Boston: Springer), pp. 3-20.

(Sharifi and Zhang 1999). Such changes are often the result of the emergence of new technologies (Thomke and Reinersten 1998). Traditionally, adoption and diffusion theory, such as Rogers' (1962), has been used as a means to explain the adoption issues surrounding external innovations. However, as new forms of network-based information systems become more complex, the role of interoperability standards as a means of enabling development requires careful consideration. Of particular importance is the emergence of the ambient intelligence (AmI) vision, which is based on a convergence of the related concepts, ubiquitous computing, ubiquitous communications, and intelligent user friendly interfaces (Ducatel et al. 2001). The concept of ubiquitous computing first emerged in the early 1990s (Weiser 1991) as a vision in which computers are removed from being objects of conscious attention. Rather than having computers operate in an environment in which people must adapt to them, they are integrated into the human environment.

A range of AmI based application spaces are currently under investigation. One such example is the development of intelligent transport systems (ITS) solutions by NEC (Maekawa 2004). Such systems rely on the integration of large numbers of sensors in the environment and in vehicles (up to 120), with integration occurring through open communications networks in order to provide services such as traffic, weather and road conditions recognition, position-based routing, and pedestrian transport services. Other examples of AmI application areas and usage scenarios are reported by Banavar and Bernstein (2002), Borriello et al.(2005), and Davies and Gellersen (2002).

The development of such systems results in a comparatively higher level of structural system complexity due to the need to integrate multiple heterogeneous devices (Garlan et al. 2002; Henricksen et al. 2001; Nakajima et al. 2002) or other system components (Davies and Gellersen 2002; Henricksen et al. 2001; Islam and Fayad 2003; Lassila 2002). While interoperability standards play a role in facilitating or inhibiting the technical development of systems, they also possess inherent economic and social characteristics which can not only impact their adoption, but also shape the future adoption and diffusion of systems based upon them.

The objective of this paper is to propose a model of open versus closed standards adoption within the context of AmI technologies. In order to clarify the technological context in which such adoption occurs, the paper first develops a categorization of network-based information systems based on their underlying structural complexity and defines three types. Following an examination of existing research on IT standards, existing extensions to DOI theory and the challenges of using such theory to account for adoption issues under certain technological contexts are then discussed. The paper then proposes an extended model for standards adoption, based on existing adoption and diffusion theory. The paper concludes by proposing that the model address issues relevant to the adoption of open or closed technical interoperability standards in the context of emergent complex network-based technologies.

The research approach used in the paper is a literature survey. Literature surveys have been employed by researchers in the past as a means of assessing the current state of the art and structuring existing knowledge. The examination of the history of previous work in an area enables the determination of progress made (Drury and Farhoomand 1999). Their use also enables reflection on what has been achieved in the past, and what work is required in the future to further develop a field of study (Alvai and Carlson 1992). It has been argued that the structured identification of required future research directions is important to conduct on an on-going basis, particularly in an emerging research area (Culnan 1987). Such an approach has been used at both a disciplinary level, for example within Information Systems (Alvai and Carlson 1992; Claver et al. 2000; Chen and Tan 2004; Drury and Farhoomand 1999; Orlikowski and Baroudi 1991), and at a thematic or subfield level (Romano and Fjermestad 2002). Earlier efforts at assessing the state of knowledge within an area (e.g., Information Systems) have limited the sample to a specific number of outlets in order to investigate the methods being used (e.g., Chen and Hirschheim 2004; Drury and Farhoomand 1999) or the paradigmatic focus into which the research falls (e.g., Chen and Hirschheim 2004; Orlikowski and Baroudi 1991). For this study, the review was limited by its aim of identifying studies that used DOI theory in a specific technological innovation context, that of base IT innovations (as per Lyytinen and Rose 2003).

2 COMPLEX NETWORK-BASED INFORMATION SYSTEMS

The use of the term *complex network-based information system* (CNIS) has its roots in complex systems literature. A complex system has been defined as one which is

> made up of a large number of parts that interact in a non-simple way. In such systems, the whole is more than the sum of the parts....[and], given the properties of the parts and the laws of their interaction, it is not a trivial matter to infer the properties of the whole (Simon 1962, p. 468).

The complexity within such a system arises from the number of distinct parts of the system (Cilliers 1998; Langlois 2002), and the nature and number of interactions between these parts (Cilliers 1998; Ethiraj and Levinthal 2004; Langlois 2002). Following this logic, the classification of CNIS according to its structural complexity, similar to Lee and Xia (2002), is proposed as occurring along two dimensions as illustrated in Figure 1. The first of these dimensions is the scope of interactions that occur within the system as facilitated by the infrastructure upon which the system is based. Infrastructure in this context is defined from a technical perspective as being the basic support systems shared among users (Sirkemaa 2002). It thus includes technologies that provide data storage, system integration, connectivity, and security (Kumar 2004) as well as a capability for shared IT services implementation (Chung et al. 2003). A key characteristic of a complex system is dynamic, nonlinear interaction (Cilliers 1998). From an information systems perspective, one level of system complexity within a network-based IS can be seen in the level of complexity of the technical infrastructure used to support its interactions (i.e., business applications and services).

The second dimension used in the classification is the magnitude of the number of elements involved in the system (Cilliers 1998; Simon 1962). In IS, these elements correspond to both the business services and their enabling hardware elements, which interact throughout the system. The term *services* here is used in place of *applications* in order to signify a higher level of granularity (Lyytinen et al. 1998) from which the varied processes of the business performed (Chung et al. 2003) are being viewed.

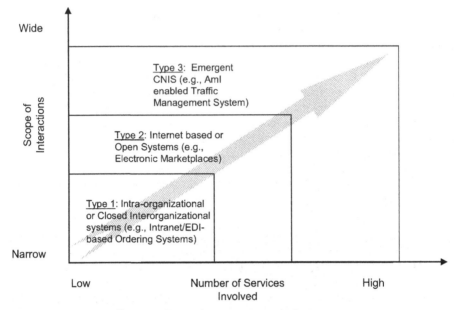

Note: The grey arrow illustrates increasing system complexity.

Figure 1. Dimensions of Structural Complexity in Network Information Systems

The application of these dimensions of complexity to network-based information systems can be seen in Figure 1, where three types of IS are represented visually as an illustration of the overlap between and changing complexity of IS of different types. The positioning of each type of IS is based on characteristics inherent in the system's design and evolution, namely, the addition of elements and the technical IT infrastructures required to facilitate element interactions. This classification offers an alternative perspective of IS by focusing on the underlying structure, rather than classification based on the types of IS users involved or the application domains. Such a perspective is useful in this context as it highlights issues relating to the underlying composition of the system, such as the role of standards.

Type 1 network IS shows the characterization of intra-organizational systems and closed interorganizational systems as having the lowest comparative level of structural complexity. The implementation of intra-organizational systems can lead to a degree of complexity. However, a degree of control can be exerted as the implementation is limited to a single organizational setting. This control is possible due to the knowledge held by those implementing the system (i.e., management services or technology vendor) and the confined nature of the system itself. Closed interorganizational systems, such as EDI-based systems, are also categorized as Type 1 due to their comparatively low level of structural complexity. This lower level of complexity is evident from the scale and type of interactions present in such networks (i.e., primarily point-to-point), as discussed by Christiaanse et al. (2004).

Type 2 systems have a higher comparative level of structural complexity. In practical terms, such systems are implemented as Internet-based or other forms of open systems that allow the ad hoc addition of network elements. The ability to facilitate ad hoc expansion requires an underlying infrastructure capable of high levels of dynamic nonlinear interaction in order to function. In the case of open systems, such an infrastructure is enabled through the use of compatibility standards and modularity in system design.

Type 3 systems have the highest comparative level of structural complexity, and are labeled complex network-based information systems (CNIS). It is within this category that emerging IS/IT supporting ambient intelligence are positioned. CNIS are based on the integration of a variety of heterogeneous technical infrastructures in order to provide a high number of services, for example, the use of multiple network communications protocols to provide a platform for multiple integrated services to users.

The structural complexity of CNIS to support AmI is evident from key features such as mobility, unobtrusiveness, and context awareness, resulting in the need for high levels of interaction and large numbers of services, as illustrated in Table 1. Mobility enables the user to move seamlessly through the environment with services changing depending on the users location (Lyytinen and Yoo 2002). Unobtrusiveness is achieved through the removal of the computer from the user's conscious attention (Abowd and Mynatt 2000; Ducatel et al. 2001). Contextual awareness refers to applications that are capable of altering their behavior in response to contextual information from the user (Abowd et al. 2002; Prekop and Burnett 2003). Interoperability standards are required to facilitate the development of such structurally complex systems. Thus diffusion theories and adoption models must consider such standards as base IT innovations.

3 TECHNICAL, BUSINESS, AND SOCIAL PERSPECTIVES ON STANDARDS

Standards as base IT innovations are the underlying technologies used by IS service providers and are antecedents to innovation in the other classifications (Lyytinen and Rose 2003).

Research in the area of standards has taken place from a variety of perspectives, with differing views of the role and impacts felt by standards adoption. Although not always mutually exclusive, these perspectives can be broadly classified as falling into one of three categories: technical, business and economic, or social. It has become evident that the integration of these perspectives is particularly important in relation to the adoption of standards for CNIS. The need for such a combined view emerges from the fact that reliance on one perspective alone can give an incomplete or inaccurate picture of how the complex issues interact (Iversen 2001; Williams 1999).

From a technical perspective, the role of standards is viewed primarily as a means of facilitating interoperability throughout a system (e.g., Christiaanse et al. 2004; Chung et al. 2003; Damsgaard and Truex 2000; Sirkemaa 2002; Strand et al. 1994), and enabling system scalability in the later stages of the technology's diffusion (Helal 2005; Strand et al. 1994). Stegwee and Rukanova (2003) identify three levels of technical interoperability standards. First, interconnectivity standards enable systems to commu-

Table 1. CNIS to Support Ambient Intelligence

CNIS Characteristics			
		Large Number of Elements	**Wide Scope of Interaction**
Ambient Intelligence Characteristics	Context Awareness	Enabled by information from combinations of sources, for example, human and software agent actors, RFID systems, environmental systems (e.g., sensor networks, CCTV), location aware systems (e.g., GPS, GSM), distributed databases, ambient displays.	• Requires interaction between geographically and technologically distinct system elements (Boddupalli et al. 2003). • Dynamic Interaction between elements required to allow changing inter-actions depending on services required.
	Mobility	Enabled by use of multiple communications systems depending on requirements (e.g., GPRS, Wi-Fi, Bluetooth).	Dynamic interaction between elements required to allow switching between multiple communications protocols depending on requirements of the user/system.
	Unobtrusiveness	Provision of unobtrusive/ uninterrupted services requires large numbers of elements embedded in the environment to allow con-sistent access to enabling systems (e.g., those described as enabling Context Awareness above).	Supports constant service access within and between environments .

nicate with each other at the network level (i.e., communication standards such as TCP/IP). Second, interchangeability standards enable systems to exchange information at the presentation level (i.e., data representation standards such as ASCII, HTML, and XML). Final interoperability standards (see also Sprott 2000; Strand et al. 1994) enable systems to operate together as one through interoperability at the application level (i.e., interaction standards such as SOAP and SMTP). Technical interoperability standards can also be classified according to the "level of openness" (West 2004). Table 2 sum-marizes the differences between the development of open and closed standards. It would be inaccurate to assume that all open or all closed standards meet all criteria within the table as standards are best placed along an open–closed continuum.

The business and economic perspective on standards-oriented research puts forward the dominant view of the roles and impacts of standards. In the development stage of new technologies, this perspective has focused on the role and impact of standards on

Table 2. Characteristics of Open Versus Closed Standard Development (Adapted from Krechmer 2005)

	Completely Open Standard	**Completely Closed Standard**
Barriers to participation	No	Yes
Discussion of interests and agreement found	Yes	Between members
Due process (use of balloting and appeals)	Yes	Between members
Global standard for the same capability	Yes	At discretion of members
IPR available to all implementers	Yes	No
Forum for presenting changes	Open	Closed
User/implementer access to draft and completed standard documents	Yes	Between members
User/implementer access to interfaces	Yes	Between members
On-going support	Through standard's life cycle	At discretion of members

issues such as competitive strategy decisions (Besen and Farrell 1994; Gabel 1991; Iversen 2001; West and Dedrick 2000), infrastructure investment costs (Christiaanse et al. 2004), the availability of complementary assets (Damsgaard and Truex 2000; Rice 2001; Tassey 2000), and their impacts on the size of production costs (Feng 2003; Iversen 2001). In the later stages of the technology's adoption and diffusion, research on the role of standards has focused on issues such as competitive advantage and network dominance through network externalities and lock-in (Funk and Mehte 2001; Sirkemaa 2002), the introduction of price competition (Besen and Farrell 1994; Farrell and Saloner 1985), and the availability of complementary assets (Funk and Mehte 2001; Tassey 2000).

Finally, from a social perspective, research in the area of standards has highlighted their role as a means to store and preserve knowledge (Damsgaard and Truex 2000; Feng 2003; King et al. 1994), influence the variety of technology available (Farrell and Saloner 1985; Jakobs 2001; Tassey 2000), impact user uncertainty and risk (Damsgaard and Truex 2000; Funk and Mehte 2001), as a means of quality control (Feng 2003; Tassey 2000), and on the alignment of users' actions (Feng 2003).

4 DOI THEORY AND BASE IT INNOVATIONS

The value of DOI theory value is well established, as evidenced by its widespread use to explain the adoption and diffusion of a range of technological innovations. When applied to certain classes of technology that do not meet the model's underlying assumptions, modification and extension of the theory is required (Fichman 2000). There have been a number of general criticisms made of DOI theory and of its underlying assumptions in the context of its application to network-based innovations and complex IS innovations, both of which are considered relevant within the context of the current paper. Following a review of these challenges to the theory's underlying assumptions, existing extensions to DOI theory in the context of base IT innovations are discussed in order to provide a basis for the proposed research framework.

4.1 Complex Innovations, Network-Based Technologies and DOI

The first of these assumptions relates to the adoption decision process related to complex IS. It has been argued that the use of DOI in the analysis of adoption issues relating to any complex organizational IS falls short because of the complexity present in the IS structure and the need for organizational rather than individual decision-making processes to adequately understand these complexities (Attewell 1992; Bayer and Melone 1989; Fichman 2000).

The lack of consideration of market characteristics and factors present within a network environment have been identified as one factor that minimizes the applicability of the theory within the context of CNIS. The impact of network effects on complex network technologies has been widely studied (see, for example, Farrell and Saloner 1985; Katz and Shapiro 1985, 1986; Shapiro and Varian 1999). The absence of consideration of the collective adoption behaviors arising in the presence of network externalities within this technology context is one area identified as being a relevant weakness of DOI theory (Fichman 1992, 2000; Gallivan 2001; Lyytinen and Damsgaard 2001).

The assumption that the innovation emerges as a complete and discrete package also comes into question in criticisms of DOI theory and its application to complex IT innovations (Fichman 2000). In complex technologies where different interrelated components and a high level of technical knowledge are required for the technology to operate, such components (for example, applications, telecommunications services, and standards; Lyytinen and Damsgaard 2001) and knowledge are often distinct from the discrete package view of an innovation. The traditional view of diffusion as a process involving the communication of information, rather than technical knowledge, means that additional demands are placed on both the supplier in terms of communication requirements and the potential adopter in terms of organizational learning (Attewell 1992, Newell et al. 2000). A point further related to this assumption is that by viewing all classes of innovation as sharing similar attributes, the complexity in certain IS innovations can be misrepresented, as not all classes of IS innovation can be described using common characteristics (Lyytinen and Damsgaard 2001).

A third assumption underlying the DOI theory is that the primary barrier to adoption is lack of information of innovation's existence and benefits (Fichman 2000). It has been argued that barriers to diffusion can be intentionally put in place to limit diffusion of innovations through the management of the elements diffusion (innovation, communication, time, and the social system), as identified by Rogers (1962) and Baskerville and Preis-Heje (1998). If this view is accepted, then a lack of information is only one aspect that can potentially act as a barrier to adoption. The complexity of the innovation, and the resulting knowledge requirements placed on the adopting organization, may also be viewed as a potential barrier to adoption (Attewell 1992, Gallivan 2001). In circumstances where organizations are aware of the existence an innovation, but lack the capabilities necessary to adopt it, again the primary barrier is not the lack of information regarding the existence of the innovation. Also, related to this assumption is the finding that adoption is not a "function of available information, preference functions, risk and adopter's properties" (Lyytinen and Damsgaard 2001, p. 10). Instead, it has been shown that other factors, such as a choice of business strategy can serve to influence adoption decisions (Lyytinen and Damsgaard 2001). Related to this point is the criticism that DOI theory exhibits a *pro-innovation bias* (Abrahamson 1991). It has been argued that DOI theory does not sufficiently take into account non-adoption decisions, a necessary factor as not every innovation is adopted (Geroski 2000).

By assuming that adoption is free from coercion (Fichman 2000; Gallivan 2001; Lyytinen and Damsgaard 2001), and is only related to relationships between the supply and demand side, interactions that allow a rational choice pose problems in the area of certain adoption IS contexts. Such a view does not fully consider the role of entities such as internal decision makers and external institutions that can mandate the adoption of an innovation (Abrahamson 1991; Lyytinen and Damsgaard 2001; King et al. 1994).

4.2 Existing Extensions to DOI Theory in the Context of Base IT Innovations

The DOI model is regarded as having a strong theoretical base and has been extensively used, with modifications and extensions, in the investigation of IS innovations of varying types. This reflects the view that the fundamental differences in adoption situation require theory development that focuses on the distinctive characteristics of the adoption context (Abrahamson 1991; Fichman 2000; Lyytinen and Damsgaard 2001; Munkvold 1998). While the dominant view of standards emerges from an economic justification of their use, the impact felt by standards and standardization covers a broader range of issues than illustrated by a discussion based in an economic or management oriented arena (Iversen 2001). Consequently, the adaptation of the DOI model to account for specific characteristics related to standards adoption is required. In order to do so, aspects of earlier studies focusing on innovations of the same type (i.e., base IT innovations), are drawn upon.

Somewhat lacking in the literature is an empirical investigation of the relationship between a system oriented technical view and the more organizationally oriented economic or strategic view of standards. While the importance of technical standards for interoperability in an ICT setting has been suggested by Williams (1999), in the context of the need for a combined innovation and economic focus on standards, there is limited empirical research evident in the area. There are a number of examples of research that have moved toward such a combination. First, Nelson and Shaw (2003) have taken an innovation diffusion view of interorganizational system standards and process innovations in order to investigate the movement away from earlier views of IOS technologies (primarily EDI) and toward modern-day IOS solutions (i.e., primarily internet enabled approaches). In addition to a focus on innovation attributes, also included are measures of organizational readiness, the external environment, and the standards development organization. By including these measures, a combined view of issues impacting standards adoption from the points of view of the technology, the organization, and the environment were examined. A second example of such research involves the investigation of a specific Internet standards (IPv6) adoption by Internet service providers conducted by Hovav et al. (2004). This work focuses on the adoption of a technical standard using an extended version of the diffusion of innovation theory. Both the perceived attributes of the standard in question and issues relating to the broader "environmental conduciveness" to the standard's adoption are examined. Here, environmental conduciveness incorporates extra-organizational economic factors, and threby moves toward a more unified view of standards adoption issues. In the case of emergent complex network information systems, substantial moves toward development remain to be completed, and as such competing paths between open and proprietary standards still exist. The existence of such competing paths means the trade-off between the technical and economic impacts of standards remains an issue. A final example of research which has moved toward a more unified view of the issues involved in standards adoption was conducted by Chau and Tam (1997), and focused on the adoption of open systems in the context of organizational IT infrastructures. A number of technology (innovation) attributes, market uncertainty, and the organization's existing technological context were considered in the research model.

While these research efforts provide a level of guidance to the development of the proposed research framework, there are important contextual differences. While these earlier efforts have related loci of adoption (i.e., organizational or interorganizational settings), the reasons for the standards adoption differ. In the identified studies, the base IT innovations have been adopted as a means to enable the development of organizational or interorganizational IT infrastructures, rather than as an input into a core product development. As such, the organizations adopting the standards can be viewed as primary users of the standard, rather than secondary users, as is the case with the AmI standards, which are of interest within the current research. While there is likely to be an overlap in the factors impacting the standards adoption decision between these types of users, the potential for difference remains.

5   TOWARD A MODEL FOR UNDERSTANDING THE ADOPTION OF CNIS STANDARDS

An extension of the Rogers' diffusion of innovation theory is required in order to explain the adoption of interoperability standards within the context of CNIS. This extension is required in order to extend the DOI theory's standalone view of the organization and to incorporate both factors relating to the context of the standard choices under consideration and the technological context in which the standards will be used. In doing so, a means of analysis may be provided for understanding the adoption choices made by technology vendors in relation to open or closed interoperability standards for

CNIS to support ambient intelligence. In particular, the factors influencing the adoption or non-adoption of interoperability standards are not confined to purely a system view in which maximum interoperability is always the objective. Rather there is a trade-off between the system oriented goal of interoperability, and the range of economic factors relating to optimal organizational performance in the market, as was illustrated through the identification of the multiple roles and impacts of standards from the technical, business and economic, and social perspectives. Figure 2 illustrates our proposed extension by illustrating that organizational, external, and innovation (standard) contexts impact the adoption process.

At the level of standard (innovation) context, Rogers' DOI model proposes five innovation attributes as being useful in predicting innovation adoption. These are relative advantage, compatibility, complexity, trialability, and observability. Following the findings of Tornatzky and Klein (1982), only the three most consistently identified attributes of relative advantage, compatibility, and complexity are included in the proposed model. In line with Rogers' view of relative advantage, it is defined here as the degree to which the adopter perceives the standard as being better than that which it supersedes. In contrast to earlier approaches, the compatibility attribute has been broken down into a number of component parts. First, the perceived strategic compatibility of the type of standards (i.e., open versus closed) being adopted is included. The decision to partake in inter-technology (i.e., within a technology class) or in intra-technology (i.e., between technology) classes is reliant on the adoption or non-adoption of compatibility standards, as proposed by Besen and Farrell (1994) and Shapiro (1998). As such, the compatibility between the candidate standards and the existing or desired approach to organizational strategy warrants investigation. Second, the technical compatibility of the standards being adopted in relation to backward compatibility (between new products based on the emerging standard and existing product offerings and internal systems) can impact the adoption decision. Finally, the compatibility between standards being adopted for inclusion within a new product requires attention. This factor is included in order to assess how interdependencies between standards of different levels (i.e., at the application, data, and network levels) can impact the adoption decision.

The complexity of the standard is considered in two ways. First, the structural complexity of the system and its relationship to the standards being adopted is included. As discussed, the structural complexity of complex network-based systems requires modularity in design to facilitate interaction between system elements. The decision to adopt open or closed interoperability standards can impact on the systems' ability to function, and as such, the organization's perception of the technical requirements of the system is an important consideration. The second aspect of complexity relates to the knowledge requirements of complex innovations and the organization's capability to respond to them. The inclusion of such a factor is line with the arguments of Attewell (1992) and Gallivan (2001), who point out that with complex innovations a high level of technical knowledge may be required, with the resulting knowledge requirements being a potential barrier to adoption.

Given the complexities involved in the decision process surrounding standards adoption, and the weakness of DOI theory in adequately understanding such complexities, the organizational context level identifies a number of factors broadly termed political issues that require consideration (see Figure 2). First, the level of support given

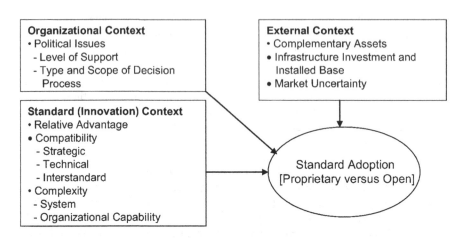

Figure 2. Model of Standards Adoption in a Complex Network-Based System

to the standards adoption process and the issue of mandated adoption can both have an effect on adoption. The scope of the decision process, as related to the extent of collaboration at an individual, organizational unit, or interorganizational level is an important consideration. Such issues may be linked to organizational or interorganizational strategy or existing participation in standards development processes. Factors surrounding organizational innovativeness were omitted following other adoption factor studies focused on similar innovation types (see Hovav et al. 2004). The inclusion of such factors may, however, be relevant as controls (for example, the use of size; Nelson and Shaw 2003), depending on the context in which the model is applied.

At the external context level, three issues are examined for their impact on adoption (see Figure 2). First is the issue of complementary assets, that is, products that can be used with the technology—for example, software is a complementary asset to an operating system, in that only certain software can be used with certain operating systems. The decision on the choice of compatibility standards made by vendors will also impact the type and number of complementary assets available for adopters of the technology. Dedrick and West (2003) have argued that a key barrier to the adoption of a new standard is the availability of complementary assets relating to the existing standard. The development of technology based on proprietary standards can limit the availability of complementary assets produced by other companies. In certain circumstances such a situation is desirable to a vendor, particularly where they intend to develop a full range of proprietary complementary assets and wish to limit competition or imitation of their products. In the area of network technologies, however, it is often the case that limiting the availability of complementary assets is not a desirable strategy. In many circumstances, one vendor does not have the capability to produce the necessary quantity and quality of complementary components required to successfully complete the construction of a network based system (Rice 2001). The lack of such a capability could, as Tassey (2000) argues, be a consequence of unwillingness to diversify operations into fields in which they have no comparative advantage, or from having limited access to resources (e.g., finance or knowledge).

The second issue relates to the issue of infrastructure investment and the existing installed base. The underlying technical infrastructure (e.g., the communications systems) for a large scale system requires substantial investment to implement and maintain. In existing complex network-based information system, the costs vary depending on the type of network involved. In the case of intra-organizational or closed inter-organizational systems this cost is borne by the organization or organizational network involved due to the proprietary nature of such systems. The implementation of network-based systems based of a proprietary nature requires up-front investment in assets (Christiaanse et al. 2004). Such a situation means that the addition of new network members is costly, leading to a limiting effect on the number of users (Afuah 2003). In order to utilize an existing infrastructure, the reliance on standards is an important issue. In the case of the Internet, the result of using a low-cost, open standard means that "anyone, anywhere" can connect to it once the required communications protocols are implemented (Afuah 2003). In relation to the installed base, given the characteristic of network effects in network-based technologies, the existence of a system based on standards of a certain type (i.e., open or closed) can be influential in the adoption decision, and as such, its consideration is warranted in the context of new standards adoption.

The final factor in the external context area relates to market uncertainty, and draws upon Chau and Tam's (1997) open systems adoption model. Markus (1987) demonstrated that the characteristics of network markets show that once a critical mass of users adopt the technology, its growth will become self-sustaining. Karlsbjerg (2002) has argued that should the technology be based on proprietary standards, the standard owner can increase switching costs leading to user lock-in, meaning that they will be less likely to move to a competing technology due to uncertainty or risk associated with leaving an established network (Damsgaard and Truex 2000), or problems with a lack of interoperability between competing standards. It is with this in mind that the consideration of market conditions such as the existing stage of market evolution and the presence of existing standards is included in the analysis of the adoption decision.

6 CONCLUSION

Using existing research on the diffusion of base IT innovations and standards, this paper has developed a model for identifying the issues surrounding the adoption of open or closed interoperability standards in the context of emerging forms of CNIS. However, the model is empirically untested, and research is needed to verify and refine it for use in practice. In order to do so, a number of operational challenges are presented. First, the selection of a unit of analysis presents choices. Given the scale of the systems under consideration, the use of a single organization or a single technology class has the potential to give misleading results. The preselection of a single standard could also limit the study by omitting non-adopting organizations, and introduce pro-innovation bias by focusing only on successful standards. It is suggested that an industry sector unit of analysis (following Reimers et al. 2004) be used in order to overcome these problems. A second challenge presented is availability of data. The area of AmI is currently underdeveloped with the majority of applications deployed as prototypes. Given the prominence of consumer electronics (CE) in the many AmI usage scenarios put forward and the fact that much AmI research and development has occurred within this area, the model will be tested within the European CE sector. In order examine such a sector, a number of stakeholders must be considered, for example, CE manufacturers, software and services development organizations, and telecommunications service providers.

This model is timely in the context of the need of organizations to assess emerging technologies used to build CNIS. Given the ongoing development of technologies capable of supporting the AmI vision, the requirement of organizations to adequately evaluate standards provides a practical outlet for such a model.

Acknowledgment

This research is based on research funded by the European Commission via IST Project 004337, CALIBRE (http://www.calibre.ie).

References

Abowd, G., and Mynatt, E. "Charting Past, Present and Future Research in Ubiquitous Computing" *ACM Transactions on Computer-human Interaction* (7), 2000, pp. 29-58.

Abowd, G., Mynatt, E., and Rodden, T. "The Human Experience," *IEEE Pervasive Computing* (1), 2002, pp. 48-57.

Abrahamson, E. "Managerial Fads and Fashions: The Diffusion and Rejection of Innovations," *Academy of Management Journal* (16), 1991, pp. 586-612.

Afuah, A. "Redefining Firm Boundaries in the Face of the Internet: Are Firms Really Shrinking?," *Academy of Management Review* (28), 2003, pp. 34-53.

Alvai, M., and Carlson, P. "A Review of MIS Research and Disciplinary Development," *Journal of Management Information Systems* (3), 1992, pp. 45-62.

Attewell, P. "Technology Diffusion and Organizational Learning: The Case of Business Computing," *Organization Science* (3), 1992, pp. 1-19.

Banavar, G., and Bernstein, A. "Software Infrastructure and Design Challenges for Ubiquitous Computing Applications," *Communications of the ACM* (45), 2002, pp. 92-96.

Baskerville, R., and Preis-Heje, J. "Information Technology Diffusion: Building Positive Barriers," *European Journal of Information Systems* (7), 1998, pp. 17-28.

Bayer, J., and Melone, N. "A Critique of Diffusion Theory as a Managerial Framework for Understanding Adoption of Software Engineering Innovations," *Journal of Systems and Software* (9), 1989, pp. 161-166.

Besen, S. M., and Farrell, J. "Choosing How to Compete: Strategies and Tactics in Standardization," *Journal of Economic Perspectives* (8), 1994, pp. 117-131.

Boddupalli, P., Al-Bin-Ali, F., Davies, N., Friday, A., Storz, O., and Wu, M. "Payment Support in Ubiquitous Computing Environments," in *Proceedings of the Fifth IEEE Workshop on Mobile Computing Systems and Applications*, Los Alamitos, CA: IEEE Computer Society Press, October 2003, p. 110.

Borriello, G., Chalmers, M., Lamarca, A., and Nixon, P. "Delivering Real-World Ubiquitous Location Systems," *Communications of the ACM* (48), 2005, pp. 36-41.

Chau, P. Y. K., and Tam, K. Y. "Factors Affecting the Adoption of Open Systems: An Exploratory Study," *MIS Quarterly* (21:1), 1997, pp. 1-24.

Chen, W., and Hirschheim, R. A. "A Paradigatic and Methodological Examination of Information Systems Research from 1991 to 2001," *Information Systems Journal* (14:3), 2004, pp. 197-235.

Chen, L., and Tan, J. "Technology Adaption in E-Commerce: Key Determinants of Virtual Stores Acceptance," *European Management Journal* (22), 2004, pp. 74-86.

Christiaanse, E., Van Diepen, T., and Damsgaard, J. "Proprietary Versus Internet Technologies and the Adoption and Impact of Electronic Marketplaces," *Journal of Strategic Information Systems* (13), 2004, pp. 151-165.

Chung, J., Lin, K., and Mathieu, R. G. "Web Services Computing: Advancing Software Interoperability," *Computer* (36), 2003, pp. 35-37.

Cilliers, P. *Complexity and Postmodernism: Understanding Complex Systems,* London: Routledge, 1998.

Claver, E., Gonzales, R., and Llopis, J. "An Analysis of Research in Information Systems," *Information and Management* (37), 2000, pp. 181-195.

Culnan, M. J. "Mapping the Intellectual Structures of MIS, 1980-1985: A Co-citation Analysis," *MIS Quarterly* (11), 1987, pp. 340-353.

Damsgaard, J., and Truex, D. "Binary Trading Relations and the Limits of EDI Standards: The Procrustean Bed of Standards," *European Journal of Information Systems* (9), 2004, pp. 173-188.

Davies, N., and Gellersen, H.-W. "Beyond Prototypes: Challenges in Deploying Ubiquitous Computing Systems," *IEEE Pervasive Computing* (1), 2002, pp. 26-35.

Dedrick, J., and West, J. "Why Firms Adopt Open Source Platforms: Grounded Theory of Innovation and Standards Adoption," in J. L. King and K. Lyytinen (eds.), *Proceedings of the MIS Quarterly Special Issue Workshop on Standard Making: A Critical Research Frontier for Information Systems,* Seattle, WA, 2003, pp. 236-257.

Drury, D. H., and Farhoomand, A. "Innovation Diffusion and Implementation," *International Journal of Innovation Management* (3), 1999, pp. 133-157.

Ducatel, K., Bogdanowicz, Scapolo, F., Leijten, J., and Burgelman, J.-C. "Scenarios for Ambient Intelligence in 2010," Technical Report, Information Society Technology Advisory Group (ISTAG), European Commission, February 2001 (available from ftp://ftp.cordis.lu/pub/ist/docs/istagscenarios2010.pdf).

Ethiraj, S. K., and Levinthal, D. "Modularity and Innovation in Complex Systems," *Management Science* (50), 2004, pp. 159-173.

Farrell, J., and Saloner, G. "Standardization, Compatibility, and Innovation," *Rand Journal of Economics* (16), 1985, pp. 70-83.

Feng, P. "Studying Standardization: A Review of the Literature," in T. M. Egyedi, K. Krechmer, and K. Jakobs (eds.), *Proceedings of the 3rd IEEE Conference on Standardization and Innovation in Information Technology,* Los Alamitos, CA: IEEE Computer Society Press, 2003.

Fichman, R. G. "Information Technology Diffusion: A Review of Empirical Research," in J. I. DeGross, J. D. Becker, and J. J. Elam (eds.), *Proceedings of the 13th International Conference on Information Systems,* Dallas, TX, December 1992, pp. 195-206.

Fichman, R. G. "The Diffusion and Assimilation of Information Technology Innovations," in R. W. Zmud (ed.), *Framing the Domains of it Management: Projecting the Future Through the Past,* Cincinnati, OH: Pinnaflex Publishing, 2000.

Funk, J. L., and Mehte, D. T. "Market- and Committee-Based Mechanisms in the Creation and Diffusion of Global Industry Standards: The Case of Mobile Communication," *Research Policy* (30), 2001, pp. 589-610.

Gabel, H. L. *Competitive Strategies for Product Standards: The Strategic Use of Compatibility Standards for Competitive Advantage,* Berkshire, England: McGraw Hill Book Company, 1991.

Gallivan, M. J. "Organizational Adoption and Assimilation of Complex Technological Innovations: Development and Application of a New Framework," *ACM SIGMIS Database* (32), 2001, pp. 51-85.

Garlan, D., Siewiorek, D., and Steenkiste, P. "Project Aura: Toward Distraction-Free Pervasive Computing," *Pervasive Computing* (1), 2002, pp. 22-31.

Geroski, P. A. "Models of Technology Diffusion," *Research Policy* (29), 2000, pp. 603-625.

Helal, S. "Programming Pervasive Spaces," *Pervasive Computing* (4), 2005, pp. 84-87.

Henricksen, K., Indulska, J., and Rakotonirainy, A. "Infrastrucure for Pervasive Computing: Challenges," in K. Bauknecht, W. Brauer, and T. A. Muck (eds.), *Proceedings of the Informatik 2001: Workshop on Pervasive Computing,* Vienna, Austria, 2001, pp. 214-222.

Hovav, A., Patnayakuni, R., and Schuff, D. "A Model of Internet Standards Adoption: The Case of IPV6," *Information Systems Journal* (14), 2004, pp. 265-294.

Islam, N., and Fayad, M. "Toward Ubiquitous Acceptance of Ubiquitous Computing," *Communications of the ACM* (46), 2003, pp. 89-92.

Iversen, E. J. "Raising Standards: Innovation and the Emerging Global Standardization Environment for ICTs," in T. D. Schoechle and C. B. Wagner (eds.), *Proceedings of the 2nd IEEE Conference on Standardization and Innovation in Information Technology*, Los Alamitos, CA: IEEE Computer Society Press, 2001, pp. 13-24.

Jakobs, K. "A Broader View on Some Forces Shaping Standardization," in T. D. Schoechle and C. B. Wagner (eds.), *Proceedings of the Second IEEE Conference on Standardization and Innovation in Information Technology*, Los Alamitos, CA: IEEE Computer Society Press, 2001, pp. 133-143.

Karlsbjerg, J. "Staying Outside the Mainstream: An Empirical Study of Standards Choices," in R. H. Sprague (ed.), *Proceedings of the 35th Hawaii International Conference on System Sciences* (Volume 8), Los Alamitos, CA: IEEE Computer Society Press, 2002, pp. 3335-3343.

Katz, M. L., and Shapiro, C. "Network Externalities, Competition, and Compatibility," *The American Economic Review* (75), 1985, pp. 424-440.

Katz, M. L., and Shapiro, C. "Technology Adoption in the Presence of Network Externalities," *Journal of Political Economy* (94), 1986, pp. 822-841.

King, J. L., Gurbaxani, V., Kraemer, K. L., McFarlan, F. W., Raman, K. S., and Yap, C. S. "Institutional Factors in Information Technology Innovation," *Information Systems Research* (5), 1994, pp. 139-169.

Krechmer, K. "The Meaning of Open Standards," in D. King and A. Dennis (eds.), *Proceedings of the 38th Hawaii International Conference on Systems Sciences*, Los Alamitos, CA: IEEE Computer Society Press, January 2005, p. 204b.

Kumar, R. L. "A Framework for Assessing the Business Value of Information Technology Infrastructures," *Journal of Management Information Systems* (21:2), 2004, pp. 11-32.

Langlois, R. N. "Modularity in Technology and Organization," *Journal of Economic Behavior and Organization* (49), 2002, pp. 19-37.

Lassila, O. "Serendipitous Interoperability," in E. Hyvonen (ed.), *Semantic Web Kick-off in Finland—Vision, Technologies, Research and Applications*, Helsinki, Finland: HIIT Publications, 2002, pp. 243-256..

Lee, G., and Xia, W. "Development of a Measure to Assess the Complexity of Information Systems Development Projects," in L. Applegate, R. Galliers, and J. I. DeGross (eds.), *Proceedings of the 23rd International Conference on Information Systems*, Barcelona, Spain, 2002, pp. 79-88.

Lyytinen, K., and Damsgaard, J. "What's Wrong with the Diffusion of Innovation Theory? The Case of a Complex and Networked Technology," in M. A. Ardis and B. L. Marcolin (eds.), *Diffusing Software Products and Process Innovations*, Boston: Kluwer Academic Publishers, 2001, pp. 173-190.

Lyytinen, K., and Rose, G. M. "Disruptive Information System Innovation: The Case of Internet Computing," *Information Systems Journal* (13), 2003, pp. 301-330.

Lyytinen, K., Rose, G. M., and Welke, R. "The Brave New World of Development in the Internetwork Computing Architecture (Internca): Or How Distributed Computing Platforms Will Change Systems Development," *Information Systems Journal* (8), 1998, pp. 241-253.

Lyytinen, K., and Yoo, Y. "The Next Wave of Nomadic Computing: A Research Agenda for Information Systems Research," *Information Systems Research* (13), 2002, pp. 377-388.

Maekawa, M. "ITS (Intelligent Transportation Systems) Solutions," *NEC Journal of Advanced Technology* (1), 2004, pp. 194-199.

Markus, M. L. "Toward a 'Critical Mass' Theory of Interactive Media: Universal Access, Interdependence and Diffusion," *Communications Research* (14), 1987, pp. 491-511.

Munkvold, B. E. "Adoption and Diffusion of Collaborative Technology in Interorganizational Networks," in J. F. Nunamaker (ed.), *Proceedings of the 31ˢᵗ Hawaii International Conference on Systems Sciences* (Volume 1), Los Alamitos, CA: IEEE Computer Society Press, 1998, pp. 424-433.

Nakajima, T., Ishikawa, H., Tokunaga, E., and Stajano, F. "Technology Challenges for Building Internet-Scale Ubiquitous Computing," *Proceedings of the Seventh IEEE Workshop on Object-Oriented Real-Time Dependable Systems (Words 2002)*, Los Alamitos, CA: IEEE Computer Society Press, 2002, pp. 171-179.

Nelson, M. L., and Shaw, M. J. "The Adoption and Diffusion of Interorganizational System Standards and Process Innovations," in J. L. King and K. Lyytinen (eds.), *Proceedings of the MIS Quarterly Special Issue Workshop on Standard Making: A Critical Research Frontier for Information Systems,* Seattle, WA, 2003, pp. 258-301.

Newell, S., Swan, J. A., and Galliers, R. D. "A Knowledge-Focused Perspective on the Diffusion and Adoption of Complex Information Technologies: The BPR Example," *Information Systems Journal* (10), 2000, pp. 239-259.

Orlikowski, W., and Baroudi, J. J. "Studying Information Technology in Organizations: Research Approaches and Assumptions," *Information Systems Research* (2), 1991, pp. 1-28.

Prekop, P., and Burnett, M. "Activities, Context and Ubiquitous Computing," *Computer Communications* (26), 2003, pp. 1168-1176.

Reimers, K., Johnston, R. B., and Klein, S. "The Shaping of Interorganizational Information Systems: Main Design Considerations of an International Comparative Research Project," in J. Gricar and G. Lenart (eds.), *Proceedings of the 17ᵗʰ Bled E-Commerce Conference, eGlobal,* Bled, Slovenia, June 21-23, 2004.

Rice, J. "Collaboration and Competition in Emerging Standards: An Assessment of the Implications for Knowledge Management," in T. D. Schoechle and C. B. Wagner (eds.), *Proceedings of the 2ⁿᵈ IEEE Conference on Standardization and Innovation in Information Technology*, Los Alamitos, CA: IEEE Computer Society Press, 2001, pp. 272-281.

Rogers, E. *Diffusion of Innovations,* New York: Free Press, 1962.

Romano, N. C., and Fjermestad, J. "Electronic Commerce Customer Relationship Management: An Assessment of Research," *International Journal of Electronic Commerce* (6), 2002, pp. 61-113.

Shapiro, C. "Setting Compatibility Standards: Cooperation or Collusion?," paper presented at the Conference of the Engelberg Center on Innovation Law and Policy, La Pietra, Italy, 1998.

Shapiro, C., and Varian, H. R. *Information Rules: A Strategic Guide to the Network Economy,* Boston: Harvard Business School Press, 1999.

Sharifi, H., and Zhang, Z. "A Methodology for Achieving Agility in Manufacturing Organizations: An Introduction," *International Journal of Production Economics* (62), 1999, pp. 7-22.

Simon, H. A. "The Architecture of Complexity," *Proceedings of the American Philosophical Society* (106), 1962, pp. 467-482.

Sirkemaa, S. "IT Infrastructure Management and Standards," in P. Srimani and H. Yu (eds.), *Proceedings of the International Conference on Information Technology: Coding and Computing*, Los Alamitos, CA: IEEE Computer Society Press, 2002, pp. 201-206.

Sprott, D. "Componentizing the Enterprise Application Packages," *Communications of the ACM* (43), 2000, pp. 63-69.

Stegwee, R. A., and Rukanova, B. D. "Identification of Different Types of Standards for Domain-Specific Interoperability," in in *Proceedings of the MIS Quarterly Special Issue*

Workshop on Standard Making: A Critical Research Frontier for Information Systems, Seattle, WA, 2003.

Strand, E. J., Mehta, R. P., and Jairam, R. "Applications Thrive on Open Systems Standards," *Standardview* (2), 1994, pp. 148-154.

Tassey, G. "Standardization in Technology-Based Markets," *Research Policy* (29), 2000, pp. 587-602.

Thomke, E., and Reinersten, D. G. "Agile Product Development: Managing Development Flexibility in Uncertain Environments," *California Management Review,* Fall 1998, pp. 8-30.

Tornatzky, L. G., and Klein, K. J. "Innovation Characteristics and Innovation Adoption Implementation: A Meta-Analysis of Findings," *IEEE Transactions on Engineering Management* (EM-29), 1982, pp. 28-45.

Weiser, M. "The Computer for the 21st Century," *Scientific American* (265), 1991, pp. 94-104.

West, J. "What Are Open Standards? Implications for Adoption, Competition and Policy," paper presented at the Standards and Public Policy Conference, Federal Reserve Bank of Chicago, Chicago, Illinois, 2004.

West, J., and Dedrick, J. "Innovation and Control in Standards Architectures: The Rise and Fall of Japan's PC-98," *Information Systems Research* (11), 2000, pp. 197-216.

Williams, R. "ICT Standard Setting from an Innovation Studies Perspective," in *First IEEE Conference on Standardization and Innovation in Information Technology,* Los Alamitos, CA: IEEE Computer Society Press, September 1999, pp. 15-17

About the Authors

David Kelly is currently pursuing a Ph.D. in Information Systems at University College Cork. His research interests include innovation adoption, ambient intelligence, standards, and open-source software. David can be reached at d.kelly@ucc.ie.

Joseph Feller is a senior lecturer in Business Information Systems, University College Cork, Ireland. His work on open source software includes coauthorship of two books (*Perspectives on Free and Open Source Software,* The MIT Press, 2005, and *Understanding Open Source Software Development,* Addison-Wesley, 2002) as well as international conference and journal papers. He coauthored "A Framework Analysis of the Open Source Software Development Paradigm," which was awarded Best Paper on Conference Theme at the 21st International Conference on Information Systems (ICIS 2000). Joseph was the lead organizer of the IEE/ACM workshop series on Open Source Software Engineering from 2001 through 2005, and has been a speaker and panelist on the topic at academic conferences, industry workshops, and European Commission briefings and roundtables. Joseph is a member of the EU FP6 Coordination action project CALIBRE (www.calibre.ie), co-leading the dissemination and awareness work package and conducting research on open source software business models. He can be reached at jfeller@afis.ucc.ie.

Patrick Finnegan holds a Ph.D. in Information Systems from the University of Warwick, and is currently a senior lecturer in Management Information Systems at University College Cork. His research interests include electronic business and IS strategy. He has published his research in a number of international journals and conferences including *The International Journal of Electronic Commerce, Information Technology & People, DataBase, Electronic Markets, The Information Systems Journal,* the European Conference on Information Systems, the International Conference on Information Systems, and the Americas Conference on Information Systems. Patrick can be reached at pfinnegan@afis.ucc.ie.

2 KNOWLEDGE EXCHANGE IN ELECTRONIC NETWORKS OF PRACTICE: Toward a Conceptual Framework

Eoin Whelan
National University of Ireland
Galway, Ireland

Abstract   *The recently developed knowledge-based view of the firm argues that knowledge is the firm's most valuable resource. Within this field of study, informal social networks are rapidly gaining attention as mechanisms that facilitate knowledge flows. Electronic networks of practice are a special case of informal networks where the sharing of practice-related knowledge occurs primarily through computer-based communication technologies. However, we know relatively little about the dynamics of knowledge exchange that occur in these electronic networks. This paper posits that there is a relationship between the structural properties of electronic networks of practice and successful knowledge exchange. The theoretical positions of social network theory and the knowledge-based view of the firm are used to support this claim.*

Keywords   Knowledge, networks of practice, electronic community, social networks

1   INTRODUCTION

Over the past two decades, as a result of managerial initiatives such as delayering, reengineering and team-based designs, most organizations have become flatter and more flexible. This has significantly changed the way work gets done. Employees are no longer constrained by the role of formally prescribed relationships in organizations. More work is being done through informal networks and "supporting collaboration and work in these informal networks is increasingly important for organizations competing on knowledge and an ability to innovate and adapt" (Cross et al. 2002). Informal relationships among employees are often far more reflective of the way work happens

Please use the following format when citing this chapter:

Whelan, Eoin, 2006, in International Federation for Information Processing (IFIP), Volume 206, The Transfer and Diffusion of Information Technology for Organizational Resilience, eds. B. Donnellan, Larsen T., Levine L., DeGross J. (Boston: Springer), pp. 21-31.

in an organization than the relationships established by position within the formal structure (Cross et al. 2002). Yet, these relationships rarely appear on formal organizational charts.

Further pressure is being placed on organizations by the increased internationalization of business resulting in collaboration and cooperation becoming more distributed. Collaboration between organizations has come into focus in recent years with the recognition that success in a global economy comes from innovation. This is the only way an organization can keep pace with the rapid developments in technology, increasingly demanding customers, and changes in the competitive environment through deregulation, social changes, and the actions of competitors. Innovation depends on the exchange of ideas and insights through trusted relationships, which depend on knowing how to collaborate effectively (Nooteboom 2004).

The diffusion of innovative knowledge has become one of the major research interests in management. Traditional organizational forms (markets and hierarchies) show serious deficits in organizing the complex nature of knowledge (Jones et al. 1997). This has led to an increased interest in the community of practice (CoP) concept. A CoP consists of a relatively tight-knit group of members who know each other, work together face-to-face, and continually negotiate, communicate, and coordinate with each other directly. CoPs are regarded as the essential building blocks of the knowledge economy and are being promoted within organizations as sources of competitive advantage (Teigland and Wasko 2004). Current research has focused on the role of CoPs for encouraging knowledge exchange and innovation *within* organizations; however, we know much less about the role that members of CoP play in creating linkages to external knowledge sources. Previous research has found that organizational members may simultaneously be members of a CoP as well as members of broader occupational communities (Van Maanen and Barley 1984). These individuals perform the dual roles of generating local knowledge within an organizational CoP while providing linkages to knowledge and innovations outside of the organization. These inter-organizational networks have been referred to as networks of practice (NoPs). NoPs are social structures linking similar individuals across organizations who are engaged in a shared practice but who do not necessarily know one another (Brown and Duguid 2000).

While the participation of individuals in NoPs is not a new phenomenon, the ability to access these networks has increased due to recent advances in information and communication technologies. Electronic networks of practice (ENoPs) are a special case of NoP where the sharing of practice-related knowledge occurs primarily through computer-based communication technologies (Wasko and Faraj 2005). In ENoPs, individuals may never get to know one another or meet face-to-face. They generally coordinate through technologies such as blogs, listservs, or bulletin boards. Previous research has shown that external knowledge trading through ENoPs is beneficial for the firm (Bouty 2000; Teigland and Wasko 2003), thus making the study of ENoPs of prime interest for researchers and practitioners.

This paper examines ENoPs through the theoretical lens of social network theory. This body of literature shows that particular structural properties of networks create or constrain possibilities for action by individuals and networks. The overarching goal of this research-in-progress is to improve our understanding of electronic networks from a business firm's perspective, and in particular to investigate issues of structure and performance, two important areas generally left by the wayside in previous NoP research. This paper posits that there is a relationship between the structural properties of ENoPs and successful knowledge exchange. To support this claim, a review of the knowledge-based view of the firm is presented in section 2. A conceptual framework, which links the roles of CoPs to ENoPs within the knowledge-based view of the firm, is presented in section 3. Section 4 gives a brief overview social network theory. Given the size constraints of this paper, we have chosen to focus on one particular structural property, core/periphery structure. The relationship between the core/periphery structure of a network and performance is explored further in this section. Finally, the mechanisms to be used to examine ENoP structure and knowledge exchange are detailed in section 5.

2 KNOWLEDGE-BASED VIEW OF THE FIRM

This study is grounded in the knowledge-based view of the firm. This recently developed theory argues that knowledge is the firm's most valuable resource. Producing unique products and services or producing them at a lower cost than competitors is based on superior knowledge of the production process and superior design. In fact, prominent authors such as Drucker (1994), Grant (1996, 2001), and Spender (2003) suggest that knowledge is perhaps the only true source of competitive advantage.

Much tension exists as to the different views of knowledge. This debate is essentially centered on whether knowledge can be captured, stored, and transferred. Many people feel that if something is to be managed, it must be able to be quantified, counted, organized, and measured (Glazer 1998), and it must be able to be built, owned, controlled and its value maximized (Davenport 1997). This view of *management* has influenced attempts to manage knowledge by quantifying, capturing and controlling it as an object. The emerging field of *knowledge management* (KM) has also attracted some criticism because of this view, much of which relates to the perceived over-emphasis on codifying and storing knowledge as data. There is a real danger that KM is just becoming another label for information systems rather than an innovative attempt to increase knowledge in the organization (Goldkuhl and Barf 2002). More recent developments have recognized that this approach to KM is too restrictive and that some aspects of knowledge cannot be captured. This debate has led to a confused picture of knowledge within the KM community as researchers and practitioners have sought to define the knowledge that can be captured and that which cannot. For example, some commentators are of the opinion that tacit knowledge can be captured (Huang 1997), some feel it is merely difficult to articulate (Teece 1998), others feel it cannot be codified without being invalidated (Buckingham Shum 1997), whereas still others feel it simply cannot be captured or codified at all (Leonard and Sensiper 1998).

There is a clear need for a different view of knowledge in order to overcome this challenge of managing knowledge that cannot be captured, codified, and stored. In this regard, Hildreth and Kimble (2002) argue that knowledge is not made up of mutually exclusive opposites of hard and soft (see Figure 1). Instead, they are mutually dependent where all knowledge is regarded as being both hard and soft. Only the proportions differ. Viewing knowledge in this way lends itself more easily to the notion that knowl-

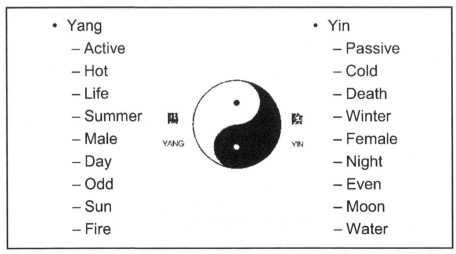

- Yang   - Yin
  - Active   - Passive
  - Hot   - Cold
  - Life   - Death
  - Summer   - Winter
  - Male   - Female
  - Day   - Night
  - Odd   - Even
  - Sun   - Moon
  - Fire   - Water

Figure 1. Knowledge Consists Simultaneously of Both "Hard" and "Soft" Knowledge (Adapted from "The Duality of Knowledge," P. Hildreth and C. Kimble, *Information Research* (8:1), 2002.)

edge can be exchanged through digital media. It recognizes that higher levels of tacit knowledge can be exchanged through face-to-face contact. However, knowledge can be made more transportable by increasing the hard/explicit element in relation to the soft/tacit element.

Assuming that knowledge is a critical input to production processes, then competitive advantage stems from the ability to integrate the specialized knowledge of individuals (Grant 1996; Nonaka 1994; Spender 2003). Therefore, one of the key issues underlying the knowledge-based view of the firm is to understand how knowledge is integrated into the firm to create competitive advantage (Hansen 1996). Informal networks such as NoPs are rapidly gaining attention within this view of the firm. Knowledge may be the organizations most valuable resource; however, no firm can possess all the knowledge it requires. Therefore, it must look outside its formal boundaries (Wasko and Faraj 2005). Nooteboom (2004) suggests that in dynamic fields, organizational innovations derive from knowledge exchange and learning from network connections that cross organizational boundaries. Organization members benefit through informal interaction by acquiring knowledge they did not have.

3   CONCEPTUAL FRAMEWORK

When individuals have a common practice, knowledge readily flows across that practice, enabling individuals to create social networks to support knowledge exchange (Brown and Duguid 2000). In fact, Brown and Duguid conclude that the key to competitive advantage is a firm's ability to coordinate autonomous CoPs internally and leverage the knowledge that flows into these communities from network connections.

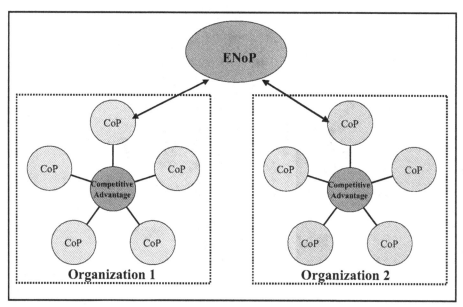

Figure 2. The Conceptual Framework

Findings from a recent study by Teigland and Wasko (2004) suggest that knowledge in a tightly knit CoP may be largely redundant, providing little additional information over what an individual may already know, thus impeding the ability to develop new and creative ideas. The highly efficient structures that support knowledge integration in a CoP may evolve into core rigidities and competency traps—inappropriate knowledge sets that preserve the status quo and limit new insights (Leonard and Sensiper 1998). One way to alleviate this concern is to use ENoPs to create "bridging links" between strong tie communities to enhance the flow of new ideas and knowledge. Electronic networks have certain advantages over social networks, mainly in rapidly transferring explicit knowledge, rapidly developing weak ties, and greatly reducing communication costs (Grandori and Soda 1995).

A conceptual framework that connects these views is presented in Figure 2. Internal to each organization are a number of CoPs. Through conversation, mentoring, war stories, etc., CoP members help each other to make sense of ambiguous, problem-centered situations. Due to the increased access of information and communication technologies, members of internal CoPs may also be members of external ENoPs. These individuals are able to acquire new knowledge from these external sources and integrate it into their internal CoPs. Through this process they are able to build competitive advantage by combining new and existing knowledge to generate novel ideas and solve complex problems.

A key question for researchers and practitioners is how to turn an empty electronic space into a vital, active forum devoted to knowledge exchange (Teigland and Wasko 2004). This research contributes to this inquiry by focusing specifically on the structural properties of ENoPs and their relationship with successful knowledge exchange. Structural property concepts are reviewed in the following section.

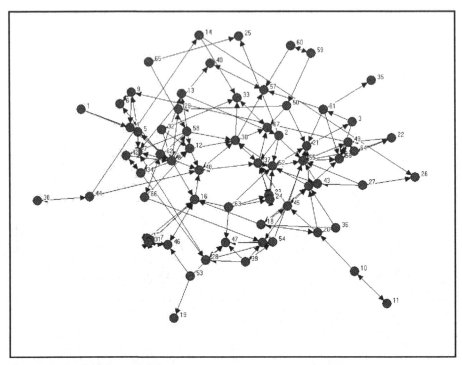

Figure 3. Social Network Map

4   SOCIAL NETWORK THEORY

In the field of social psychology, an important tradition of study on networks is that of social network theory. Social network theory views social relationships in terms of nodes and ties. Nodes are the individual actors within the networks, and ties are the relationships between the actors. Social network theory indicates the ways in which they are connected through various social familiarities ranging from casual acquaintance to close familial bonds. In its most simple form, a social network is a map of all of the relevant ties between the nodes being studied (see Figure 3).

The power of social network theory stems from its difference from traditional sociological studies, which assume that it is the attributes of individual actors that matter. Social network theory produces an alternate view, where the attributes of individuals are less important than their relationships and ties with other actors within the network. It suggests that at least some properties and outcomes of a social network are a function of its complete structure and are not reducible to either an individual actor or a single link (Degenne and Forse 1999).

The structural properties of the social network help determine the network's usefulness to its individuals. When talking about the structural properties, what is meant is the impact of group communication structure on collective performance outcomes. Structural properties refer to concepts such as density, connectedness, centrality, core/

periphery structure, coreness, etc. Due to the length requirements of this paper, one structural property is selected—core/periphery structure—and its relationship with network performance is examined.

A network has a core/periphery structure if it can be partitioned into two sets: a core whose members are densely tied to each other, and a periphery, whose members have more ties to core members than each other (Borgatti and Everett 1999). Research into core/periphery structure has a long tradition dating back to 1940s and 1950s. This body of literature consistently shows that networks with a strong core/periphery structure are better for the diffusion of routine information, while networks with a weak core/periphery structure are better for solving complex tasks (see Figures 4 and 5). For example, Bavelas (1948) showed that *communication nets* with centralized structures (e.g., wheel) improved the diffusion of information in simple tasks while decentralized structures (e.g., circle) delayed the diffusion of information. Groups with decentralized communication nets took less time to finish complex tasks than groups with a centralized structure (Shaw 1964). More recently, Cummings and Cross (2003) found that a strong core/periphery structure was negatively related to group performance for complex, nonroutine work.

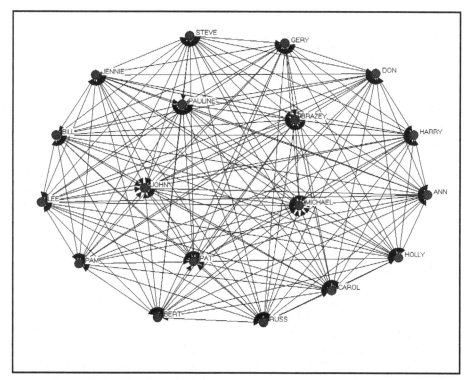

Figure 4. Weak Core/Periphery Structure

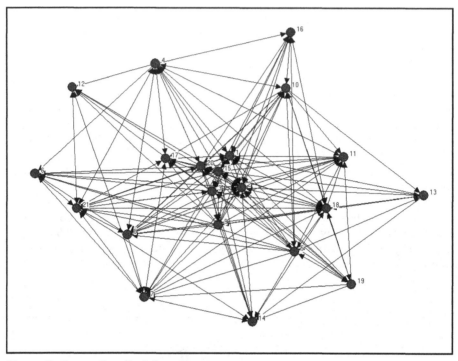

Figure 5. Strong Core/Periphery Structure

It has only been in recent years that network analysis has captured the attention of the business world on a broad scale. Yet despite the increase in the use of work groups in organizations, there has been relatively little social network research on the structural properties of natural work groups and the consequences for performance (Cummings and Cross 2003; Schenkel et al. 2001). Social network scholars have tended to focus on structural properties of ego-centric networks or bounded networks within an organization. Cummings and Cross also suggest that field work is needed to revisit which structures have meaningful consequences for performance.

5 METHODOLOGY

ENoP research is still in its infancy and we know little about the dynamics of knowledge exchange in these significant organizational forms. Previous research has been limited by the fact that researchers have tended to concentrate on only one ENoP, usually internal to one organization (Teigland and Wasko 2003, 2004; Wasko and Faraj 2005). Empirical evidence that links ENoP structures to performance is needed as previous research in the social network field shows that informal methods of knowledge transfer are more effective than formal processes (Burt 1992; Grant 1996). As a step in this direction, this research will address the following question: *What is the relationship between ENoP structural properties and successful knowledge exchange for complex, non-routine work?* A set of hypotheses relating the two variables (i.e., ENoP structural properties and successful knowledge exchange) will be developed and tested. Previous research will be extended by analyzing multiple categories of knowledge workers across multiple organizations.

The first stage of this research will be to identify six to eight interorganizational ENoPs. For example, one might be an open-source software network; another might be a discussion forum for chemical engineers. Once identified, the structural properties of the ENoPs will be measured using a tool called social network analysis. This tool provides both a graphical display of the network as well as precise mathematical measures of its structure (i.e., density, connectedness, centrality, core/periphery structure, coreness). The second stage will involve measuring the success of the knowledge exchanged through these electronic networks. Successful knowledge exchange in ENoPs is determined by both the quantity of knowledge exchanged as well as the quality. Knowledge quantity will be measured by a process called content analysis. To measure the quality of knowledge exchanged in an ENoP, an expert from each field will rate the usefulness of responses posted. A survey of ENoP participants will serve as a second measure of knowledge quality. For example, participants can be asked how useful they found the ENoP for solving complex problems. To test the hypotheses, the various measures of ENoP structural properties will be related to the measures for successful knowledge exchange.

6 CONCLUSION

This paper posits that there is a relationship between the structural properties of ENoPs and successful knowledge exchange. The knowledge-based view of the firm and social network theory are used to justify this claim. The knowledge-based view of the firm argues that knowledge is the firm's most important strategic asset while social network theory shows that network outcomes are determined by its structure. A conceptual framework linking a firm's competitive advantage to the interaction of face-to-face CoPs and interorganizational ENoPs has been presented. Further research will involve developing hypotheses that relate ENoP structures to successful knowledge exchange. These hypotheses will be applied to multiple categories of ENoPs and tested.

References

Bavelas, A. "A Mathematical Model for Group Structure," *Human Organizations* (7), 1948, pp. 17-30.
Borgatti, S. P., and Everett , M. G. "Models of Core/Periphery Structures," *Social Networks* (21), 1999, pp. 375-395.
Bouty, I. "Interpersonal and Interaction Influences on Informal Resource Exchanges Between R&D Researchers Across Organizational Boundaries," *Academy of Management Journal* (43:1), 2000, pp. 50-66.
Brown, J. S., and Duguid, P. *The Social Life of Information*, Boston: Harvard Business School Press, 2000.

Buckingham Shum, S. "Negotiating the Construction and Reconstruction of Organizational Memories," *Journal of Universal Computer Science* (3:8), 1997, pp. 899-928.

Burt, R. *Structural Holes: The Social Structure of Competition*, Cambridge, MA: Harvard University Press, 1992.

Cross, R., Borgatti, S. P., and Parker, A. "Making Invisible Work Visible: Using Social Network Analysis to Support Strategic Collaboration," *California Management Review* (44:2), Winter 2002, pp. 25-46.

Cummings, J., and Cross, R. "Structural Properties of Work Groups and Their Consequences for Performance," *Social Networks* (25), 2003, pp. 197-210.

Davenport, T. H. *Information Ecology*, New York: Oxford University Press, 1997.

Degenne, A., and Forse, M. *Introducing Social Networks*, Thousand Oaks, CA: Sage Publications, 1999.

Drucker, P. *Post-Capitalist Society*, New York: Harper Business, 1994.

Glazer, R. "Measuring the Knower: Toward a Theory of Knowledge Equity," *California Management Review* (40:3), 1998, pp. 175-194.

Goldkuhl, G., and Barf, E. "Organizational Ability: Constituents and Congruencies," in *Knowledge Management in the Sociotechnical World.: The Graffiti Continues*, E. Coakes, D. Willis, and S. Clarke (eds.), London: Springer, 2002, pp. 30-42.

Grandori, A., and Soda, G. "Inter-Firm Networks: Antecedents, Mechanisms and Forms," *Organization Studies* (16:2), 1995, pp. 183-214.

Grant, R. M. "Knowledge and Organization," in *Managing Industrial Knowledge: Creation, Transfer and Utilization*, I. Nonaka and D. J. Teece (eds.), London: Sage Publications, 2001.

Grant, R. M. "Toward a Knowledge-Based Theory of the Firm," *Strategic Management Journal* (17), 1996, pp. 109-122.

Hansen, M. T. *Knowledge Integration in Organizations*, Boston: Harvard Business School Press, 1996.

Hildreth, P., and Kimble, C. "The Duality of Knowledge," *Information Research* (8:1), Paper Number 142, 2002 (available online at http://InformationR.net/ir/8-1/paper142.html).

Huang, K. "Capitalizing Collective Knowledge for Winning Execution and Teamwork," *Journal of Knowledge Management* (1:2), 1997, pp. 149-209.

Jones, C., Hesterly, W. S., and Borgatti, S. P. "A General Theory of Network Governance: Exchange Conditions and Social Mechanisms," *Academy of Management Review* (22:4), 1997, pp. 911-945.

Leonard, D., and Sensiper, S. "The Role of Tacit Knowledge in Group Innovation," *California Management Review* (40:3), 1998, pp. 112-131.

Nonaka, I. "A Dynamic Theory of Organizational Knowledge Creation," *Organization Science* (5:1), 1994, pp. 14-37.

Nooteboom, B. *Inter-Firm Collabortion, Learning and Networks*, London: Routledge, 2004.

Schenkel, A., Teigland, R., and Borgatti, S. P. "Theorizing Structural Properties of Communities of Practice: A Social Network Approach," paper presented at the Academy of Management Conference, Organization and Management Division, Washington DC, 2001.

Shaw, M. E. (ed.). *Communication Networks*, New York: Academic Press, 1964.

Spender, J. C. "Knowledge Fields: Some Post–9/11 Thoughts About the Knowledge-Based Theory of the Firm," in *Handbook on Knowledge Management*, C. W. Holsapple (ed.), New York: Springer, 2003, pp. 59-72.

Teece, D. J. "Research Directions for Knowledge Management," *California Management Review* (40:3), 1998, pp. 289-292.

Teigland, R., and Wasko, M. "Integrating Knowledge Through Information Trading: Examining the Relationship Between Boundary Spanning Communication and Individual Performance," *Decision Sciences* (34:2), Spring 2003, pp. 261-287.

Teigland, R., and Wasko, M. "Extending Richness with Reach: Participation and Knowledge Exchange in Electronic Networks of Practice," in *Knowledge Networks: Innovation Through Communities of Practice,* P. Hildreth and C. Kimble (eds.), London: Idea Group, 2004.

Van Maanen, J., and Barley, S. R. "Occupational Communities: Culture and Control in Organizations," in *Research in Organizational Behavior,* B. M. Staw and L. L. Cummings (eds.), Greenwich, CT: JAI Press, 1984.

Wasko, M. M., and Faraj, S. "Why Should I Share? Examining Social Capital and Knowledge Contribution in Electronic Networks of Practice," *MIS Quarterly* (29:1), March 2005, pp. 35-57.

About the Author

Eoin Whelan is a lecturer in information systems at the National University of Ireland, Galway, where he teaches information systems strategy, e-commerce, and computer programming. He is also undertaking a Ph.D. with the Centre for Innovation & Structural Change at the same institution. Prior to commencing his Ph.D., Eoin worked as a management accountant in Ireland, New Zealand, and the United States. He earned his Master's degree by research from the University of Limerick in 2002 and was awarded the Government of Ireland Scholarship in Humanities and Social Sciences for this research. Eoin can be reached at eoin.whelan@ nuigalway.ie.

3 THE IMPACTS OF INFORMATION TECHNOLOGY AND MANAGERIAL PROACTIVENESS IN BUILDING NET-ENABLED ORGANIZATIONAL RESILIENCE

Lih-Bin Oh
Hock-Hai Teo
National University of Singapore
Singapore

Abstract   *The ability of an organization to generate variety is important for enhancing its organizational resilience when faced with volatilities from the environment. Using the context of integrated multichannel net-enabled retail organizations, we conceptualized organizational resilience as a higher-order capability comprising of two capabilities in terms of innovativeness and agility. Innovativeness reflects the scope aspect while agility represents the speed aspect of resilience. Based on a survey of 125 net-enabled retail organizations, we found that high levels of information technology capability and managerial proactiveness both significantly enhance organizational resilience. In addition, more resilient organizations perform better under turbulent environments. The construction of metrics to measure organizational resilience and the development of a structural model to elucidate the resilience building process and its performance consequences provide useful managerial and research implications.*

Keywords   Information technology, managerial proactiveness, net-enabled organization, multichannel retailing, organizational resilience, innovative capability, agility capability

1   INTRODUCTION

The retailing industry is currently operating in a dynamic environment and experiencing significant structural changes (Sambamurthy et al. 2003). To remain viable amidst this turbulence, retail organizations need to reexamine their organizational

Please use the following format when citing this chapter:

Oh, Lih-Bin, Teo, Hock-Hai, 2006, in International Federation for Information Processing (IFIP), Volume 206, The Transfer and Diffusion of Information Technology for Organizational Resilience, eds. B. Donnellan, Larsen T., Levine L., DeGross J. (Boston: Springer), pp. 33-50.

strategy, structure, and processes to keep themselves in pace with the competition. They need to nurture core competences for enhancing their organizational resilience to better withstand the environmental volatilities. In this digital economy, the chances of survival for retail businesses with only brick-and-mortar stores or pure Internet presence are ominous due to their low readiness to meet the expectations of the Net-generation consumers. Technology savvy consumers are increasingly demanding the ability to reach out to retailers using a wide range of technologies. They freely exchange information about products and retailers with other consumers through various interactive media. In addition, they expect retailers to offer presale, purchase, and after-sale services through a retail channel most convenient to them.

Such evolving environmental and consumer forces have intensified the imperative for retailers to expedite their transformations into multichannel net-enabled retail organizations (NERO). A net-enabled organization coordinates its activities and interacts with its stakeholders by exchanging messages over electronic networks (Straub and Watson 2001). It provides new channels for accessing customers and engages in innovation to offer new digital products or services that align the firm to its competitive environment (Wheeler 2002). Retail organizations such as Sears, CompUSA, Staples, Circuit City, and Best Buy in the United States and Tesco in the United Kingdom are certainly aware of the need for this e-transformation. These organizations and many others have been aggressively building up their cross-channel capabilities.

Undoubtedly, advancements in information technologies such as Internet connectivity, data warehousing, and customer relationship management systems are pivotal in presenting retailing firms with immense options to speed up the convergence of their retail channels. However, a fully integrated NERO is not about having separate physical and online retail channels with disparate business processes. Instead, it entails the effective exploitation of IT to integrate informational content and reconfigure processes in both channels.

Given the organizational complexity present in such a multichannel retailing firm, it is thus important to advance our understanding of the role in which IT affects the net-enablement and capability-building processes. Recent thinking about the performance enhancing role of IT in organizations suggests that IT alone does not have a direct and unequivocal impact on firm performance. Rather, it is the complementary effect of IT with other organizational resources that results in improved organizational performance (Melville et al. 2004; Wade and Hulland 2004). A complementary organizational resource that is critical to reinforce the role of IT is the top management's level of proactiveness in formulating forward-looking strategies for organizational survival. This managerial characteristic is necessary for the organization to be able to sense and detect IT-enabled market opportunities to innovate rapidly under a turbulent environment.

In this study, we employ the context of business model and technology innovations in retail organizations to explore the impacts of IT and managerial proactiveness in enhancing organizational resilience for multichannel retailers. We also further examine the performance implications of net-enabled organizational resilience under turbulent environments. The rest of the paper is organized as follows. First, we provide a background of the study context and then introduce our conceptualization of organizational resilience and relate its relevance to NERO. Next, we discuss the hypotheses development and research method. Finally, we present the results and elaborate on our findings and contributions.

2   INTEGRATED RETAIL OPERATIONS MANAGEMENT

According to *The Economist* (2004), one in five customers who enters a major U.S. department store has researched their purchase online. Half of the 60 million European consumers bought products offline after having investigated prices and details online. Multichannel consumers are found to spend more and are more loyal to retailers than single channel consumers (Forrester Research 2004). In response to consumers' expectations for multichannel shopping and the realization that physical retail channels are important in complementing the virtual channels, retail organizations are increasingly integrating their retail operations across channels.

After conducting an extensive review of the extant literature in traditional retailing, electronic commerce, and multichannel retailing (Keeney 1999; Mason et al. 1993; Samli 1989; Steinfield et al. 2002), we identified six areas of integrated retail operations management. These are briefly described below to provide a background for our study about building organizational resilience through innovations in retail channels.

- *Integrated promotion* is the advertising and publicity of one channel by the other channel in order to encourage customers of one to use the other as well as to increase awareness of both channels (Bahn and Fischer 2003). The physical store can be used as an advertising medium for the Website through brochures, receipts, carrying bags, posters and in-store promotions. Similarly, the Website can provide information about the locations of the physical stores and announcements of in-store events (Steinfield et al 2002). Spillover effects are increased as promotions in each channel draw attention to the other.

- *Integrated transaction information management* involves collecting customers' online and offline transaction information, managing this integrated information, and making it available across multiple channels (Goersch 2002). Integrated transaction information would increase the richness of the information available and the quality of the services that can be provided based on this information. Retailers would be able to offer many value-added, personalized services such as customized Web pages, allowing customers to review their previous purchases and providing them with suggestions for future purchases.

- *Integrated product and pricing information management* involves ensuring the consistency of product and pricing information in both retail channels. This can be achieved by integrating product catalogs and ensuring that information related to product descriptions, product categories, prices, and discounts are consistent in both channels (Daniel and Wilson 2003). This would lead to a transparent flow of information between the processes and reduce consumers' confusion due to information inconsistencies.

- *Integrated information access* provides customers with the ability to access information available in one channel from another channel. With integrated information access, the Website can allow customers to search for products available in the physical store through an integrated database. Information on real-time inventory can be made available online so that customers will not make wasted trips to the store when the product is out of stock (Prasarnphanich and Gillenson 2003). Information kiosks at the physical store can help customers search for the availability and location of products from an online database while they are at the physical store (Gulati and Garino 2000).

• *Integrated order fulfillment* is the provision of support for customers to choose their preferred channel to complete their purchases. It includes allowing customers to use the online channel to order products and pick them up at local physical outlets and allowing gift coupons issued by the store to be redeemed either online or offline (Wallace et al. 2004). Consumers can also choose to make payment for their online purchases in the physical stores. An integrated product cataloging system can allow customers to quickly place online orders based on catalog numbers.

• *Integrated customer service* is the provision of services for customers to access service support in either channel. Self-serve Internet kiosks can be used for customers to access information on the Website or to place orders for out-of-stock items. Support can be provided at the physical stores for problems related to the online purchases such as allowing customers to return goods ordered online at the physical store (Prasarnphanich and Gillenson 2003). It also involves having an integrated communication channel where the Website provides after-sale services such as e-mail support for products bought in physical stores as well as real-time live chat, where online customers have access to in-store customer service assistants (Amit and Zott 2001).

3   BUILDING BLOCKS OF ORGANIZATIONAL RESILIENCE

The concept of resilience has its origins in the field of ecology and refers to "the magnitude of disturbance that a system can absorb before the system redefines its structure by changing the variables and processes that control behavior" (Gunderson 2000, p. 426). This suggests that sustainability of a system is contingent on its variety. The degree of variety in a system guards against unexpected events in the environment. Therefore, a high degree of biological diversity ensures that no matter what the future unfolds, there will be at least some organisms that are well-suited to the new circumstances (Hamel and Valikangas 2003).

This capability to generate variety so that options are available to do things differently or do something else if the need arises is not only valuable to biological systems, but in fact to any system. Increasingly, organizations competing in dynamic environments are being viewed as systems making up of a collection of subsystems that are integrated to achieve organizational goals of the system (Sanchez 2001). Hence, the variety-generating capabilities of an organization are critical in enhancing its resilience (SubbaNarasimha 2001). The larger the variety of actions available to a system, the larger the variety of perturbations it is able to accommodate. If an organization's range of strategic alternatives is significantly narrower than the breadth of changes in the environment, the organization is going to be a victim of turbulence (Hamel and Valikangas 2003). By applying Ashby's (1958) "law of requisite variety" to organizations, Weick (1979) suggests that because of requisite variety, organizations have to keep sufficient diversity inside the organization to sense accurately the variety present in ecological changes outside it.

For the case of net-enabled retail organizations, we expect the ability to offer a variety of innovative products and services rapidly as being crucial to building up its organizational resilience. This is achieved by integrating the unique capabilities of an Internet Website and the advantages of a physical store such as personal contact and instant gratification. Our conceptualization of this form of net-enabled organizational resilience concurs with Hamel and Valikangas (2003), who define resilience as the capability of the organization to innovate with respect to organizational values, processes, and behaviors for continuous reconstruction. It also encompasses an organization's ability and capacity to endure systemic discontinuities and adapt to new risk environments (Starr et al. 2003).

Innovative capability represents one engine of organizational resilience building. In line with the thinking of Volberda (1996) on flexible organizational form, we believe that the speed to detect opportunities and threats, mobilize resources and generate innovations is equally important. Hence, we conceptualized organizational resilience as a second-order construct with two first-order constructs: *innovative capability* contributing to the scope aspect and *agility capability* contributing to the speed aspect of organizational resilience. Accordingly, we define *net-enabled organizational resilience* in this study as follows:

> Net-enabled organizational resilience is the capacity of an organization to sense environmental changes and response swiftly with business model and technology innovations through the use of electronic networks to effectively withstand turbulence in the environment.

Organizations combine business model change and technology change to create innovations (Davila et al. 2005). In our study context, the value creation potential of innovations can be in the form of new products or services, new methods of distribution or marketing, tapping of new markets, or re-structuring transactions (Amit and Zott 2001). Access to resources from both channels provides the NERO an unprecedented opportunity to create new combination of product and service offerings and bundling. The improved quality of information about customers gathered allows the firm to come out with a variety of novel business processes that is not possible in a single-channel business. By innovating in the way business is done, firms can hope to differentiate themselves and gain additional market share.

Enhanced capabilities in innovativeness represent the scope of a firm's ability to launch competitive actions. Another area that is gaining prominence for firms to compete in a dynamic business environment is their ability to be agile (Oosterhout et al. 2005). Agility is the ability of a firm to continually sense and explore customer and marketplace enrichment opportunities and respond with the appropriate configurations of capabilities and capacities to exploit these opportunities rapidly and successfully (Sambamurthy et al. 2003). In order to actively respond to an accelerated and turbulent environment, firms need to develop competitive agility to be able to act quickly so as to manifest a high variety of competitive actions (Nayyar and Bantel 1994). An inte-

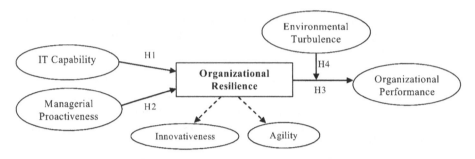

Figure 1. Research Model

grated retail channel provides the NERO with access to a pool of flexible resources that it can freely reallocate and reconfigure. This will enhance its ability to respond to competition quickly.

4   RESEARCH MODEL AND HYPOTHESES DEVELOPMENT

Figure 1 depicts the research model.

4.1 Antecedents of Organizational Resilience

Information technology serves as a critical antecedent for firms to generate more competitive actions through integrating their channels. In the retail industry, complementarities between IT, human, and business resources have been found to lead to sustainable performance advantages (Powell and Dent-Micallef 1997). An organization's IT capability can be defined as its organizational base of IT resources and capabilities. IT capabilities determine a firm's capacity for IT-based innovation as a result of available *IT resources* and the *ability to convert IT assets* into strategic applications (Sambamurthy et al. 2003). In a multichannel NERO context, an organization's IT infrastructure capability can be regarded as the degree to which its computer and communication technologies, technical platforms and databases are shareable and reusable (Duncan 1995). This is necessary to enable business process synthesis and integration across disparate physical and organizational boundaries (Basu and Blanning 2003). Successful Internet-enabled business requires the seamless flow and sharing of order and customer information across all channels so that data about customers and stocks are synchronized across databases to ensure consistency. This enhances an organization's ability to innovate and respond to its environment rapidly. Therefore, we expect that firms with a higher level of IT infrastructure capabilities would be able to achieve a higher level of organizational resilience.

> *H1: Information technology capability positively influences organizational resilience.*

From the viewpoint of resource complementarity, it is equally critical for the top management to have the strategic foresight to integrate the IT and business processes effectively (Sambamurthy et al. 2003). The entrepreneurial characteristic of proactiveness provides the ability to generate competitive actions. Proactiveness refers to an organization's strategic orientation to seek new opportunities and introduce new products and services ahead of the competition (Venkatraman 1989). Firms that are proactive are the quickest to innovate and first to introduce new products and services (Lumpkin and Dess 1996). Strategic resilience is about continuously anticipating, making adjustments, and possessing the capacity to change before it is obvious (Hamel and Valikangas 2003). This suggests that strong proactive behavior by management is critical in enhancing organization resilience. In Miles and Snow's (1978) business strategy typology, prospectors are found to enact a more dynamic environment and to place more emphasis on innovation. Proactiveness is a distinguishing characteristic of prospector organizations (Sabherwal and Chan 2001). Hence, we expect firms that are more proactive in their strategic orientation would be able to achieve a higher level of organizational resilience.

H2: Managerial proactiveness positively influences organizational resilience.

4.2 Impact of Organizational Resilience on Performance

In our context, by enhancing its level of innovativeness through providing a greater range of new offerings to its customers, the organization can retain its existing customers as well as attract new customers. As a result, it increases its market share and profits. By being more agile, firms can act quickly so as to manifest a high variety of competitive actions (Nayyar and Bantel 1994). This is an essential capability for organizations operating in high-velocity industries with rapidly shifting competitive landscapes. In line with previous studies in marketing (e.g., Grewal and Tansuhaj 2001; Johnson et al. 2003) and manufacturing (e.g., Vickery et al. 1997), we hypothesize that organizational resilience will have a positive impact on organizational performance.

H3: Organizational resilience positively influences organizational performance.

Consistent with current theory (e.g., Grewal and Tansuhaj 2001), we posit that the impact of organizational resilience on organizational performance is contingent on the level of turbulence in the macro environment. This is because turbulent environments reward organizational resilience since such environments demand anticipating the unexpected and competing in uncertain conditions (Sambamurthy et al. 2003; Volberda 1996). Environmental turbulence increases the likelihood that organizational resilience would create valuable outcomes for the firm. This argument is premised on the notion of performance advantages accruing to a firm that is in strategic alignment with its environment (Zajac et al. 2000). Building organizational resilience through enhanced innovative capabilities and agility capabilities can be viewed as strategic options (Kogut and Zander 1996), which offer the firm a choice to pursue new opportunities leading to enhanced performance when the environment calls for them. Hence, the higher the environmental turbulence, the more likely these options will be valuable in enhancing firm performance (Sambamurthy et al. 2003).

H4: The relationship between organizational resilience and organizational performance is positively moderated by environmental turbulence.

4.3 Control Variables

Following prior research on business value of IT and organizational performance, we expect that organizational performance would be influenced by its firm size and number of years since it first established a Website (net-enablement). Next, the extent to which a firm achieves superior performance through implementing various multi-channel strategies would likely be affected by the size of the physical store network since a large chain store would have more advantages to tap into their extensive physical store infrastructure to complement their online activities. Furthermore, integration of some activities might be less important for certain retail industry sectors and this might influence the performance. These four factors were used as control variables for organizational performance.

5   RESEARCH METHOD

5.1 Survey Data Collection

The unit of analysis is retail organization with both physical store(s) and an online Website. The sampling frame was drawn from Dun and Bradstreet directories and included retail trade companies in Singapore with standard industrial classification (SIC) codes starting from 5211 through 5999. The final sampling frame comprises of 562 companies. The survey that was conducted between March and May 2005 employed a three-wave mailing procedures advocated by Dillman (1999). A survey package with a postage-paid return envelope was mailed to the top executive of each company. One week after the initial mailing, a reminder postcard was sent to the companies. After about another week, a complete survey package was remailed to them. After accounting for 20 undelivered packages, and discarding 8 incomplete responses, we obtained a final usable sample of 125. The response rate of 24.5 percent is considered reasonable since the survey was unsolicited and involved participation of senior management. We motivated the respondents to provide valid data by offering a summary of the research results and an invitation to a free workshop on the research findings. These helped to ensure that respondents become professionally interested and committed to provide accurate data. We assessed nonresponse bias by verifying that early and late respondents did not significantly differ in their demographic characteristics and responses on principal constructs (Armstrong and Overton 1977). We also checked for existence of any common method bias with Harman's single-factor test since response comes from a single key informant (Podsakoff et al. 2003). We found no significant biases in our dataset. Table 1 shows our sample characteristics.

Table 1. Characteristics of Survey Sample

	Category	Number	%
Respondent Position	CEO, CFO, CIO, Managing Director	80	64.0
	Sales and Marketing Directors/Managers	29	23.2
	Executives	10	8.0
	Others	6	4.8
Retail Industry Sector	Apparels, Accessories and Jewelry	23	18.4
	Cars and Automotive Products	9	7.2
	Book and Stationery Stores	5	4.0
	Furniture, Home Furnishings and Building Hardware	13	10.4
	Eating and Drinking Places	12	9.6
	Florists and Gifts Shop	15	12.0
	Grocery Stores and Health Products	13	10.4
	Home Appliances, Computers and Electronics	25	20.0
	Departmental Stores and Other Merchandise	10	8.0
Number of employees	<50	77	61.6
	50-100	19	15.2
	101-200	14	11.2
	>201	15	12.0
Number of physical retail stores	<5	84	67.2
	5-10	16	12.8
	11-20	15	12.0
	>20	10	8.0

5.2 Operationalization of Constructs

All constructs were measured on seven-point Likert-type scales. The four-item scale used to measure *IT capability* was adapted from Byrd and Turner (2000) to assess the firm's technical IT infrastructure in terms of communication network connectivity, inventory, and customer database integration. The three items used to measure *managerial proactiveness* were adopted from Sabherwal and Chan (2001), which was based on Venkatraman's (1989) strategic orientation of business enterprises (STROBE) scale. This scale assesses the proactive behavior of increasing capacity before competitors and being a first-mover to introduce products and services. *Organizational resilience* was conceptualized as a second-order construct comprising of two first-order constructs of innovative capability and agility capability. Due to the unavailability of scales suitable for our study context, the three-item scale used to measure innovative capability was self-developed based on conceptual developments by Amit and Zott (2001) and Hamel and Valikangas (2003). It assesses the net-enabled organization's ability to offer new services and products. The three items used to measure agility capability were self-developed based on Sambamurthy et al. (2003), and measure the organization's ability to detect opportunities and respond quickly to business environment and competitor's market actions. We used a seven-item scale to measure environmental turbulence by assessing the organization's market and technological turbulence. This scale was adapted from Jaworski and Kohli (1993).

Many variables including productivity, efficiency, profitability, and competitive advantage have been used to measure IT-enabled organizational performance (Melville et al. 2004). Tallon et al. (2000) suggest that perceptual measures of firm performance correlate strongly with objective measures and in the absence of objective data on IT payoffs, executives' perceptions can identify areas where IT is creating value. Management assessments are generally consistent with secondary published performance data external to the organization. Following Wade and Hulland's (2004) recommendation that the dependent variable used to measure performance should incorporate a competitive assessment of performance, we measured *organizational performance* as an aggregated metric comprising of market share gains, net profits, revenue growth, return on investments, and return on assets, measured relative to major competitors.

5.3 Control Variables

Firm size was coded as the *log* of the number of employees, and net-enablement age was represented as the *log* of the number of years since the firm first established its Website, using year 2005 as a base. Industry sector was coded as a dummy variable for different industry sectors, while the size of the physical network was coded as the *log* of the number of physical retail store(s).

6   DATA ANALYSES AND RESULTS

The structural equation modeling technique, partial least squares (PLS) as implemented in PLS-Graph Version 3.0, was used for data analyses (Chin 2001). It is an appropriate method for testing complex predictive research models (Joreskög and Wold 1982) as it can assess the measurement model (relationships between questions and constructs) within the context of the structural model (relationships among constructs). It maximizes the explanation of variance and prediction in the theoretical model, does not demand multivariate normal distributions, and is suitable for small sample size exploratory studies. Although a series of multiple regression analyses could be used to test our research model, PLS is a better approach as it can account for measurement errors in unobserved constructs and examine the significance of structural paths simultaneously. Furthermore, due to the lack of ability to account for measurement errors, techniques such as moderated regression are unable to accurately detect the strength of moderating effects between continuous variables (McClelland and Judd 1993).

6.1 Validity and Reliability of Organizational Resilience Construct

Based on the conceptual model presented in Figure 1, two factors were created from indicators of innovative capability and agility capability to represent organizational resilience as a second-order construct. The factor analysis confirmed that the organizational resilience indicators loaded well onto the two corresponding factors: innovative capability and agility capability. As shown in Table 2, this indicates good validity and reliability of the first-order factors.

As theorized earlier, organizational resilience is a higher-order construct across two dimensions of innovative capability and agility capability. The correlations between the two first-order factors are statistically significant and of high magnitude (Pearson's coefficient = 0.668, p < 0.001). This suggests the existence of such a higher-order factor structure consistent with our conceptualization. The factor scores of the two first-order constructs were used to assess the validity and reliability of the second-order construct. As shown in Table 3, all structural coefficients exhibit significant critical ratios, providing evidence of convergent validity. The composite reliability was estimated from path loadings to be 0.773, indicating sufficient reliability for the second-order construct. Therefore, on both theoretical and empirical grounds, our conceptualization of organizational resilience as a higher-order, multidimensional construct seems justified.

Table 2. Measurement Properties of First-Order Organizational Resilience Constructs

Construct	Item	Factor Loading	Cronbach's Alpha
Innovative Capability (IC)	IC1: Provide unique products and services to our customers.	0.855	0.928
	IC2: Bundle products and services creatively.	0.893	
	IC3: Offer new customer support services.	0.859	
Agility Capability (AC)	AC1: Continually sense and detect customer and marketplace opportunities.	0.866	0.956
	AC2: Respond quickly to dynamic business environment.	0.882	
	AC3: React rapidly to competitors' market actions.	0.911	

Table 3. Estimation of the Second-Order Construct

Second-order Construct	First-order Constructs	Standard Loading	*t*-statistic	Composite Reliability
Organizational Resilience (RESILIENCE)	Innovative Capability (IC)	0.798	7.015***	0.773
	Agility Capability (AC)	0.752	6.841***	
*** p < 0.001				

Table 4. Psychometric Properties and Descriptive Statistics of Measurement Model

Construct	Item Loading	Composite Reliability	AVE	Mean	SD
IT Capability (IT)					
IT1: Our Web-based systems arc tightly linked to our existing computer systems in the physical stores via real-time communication networks.	0.916	0.943	0.806	3.440	1.511
IT2: The physical stores and the Website access to a common inventory database.	0.930				
IT3: The physical stores and the Website access to common customer database.	0.881				
IT4: Information is shared seamlessly across our organization, regardless of location.	0.862				
Managerial Proactiveness (PROACT)					
PROACT1: We generally increase capacity (i.e., prepare to handle a greater volume of business) before our competitors do the same.	0.889	0.952	0.869	4.650	1.411
PROACT2: We are usually the first ones to introduce various products and/or services in the market.	0.957				
PROACT3: We adopt innovations early.	0.950				
Environmental Turbulence (ENV)					
ENV1: Environmental changes in our industry are very difficult to forecast.	0.661	0.904	0.577	4.880	0.994
ENV2: The business environment in which we operate is continuously changing.	0.766				
ENV3: In our kind of business, customers' product preferences change a lot over time.	0.793				
ENV4: Marketing practices in our product areas arc constantly changing.	0.814				
ENV5: New product introductions are very frequent in this market.	0.862				
ENV6: The technology used to provide our products and services changes rapidly.	0.736				
ENV7: Many new products and services ideas have been made possible through technology breakthroughs in this industry.	0.663				
Organizational Performance (PERFORM)					
PERFORM1: Market share gains	0.809	0.939	0.756	4.420	0.915
PERFORM2: Net profits	0.870				
PERFORM3: Revenue growth	0.897				
PERFORM4: Return on investment	0.874				
PERFORM5: Return on assets	0.894				

Table 5. Discriminant Validity of Reflective Constructs

Construct	IT	PROACT	RESILIENCE	ENV	PERFORM
IT	0.806				
PROACT	0.108	0.869			
RESILIENCE	0.272	0.215	0.574		
ENV	0.070	0.123	0.098	0.577	
PERFORM	0.208	0.403	0.215	0.052	0.756

6.2 Evaluating the Measurement Model

We used three tests to determine the convergent validity and internal consistency of the four other reflective constructs in our model: item loading, composite reliability of constructs, and the average variance extracted (AVE) by construct. Table 4 presents the psychometric properties and descriptive statistics. All item loadings between an indicator and its posited underlying construct factor were greater than 0.7. Composite reliability of constructs all exceeded Nunnally and Bernstein's (1994) criterion of 0.7, while the average variances extracted were above the recommended threshold of 0.5, adequately demonstrating convergent validity. Table 5 reports the test for discriminant validity of reflective constructs. Diagonal elements are AVE for each construct, which, for discriminant validity, should be greater than the off-diagonal elements of the square of inter-construct correlations. All our constructs fulfilled these criteria.

6.3 Testing the Structural Model

With assurance of good psychometric properties in the measurement model, the PLS structural model was next assessed to determine its explanatory power and the significance of the hypothesized paths. The explanatory power of the structural model was determined based on the amount of variance in the endogenous constructs for which the model could account. To assess the moderating role of environment turbulence on the relationship between organizational resilience and firm performance using PLS, we followed the method proposed by Chin et al. (2003). First, product indicators for the interaction construct (RESILIENCE × ENV) were created by multiplying each of the two indicators for organization resilience (factor scores of IC and AC) with each of the seven indicators for environment turbulence (ENV1 to ENV7). Hence, the interaction construct comprises of 14 product indicators. A boot-strapping resampling procedure was used to estimate the standard errors and to determine the significance of the path coefficients.

Our variables in the research model could explain 32.5 percent of variance in performance. All hypotheses were supported. Both IT capability and managerial proactiveness significantly impact organizational resilience but the level of IT capability ($b = 0.431, p < 0.001$) had a greater impact on organizational resilience compared to managerial proactiveness ($b = 0.308, p < 0.001$). These two antecedents accounted for 37.8 percent of the variance in organizational resilience. Before including the moderating variable environmental turbulence into the structural model, we separately tested a base model whereby organizational resilience directly impacts organizational performance. This relationship is significant at $p < 0.01$ but the variance explained for organizational performance in this base model is only 23.2 percent. This suggests that by adding environmental turbulence as a moderator into the model, we have substantially increased the variance explained in performance by 9.3 percent. In the full model, organizational resilience has a direct impact on organizational performance (H3: $b = 0.446, p < 0.01$), but this relationship is significantly moderated by environmental turbulence (H4: $b = 0.263, p < 0.01$). All control variables were insignificant at $p < 0.05$.

7   DISCUSSION

This research attempts to understand the impacts of information technology and managerial proactiveness in nurturing net-enabled organizational resilience in the context of multichannel retail organizations. Drawing on the ecological survival perspective, we argue that creation of organizational resilience hinges on the firm's ability to generate variety in the organization. This is because formulating organizational strategy for turbulent environments requires the development of variety-generating capability in the organization (SubbaNarasimha 2001). The results from our empirical study demonstrate evidence to support this proposition.

Foremost, our findings explicate the roles of IT and managerial proactiveness in enhancing organizational resilience. We found that IT capability has a stronger impact on organizational resilience compared to managerial proactiveness. An integrated IT infrastructure across the organization links various units and provides a seamless flow of accurate, consistent, and timely information to employees and customers. Information is the key to formulating IT-enabled strategies for competing in turbulent environments. Hence, a high level of IT capability is a prerequisite to provide the foundation for developing core organizational competences. However, based on the organizational resource complementarity perspective, the business value of IT depends on the presence and influence of other organizational, business, and technical resources. Organizational resources such as organizational culture and human resource capability have been found to affect innovation and agility (Oosterhout et al. 2005). Increasingly, there is an expectation for organizations to exhibit an entrepreneurial orientation in order to achieve superior performance (Lumpkin and Dess 1996). In our research context of multichannel retailing, the degree of proactiveness is an essential entrepreneurial characteristic for executing managerial foresight to seize new opportunities in the competitive retailing environment.

Our results revealed that organizations attain resilience when they are able to sense environmental changes and respond swiftly with innovations in channel arrangements, products, and services. This results from the expansion of the repertoire of actions available to react to unforeseen threats and unanticipated changes in the environment. Organizations that are more resilient were found to exhibit better organizational performance. Furthermore, the findings also indicate that under turbulent environments, organizations with a higher level of organizational resilience achieve more superior performance. This highlights the point that organizations that have invested heavily in IT and manifest proactive behavior to build up their resilience capacity will be able to leverage on the strategic options of doing so when the opportunities arise or when crisis happens.

Before discussing the implications of our research, some limitations must be acknowledged. First, even though we have carried out statistical tests to address potential biases, interpretation of our results needs to take into consideration that data were collected through a single informant. Second, the dataset comprising of only Singaporean retail firms might limit the generalizability of our results. Third, we have developed and examined the notion of organizational resilience in the context of net-enabled retail organizations. Our conceptualization of this construct in terms of innovative capabilities is based on a retailing context and hence this could reduce its applicability to other types of organizations. Finally, even though our sample size is of sufficient power to detect meaningful effects, future research should be conducted with a larger sample.

Despite these limitations, we believe that our substantial findings through this exploratory effort provide numerous implications for practice and future research. The validation that IT and proactiveness are complementary in building organizational resilience should serve as a reminder to managers that they need to ramp up the integrative capabilities of their IT infrastructure. The subunits and functional areas across the organizations should be tightly linked with IT to facilitate communications and information flow. This is critical for sensing opportunities and disruptive irregularities in the organization system. Next, our results also attest to the importance of cultivating a proactive behavior in the top management for building a resilient organization. Our conceptualization of organizational resilience as a higher-order construct comprising of innovative capability and agility capability provides some relevant managerial insights. The empirical validation of the metrics for this construct suggests that the level of resilience in an organization may be measured through assessing its innovative capabilities in making changes to its business model, products, and services as well as its agility capabilities in terms of how well it is able to sense and respond to environmental threats and opportunities. It is also noteworthy that the rewards for building resilience are greater for organizations existing in highly dynamic environments.

The development of a structural model to understand organizational resilience building a under turbulent environment is a significant theoretical contribution. This should serves as a useful first step in advancing our knowledge of the capability-building process of resilience and its performance implications. Our theoretical conceptualization of organizational resilience converges with Gunderson (2000)'s idea that the resilience of a system can be increased by increasing the buffering capacity of the system through nurturing sources of renewal (i.e., increasing scope through innovating) and mitigating the effects of unwanted variation in the system in order to shorten the return time to a desired equilibrium (i.e., increasing the response speed by being more agile). We find empirical support for our two-dimensional higher-order construct of organizational resilience. Nevertheless, we believe that organizational resilience is likely to be a multi-faceted construct that manifests itself differently under different context. The approach that we have employed in this research should be invaluable to future researchers who are interested in constructing multidimensional representations of organizational resilience in other net-enabled organizations to measure and understand the challenges involved in building this important organizational capability.

References

Amit, R., and Zott, C. "Value Creation in E-business," *Strategic Management Journal* (22), 2001, pp. 493-520.

Armstrong, J. S., and Overton, T. S. "Estimating Nonresponse Bias in Mail Surveys," *Journal of Marketing Research* (14), August 1977, pp. 396-402.

Ashby, W. "Requisite Variety and its Implications for the Control of Complex Systems," *Cybernetica* (1), 1958, pp. 83-99.

Bahn, D. L., and Fischer, P. P. "Clicks and Mortar: Balancing Brick and Mortar Business Strategy and Operations with Auxiliary Electronic Commerce," *Information Technology and Management* (4), 2003, pp. 319-334.

Basu, A., and Blanning, R. "Synthesis and Decomposition of Processes in Organizations," *Information Systems Research* (14:14), 2003, pp. 337-355.

Byrd, T.A., and Turner, D.E. "Measuring the Flexibility of Information Technology Infrastructure: Exploratory Analysis of a Construct," *Journal of Management Information Systems* (17:1), Summer 2000, pp. 167-208.

Chin, W. W. *PLS-Graph User's Guide Verison 3.0*, Soft Modeling Inc., 2001.

Chin, W. W., Marcolin, B. L., and Newsted, P. R. "A Partial Least Squares Latent Variable Modeling Approach for Measuring Interaction Effects: Results from a Monte Carlo Simulation Study and an Electronic-Mail Emotion/Adoption Study," *Information Systems Research* (14:2), 2003, pp. 189-217.

Daniel, E. M., and Wilson, H. N. "The Role of Dynamic Capabilities in E-Business Transformation," *European Journal of Information Systems* (12), 2003, pp. 282-296.

Davila, T., Epstein, M. J., and Shelton, R. *Making Innovation Work: How to Manage It, Measure It, and Profit from It*, Upper Saddle River, NJ: Wharton School Publishing, 2005.

Dillman, D. *Mail and Internet Surveys: The Tailored Design Method* (2nd ed.), New York: John Wiley, 1999.

Duncan, N. B. "Capturing Flexibility of Information Technology Infrastructure: A Study of Resource Characteristics and Their Measure," *Journal of Management Information Systems* (12:2), Fall 1995, pp. 37-57.

The Economist. "A Perfect Market," May 15, 2004, pp. 3-5.

Forrester Research. "The State of Retailing Online 7.0," Cambridge, MA, 2004.

Goersch, D. "Multichannel Integration and Its Implications For Retail Web Sites," paper presented at the European Conference on Information Systems (ECIS), Gdansk, Poland, 2002.

Grewal, R., and Tansuhaj, P. "Building Organizational Capabilities for Managing Economic Crisis: The Role of Market Orientation and Strategic Flexibility," *Journal of Marketing* (65), April 2001, pp. 1-28.

Gulati, R., and Garino, J. "Get the Right Mix of Bricks and Clicks," *Harvard Business Review* (78:3), May/June 2000, pp. 107-114.

Gunderson, L. H. "Ecological Resilience: In Theory and Application," *Annual Review of Ecological Systems* (31), 2000, pp. 425-439.

Hamel, G., and Valikangas, L. "The Quest for Resilience," *Harvard Business Review* (81:9), September 2003, pp. 52-63.

Jaworski, B., and Kohli, A. "Market Orientation: Antecedents and Consequences," *Journal of Marketing* (57), July 1993, pp. 53-70.

Johnson, J. L., Lee, R. P., Saini, A., and Grohmann, B. "Market-Focused Strategic Flexibility: Conceptual Advances and an Integrative Model," *Journal of Academy of Marketing Science* (31:1), 2003, pp. 74-89.

Joreskög, K., and Wold, H. *Systems Under Indirect Observation: Causality, Structure, and Prediction*, Amsterdam: North-Holland, 1982.

Keeney, R. "The Value of Internet Commerce to the Customer," *Management Science* (45:4), April 1999, pp. 533-542.

Kogut, B., and Zander, U. "What Do Firms Do? Coordination, Identity, and Learning," *Organization Science* (7), 1996, pp. 502-518.

Lumpkin, G., and Dess, G. G. "Clarifying the Entrepreneurial Orientation Construct and Linking it to Performance," *Academy of Management Review* (21:1), 1996, pp. 135-172.

Mason, J. B., Mayer, M. L., and Wilkinson, J. B. *Modern Retailing: Theory and Practice* (6th ed.), Homewood, IL: Irwin, 1993.

McClelland, G., and Judd, C. "Statistical Difficulties of Detecting Interactions and Moderator Effects," *Psychological Bulletin* (114:2), 1993, pp. 376-390.

Melville, N., Kraemer, K., and Gurbaxani, V. "*Review*: Information Technology and Organizational Performance: An Integrative Model of IT Business Value," *MIS Quarterly* (28:2), June 2004, pp. 283-322.

Miles, R. E., and Snow, C. C. *Organizational Strategy, Structure, and Process*, New York: McGraw-Hill, 1978.

Nayyar, P., and Bantel, K. "Competitive Agility: A Source of Competitive Advantage Based on Speed and Variety," *Advances in Strategic Management* (10A), 1994, pp. 193-222.

Nunnally, J., and Bernstein, I. *Psychometric Theory* (3rd ed.), New York: McGraw-Hill, 1994.

Oosterhout, M. V., Waarts, E., and Hillegersberg, J. V. "Assessing Business Agility: A Multi-Industry Study in the Netherlands," in R. Baskerville, L. Mathiassen, J. Pries-Heje, and J. I. DeGross (eds.), *Business Agility and Information Technology Diffusion*, New York: Springer Science and Business Media, 2005, pp. 275-294.

Podsakoff, P. M., MacKenzie, S. B., Lee, J.-Y. , and Podsakoff, N. P. "Common Method Bias in Behavioral Research: A Critical Review of the Literature and Recommended Remedies," *Journal of Applied Psychology* (88:5), 2003, pp. 879-903.

Powell, T., and Dent-Micallef, A. "Information Technology as Competitive Advantage: The Role of Human, Business and technology Resources," *Strategic Management Journal* (18:5), 1997, pp. 375-405.

Prasarnphanich, P., and Gillenson, M. "The Hybrid Click and Bricks Business Model," *Communications of the ACM* (46:2), 2003, pp. 178-185.

Sabherwal, R., and Chan, Y. E. "Alignment Between Business and IS Strategies: A Study of Prospectors, Analyzers, and Defenders," *Information Systems Research* (12:1), March 2001, pp. 11-33.

Sambamurthy, V., Bharadwaj, A.S., and Grover, V. "Shaping Agility Through Digital Options: Reconceptualizing The Role of Information Technology in Contemporary Firms," *MIS Quarterly* (27:2), June 2003, pp. 237-263.

Samli, A. *Retail Marketing Strategy: Planning, Implementation, and Control*, New York: Quorum Books, 1989.

Sanchez, R. "Building Blocks for Strategy Theory: Resources, Dynamic Capabilities and Competences," in T. Elfring and H. W. Volberda (eds.), *Rethinking Strategy*, Thousand Oaks, CA: Sage Publications, 2001.

Starr, R., Newfrock, J., and Delurey, M. "Enterprise Resilience: Managing Risk in the Network Economy," *Strategy+Business*, Spring 2003, pp. 1-10. (retrieved on February 22, 2006 from www.boozallen.de/scm/downloads/201.pdf).

Steinfield, C., Bouwman, H., and Adelaar, T. "The Dynamics of Click-And-Mortar Electronic Commerce: Opportunities And Management Strategies," *International Journal of Electronic Commerce* (7:1), 2002, pp. 93-119.

Straub, D. W., and Watson, R. T. "Research Commentary: Transformational Issues in Researching IS and Net-enabled Organizations," *Information Systems Research* (12:4), 2001, pp. 337-345.

SubbaNarasimha, P. "Strategy in Turbulent Environments: The Role of Dynamic Competence," *Managerial and Decision Economics* (22), 2001, pp. 201-212.

Tallon, P. P., Kraemer, K. L., and Gurbaxani, V. "Executives' Perceptions of the Business Value of Information Technology: A Process-Oriented Approach," *Journal of Management Information Systems* (16:4), Spring 2000, pp. 145-173.

Venkatraman, N. "Strategic Orientation of Business Enterprises: The Construct, Dimensionality, and Measurement," *Management Science* (35:8), August 1989, pp. 942-962.

Vickery, S., Droge, C., and Markland, R. "Dimensions of Manufacturing Strength in the Furniture Industry," *Journal of Operations Management* (15:4) 1997, pp. 317-330.

Volberda, H. W. "Toward the Flexible Form: How to Remain Vital in Hypercompetitive Environments," *Organization Science* (7:4), July-August 1996, pp. 359-374.

Wade, M., and Hulland, J. *"Review:* The Resource-Based View and Information Systems Research: Review, Extension, and Suggestions for Future Research," *MIS Quarterly* (28:1), March 2004, pp. 107-142.

Wallace, D. W., Giese, J. L., and Johnson, J. L. "Customer Retailer Loyalty in the Context of Multiple Channel Strategies," *Journal of Retailing* (80), 2004, pp. 249-263.

Weick, K. *The Social Psychology of Organizing*, New York: McGraw-Hill, 1979.

Wheeler, B. C. "NEBIC: A Dynamic Capabilities Theory for Assessing Net-Enablement," *Information Systems Research* (13:2), June 2002, pp. 125-146.

Zajac, E. J., Kraatz, M. S., and Bresser, K. "Modeling the Dynamics of Strategic Fit: A Normative Approach to Strategic Change," *Strategic Management Journal* (21), 2000, pp. 429-453.

About the Authors

Lih-Bin Oh is an instructor and doctoral candidate in the Department of Information Systems at the National University of Singapore. He obtained his M.Sc. in Information Systems and B.Sc. (First Class Honors) in Computer and Information Sciences from NUS in 2000 and 1998 respectively. He was a visiting scholar at the Eli Broad Graduate School of Management, Michigan State University, from August to December 2005. Prior to pursuing an academic career, he worked as a program officer in the division of information and communications sciences for the Agency for Science, Technology and Research (A*STAR). His current research interest is in the area of business value of IT in net-enabled organizations. Lih-Bin can be reached at ohlb@comp.nus.edu.sg.

Hock-Hai Teo is an associate professor of Information Systems in the Department of Information Systems at the National University of Singapore. He received his Ph.D. in MIS from NUS in 1998. He was a visiting scholar at the Wharton Business School, University of Pennsylvania from 1999 to 2000. He has published in the *MIS Quarterly*, *Journal of Management Information Systems*, *IEEE Transactions on Engineering Management*, *International Journal of Human-Computer Studies*, *Journal of the American Society for Information Science and Technology*, *Journal of Educational Computing Research*, *Information and Management*, and *Journal of Database Management*. He was the winner of the *MIS Quarterly* Reviewer of the Year Award (2004). He is currently serving on the editorial boards of *MIS Quarterly*, *IEEE Transactions on Engineering Management*, and the *Journal of Electronic Commerce Research*. Hock-Hai can be reached at teohh@comp.nus.edu.sg.

Part 2

IT Adoption and Diffusion

4 THE ROLE OF VALUE COMPATIBILITY IN INFORMATION TECHNOLOGY ADOPTION

Deborah Bunker
University of New South Wales
Sydney, Australia

Karlheinz Kautz
Copenhagen Business School
Frederiksberg, Denmark

Anne Luu Thanh Nguyen
University of New South Wales
Sydney, Australia

Abstract   *Compatibility has been recognized as an important element in the adoption of IT innovations in organizations but as a concept it has been generally limited to technical or functional factors. Compatibility is also significant, however, with regard to value compatibility between the organization and the adopted IT innovation. We propose a framework to determine value compatibility analyzing the organization's and information system's structure, practices, and culture and to explore the value compatibility of an organization with its adopted self-service computer-based information system. A case study was conducted to determine the congruence of an organization's value and IT value compatibility. This study found that while there was a high correspondence in the organizational structure and practices dimensions, there were organizational culture disparities. The cultural disparities reflected the self-service acceptance and training issues experienced by the case organization. These findings explain the problems experienced with value compatibility and the adoption of the information systems and show the suitability of the framework for the detection of such problems.*

Keywords   Value compatibility, IT innovation

Please use the following format when citing this chapter:

Bunker, Deborah, Kautz, Karlheinz, Thanh Nguyen, Anne Luu, 2006, in International Federation for Information Processing (IFIP), Volume 206, The Transfer and Diffusion of Information Technology for Organizational Resilience, eds. B. Donnellan, Larsen T., Levine L., DeGross J. (Boston: Springer), pp. 53-70.

1   INTRODUCTION

The idea that innovations may be compatible or incompatible with an organization's existing (information) systems or resources has been long advocated in the innovation literature by, for example, Rogers (1995), whose definition of compatibility highlights the traditional view of the concept:

> compatibility is the degree to which an innovation is perceived as consistent with the existing values, past experiences, and needs of potential adopters. An innovation can be compatible or incompatible: with socio-cultural values and beliefs, with previously introduced ideas, or with clients needs for innovations (p. 224).

The incompatibility of the potential adopters' cultural values with the innovation will hinder the adoption process and there is the belief that the higher the compatibility of an idea, the lower the uncertainty felt by the potential adopters (Rogers 1995). Among those who have researched organizational values and have found that they influence the successful adoption of IT innovations are Orlikowski (1993) and Zammuto and O'Connor (1992).

The traditional view of compatibility has, however, been criticized by Tornatsky and Klein (1982) as being too broad. In their meta-analysis of innovation adoption and implementation, they argue that it is more appropriate to distinguish between value compatibility and practical compatibility. Value compatibility refers to the suitability of the innovation with the norms or values of the potential adopters. Practical compatibility refers to the suitability of the innovation with the current practices of the adopters. Klein and Sorra (1996) reinforce this view in their model of innovation implementation success. Their proposed model explains that successful innovation implementation is due to both the formal mechanisms creating a climate for the innovation's implementation, which can be understood as practical compatibility, and value compatibility, which they define as the fit of an innovation to the targeted users' values at the organizational and group levels. Harrington and Ruppel (1999) also acknowledge the dual nature of compatibility. They motivate their work by relating to Cooper (1994), who suggests that organizational culture and its associated values comprise an area that has largely been ignored by IT implementation researchers. Supported by Romm et al. (1991), they make the argument that without a match between the values of an organization and the value assumptions embedded in an IT innovation, a costly implementation failure is likely to occur.

This argument is central to this paper and we try to fill this gap by providing a study of value compatibility between an organization and a computer-based information system and its influence on the adoption of the information system. For this purpose we develop a research framework, which emphasizes organizational structure, practices, and culture and their embeddedness in an information system and application to a specific case.

In the remainder of the paper we present our framework, our research method, and our case organization as well as the information system. We then describe and discuss our findings and finish with some conclusions.

2   A FRAMEWORK TO STUDY VALUE COMPATIBILITY

Organizational values are a defining part of organizational culture (Schein 1984). According to Robbins and Langton (2001), researchers in the field agree that the following seven dimensions jointly explain organizational culture: innovation and risk-taking; attention to detail; outcome orientation; people orientation; team orientation; aggressiveness; and stability. The dimensions describe the degree to which employees are encouraged and expected to act in certain ways, the level of management focus on outcomes and people, the way employees interact with each other and externally, as well as the level of drive of the company to maintain the status quo or to change with the times (Robbins and Langton 2001). These seven dimensions form the first part of our framework.

While values are the invisible manifestations of organizational culture, organizational practices are their visible counterpart. Therefore, organizational practices have to be taken into account when studying organizational values and culture. Hofstede (1994), beyond heroes and symbols, considers rituals as important expressions of practices and he distinguishes six dimensions, which are helpful for their detailed investigation: process-orientated versus results-orientated; employee-orientated versus job-orientated; parochial versus professional; open systems versus closed systems; loose control versus tight control; and normative versus pragmatic organizations. While the first two dimensions are rather self-explanatory, the others require some elaboration. The parochial versus professional dimension refers to the level to which the employee's identity is derived from the organization as opposed to deriving their identity from the type of job they hold. Furthermore, parochial companies may take into consideration social and familial background as much as the job competence in the hiring process. In contrast, professional organizations hire solely on the basis of job competence and employees' private details are not considered. Open systems versus closed systems may be referred to as the *communication climate* of the company. The image of welcoming organizations where employees feel part of the team may be contrasted with a very secretive organization where only special people will feel accepted. Loose versus tight control refers to the restraint or checks with regard to budgets, meeting times, and level of formalness. Finally, normative versus pragmatic practices deal with the notion of customer orientation. Pragmatic organizations are market driven as opposed to normative organizations, which place high importance in following organizational procedures and ensuring that the ethical standards and honesty are upheld. The image of a private sector organization as opposed to a government organization may be helpful in understanding this practice dimension (Hofstede 1994). The dimensions form the second part of our framework.

Organizational culture and its values, however, also become visible in organizational structures (Mintzberg 1989), which we take into account when studying compatibility between the organization and its computer-based information systems. Again following Robbins and Langton (2001), the key elements that need to be addressed in the design of an organization's structure include: work specialization; departmentalization; chain of command; span of control; centralization and decentralization; and formalization. Work specialization may also be called the division of labor. Robbins and Langton refer to "the degree [with] which tasks in the organization are subdivided

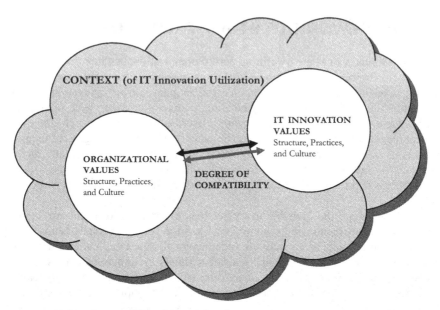

Figure 1. Value Compatibility in IT Adoption

into separate jobs." Departmentalization is the "basis on which jobs are grouped together." Typical forms of departmentalization include, by function, type of product, geography, process and type of customer. The chain of command refers to the "unbroken line of authority that extends from the top of the organization to the lowest echelon and clarifies who reports to whom." The span of control refers to "the number of employees which a manager can effectively and efficiently direct." Centralization refers to the "degree to which decision making is concentrated at a single point in the organization." On the other hand, decentralization occurs when the "decision discretion is pushed down to lower-level employees." Finally, formalization refers to the level in which "jobs within the organization are standardized."

In summary, our framework (see Figure 1) to study value compatibility between information systems and organizations consists of three dimensions. The context for which IT innovations are utilized is entrenched in the organizational values, which are reflected in the structure, practices, and culture of an organization. In the following, we will illustrate the suitability of our framework and the importance of value compatibility through the analysis of a particular case.

3   THE RESEARCH METHOD

As the research aims at exploring the value compatibility of an organization with a computer-based information system in terms of its structure, practices, and culture, an interpretive, qualitative case study is, in this instance, more appropriate to study these dimensions than undertaking a positivist quantitative study. The descriptive com-plexities of organizational structure, practices, and culture mean that a qualitative approach can better cater to describing nuances as well as exploring information that would otherwise not be possible if restricted to certain quantitative criteria. This is especially important as our work aimed to also discover organizational issues that may have hindered the adoption of the system by the members of the organization. Myers (1997) categorizes qualitative research into the underlying epistemology that influences and guides the research: positivist, interpretive and critical. Although organizational issues have become a major focus for information system researchers in recent years, "much of this literature reflects a rational–economic interpretation of organizational processes, and a positivist methodology which is based on the view that the world exhibits an objective cause-effect relationship which can be discovered, at least partially, by structured observation" (Walsham 1993, p. 4). While these methods are powerful, other researchers have highlighted some inherent limitations of a positivist approach, which are summed up by Kraemer and King (1990) as the inability to "explain the variance observed in the patterns and processes of adoption and routinization of information technology in various tasks" and "the differences in successful use of the technology across organizations" (p. 583). Other information system researchers have advocated the interpretive epistemology of research as it

> can help information system researchers to understand human thought and action in social and organizational contexts; it has the potential to produce deep insights into information systems phenomena including the management of information systems and information systems development (Klein and Myers 1999, p. 67).

The interpretive epistemology aims "at producing an understanding of the context of the information system, and the process whereby the information system influences and is influenced by its context" (Walsham 1993, pp. 4-5). Hence, the interpretive epistemology is very apt for our research as the context in which the information system is utilized is significant for the exploration of value compatibility between the adopting organization and the information system. In the interpretive tradition, theories are neither correct nor incorrect. These theories are compared, evaluated, and improved upon with the aim of creating "intersubjectively tested theoretical approaches, considered of value to a broader group than a single individual" (Walsham 1993, p. 6).

The research itself was conducted as a case study that utilized 12 semi-structured, open-ended interviews with 3 systems administrators and 9 system users from 5 different departments, as well as observations and analysis of artefacts such as employee newsletters, employee manuals, company posters and ornaments, systems development documents, training manuals, employee advertisements, and signage in the exploration of the context.

4 THE CASE

The case organization is a beverage company, which manufactures, sells and distributes a wide range of nonalcoholic ready-to-drink beverages. In the Asia Pacific region, it is the largest bottler, spanning six countries. The Beverage Company's (TBC) flagship licensed drink is also the market leader in the leisure industry. Marketing for the drink is high, often associated with youthful, fun, and jovial images. TBC's presence in Australia began in the early 1900s and since then has undergone many acquisitions and mergers. Today it is a public company and employs approximately 3,500 people.

The business owner of the system under investigation is the Accounts Payable department. The Non-Inventory Purchasing System (NIPS) is a PC-based e-commerce information system for the procurement of TBC's non-inventory items in Australia. Non-inventory goods are items that are not direct inputs into the production of the beverages produced by the company. NIPS is a web-based purchasing software package and is the only mechanism for obtaining non-inventory goods at TBC. As part of the system implementation, the Accounts Payable department was centralized nationally. The purchasing job functions of the administrative employees, for example executive assistants and purchasing officers, were transferred to the employee population for self-service and self-maintenance.

NIPS contains on-line catalogs that assist the approximately 2,500 system users in making electronic requests. For strategic items, there is a fully integrated approval process. Corporate purchasing cards, of which approximately 1,700 are issued, are usually of low value and are used in conjunction with the system for nonstrategic items. The purchasing card is similar to a credit card with limits imposed. The system also provides functionality to manage the corporate purchasing cards. Limits on the cards are hierarchically allocated based on the employee's position as well as their specific needs. The system allows employees to verify purchases made with their purchasing card. A database of all non-inventory purchases provides information on purchasing patterns and can assist the company in its supplier negotiations. In parallel with business rules, features such as automatic routing to approvers, automatic creation of purchase orders, and dispatch to the vendors (via the nominated method, including e-mail), eliminates clumsy communication channels and also the need for purchase officers. The benefits, which were presented by the NIPS business case, included empowering employees and enabling them to get on with the job; savings as a direct result of reduced headcount; lower time and effort required by the business to make a purchase; enforced time control for approvals to be made; ability to enforce the standards of products; ability to obtain the whole picture of purchasing patterns; and data to assist in the negotiation of supplier agreements. The system owners, however, were dissatisfied with the adoption and use of the system and a commissioned pilot study highlighted problems and showed that the expected benefits were not realized.

5   CASE STUDY FINDINGS

Our framework for analyzing value compatibility as a prerequisite for IT adoption emphasizes the concepts of organizational structure, practices, and culture and their embeddedness in information technology artefacts and information systems. Applying these concepts, our findings are next outlined with regard to the value compatibility of TBC and the NIPS (the information system) that the organization had implemented to support its purchasing processes.

5.1 TBC Structure and Value Compatibility with NIPS

5.1.1 TBC Structure

Work specialization is relatively high at TBC; however, the jobs are not unfulfilling and meaningless. For example, within the Accounting department, the accounting concerns of the company are subdivided into accounts payable, payroll, operations accounting, revenue accounting, etc. Within each functional department the roles are specialized to the skill-level required and a Projects Portfolio Team documents the skills, knowledge of technologies, experience, and basic level of competency required for the team members.

TBC is organized in eight departments—Finance, Operations and Logistics, Employee Relations, Corporate Affairs, Strategic Programs, Sales and Customer Service–Field Operations, Sales and Customer Service–National Business, and Information Systems—thus there is high departmentalization and within departments there are further groupings by state, type of customer, type of product, and type of process. For example, within Employee Relations, the function has regional departmentalization by states and also by the functional speciality such as operations and logistics, commercial, business support services, and learning and development on a national level. Within the National Business department, there are two subdepartments.

Departmentalization has led to a chain of command that is fairly clear, especially in the traditional operations and accounting departments, whereas the introduction of cross-functional teams resulted, for example, in multiple reporting paths and wide access to information through technology. This has made the employees less reliant on their immediate managers for information.

The span of control at TBC differs with many functions revolving around teamwork. By using team leaders as intermediaries, managers can also manage a greater number of employees. Therefore, there is no standard number of employees for a span of control.

On the whole, TBC is mostly centralized with the majority of the business support activities operating out of the head office and one plant site. Departments such as Employee Relations that require physical presence in the state regions are more decentralized with groupware technologies such as Lotus Notes allowing control at the head office to be preserved. It is highly evident that the decision discretion for items such as marketing, information system projects, and financial analysis is planned and conducted in the head office and subsequently executed elsewhere. The production of beverages, on the other hand, is the responsibility of individual states.

Manufacturing, accounting and customer services are fairly standardized and formalized, while more creative activities such as planning for and marketing are less standardized, allowing employees to use their own judgement. Standardization occurs not just within the company premises but also throughout the areas in which TBC supplies its products. In supermarkets and smaller outlets, the shelf location and placement of the drinks follow a specific pattern to increase sales.

In summary, TBC is a combination of a bureaucracy, a matrix, and team structure. The bureaucratic nature of TBC is very evident in the ways in which protocols such as issues escalation are adhered to. Furthermore, there is the perception that the "*buck stops with senior executives*." The matrix is often seen in project-related work, whereas the team structure is present in most departments. In this environment, TBC utilizes information technology heavily in many facets of work.

5.1.2 NIPS Structure

NIPS has been designed for nonspecialists to perform procurement activities, which in the past has been an accounting domain. In terms of work specialization, although it is a system for a specific purpose, it can be characterized as exhibiting low specialization.

Departmentalization is evident in the types of financial approvals given to the purchase requests. Financial approvals may be by project, category, or cost center with different approval procedures. For each category or cost center, the approvers only see and approve the items to which they are assigned.

The chain of command is an important concept of the information system and its operation. On the simplest level, there are four user access levels. All users of NIPS can raise a request; however, the difference in user access levels determines their ability to make approvals, view requests from others, view all details in the system, create specific reports, add users, alter details, suspend cards, and conduct other system administration activities. The systems administrator has the highest access level and is able to perform most of the activities. The approval process also reflects the chain of command. Approvals may be associated with a user or position and the methods used may be sequential, direct, hierarchical, or group. An approval of a request will be sent to the manager of the requester and then on to the next person in the chain of command until approval is reached. Within this type of approval there are two choices: sequential or direct. In any case, the chain of command is clearly defined through the systems.

Span of control is another fundamental concept in NIPS. Each employee has a credit limit for what they can purchase. These values are determined on an as-needed basis, not solely depending on the employee level. A manager in one department may have a different credit limit than a manager on the same level in another department. Managers also have a limit on the amount to which they may make approvals and again different procedures are used depending on the different but clearly defined range of mandates that are implemented.

The structure of the system is both centralized and decentralized. Thus, although being rather bureaucratic, NIPS allows the accounts personnel at the head office to stay in control and to centrally maintain the administration of the system and purchases. Thus, the systems administrator residing at the head office is, for example, responsible for issuing and suspending purchase cards for all the states. The decentralization allows individuals to maintain and administer purchases themselves rather than relying on an accounts payable officer. Furthermore, a state-based purchasing administrator provides assistance for each state.

Finally, another significant component of the system is the formalization of rules and system procedures to ensure control and that correct actions take place. When employees want to make a purchase, they must follow the defined five step process. Skipping one phase, namely confirming the receipt of the goods, before creating an invoice as practiced by many employees is not tolerated by the system. A key respon-

Table 1. Organizational Structure of TBC and as Embedded in NIPS

Structural Dimension	The Beverage Company	NIPS
Work Specialization	High	Low
Departmentalization	High	High
Chain of Command	Clear	Clear
Span of Control	Varying	Varying
Centralization/ Decentralization	Centralization of support activities at head office Decentralization of information dissemination and manufacturing of products	Centralization of administrative functions Decentralization of usage (self-service procurement)
Formalization	High	High

sibility of the systems administrators is thus to educate users so that the rules are properly followed. Table 1 presents a summary of the structural dimension of value compatibility between TBC and the NIPS.

5.2 TBC Practices and Value Compatibility with NIPS

5.2.1 TBC Practices

The employees perceive that the company focuses heavily on clear, quantifiable practices, with process also being an important factor. An employee summed up the driving force in the work that they do as *objective driven*. In different departments, the objective may differ, but the employees focus on, and work toward, achieving that objective. For example, in Sales, the objective is to increase profit and volume. The primary objective of the Information Systems department is to deliver outcomes within the deadlines agreed to and to meet expectations. In both departments, although there is high focus on achieving results, the processes used to ensure the quality of results are significant. Thus, the Project Portfolio Team in the Information Systems department must follow a project life cycle methodology to ensure the completeness of the systems they implement and also to minimize risks and problems.

TBC shows concern and trust for its employees and in return employees are highly dedicated in their work. Within the business support departments, the work hours are flexible, allowing employee discretion and trust that they complete their work. There is no set time or duration for lunch. When there are high workloads, the employees are expected to work harder and have shorter breaks; during quiet times, the employees may have longer breaks within reason. TBC provides on-site food services at subsidized rates. On every floor of the buildings, employees are provided with drinks, coffee, and fruit. Social activities are organized to encourage employee morale and camaraderie.

Putting these benefits aside, employees are aware of their job role and accountabilities. They like to "*get on with the job*" and are highly dedicated. In summary, TBC puts equal emphasis on the employees and on their jobs.

When identifying themselves, the employees are proud to be associated with the company values more than those of their profession. When asked what they do, they initially reveal the company and then what they do there. Many employees are often seen wearing clothes displaying the company logo. The high pride in the company is further fostered and encouraged subtly through the many posters displaying the company's flagship drink in history. The parochial attitude becomes more obvious with the number of years an employee has spent with the organization. TBC experiences low turnover and many employees have spent in excess of 5 years at the company; it is not surprising that they tend to identify with the company rather than their profession. It must be noted, however, that within the company, the employees identify and distinguish themselves via the department in which they work or their job role. Moreover, although employees derive their identity from the organization, the recruitment practices of the company are professional. The company hires based on job competence and whether the individual shares the same values as the company. It does not take into account any social or familial factors. On the whole, though, parochial values prevail over professional ones.

When new employees join the company, they are warmly welcomed. The communication climate is generally one of openness and there is the sentiment that everyone can make a difference and is important in the company's success. During recruitment interviews, employee relations officers are concerned if the employee will fit in with the values and culture of the company; however, once someone joins TBC, the atmosphere is one of high acceptance rather than one where only very special people will fit in. The company celebrates the diversity of its employees. Furthermore, employees of all levels are highly approachable and on a first-name basis. Yet sensitive information is kept to management, which indicates, at least with respect to information flow, a partly closed system is in place.

With regard to control, TBC has established the necessary limitations to ensure that physical and intellectual security is maintained and unnecessary costs and time wastage are minimized, thus ensuring efficient functioning of systems. There is tight control over access to the company's work areas; security personnel are responsible for inspecting and allowing access to visitors. Employees are subjected to controls such as Internet usage, software access, database access, and credit limit for purchase cards on a needs-only basis.

Managers must authorize documents and provide reasons for the need. These strict controls are contrasted with the employees' attitude and flexibility of working hours as described earlier and their approach to scheduled meetings where meeting times are only kept approximately. No formal and stern work environment is enforced, informal conversations between colleagues are audible, and employees are free to decorate their personal work spaces. Furthermore, employees have the opportunity to dress "smart casual" rather than in strictly business attire. This reflects a comfortable workplace where the employees balance tight cost and procedural controls with fun and flexibility of their work spaces.

TBC employee newsletters and magazines often celebrate employees and initiatives that improve customer satisfaction. A challenge of the business is to meet the evolving needs of their customers and consumers. In the manufacturing function, this is translated to increasing their efficiency. TBC launched a "Changeover Challenge," aimed to "*question[ing] the current production processes and mindsets, and encouraged employees to find better ways of changing lines over from one flavor or package to another, and to share that information between operations.*" Although the ultimate goal is to meet the needs of customers, the employees also have to ensure that quality and safety are not compromised in the new processes. Hence procedures and standards-compliance are important facets of the company. In business support services, policies are also important in their day-to-day jobs. For example, the computer usage policy is strictly enforced and usage will not be tolerated if it does not fall within policy guidelines. Theses policies ensure the security of the company systems and protect their intellectual property. Therefore, the compliance of procedures and standards must be met in the quest and response to customer and market request and forces. In conclusion, normative and pragmatic practices are equally followed.

5.2.2 NIPS Practices

NIPS successful function requires a strict adherence to the rules for raising a purchase request through to the invoicing of the order, and therefore the information system shows a high process-orientated nature. With regard to the business benefits, it was supposed to be a symbol for accuracy and for achieving better procurement results. To achieve this, there was a need to streamline the procurement process. The processes imperative for correct utilization of the system are highly documented and easily accessed by users through TBC's intranet. Although giving the employees the respon-sibility for their purchases, NIPS is completely orientated toward their jobs and noticeably exhibits a professional image.

NIPS is a highly open system in the sense that all employees can use it. However, this openness is not a universal concept. All users have a password and can only view their procurement activities and any approvals that they are required to make. Hence visibility of procurement activities is closed to the individuals' activities, the activity of inferiors, and administrator-level access.

In conjunction with the rules of the system, there are tight controls that ensure the compliance of users and effective operation of the system. The employees are respon-sible for submitting their purchase card statements by the end of the month. If this is not undertaken, they will have their card suspended until the statement is submitted. There is a mechanism for explaining any difference between the quoted cost of the purchase and what was actually charged and the employees are required to enter the reason for any discrepancy. A formalized interface ensures conformity of any input of purchase data.

Finally, the strict request for process rules and standards compliance shows the normative design of NIPS. Table 2 presents a summary of the practice dimension of value compatibility between TBC and the NIPS.

Table 2. Organizational Practices at TBC and as Embedded in NIPS

Practice Dimension	The Beverage Company	NIPS
Process- versus Results-orientation	Mainly results-orientated, Less process-orientated	Process-orientated
Employee versus Job orientation	Equally employee- and Job-orientated	Job-orientated
Parochial versus Professional	Mainly parochial, Still professional	Professional
Open Systems versus Closed Systems	Generally openness Partly closed system with regard to sensitive information kept to management	General open for all to use. Closed system through password security and limited access to purchase and approval data
Loose Control versus Tight Control	Cost: Tight Time: Low Punctuality Language and Dress: Informal	Cost: Tight Time: High Punctuality Language: Formal
Normative versus Pragmatic Practices	Equally normative and pragmatic	Normative

5.3 TBC Culture and Value Compatibility with NIPS

5.3.1   TBC Culture

TBC sees itself as being responsive to the changing needs of its customers and consumers. It tries to be innovative to some extent, but it also acknowledges that it is the market leader and does not feel the need to be extremely innovative and to take unnecessary risks. Innovativeness is often geared toward marketing. For example, the company was the first to implement vending machines that can dispatch a can of drink using a mobile phone. Within the company, TBC also tries to be innovative to keep up with the changing times. In total, TBC prefers to take calculated and educated risks. Many months of planning and risk management procedures are conducted prior to the start of projects, new product developments, and acquisitions of other companies.

The level of attention to detail is set by the managers of the departments and an employee described it as a "*as we need to*" basis. This is reemphasized when it is felt that "*we are out of control.*" The level of attention to detail differs between departments; the Finance and Accounting departments are more accurate than the Information System department. When making major decisions, such as selecting a vendor, the employees try to minimize risks and are expected to fully document the decision, providing objective data to support their recommendation.

TBC has a strong emphasis on outcome and the quality of the outcome. However, the processes and techniques used to achieve these outcomes must comply with policies and principles, such as safety and quality standards in the production of the drinks.

Furthermore, the type of outcome or objective depends on the department; for example, Sales people are highly focused on selling drinks and thus on achieving volume and profit whereas the Finance department is focused on ensuring that reports are completed within deadlines.

While TBC is concerned with high productivity, it also believes that this comes through treating its people in the proper manner. There are many benefits and facilities that aim to make the workplace comfortable for employees. The level of concern at TBC for its employees and the level at which employees are valued appear to be higher than other organizations as shown by the loyalty of its employees. However, it also has to be stated that when decisions are made, people are not always the primary concern and while there is concern for people, the level of thought on the implications to employees is often not fully considered. For example in information systems implementations, technological approaches generally dominate with the level of concern for employees being restricted to the issue of systems training.

Work teams are enforced on every level of TBC. They enable high interaction between the team members and team meetings are usually held on a weekly basis.

The relationship of employees, by and large, is easy-going and everyone is willing to lend a hand. However, politics and aggressiveness occur especially in the event of crises, where political battles are waged so as to avoid blame.

Finally, TBC has been a reputable and stable organization with a long tradition and history and its employees are not very comfortable with widespread and extreme change. This is not in contradiction to organizational activities that emphasize growth and the quest to continually improve, as the employees largely accept a certain level of uneasiness and uncertainty, and they support the notion that to survive and improve productivity, TBC needs to be dynamic and continually evolving.

5.3.2 NIPS Culture

With regard to innovation and risk taking, the NIPS certainly represents enormous innovation and a high risk, as it was one of the first e-procurement systems to be implemented in Australia. The system exploits the capabilities provided by Internet browsers and networking. The embedded online training reflects the digital age as it, in a sense, replaces face-to-face training with interface-to-face training.

The attention to detail, and in this case cost details, is very high as NIPS emphasizes the need for accuracy in selecting account codes and prices for articles purchased. Although there is high attention to detail expected of the users, the prices listed on the system are only indicative as some products such as computing goods have frequent price fluctuations and it is difficult to update the cost tables accordingly in a timely manner. Reasons must be provided, however, for discrepancies in expected purchase prices and what was actually paid.

With regard to the outcome dimension, it can be stated the NIPS is a system that relies heavily on processes to obtain the final result. It is vital that the employees complete all components of the process; otherwise the system will not function accurately. Thus, the NIPS has a strong emphasis on process, although aiming at a correct and efficient purchase as an outcome, so the outcome orientation has to be considered as low.

The people orientation of NIPS rests on its promotion as a self-service system that empowers users. Although this is marketed as a benefit, it has both positive and negative consequences. Employees can now get on with the procurement job without relying on another person. However, this assumes that employees have the competence to use the system. This assumption, however, provides space for errors. The low orientation toward people is also mirrored in the online training, aimed at minimizing face-to-face interaction. The human–computer interaction features of NIPS show a low concern for users and there are no means for obtaining and judging what are effective skills. Despite providing some help facilities, the low intuitiveness of NIPS reflects little consideration of nonspecialist users. This all contributes to an overall low people-orientation.

NIPS is very much orientated toward individuals rather than being team focused. The individual employees are responsible for their purchases and the approvals for their chain of command.

The aggressiveness of NIPS lies mainly in the actions of the systems administrator when employees show little regard for submitting their purchase card statements on time or abuse features of the system. In order to ensure proper usage of the system, the systems administrator must use tactics such as suspension of purchase cards to force compliance.

Finally, NIPS is not considered by employees to be a stable system, with down times and a lack of accessibility occurring regularly. Table 3 presents a summary of the cultural dimension of value compatibility between TBC and the NIPS.

6   DISCUSSION

The comparison of TBC and NIPS along the structural, practice, and cultural dimensions shows that the highest correspondence is between the structure of the organization and the structure of the information system. This is, however, not that astonishing as the structure of the organization, with its levels of authorization and its spans of control, was

Table 3. Organizational Culture of TBC as Embedded in NIPS

Cultural Dimension	The Beverage Company	NIPS
Innovation and Risk-Taking	Low innovativeness and Calculated risk taking	Highly innovative—one of the first e-procurement systems implemented in Australia
Attention To Detail	Medium in general High in specific area	High
Outcome Orientation	High	Low
People Orientation	High in general Medium to low in specific areas	Low
Team Orientation	High	Low
Aggressiveness	Low	Low
Stability	High	Low

apparently the basis for the system. Yet, the company and information system differ with regard to the work specialization dimension. While the work of employees is generally specialized, the information system requires everyone to perform an activity, namely procurement (which was formerly performed by the accounting domain), for which they are not specialists.

Like many other computer-based information systems, NIPS has been constructed around the formal aspects of organizational structure, which the company exhibits. These reveal the underlying economic ambition and control of the corporation. With regard to practices, on each of the scales, the information system displays partial similarities with the practices of the organization. The regimented aspects, in which the system resembles the organization most, are job-orientation, with its orientation toward normative practices and cost control. To a lesser extent as opposed to the information system, the organization also displays process-orientation and an orientation towards professionalism. These elements are in line with the bureaucratic character of the organization's structure. With regard to control, however, the system exceeds the organization by implementing strict time control and a more formal form of interaction.

The organizational culture shows the least congruence between TBC and the information system. Organizational culture as the invisible force behind the tangibles and observables in any organization is the most difficult of the three to capture. Therefore, an externally produced information system is generally hard to align with the culture of an organization.

TBC and NIPS correspond with low aggressiveness. For the attention to detail, they partially correspond. However, in other areas there are major contrasts. Where the company takes very calculated risks and has low innovativeness, for TBC NIPS is quite an innovation; where the company values outcome, NIPS is rather process-orientated; where the company is built upon a high people orientation, the information system exhibits a low concern with human aspects; where the company emphasizes teams, the information system stresses individuals, and where TBC appears to be a stable organization, NIPS shows evidence of instability due to numerous technical problems.

In particular, the difference with regard to people orientation deserves more detailed consideration. It becomes apparent in two major issues, namely self-service and online training.

Self-service is an integral part of the promotion and operation of the system. The shift away from reliance on accounting personnel toward an inclusion of purchasing activities into everyone's day-to-day responsibilities has been one of the main challenges and a source of dissatisfaction among the employees. While self-service has been accepted by some groups of employees, others have not accepted it. The amount of time spent on the system by executives and sales personnel does not correspond to the benefits that NIPS provides to the company. Thus, the savings expected by self-service and the anticipated reductions of staff were not achieved. The eliminated purchasing officers were replaced with personal administrators or even dedicated purchase administrators for each department. Instead of being self-service, it has become peer-service, as the employees would identify a person who was the expert in the use of the system in their work area and nominate that person to conduct the purchasing activities. When they did have to use the system, they would request their colleague's assistance. Some departments have also felt the need to formally hire dedicated personnel to deal with the new procurement or added it to the workload of the existing personal assistants.

There was the assumption that self-service would be welcomed and accepted by all employees. Instead it resulted in unintended system usage and new requirements for the hiring of new personnel. Hence, the self-service has only been accepted to a limited extent and has hindered the effective adoption of the system.

The self-service concept, however, is not limited to the usage of the system, but extends to the online training for the system. This too was a major problem, showing lack of genuine concern for the employees' ability to use the system, further encumbered the effective adoption process. Our interviews indicated that there is quite an effort involved to confidently use the system. Only a small number of dedicated key users got the opportunity to practice system use and had access to the necessary support during the initial pilot stages of the system implementation, which enabled them to grasp the complexities of the system. The training software was difficult to understand in itself (let alone the actual NIPS). Training for the system was often put-off by the employees, as many perceived that performing their work had higher priority than taking the time to complete the training. Even those who completed the training, however, reported that it did not provide a "feel" for what the information system was about. The training consisted largely of the employees sitting in front the computer and clicking buttons for the length of the session. The frustrations generated through the lack of understanding of the NIPS resulted in an increased negative perception of the system, affected its acceptance, and lead to only limited adoption.

In summary, we found a certain value compatibility mostly with regard to structure, less so with regard to practices, and least so with respect to culture. The lack of congruence with culture has caused considerable dissatisfaction. Depending on the nature and level of discontent, some employees have voiced their disgruntlement, but have shown hopefulness and loyalty, while others have become indifferent, neglected the system, and avoided using it. The avoidance of the system has been the most common reaction with the consequences described above. However, no one has left the company because of the system. Perhaps the extent of the compatibility is sufficient to prevent open resistance and rejection and accounts for why the dissatisfied employees only project tame or passive expressions of discontent and tolerate the system. However, alleviation of the disparities might ensure a better fit between TBC and the information system and subsequently more effective adoption of the system with better results for the company.

7   CONCLUSIONS

While there have been many studies on the compatibility of innovations, there has been little research specifically focused on the area of value compatibility of IT innovation. There are issues beyond value compatibility that influence adoption of IT innovations in organizations, but value compatibility is essential for the adoption of IT innovations. Value compatibility assessments provide insights to key areas and issues that are necessary for the successful adoption of IT innovations. This research provides one way of analyzing the value compatibility of organizations and computer-based information systems. The investigated case (TBC) has highlighted areas of disparities that had an influence on the effective adoption of the IT innovation. The concept of value compatibility was studied in the context of packaged standard systems (NIPS), independent of taking into account who built the system and the underlying development process. Future studies should also take these aspects into account.

The research found that the structural and practices dimensions of the organization and system had a higher fit than the cultural dimensions. The major issues were related to the self-service aspect of the system and the method of training. The ways in which the users have responded to these issues show that while they were dissatisfied, they were still able to tolerate the information system as there was some value compatibility between the organization and the information system.

The study has shed light on the practice of IT innovation adoption. There have been 30 years of research on the impact of information technology on organizations and the need for contextual analysis. Although there have been many successful IT innovations, the high failure rate of IT innovations continues to haunt the field. It is, therefore, necessary to ask why organizations are still underestimating the effects of organizational values on the success of the information system adoption. In a world dominated by rational, economical, and technology deterministic views, much education of organizational and social theories at the grassroots level of the practitioners' career paths may help to sway the tide to embrace organizational issues.

References

Cooper, R. "The Inertial Impact of Culture on IT Implementation," *Information and Management* (27), 1994, pp. 17-31.

Harrington, S .J., and Ruppel, C. P. "Practical and Value Compatibility: Their Roles in the Adoption, Diffusion, and Success of Telecommuting," in P. De and J. I. DeGross (eds.), *Proceedings of the 20th International Conference on Information Systems*, Charlotte, NC, 1999, pp. 103-112.

Hofstede, G. *Cultures and Organizations: Software of the Mind*, London: Harper Collins Business, 1994.

Klein, H. K., and Myers, M. D. "A Set of Principles for Conducting and Evaluating Interpretive Field Studies in Information Systems," *MIS Quarterly* (23:1), 1999, pp. 67-94.

Klein, K. J., and Sorra, J. S. "The Challenge of Innovation Implementation," *Academy of Management Review* (21:4), 1996, pp. 1055-1080.

Kraemer, K. L., and King, J. L. "Social Analysis in MIS: The Irvine School, 1970–1990," in J. F. Nunamaker (ed.), *Proceedings of the 27th Hawaii International Conference on System Sciences*, Los Alamitos, CA: IEEE Computer Society Press, 1990, Volume 3, pp. 582-590.

Mintzberg, H. *Mintzberg on Management: Inside Our Strange World of Organizations*, New York: The Free Press, 1989.

Myers, M. D. "Qualitative Research in Information Systems," MISQ Discovery, archival version, June 1997 (available online at http://www.misq.org/discovery/ MISQD_isworld/index.html).

Orlikowski, W. "Learning from Notes: Organizational Issues in Groupware Implementation," *The Information Society* (9:3), 1993, pp. 237-250.

Robbins, S. P., and Langton, N. *Organizational Behavior: Concepts, Controversies, Applications*, Toronto: Pearson Education Canada Inc., 1995.

Rogers, E. M. *Diffusion of Innovations* (4th ed.), New York: The Free Press, 1995.

Romm, C. T., Pliskin, N., Weber, Y., and Lee, A. "Identifying Organizational Culture Clash in MIS Implementation: When Is it Worth the Effort," *Information & Management* (21), 1991, pp. 99-109.

Schein, E. H. "Coming to a New Awareness of Organizational Culture," *Sloan Management Review* (25:2), 1984, pp. 3-16.

Tornatzky, L. G., and Klein, K. J. "Innovation Characteristics and Innovation Adoption-Implementation: A Meta-Analysis of Findings," *IEEE Transactions on Engineering Management* (EM-29:1), February 1982, pp. 28-45.

Walsham, G. *Interpreting Information Systems in Organizations*, Chichester, UK: John Wiley & Sons, 1993.

Zammuto, R. F., and O'Connor, E. J. "Gaining Advanced Manufacturing Technologies' Benefits: The Roles of Organization Design and Culture," *Academy of Management Review* (17:4), 1992, pp. 701-728.

About the Authors

Deborah Bunker is a senior lecturer and associate head of school at the School of Information Systems, Technology and Management at the University of New South Wales. She holds a Ph.D. in Information Systems Management. Her research interests are in IS philosophy, IS management, IS diffusion and e-commerce/e-business. She has widely published in these areas. Deborah is a founding member and the secretary of IFIP TC 8 WG 8.6 on the adoption and diffusion of IT. Deborah can be reached by e-mail at d.bunker@unsw.edu.au.

Karlheinz Kautz is professor in systems development and software engineering at the Department for Informatics at the Copenhagen Business School. He holds a Ph.D. in systems development. His research interests are in the diffusion and adoption of information technology innovations, evolutionary systems development, and system development methodologies for advanced application areas, the organizational impact of IT, knowledge management, and software quality and process improvement. He has widely published in these areas. Karl is a founding member and the chairman of the IFIP TC 8 WG 8.6 on the adoption and diffusion of IT. Karlheinz can be reached by e-mail at khk.inf@cbs.edu.

Anne Luu Thanh Nguyen has been a student for the degree of Business Information Technology (Honours) at the University of New South Wales and has been a research assistant for the project, which builds the basis for the research described here.

5 THE POLITICS OF INFORMATION AND COMMUNICATION TECHNOLOGY DIFFUSION: A Case Study in a UK Primary Health Care Trust

David W. Wainwright
University of Northumbria
Newcastle upon Tyne, UK

Teresa S. Waring
University of Sunderland
Sunderland, UK

Abstract   *This paper investigates the politics of ICT diffusion and presents the findings from a pilot study conducted across general medical practices based within a Primary Care Trust in the North East of England. An overview is provided of the macro level politics of ICT adoption in a UK primary health care and the applicability of diffusion of innovation research within the healthcare context. A research approach, based on phenomenology, semi-structured interviews, and template analysis is adopted in the study in order to conduct and provide a rich analysis of the data. The findings are discussed using a modified diffusion of innovation framework. Conclusions highlight how ICT innovation is politically constrained, perceived, and motivated within primary healthcare environments and how in this case it might influence organizational resilience.*

Keywords   Diffusion of innovation, ICT, primary health care, general medical practice, template analysis, organization resilience

1   INTRODUCTION

Computer information and communication technology (ICT) entered medical general practice in the UK in 1970 when John Preece became the first British medical general practitioner to use a computer in his consulting room. Five years later, the

Please use the following format when citing this chapter:

Wainwright, David, W., Waring, Teresa, S., 2006, in International Federation for Information Processing (IFIP), Volume 206, The Transfer and Diffusion of Information Technology for Organizational Resilience, eds. B. Donnellan, Larsen T., Levine L., DeGross J. (Boston: Springer), pp. 71-90.

health center at Ottery St Mary, near Exeter, was the world's first paperless general practice. During the 1980s, GPs could participate in the "Micros for GPs" scheme where subsidized technology was supplied by the government to encourage innovation. This was followed by two general practice ICT suppliers offering free computer schemes which eventually covered 20 percent of all English GP practices. After a period of stagnation in the 1990s, most GPs are now connected to the NHS net, the internal National Health Service (NHS) network, and many are using e-mail and the Internet (Benson 2002). Thus there has been a 35 year period where ICT in general practice has had the potential to grow, develop in sophistication, support innovation, and become normalized throughout the GP community. Nevertheless, despite numerous versions of the UK government's NHS IT strategy, and various funding initiatives, this has yet to happen. The future organizational resilience of the NHS in general, and primary care in particular, is a growing concern, especially in relation to the new and massive investment in ICT innovations. Successive reforms of the healthcare system are becoming increasingly dependent on efficiency gains achieved through organizational change, the modernization of professional work practices, and the increasingly ambitious levels of ICT adoption. Organizational resilience within the healthcare sector has become integrally linked with modernization that, in turn, depends on effective ICT adoption practices.

In this context, a useful definition of organizational resilience is provided by Riolli and Savicki (2003, p. 227) who adopt the definition as provided by Horne and Orr (1998):

Resilience is the fundamental quality of individuals, groups, organizations, and systems as a whole to respond productively to significant change that disrupts the expected pattern of events without engaging in an extended period of regressive behavior.

They particularly focus on factors related to information systems adoption with respect to vulnerabilities and stress at both the level of the individual and the organization.

This paper investigates the politics of ICT diffusion and presents the findings from a pilot study conducted with GP practices in a Primary Care Trust in the North East of England. In the context of our research general medical practices in the UK can be viewed as small businesses (GPs are self employed and have a contractual arrangement with the English NHS). The first section provides an overview of the macro level politics of ICT adoption in UK primary health care and then, in the second section, goes on to consider diffusion of innovation (DOI) research and its applicability in the healthcare context. The third section explores the research methodology, the template analysis adopted in the study, and the findings that emerged from the large amount of rich data collected through semi-structured interviews. The final section, comprising discussion and conclusions, highlights the findings in relation to how the process of diffusion of innovation, in this case healthcare ICT, might determine future organizational resilience together with a reflection on the approach chosen and its appropriateness to the study.

2   ICT AND THE MACRO POLITICS OF THE NHS

The ICT strategy of the English NHS has a long and checkered history—not least because it changes its objectives, scope, and emphasis at very frequent intervals. This mirrors the dominant government political ideologies (for a more detailed account see Wainwright and Waring 2000). The strategy, throughout the 1990s and up until the present, has evolved from a focus on resource management, integrated hospital information support systems (HISS), the electronic patient record (EPR), to what is now a lifetime "cradle to grave" record termed the electronic health record (EHR). Lately, after the millennium, a major step change in ICT investment has taken place in parallel with government policies for modernization of the entire health service organization. There are official estimates of £6.5 billion and unofficial, but not really disputed, forecasts of up to £30 billion of investment in ICT hardware, software, consultancy services, training, and infrastructure over an initial 8 year period with a fully integrated ICT enabled health service targeted for 2010. This is governed under the organizational umbrella of the National Programme for Information Technology (NPfIT, www.npfit.nhs.uk), initiated in October 2002. In 2005 this became known as Connecting for Health (DOH 2005), a government agency, which is tasked with developing and implementing a new care records service (CRS) to connect secondary care hospitals with primary care healthcare providers (general medical practices).

There is a paucity of research that examines ICT adoption within both the UK NHS generally (Wainwright and Waring 2000) and primary care services specifically (Newton et al. 2003). The politics of diffusion of ICT, and the impact of managerial instrumentalism within a professional service culture, has been the focus of a small number of interpretive and critical theoretical studies over the past decade (for example, Bloomfield et al. 1997; Doherty, Coombs, and Loan-Clark 2004; Doherty, King, andMarples 2000; Packwood et al. 1998; Pettigrew et al. 1994; Waring and Wainwright 2002). These studies have examined how political agendas have been the driving force for a process of modernization or significant healthcare reforms—often viewed as the rise of managerialism, centralized control, and an assault on, or an erosion of, power of the medical profession. The NHS itself has kept a very tight control on the dissemination of information about the progress of the national ICT strategy. This has caused problems for many independent researchers who have requested access to the NHS over the last 8 years.

3   DIFFUSION OF INNOVATION RESEARCH AND ITS APPLICABILITY TO HEALTHCARE

Diffusion of innovation research and practice originates from many diverse fields of study. These include sociology, anthropology, healthcare, medicine, social policy, psychology, strategic management, economics, marketing, entrepreneurship, organizational behavior, research and development, and technology management. An innovation is not just an outcome but a process and is the effort to create purposeful, focused change in an enterprise's economic or social potential (Drucker 1985). It may be viewed as something that is new to an adopting organization but not necessarily new in its own right. Rogers (1995) over the course of many decades has developed and refined a diffusion of innovation (DOI) framework. He defines diffusion as the process by which an innovation is communicated through certain channels over time among the members of a social system and that an innovation is an idea, practice, or object perceived as new by an individual or other unit of adoption. Also, that there are five attributes of innovation: relative advantage, compatibility, complexity, trialability, and observability. Similarly, five steps are involved in the innovation decision process: knowledge, persuasion, decision, implementation, and confirmation. Five adopter categories based on innovativeness are identified: innovators, adopters, early majority, late majority, and laggards, where the rate of adoption is the relative speed at which an innovation is adopted by members of a social system. The social and communication structure of a system is seen to either facilitate or impede diffusion where norms, opinion leadership, change agentry, and aides are seen as key variables in the process. Finally, four types of innovation decisions are identified: optional (independent choices), collective (consensus), authority (power enforced by a few members), and contingent (choices made after a prior decision). The main corpus of work related to DOI studies provides useful generic theories, based on the innovation definitions and processes identified, to explain technology adoption in many diverse fields. Most of this work relates to studies of large organizations. However, there is a growing interest in research on IT adoption and e-business specifically in small to medium, private sector businesses (Caldeira and Ward 2003; Cragg 2002; Grandon and Pearson 2004; Poon and Swatman 1999; Southern and Tilley 2000). These studies tend to adopt a case study approach, building competing theories of ICT adoption but not specifically utilizing any DOI framework. More recent studies and particularly those in the area of Information Systems research, attempt to explain ICT adoption and use by building on and extending the classic Rogers DOI framework. These adapted theories may, therefore, be more applicable to aid understanding and knowledge related to ICT adoption in healthcare environments.

3.1 Diffusion of Innovation Research and Information Systems

It is apparent that in the area of Information Systems there is a growing body of academic literature related to diffusion of innovation theory and that this ranges from macro-industry level studies of Internet adoption through to organizational and micro-level individual adoption of technologies such as software process improvements (Mustonen-Ollila and Lyytinen 2003). Kim and Galliers (2004) provide a comprehensive review of diffusion studies related to IS and also provide a model to explain the diffusion of Internet systems comprising four dimensions: external market factors, external technical factors, internal organizational factors, and internal systems factors. Although useful for broadly explaining the diffusion of ICT and Internet systems at the macro (industry) and micro (organizational and individual) levels the model does not provide an adequate theoretical basis for exploring more complex diffusion processes associated with organizations and their associated power and political dimensions. Other studies, however, attempt to more directly examine information systems process innovations and retrospectively apply them to primary longitudinal case data utilizing DOI theory.

One such study by Kautz and Larsen (2000) utilizes and adapts the original DOI framework of Rogers. They use this to examine the diffusion of software process innovations by utilizing some key elements of the DOI framework to revisit and reanalyze the findings from the European Software Process Improvement Training Initiative (ESPITI) in Norway. A key aim of this research was to discuss the suitability and limitations of Roger's framework as retrospectively applied to this project. The case analysis adopted categories of innovation content and context, information needs and target audience, change agents and opinion leaders, and finally innovation consequences and countermeasures. Kautz and Larsen conclude that the conscious use of Rogers' DOI framework might have resulted in a better dissemination strategy and might have been beneficial for the project. A criticism, however, was that the model does not adequately address the dynamic relationship between all stakeholders involved in the ESPITI project: the "classic" diffusion process, often being perceived as too instrumental, driven by the needs of potential adopters and also as overly sequential in nature.

A second study by Baskerville and Pries-Heje (2001) utilizes three innovation diffusion models: the interactive model, the linked-chain model, and the emergent model to produce distinctive but complementary knowledge (a retrospective analysis using competing theories) about three information technology case settings. Importantly, they describe the diffusion of innovation process in terms of an "ecological" view (centralizes conflict and competition in the diffusion setting) and a "genealogical" view (centralizes consensus and regulation). This is where the micro perspective is a genealogical view based on economics and innovation theory and the meso and macro perspectives are ecological views that use power dependency analysis on networks of interacting agencies to understand how extra-organizational power dependencies shape the diffusion process (Baskerville and Pries-Heje (2001, p. 182). The classic innovation literature is seen to typically adopt the genealogical view. Innovation is, therefore, seen as a linear process, either as technology push, (market/adopter) need-pull, or interactive (both technology linking and need linking). The linked chain model is also positioned within the genealogical view but incorporates a knowledge dimension as the base of the innovation and its diffusion. Emergent or ecological models of innovation are based on conflict theories where innovation may be stimulated by internal or external shocks to the organization: unpredictable setbacks and surprises are inevitable and restructuring of the organization often occurs.

> So, like a social culture, innovation evolves as mixture of old and new ideas, directions and stakeholders; outcomes, evaluation and histories of events are "reframed," contemporaneously conflated or partitioned in order to rationalize "the messy and complex progression of ideas observed in the innovation cases" (Baskerville and Pries-Heje 2001, p. 187, quoting Schroeder et al. 1989).

Interestingly, each DOI theory utilized proved equally meritorious and provided complementary and distinctive knowledge; there was no one best model. In terms of advice to other researchers, therefore, the ecological view is recommended in research focused on multiple entities involving evolution or confrontation and dialectic. This is certainly more characteristic of healthcare environments, which exhibit multiple organization structures, have a long history of power struggles between professional groupings, and are shaped by a very intense political macro environment.

These studies present important findings in relation to the application of DOI theoretical frameworks to explain complex organizational scenarios for information systems process innovations. In order to perform a more detailed case analysis, however, a more structured framework would provide advantages in terms of developing or complementing an analytical template to explain and understand ICT diffusion studies. More recently, Mustonen-Ollila and Lyttinen (2003) attempt to develop such a framework in order to undertake a longitudinal analysis of process innovations. They expand, adopt, and adapt Rogers' DOI theory and the original list of five factors that affect innovation adoption: innovation, individual, task, environmental, and organizational. Based on these original categories, and from a review of relevant IS diffusion studies literature, 28 attributes are identified that represent independent variables; the dependent variable being the likelihood to adopt an innovation. This can be viewed in Table 1.

Table 1. Diffusion of Innovation Factors (adapted from Mustonen-Ollila and Lyytinen 2003, p. 282).

DOI Factor	Characteristic	Explanation
Innovation	• Relative advantage • Ease of use • Compatibility • Visibility • Trialability • Price • Problem solver • Standard • Technological edge	• It is thought better than the idea it replaces. • Is it difficult to use or understand. • The degree to which an innovation is perceived consistent with the existing values, past experiences and the needs of potential adopters, similar to suitability. • Is it experimental. • Is the cost of the innovation excessive. • Does the innovation solve a problem not currently dealt with. • The innovation becomes the standard in the sector and clients are forced to use. • Superiority to other innovations.
Task	• Commercial advantage • User need recognition • User resistance	• The internal or external vendor sells an innovation in a form of a useful product. Later on this product is commercialized. • An innovation must match the user needs in the task. • Innovations must simplify tasks to avoid resistance.
Individual	• Own testing • Personal contact network • Own rules and control of own work • Learning by doing	• Innovation used experimentally by individual. • People use their own networks to disseminate innovation. • The innovator has to conduct experimentation with the new idea in order to assure itself that innovation is advantageous. • Learning to evaluate the innovations on the basis of experience.

DOI Factor	Characteristic	Explanation
Environmental	• Cultural values • Technological infrastructure • Community norms • Funding	• Cultural beliefs concerning change. • The maturity of the technological infrastructure. • To what extent will all conform. • Are resources available to help in the diffusion
Organizational	• Interpersonal networks • Peer networks • Informal communication • Technological experience • Working teams • Opinion leaders and change agents • Interdependence from others • Adopter type • Management hierarchy	• Evaluations of innovations are shared between individuals. • Social relationships. • Exchange of information is informal and unplanned. • Technological experience over a long period of time—good or bad. • Team members keeping primary control over their management. • An individual who influences clients' innovation decisions—are they present? • Each adopter increases the utility of the innovation for both future adopters. • The degree to which an individual is earlier in adopting new ideas than others. • Do management determine the adoption of an innovation.

3.2 Selecting a Diffusion of Innovation Research Model to Explain ICT Adoption in Healthcare

The diffusion, spread, and sustainability of ICT innovations within health service delivery and organization may be examined from multiple perspectives of innovation in terms of organization structure, work processes, professional cultures, services delivery, clinical working, products, processes, and technologies. After a review of relevant literature, it appears that many competing DOI theories (Baskerville and Pries-Heje 2001) could be used; each would provide an interesting and a potentially complementary account of our research project. However, in the spirit of our particular pilot study, which was exploratory in nature, it would seem prudent to commence by using elements from the classic DOI framework as articulated by Rogers. Also, as the research was focused on determining diffusion behaviors, politics, and processes across a complex social network (healthcare) there was a need to utilize a framework that more clearly articulated a range of relevant factors mapped to Rogers' DOI theory. Having explored a number of adaptations of DOI theory, the framework developed by Mustonen-Ollila and Lyttinen, in their study of information system process innovations, was, from our perspective, the most comprehensive and suitable structure upon which to base our analysis. It also provided the possibility to incorporate elements related both the genealogical and also ecological views (Baskerville and Pries-Heje 2001), as innovation occurs at different levels of resolution. Therefore, issues related to the individual, as well as the social unit and the enterprise system, should be examined. Our focus is on the politics of ICT diffusion but also incorporates a much broader view of the concept of innovation and diffusion within complex social networks. The next section deals with the primary research and the methodology used.

4   THE RESEARCH METHODOLOGY

The methodology that we adopted in this research was that of phenomenology based on template analysis. According to King (2004, p. 256),

The essence of template analysis is that the researcher produces a list of codes representing themes identified in their textual data. Some of these will usually be identified a priori, they will be modified and added to as the researcher reads and interprets the texts.

The approach may be considered sympathetic to grounded theory but is not as prescriptive in terms of rigorously following a purely inductive pathway. Its advantages include the ability to develop conceptual themes and the clustering into broader groupings with the eventual identification across cases of master themes. Template analysis works particularly well when the aim is to compare the perspectives of different groups of staff within a specific context (King 2004, p. 257).

4.1 The Study: The Use of ICT in Primary Care

The project described here explores the impact of NHS information and communication technology (ICT) initiatives at the level of general practice organizations. There is little empirical research exploring current issues concerning ICT strategy adoption and usage within primary care from the user as opposed to policy maker perspective. We wanted to define key issues impacting upon the adoption of new ICT within primary care practice from clinician, management, and administrative stakeholder perspectives. We then aimed to evaluate the progress of ICT adoption and its diffusion relative to targets defined within the current NHS information strategy. The research was designed and carried out by the authors. Two main research questions were posed.

*   To what extent has the current NHS ICT strategy and diffusion of ICT impacted on working lives at the level of the general medical practice?

*   What are general medical practices' experiences of engaging in ICT initiatives and how will this affect future adoption of ICT within primary care organizations?

Initially we approached Gateshead Primary Care Trust (PCT), in the North of England, to explore whether we could carry out the research with a number of their GP practices. The PCT was a relatively new organization, created under the most recent wave of NHS and labor government organizational reforms. The staff in the PCT were only beginning to establish an understanding of the ICT issues within the Trust. The senior management of the PCT were very supportive of the research and we were asked to submit our research proposal to both the Gateshead PCT ethics and research and development committees. Eventually, after almost 12 months and further revisions, we were given clearance to carry out the research (this is not unusual in English health services research).

Initially a pilot site was selected for the first trial run of the data collection. This enabled the research design to be reviewed, assessed, and refined prior to expanding it across a wider range of respondents and organizations. The study was conducted between January and September 2004 and aided by a small university research grant.

In discussion with the PCT, we thought that we would like the study to include GP practices that fit the following profile in order to get a representative cross-section across the PCT:

- Opportunity, willingness and potential for good collaboration
- Mix of local general medical practices
- Levels of ICT usage and maturity (paper-heavy to paper-lite)
- Involvement in specific ICT projects, electronic health records, Prodigy (decision support systems for doctors and nurses), pathology and laboratory results reporting, hospital booked patient admissions, etc.

However, after some discussion we agreed with the PCT that GP practices should be sent a letter by the PCT inviting them to participate in the pilot research project. From the responses to these letters, five practices were identified. Obviously these practices were self-selecting and this poses issues for the validity of the study and the findings that have emerged. However, this was the best situation available and it may not reflect the PCT as a whole. The method of data collection for this study was that of the semi-structured interview. At each of the five research sites, tape recorded interviews were carried out with a core set of staff: a general practitioner (doctor), practice manager, and practice nurse. The interviews were based around a broad set of topic headings to guide the interviews but we tried as far as possible to allow the participants to lead the discussion. Research consent forms and information leaflets were provided in advance of the study.

Interviews took place at a time and place convenient to the respondent and ideally were limited to a maximum of 1 hour duration. All data has been made anonymous and all confidences respected. Transcripts (verbatim) were presented back for verification by each respondent. Wherever possible, the two researchers were present to enable consistency of the data collection approach and to enable peer reflexivity at a later date in terms of the data analysis and also the research process itself.

4.2 Developing the Template

In this section we will describe the development of the analytical template but it is essential to recognize that the development of the template is not a separate stage from its usage in the analysis of texts.

Defining the codes and creating the initial template: Template analysis normally starts with some predefined codes intended to help guide analysis. The first issue we faced was how extensive the initial template should be. King (2004) suggests that if you start with too many predefined codes, then the template might blinker analysis and prevent exploration of more pertinent issues. On the other hand, too few codes may lead to an overwhelming mass of rich and complex data.

Our approach and starting point was the letter sent out to the GP practices introducing the research topic and some of the government and department of health concerns. From these we constructed a template in a graphical format (see Figure 1). This took a period of time and reflection to ensure we agreed on the initial codes. The template was used as a prompt for the respondent and adapted for use if necessary. The key words have been derived from the research literature, NHS documentation related to ICT strategy initiatives, and the personal research experience of the researchers. This approach has a proven record of successful use in qualitative research in healthcare settings specifically investigating "soft" organizational issues (Clarke and Wilcockson 2001, 2002).

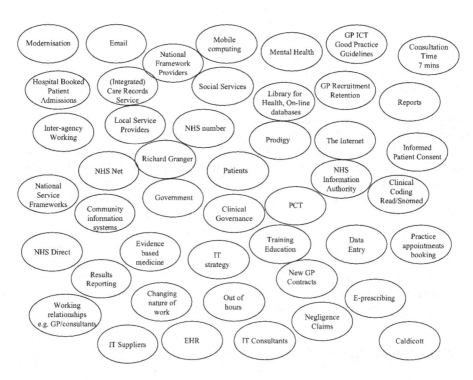

Figure 1. Template for Key Issues Associated with ICT in English General Medical Practices

Revising the template: It is important to realize that the template must be revised in response to the concerns of the interviewees. Respondents were able to suggest other key words that they thought should be included and enlarged on them if they felt it necessary. They were provided with the template at least 1 week prior to the interview. As part of the research we soon discovered that many of the key issues, words, and phrases that we identified initially were not relevant to all of the interviewees and a number could be deleted. It was also apparent that GPs had issues and perspectives different from nurses and practice managers even when they came from the same organization practice.

5 FINDINGS

In order to analyze our results we have used the diffusion of innovation factors as developed by Rogers (1995) and have addressed, to a greater extent, the attributes of these factors as set out by Mustonen-Ollila and Lyytinen (2003). Unfortunately, the large amount of rich data collected in this study is difficult to encapsulate in such a short paper and so we have developed a framework as shown in Table 2 that highlights the factors but also incorporates political issues that are intrinsically linked to the diffusion agenda within the study.

If we now consider each section in turn we will be able to highlight some of the key issues that have emerged and determine the extent to which policy and reality are mirrored at the level of the GP practice.

Innovation: The term innovation has connotations with leading-edge technology and new and better ways of doing tasks. Yet Rogers recognized that innovation can have many meanings in different stakeholder contexts. In the case of Gateshead PCT, and the pilot practices therein, innovation means optimizing the use of EMIS (this is the medical practice computer system used by all the practices sampled and also by 55 percent of doctors in England; see emis-online.com). EMIS is constantly evolving and has many features, a number of which have not previously been used by the staff in the practices. However, the new environment of the GP contract (a new NHS government reform related to the adoption of new working practices for doctors allied to significantly enhanced financial incentives) means they have to engage more with the data to meet targets, demonstrate quality, and enable financial probity. There is also the ambition of some practices, driven by PCT "e-rhetoric," to implement full electronic patient records systems and become "paper-lite." Nevertheless, when this was explored further, it was difficult to establish to what extent staff in a practice understood these terms.

One interesting aspect of the PCT was the use of mobile technology. Community nurses based centrally at the PCT headquarters used notebook computers with wireless technology when visiting patients' homes. Instead of supporting the work of the GPs, this was a cause for some concern as practices were not consistent in their data entry requirements and community nurses appeared to have a limited appreciation of their obligations. Staff at the practices often had to re-input data entries for consistency. Only one of the doctors we interviewed had used mobile technology (a type of Palm Pilot) while visiting patients and it had limited appeal:

Table 2. Diffusion of Innovation Factors Applied to the Political Issues of the Process in the GP Research Sites[1]

	GPs (Doctors)	Nurses	Practice Managers
Innovation	• Mobile technology • New use of EMIS—Population Manager • Results reporting • Internet	• Internet • Results reporting • EMIS—Population Manager, templates • Results reporting	• Paper-lite systems • E-communications • EMIS Population Manager • Results reporting
Task	• Evidence-based medicine • GMS contract and collection of data • Patient consultation (10 mins)	• Community medicine/nursing • Nurse as practitioner • Practice nursing • Interfacing with GPs • EMIS—developing templates	• Statistical returns • Management of practice • EMIS management • Training staff • Manager as IT manager
Individual	• Targeted health intervention • Deskilling/reskilling • Experiential learning and the impact on job • Strong financial incentives	• Email at work • Patient interpreter • Lack of training • Limited financial incentive	• Manager as trainer • Under-valued • More e-mail contact with patients • Learning by doing • Limited financial incentives
Environmental	• No real understanding of strategy • Patient Choice—Choose and Book—politically driven • Comparative performance • Normalization of practice • Doctors know best	• No real understanding of strategy • Culture of sharing—training by practice staff • Hierarchy/nurse profession • Challenges to hierarchy/norms	• Limited understanding of strategy • Impact of new staff from private sector—values, culture • EMIS/Lorenzo debate and consequences • Limited funds for investment
Organizational	• PCT—formal GPs network • Doctor as IT champion • Luddites not visible • Change in response to new contracts • Informal peer network to keep abreast	• No real sharing of experience with other nurses • Part of practice team • Formal nurse practitioner network, education program • Nurse practitioners leaders in new quasi medical role	• Practice managers network formalized—inadequate for needs • Ownership of IT • PCT as IT champions • Change ordered from above

[1]Table 2 shows contextualized attributes for key stakeholders in GP practices, adapted from "Why Organizations Adopt Information System Process Innovations: A Longitudinal Study Using Diffusion of Innovation Theory," E. Mustonen-Ollila and K. Lyytinen, *Information Systems Journal* (13), 2003, p. 282.

I decided to review the medication of everybody over 75, a certain percentage of which were housebound. They gave me a Palm Pilot, it was too cumbersome...we've printed off some forms....we all know how to use that....it's a lot easier.

Taking hard copy out to patients was far more efficient in their eyes. This was also reinforced by new NHS structural reforms that enabled unsocial "out of hours" services to be outsourced to a collective of locum tenentes GPs. This resulted in GPs doing for fewer home visits to patients.

The Internet is becoming a resource that is encroaching on GP practices in varying degrees. The GPs saw it as a useful resource for information but did not use it extensively in consultations. However, the nurse practitioners found it extremely helpful when dealing with patients and often used it to support the management of illness.

A final innovation in the pilot practices was the recent ability to receive results of patients' tests (blood, etc.) directly into the surgery from the local hospital via e-mail. This is not at the forefront of technological innovation but for these individuals it has been one of the major developments in supporting their work and when it malfunctions they are distraught. One nurse commented:

We didn't get any results! We got no results for a long time, we couldn't download it...we had to go back to paper copies.

Task: Although ICT has been around for many years and GPs have used it to a greater or lesser extent, it is now evident that it is becoming ubiquitous in these pilot practices. The increasing dependence is illustrated by one GP:

Recently we've become paper-lite so we're now so dependent on the computer and we use it so frequently it's integral to every consultation.

The new GP contract has acted as a catalyst for engagement with the technology because payment for work done is by results and needs to be evidence-based. The PCT has on-line access into GP systems and can download data at will. It is no longer sufficient to leave the practice administrative staff to do the data entry as clinical data must be collected at each consultation.

This has led to a number of issues impacting on the practices. Training of all staff in the use of the systems is essential. Doctors need to understand the finer points of clinical coding to ensure that the correct data is captured at the source. This has been difficult for some. Nevertheless, if done well, it can provide a great deal of data for evidence-based medicine and may contribute to the future health of the population, something which the government insists on happening. The nurse practitioners (higher grade nurses who have the authority to perform delegated diagnostic work and prescribe certain drugs) have been instrumental in developing protocols for collection of clinical data on EMIS and the management of patient treatment for long-term conditions such as diabetes. This has caused some growing tensions in the practices where they are based as their new roles have yet to be clearly defined and the interface with GPs has the potential to be politically contested ground.

Individual: From the perspective of the individual within the pilot practices, there are some major issues if the diffusion of ICT is to progress and be used innovatively. First, the practice managers generally felt that the onus was on them to deliver much of the data and this meant they relied on being up to date with all aspects of the EMIS system pertaining to their area. They have limited budgets for staff training and therefore undertook on-the-job training with all staff, including doctors, in their practice. Two comments from practice managers:

In the private sector there is a lot more training, development and coaching regarding change.

I've never had any formal training on the computer system.

This lack of training and resource was putting them under a lot of pressure at work and leading to feelings of being under valued. Although paid at a reasonable rate, they were unsure how the new GP contract payment system would work and suggested that it would generally only financially benefit the GPs.

The practice managers were also in the front line in terms of patient contact and, although not extensive, were increasingly using e-mail to communicate with patients. They saw this as beneficial to both practice and patient. However, the GPs did not want e-mail communication with patients and did not see any benefits to themselves. On the contrary, they felt this would add an unacceptable burden to workloads.

From the clinical practitioner perspective, ICT was impacting on them in different ways. One GP, who had been in practice for about 25 years, felt that the ICT was causing some difficulty and was becoming a barrier in the consultation room, leading to a poorer level of service to patients. She stated:

Consultation time is just 10 minutes, it's barely enough time to speak to someone without turning around and start working on the computer....I'm doing a 4 hour surgery in the morning and 4 hours in the afternoon, and absolutely brain dead at the end of it.

There was also a feeling among the GPs that GP medicine was becoming much more mundane and they were seeing less acute cases due to the way out-of-hours medicine was now being managed and the intervention of NHS direct. Also with the government's initiative on targeted interventions and possibly the role of the nurse practitioners, some GPs believed they could be deskilled. The nurse practitioners, however, were very upbeat about their emerging roles and saw themselves as advocates of ICT, one stating:

I think we are taking on a lot of new roles, taking over a lot of things that doctors would be doing.

Their nurse practitioner education program was underpinned by ICT and its use to support the patient consultation. Many used the decision support system Prodigy for advice on drug prescribing and drug conflicts when dealing with patients. The doctors interviewed did not use Prodigy. It was not on their horizon at all, even though it had been initially developed in the North East of England with GPs.

Environment: For the vast majority of those interviewed, the NHS national strategy on ICT had passed them by. Their horizon was the PCT and only those who were part of some external network had any idea that there was a national strategy. The practice managers generally met regularly at the PCT headquarters and were exposed only to relevant issues from the strategy. However, these were generally contextualized for the PCT. They did not see the big picture nor that they were part of a much larger initiative. An example of this was when we asked whether they were familiar with the current debate around local service providers (there are five clusters of LSPs in England, spread across geographical sectors and comprised of major consortia of consultancy companies and ICT vendors; Accenture heads the North East LSP), and that if the various contracts were signed they might lose EMIS, their current GP system, for a new one called Lorenzo (Accenture's preferred system). Only one interviewee was aware of this and the others were quite shocked that there had been no consultation on the decision, particularly when they were perfectly happy with EMIS.

Another initiative that was looming large on the government's agenda was "Choose and Book," where needy patients could, during a GP consultation, be referred through an ICT link to a hospital and consultant of their choice. None of the practices we visited had begun any form of discussion with local hospitals about how this would be implemented locally or even knew whether there was a system in place that could facilitate the process. This system was due to be implemented by December 2005 with current indications that the system may now not be ready for another year at the earliest.

Culture within organizations can often determine whether ICT diffusion will succeed. In the pilot practices studied, it was apparent that a culture change was emerging through a number of factors. A major factor was the introduction of new staff into the practices. Three of the practice managers had come from the private sector and were used to working in different ways. This "can do" approach was having a dramatic impact on how the surgery worked. Practices were working in more effective and efficient ways and tasks were getting done. The hierarchy within these practices is also changing and becoming much more team based with nurses working alongside the administrators to address patients' needs. Some doctors are aligning with this approach but other still need to maintain the status quo. ICT and the need for common shared goals such as standardized patient data are also facilitating this culture change but the evidence for this is only emerging. The difficulty for the PCTs will be keeping these champions of change and ICT diffusion and, on limited budgets, rewarding their efforts.

Organization: It is important for all concerned that innovations or ICT diffusion experience is communicated to share good practice and discuss future developments. To some extent, each of the three groups interviewed were part of networks but these networks were not ICT focused nor did they have ICT as an agenda item when formally constituted. The doctors met formally at the PCT to discuss clinical issues and new medical developments. They also were part of an informal network as many went to medical school together around the same time. What is obvious from our study is that GP practices are not all embracing ICT is the same way and the PCT was unable to engage any of the Luddites in our research. Even though the new GP contract expects GPs to work in certain ways, a number are not necessarily using EMIS to deliver requirements. How this will evolve and how the PCT will deal with transgressors is still to be determined.

The nurses do not appear to be well networked and only those who are studying in the nurse practitioners program have access to other similar individuals at a regional or national level. Thus they get to discuss more strategic issues but out of context to their local issues. In their practice they see themselves as part of the practice team and share information across the practice rather than across the PCT.

The practice managers are at the forefront of the ICT initiative and changes in the PCT. They meet regularly at the PCT but agendas are determined by the PCT management and generally relate to financial data and the new contract. The practice managers would like to network further to discuss their issues and share good practice and this may evolve through the efforts of new entrants into the arena. If practices are to further develop ICT and related systems, these individuals are the champions and the change agents. It will be through their efforts that diffusion will benefit the patients and bring about the evidence-based practice that the government believes is worthwhile.

Implications for organizational resilience: In relation to the work of Riolli and Savicki (2003), our research findings show that there are significant vulnerabilities and stresses related to the rapid and enforced diffusion of ICTs throughout the NHS and among staff in general medical practices. At the level of the individual, staff are coping by adopting processes of informal learning and modifying the technologies in use, such as the creation of templates by practice nurses. Formal and informal groups, such as GP committees within the PCT and also the practice managers' forums, are enabling sharing of good practice, ideas, advice, and dissemination of the official strategies and policies in a second-hand way—often making up for a lack of official communications. The organization as a whole, however, is not as agile in terms of responding to the innovations and changes required within the time scales stipulated by the government's political agenda. The net result is that the diffusion of ICT within general medical practices and across the PCT is problematic and slower than expected.

6   DISCUSSION AND CONCLUSION

This section explores some of the pertinent issues highlighted by this research project and reflects on the political process that influences the diffusion of ICT and modernized working practices in the NHS; the outcomes of which will determine the level of organizational resilience.

The macro politics of ICT adoption and diffusion: Our research has shown that in the PCT very few of the staff in the study were aware of either the political or technology driven agendas. They did not see themselves as part of a major ICT initiative nor as using innovative technology. They were generally unaware that their GP system, EMIS, was likely to be replaced by another due to contract negotiations at a national level. They were shocked that they had not been consulted. Another major government innovation, the Choose and Book scheme, whereby patients could be referred electronically for consultation to a hospital, had hardly been explored in the PCT. Yet this system was intended to be live across the UK by December 2005. Thus the government rhetoric and local reality of DOI are completely incongruent in this PCT. Patient choice is seen as a cornerstone of the strategy alongside a modern technologically driven health service. The government has used this message extensively to gain votes but at a cost, perhaps, of totally unrealistic expectations from the public.

Micro-politics: the impact of the NHS ICT strategy on GPs and their practices: As has already been stated above, the strategy per se has hardly entered the consciousness of the local GP practices. However, the new GP contract has had a much bigger impact and has brought ICT adoption and innovation, to a lesser extent, to the fore. The reason for this is the requirement to collect management information at the source to ensure funding for primary care at the GP level. However, some aspects of ICT innovations that have been assimilated into the normal working life of many organizations such as e-mail, electronic booking systems, and mobile computing are being resisted by GPs in the pilot study.

It is evident that many individual and task related factors are influencing the diffusion process. User resistance is not overt in many cases, but just manifested through lack of engagement with the new technologies and protectionism due to maintaining traditional professional boundaries. Much learning is taking place on an individual basis with the importance of peer to peer training underestimated. The national agenda for modernization is being pushed through the organization by the strict imposition of quality indices, targets, and monitoring. The lure of financial rewards for doctors and increased esteem through enhanced professional status of nurse practitioners are significant factors. ICT plays a vital role in achieving targets and supporting the decision making processes of less qualified health professionals.

The contribution to IS theory and the research approach adopted: From our perspective, this was the first detailed study that used a DOI research framework to analyze complex political processes within small organizations in healthcare. This contributes to our understanding of IT adoption within professionally dominated cultures. It also presents an alternative or complimentary approach to other organizational research in IS such as actor network theory (Latour 1991; Munir and Jones 2004), structuration theory (Jones 1999; Walsham 2002) and soft systems methodology (Checkland 1981).

The use of semi-structured interviews to gather data from three key perspectives within general medical practices provided a rich insight into the actual politics of ICT adoption and diffusion. The independence of the researchers was critical to the success of this exercise alongside the protection of anonymity for the respondents. The template methodology was also successful in determining key categories and codes around which to base both the interviews and also the initial data analysis. The literature on diffusion of innovation research, however, provided a different and alternative avenue upon which to examine and analyze the data. In particular, the adapted framework extracted from Mustonen-Ollila and Lyytinnen (2003) enabled a more sophisticated understanding of the data and provided a new structure from which to explain the politics of the diffusion process. This was more congruent with Baskerville and Pries-Heje's (2001) view that complex political processes associated with DOI studies may be better understood by adopting an interactive and ecological model of diffusion. There are limitations to our study, however. This is mainly due to it being on a small scale across five practices within one PCT organization, and also due to the self selecting bias as a result of having to solicit volunteers as opposed to selecting a more representative sample.

References

Baskerville, R., and Pries-Heje, J. "A Multiple-Theory Analysis of a Diffusion of Information Technology Case," *Information Systems Journal* (11), 2001, pp. 181-212.

Benson, T "Why General Practitioners Use Computers and Hospital Doctors Do Not—Part 1: Incentives, *British Journal of Medicine* (325), November 9, 2002, pp. 1086-1089.

Bloomfield, B. P., Coombs R., Owen, J., and Taylor, P. "Doctors as Managers: Constructing Systems and Users," in B. Bloomfield, R. Coombs, D. Knights, and Littler (eds.), *The National Health Service in IT and Organizations*, Oxford, UK: Oxford University Press, 1997, pp. 112- 132.

Caldeira, M. M., and Ward, J. M. "Using Resource-Based Theory to Interpret the Successful Adoption and Use of Information Systems and Technology in Manufacturing Small and Medium Sized Enterprises," *European Journal of Information Systems* (12), 2003, pp. 127-141.

Checkland, P. *Systems Thinking, Systems Practice*, Chichester, UK: Wiley, 1981.

Clarke C. L., and Wilcockson, J. "Professional and Organizational Learning: Analyzing the Relationship with the Development of Practice," *Journal of Advanced Nursing* (34:2), 2002, pp. 264-272.

Clarke C. L., and Wilcockson J. "Seeing Need and Developing Care: Exploring Knowledge for and from Practice," *International Journal of Nursing Studies* (39:4), 2001, pp. 397-406.

Cragg, P. B. "Benchmarking Information Technology Practices in Small Firms," *European Journal of Information Systems* (11), 2002, pp. 267-282.

DOH. "Delivering 21st Century IT Support for the NHS," Department of Health National Strategic Program, 2005 (available online through http://www.connectingforhealth.nhs.uk/publications/).

Drucker, P. "The Discipline of Innovation," *Harvard Business Review*, May-June 1985, pp. 67-72.

Doherty, N. F., Coombs, C., and Loan-Clarke, J. "Exploring the Duality of Information Technology in Community Health Trusts," Research Series Working Paper, Business School, Loughborough University, 2004.

Doherty, N. F., King, M., and Marples, C. G. "The Impact of Hospital Information Support Systems on the Operation and Performance of Hospitals," *Information Systems Review* (1:1), 2000, pp. 97-107.

Grandon, E. E., and Pearson, M. J. "Electronic Commerce Adoption: An Empirical Study of Small and Medium US Businesses," *Information and Management* (42), 2004, pp. 197-216.

Horne, J. F., and Orr, J. E "Assessing Behaviors that Create Resilient Organizations," *Employment Relations Today* (24), 1998, pp. 29-39.

Jones, M. "Structuration Theory," in W. Currie and R. D. Galliers (eds.), *Rethinking Management Information Systems: An Interdisciplinary Perspective*, Oxford, UK: Oxford University Press, 1999.

Kautz, K., and Larsen, E. A. "Diffusion Theory and Practice: Disseminating Quality Management and Software Process Innovations," *Information Technology and People* (13:1), 2000, pp. 11-26.

Kim, C., and Galliers, R. D. "Toward a Diffusion Model for Internet Systems," *Internet Research* (14:2), 2004, pp. 155-166.

King, N. "Using Templates in Thematic Analysis of Text," in C. Cassell and G. Symon (eds.), *Essential Guide to Qualitative Methods in Organizational Research*, London: Sage Publications, 2004.

Latour, B. "Technology is Society Made Durablem" in J. Law (ed.), *A Sociology of Monsters: Essays on Power, Technology and Domination*, London: Routledge, 1991, pp. 103-131.

Munir, K. A., and Jones, M. "Discontinuity and After: The Social Dynamics of Technology Evolution and Dominance," *Organization Studies* (25:4), 2004, pp. 561-581.

Mustonen-Ollila, E., and Lyytinen, K. "Why Organizations Adopt Information System Process Innovations: A Longitudinal Study Using Diffusion of Innovation Theory, *Information Systems Journal* (13), 2003, pp. 275-297.

Newton, J., Graham, J., McLoughlin, K., and Moore, A. "Receptivity to Change in a General Medical Practice," *British Journal of Management* (14), 2003, pp. 143-153.

Packwood, T., Pollit. C., and Roberts, S. "Good Medicine? A Case Study of Business Process Re-engineering in a Hospital," *Policy and Politics* (26:4), 1998, pp. 401-415.

Pettigrew, A., Ferlie, E., and McKee, L. *Shaping Strategic Change*, London: Sage Publications, 1994.

Poon, S., and Swatman, M. C. "An Exploratory Study of Small Business Internet Commerce Issues, *Information and Management* (35), 1999, pp. 9-18.

Riolli, L., and Savicki, V. "Information System Organizational Resilience," *Omega* (31), 2003, pp. 227-223.

Rogers, E. M. *Diffusion of Innovations* (4th ed.), New York: The Free Press, 1995.

Schroeder, R. G., Van de Ven, A. H., Scudder, G. D., and Polley, D. "The Development of Innovation Ideas," in A. H. Van de Ven, H. L. Angle, and M. S. Scott Poole (eds.), *Research on the Management If innovations: The Minnesota Studies*, New York: harper and Row, 1989, pp. 107-134.

Southern, A., and Tilley, F. "Small Firms and Information and Communication Technologies (ICTs): Toward a Typology of ICTs Usage," *New Technology Work and Employment* (15:2), 2000, pp. 138-153.

Wainwright, D., and Waring, T. "The Information Management and Technology Strategy of the UK National Health Service: Determining Progress in the NHS Acute Hospital Sector," *The International Journal of Public Sector Management* (13:3), 2000, pp. 242-259.

Walsham, G. "Cross Cultural Software Production and Use: A Structurational Analysis," *MIS Quarterly* (26:4), 2002, pp. 359-380.

Waring, T., and Wainwright, D. "Communicating the Complexity of Computer-Integrated Operations: An Innovative Use of Process Modeling in a North East Hospital Trust," *International Journal of Operations and Production Management* (22:4), Special Issue on Healthcare Systems, 2002, pp. 394-411.

About the Authors

David Wainwright is a reader in Information Systems and Head of Collaborative Research at the School of Computing, Engineering and Information Sciences, Northumbria University, Newcastle upon Tyne. He has a Ph.D. in Information Systems and his main area of research focuses on developing organizational approaches to information systems integration and implementation. David has extensive high level experience of consulting with large and small organizations, both in commercial businesses and also the healthcare sector. David has an extensive portfolio of internationally refereed articles and has published in many major journals. He has been invited as keynote speaker at many international conferences. He received a highly commended award for his paper in the *International Journal of Operations and Production Management*. David is a member of the British Computer Society and also serves as an elected board member of the UK Academy for Information Systems (UKAIS). David was the organizing and program chair for the UKAIS 2005 conference. He can be reached at david.wainwright@unn.ac.uk.

Teresa Waring is Associate Dean of Business and Management at Sunderland University Business School and is Director of Research for the subject area. Her research is in the area of critical information systems with a focus on systems integration. She has a Ph.D. and an M.Sc. in computer-based information systems and her main research area of interest is the implementation of information systems. Although Teresa has spent most of her career in education, she has acted as a consultant to a large number of organizations both in the private and public sectors and retains close links with many of them. She has presented research papers at many conferences, both in the UK and Europe, and has a number of internationally refereed articles. In 2002, she won the best paper award at the Business Innovation in the Knowledge Economy Conference at IBM Warwick, UK, and was highly commended for her paper in the *International Journal of Operations and Production Management*.   She can be reached at teresa.waring@ sunderland.ac.uk.

Part 3

Product Development Cases

6 LEVERAGING INFORMATION TECHNOLOGY FOR ORGANIZATIONAL RESILIENCE IN DESIGN OF COMPLEX PRODUCTS: A Case Study

Rajeev Lal
Infotech Enterprises Ltd.
Hyderabad, India

Avinash Samrit
Infotech Enterprises Ltd.
Singapore

Abstract   *Infotech Enterprises Ltd. provides IT and engineering design services, and is certified for CMMI level 5, ISO 9000-2000, BS 7799, and AS9100. One of our major customers is a leading aero engines design and manufacturing company in the United States. The customer designs and manufactures jet engines, the most sophisticated breakthrough of the 20th century. Around 2001, this customer initiated work on development of an engineering design framework for constant innovation, greater productivity, and better success and profitability. It also aimed at resilience against serious loss of knowledge and experience as employees retire or leave suddenly. It is important for organizations to have the resilience to muster up the required size and skill mix of teams based on need, sometimes at a very short notice. An important component for this resilience is a framework that enables new entrants in the projects, whether employees or companies to which work is assigned, to quickly come up to speed as well as be able to do their work correctly. The framework consists of knowledge repository, design process, visual representation, quick navigation, standardization, and easy workflow.*

One of our large customers, a leading aero engine design and manufacturing company, under relentless pressure from customers and competitors, had been trying a radical change in the engineering design process. We started working on a solution jointly in 2002. The challenge was to develop a framework that is easy to learn and use, and has the capability for global deployment. We set up a team of IT specialists who were adept at grasping new technologies quickly. The first decision taken was to use a web browser

Please use the following format when citing this chapter:

Lal, Rajeev, Samrit, Avinash, 2006, in International Federation for Information Processing (IFIP), Volume 206, The Transfer and Diffusion of Information Technology for Organizational Resilience, eds. B. Donnellan, Larsen T., Levine L., DeGross J. (Boston: Springer), pp. 93-99.

interface that is commonly used. A standard document storage mechanism based on XML was decided upon. A unique and very convenient method of quickly navigating to the desired point from within a large diagram was developed on the browser. The first version was ready for deployment in 18 months.

A 30 percent improvement in engineering design productivity had taken place once the implementation stabilized. By that time, all 4,000 design engineers in the organization were using the framework. Extracts relating to work outsourced to external companies were passed on to the suppliers, resulting in improvements. This increased organizational resilience in effectively managing varying levels of manpower resource requirement. Other companies of the group are now initiating similar frameworks. IT tools, especially web technologies and connectivity, now make it possible for an organization to implement such a framework within and across engineering design teams, both internal and external. IT should be leveraged by large companies to attain and maintain competitive leadership through resilience.

Keywords   Organizational resilience, knowledge repository, engineering design productivity, competitive leadership

1   INTRODUCTION

Infotech Enterprises Ltd. provides information technology and engineering design services, and is certified for CMMI level 5, ISO 9000-2000, BS 7799, and AS9100. One of our major customers is a leading aero engines design and manufacturing company in the United States. The customer designs and manufactures jet engines, the most sophisticated breakthrough of the 20th century. The product design process is highly manpower intensive, with a combination of creativity and diligent analysis and validation. Around 2001, this customer initiated work on development of an engineering design framework for constant innovation, greater productivity, and better success and profitability. It also aimed at resilience against serious loss of knowledge and experience as employees retire or leave suddenly. All parts of the design activity that did not involve pushing the envelope were standardized. To build on lessons from past experiences, the organization wanted a system to identify and convert individual expertise, skills, and experience into organizational resources.

The customer found good results in meeting the need to shorten development time, use fewer resources and have fewer quality problems using a framework that it called engineering standard work (ESW). The framework enabled robust results under conditions of stress and change. The stress is caused by difficulties in quickly generating new strategic options (e.g., effectively deploying large teams at short notice and imparting them with knowledge traditionally documented and stored on the desks of individual practitioners). A major facilitator of this resilience is the ability to outsource part of the work. This ability enables use of external help in a profitable manner. Lack of it results in the organization sometimes spending more effort in getting work done from outside than it would have spent in doing it internally.

ESW expedited controlled innovation, and brought about a radical change in the engineering design process. For producing good results, engineers require subject knowledge in product domain and engineering disciplines like modeling, analysis of various types (structural, dynamic, thermal), and product testing. ESW integrated the disciplinary functions and formalized the design, development, and review processes.

The benefits of ESW were clearly noticed wherever it was introduced. The customer, however, had no mechanism in place to ensure that it was used, sustained, and improved. Methodologies were locally documented in different formats. Lessons learned for not captured formally. If the department chief or a few experts left, there was trouble at hand. It was decided to use technology as a tool for capturing and organizing organizational knowledge and diffusing it.

2   FRAMEWORK DEFINED

The following elements were identified in ESW by the customer:

- Workflow maps
- Tools and methods
- Design criteria
- Design standards
- Lessons learned
- Practitioner proficiency assessments

Workflow maps depicted the design process at the system, module, and part levels. The maps captured inputs, outputs, and dependencies between tasks and activities.

An activity page prescribed each discrete task on the map. The page contained a task description, work instructions and tools, the range of applicability of each tool and method, required inputs and outputs (from whom and to whom), design criteria, documentation and sign-offs, design standards, and a resource plan.

Tools and methods included "how to" work instructions, their range of applicability, modeling standards, and validation.

Lessons learned emphasized constant improvement of ESW as better tools, methodologies, and work instructions evolved.

An assessment found that for every $1 spent on ESW, the customer achieved a cost savings of nearly $4.

3   RESILIENT FRAMEWORK

The customer used Infotech's services to develop an IT solution that would enable the implementation and diffusion of ESW across its organization. We examined the possibility of a ready-made solution, but could not identify one that would meet the customers' requirements. Functionality required in the solution consisted of the following:

- **Knowledge repository:** A database to serve as a repository for standards, guidelines, etc. There should be a process to add, change, or remove items in the repository with appropriate authorization and access control.

- **Design process:** A convenient way of specifying and design process. Each design process will be a subset taken out of the options available in the organization.

- **Visual representation:** A flow chart or a diagram is the easiest way to communicate a process and its components. Some flow charts were already in use. If the complete engineering design process can be put in a flow diagram, it can be easily understood by any one required to use it.

- **Quick navigation:** In a large flow diagram, there should be a quick way to reach a selected section. Within the chosen section, it should be easily possible to access all of the related design processes and documents.

- **Standardization:** As the system will be used by a large number of people whose work will be integrated in various ways, it is necessary to standardize the process representation, the documents, and the norms for design.

- **Easy workflow:** Review and approval is an important component of a robust design process. It should be possible to store results of the work done, and for a specialist or manager to review it conveniently.

4   VIRTUAL SOLUTION LEVERAGING IT

We started working on a solution jointly with the customer in 2002. The design team was already using computers and design software. The challenge was to develop a framework that is easy to learn and use, and that has the capability for global deployment. We set up a team of IT specialists who were adept at grasping new technologies quickly and in finding innovative ways to use them in solutions. The first decision taken was to use a browser interface, which is commonly used and hence does not require any training to start. While the concept of the framework was under discussion for some time, there was no detailed description or specification on which the IT solution could be developed.

The entire user interface was developed in industry standard HTML and XML with standard client-side scripting. Despite the flexibility and ease of development in image based interactive user interface, Java applets were not used in order to comply with the security standards.

The Java application implemented model view controller (MVC) architecture, providing segregation of business logic and presentation layer. This has higher maintainability and extensibility.

Microsoft Visio was the incumbent tool used by the engineers for drawing the process flow maps. It was decided to continue with the same tool for flow maps. An innovative add-on, Remote Visio, was developed to access and edit the Visio map from the central servers with the security mechanism built into it. Visio templates with built-in macros to capture the process flow map coordinates and underlying data were developed to provide the required task-specific data to the Java application.

Documentum is used in this implementation for document management. Web based ESW leverages the powerful features of Documentum viz document lifecycle and document workflow by integrating them with the web-based application using Java interfaces. Users having creator, reviewer, or approver status can create, review, and approve the technical content respectively.

Although the documents are maintained in XML format and rendered on a web browser, the look and feel of the documents were maintained identical to that of the customer's recent Microsoft Word template. This not only improved the user acceptance but also reduced the user training effort.

Various engineers created the standard work technical content (activity pages, work instructions, etc.) over more than 30 years. With the advent of new processes, materials, and practices, these were updated many times. The content existed in various file formats following different templates. A set of data migration tools using Visual Basic, Pro C, and VC++ were developed to import this technical content into the standard XML templates.

The first version was available in 18 months from the date of starting work and was implemented as per schedule. The iterative method of finalizing specifications resulted in continuous flow of new requirements and changes. It was therefore decided to freeze specifications at some stage so that the original schedule for deployment could be maintained. Requirements and specifications were collated for subsequent changes after a roll out of the first fully tested version.

5   APPLICATION PERFORMANCE

Web based applications often have challenges in the area of application performance. Some of the challenges we faced were

*   **Delayed loading of the flow maps on the browser**: The workflow maps are viewed in two sections, one section provides a bird's eye miniature view with a tracker for locating the user's view and the other section a zoomed in flow map that can be scrolled to view and get the required information. The initial version of the application created the miniature view, a resource intensive task, on the fly. The miniature map is now created at the time of saving the Visio map by the creator. This is stored along with the "real" map.

*   **Overall slow response**: On analysis it was found that whichever page referred to LDAP, which has more than 150,000 users, was slow. Some tweaking of the code and caching algorithms helped in solving this problem.

Documentum settings and workflow options were found to have a significant bearing on the performance. In a trade-off between some "nice-to-have" features and performance, some low priority not-so-important features were restricted.

6   IMPLEMENTATION AND SUCCESS

The deployment was driven by high customer initiative and was effectively done. On a monthly basis, the organization began to report their progress to senior management. Finally, a central ESW office was created to conduct ESW process assessments, provide IT infrastructure support and a framework for the ESW documentation process, and establish a robust ESW content creation and revision process.

An audit was conducted by the customer after the implementation had stabilized concluding that a 30 percent improvement in engineering design productivity had taken place. By that time, all 4,000 engineers in the organization were using the framework. Improvements had occurred because

- Engineers were able to easily locate the standard method to be followed for a new design or design improvement

- The reduction in rework as all instructions were available clearly in advance before the work was started

- Quick information was provided to managers and subject matter experts to check the results of work done and provide timely feedback by e-mail and a workflow process

- Ease in storing the results of the work done for checking and confirmation

No instances of engineers in a group referring to different versions of technical content were reported. A major cause of concern was thus addressed. Engineers with relatively less experience were able to take up tasks that were otherwise performed by highly experienced engineers only.

The major benefit derived by the organization was that knowledge, which was otherwise maintained by and confined to experienced personnel, became easily available to all engineers almost instantaneously. Knowledge was retained in the organization even if the person who created it went away. The framework provides a dynamic platform for innovation through continuous improvement. The quality of the first result is much higher because very few assumptions were made; detailed information is available for the engineer at the time of starting work. Extracts relating to work outsourced to external companies were passed on to the suppliers, resulting in improvements. The organization's capability to outsource work is greatly enhanced, and managing this outsourcing became easier and less prone to risk.

7   SECURITY

Virtual business and virtual work require vigilant attention. Hundreds of users are developing discussing and completing their work through e-mail, collaboration tools, etc. Unauthorized people may peer into crucial data.

The customer already had a robust security and access control mechanism for its intranet, and it was incorporated in the ESW application. User authentication and access roles have been implemented in light weight directory access protocol (LDAP). The application has been integrated with Netscape LDAP server. The super user manages the access control list (ACL) using a web-based interface. The LDAP access control list works seamlessly with Documentum as well. Hence security and access control are centralized and robust.

8 EVOLVING SOLUTION

The use of ESW generated suggestions for enhancements and improvements. Some of the improvements in later version include

- Provision for integrating lessons learned and suggestions into the mainstream workflow
- Reports for process performance measurement
- Resource planning feature
- ESW usage measurement
- Further refinement of Remote Visio

9 CONCLUSION

IT tools, especially web technologies and connectivity, now make it possible for an organization to implement a framework like ESW within and across engineering design teams. The ESW framework for the product design and engineering process leads to organizational resilience in effectively managing varying levels of manpower resource requirements and meeting the challenge of sudden loss of expertise. It enables optimum cost and schedule in product development.

Based on the success achieved by the customer, other companies in its group have initiated similar exercises. Our other large customers have also shown keen interest in developing and implementing similar frameworks. Such implementations can be leveraged by large companies to attain and maintain competitive leadership through organizational resilience.

About the Authors

Rajeev Lal is President, Strategic & New Business Initiatives, at Infotech Enterprises Ltd., Hyderabad, India. Founded in 1991, Infotech (www.infotechsw.com) is a leading provider of engineering, software, and geospatial services to manufacturing, utility, and government verticals worldwide. Infotech currently employs about 4,000 people across 17 global locations. Rajeev has been in information services for over 33 years and has worked at a number of renowned companies. In Infotech he led the initiative for successful certification of the software development business to ISO 9001 in 1999, SEI CMM Level 5 in 2002, and CMMi Level 5 in 2003. He is chairman of the company's Security Forum. He is a Fellow of The Institution of Engineers (India) and has been a member of American Management Association. Rajeev can be reached at rajeevl@infotechsw.com.

Avinash Samrit has a bachelor's degree in mechanical engineering, a top ranker in his class. Avinash has been associated with the IT industry for more than 13 years. He has played various technical and leadership roles in IT organizations, with eBusiness portals and relational databases being his areas of technical expertise. Avinash joined Infotech Enterprises Ltd. in 2000, managing large teams and complex IT projects for some Fortune 100 clients. Avinash is currently Assistant General Manager responsible for Singapore operations of Infotech. He has been the project manager for the Engineering Standard Work IT solution developed by Infotech. He can be reached at avinashs@infotechsw.com.

7 AN INTEGRAL APPROACH TO INFORMATION TECHNOLOGY DIFFUSION: Innovation in the Product Life Cycles of a Large Technology Company

Michael L. Ginn
Fielding Graduate University
Santa Barbara, CA U.S.A.

Abstract   *A practitioner in a large technology company reflects on a successfully designed and implemented enterprise-wide IT diffusion, which exemplifies both integral and action research approaches. An online tool, in use in one part of the company, was modified and extended to support a standard and customizable product life cycle methodology. In addition, this diffusion approach addressed the broader system of work, including culture and the intentions and behaviors of organization members. Other lessons learned are captured as key success factors, change agent attributes, and useful research methods.*

Keywords   Integral, diffusion, action research, product life cycle, culture change, Sun Microsystems

1   INTRODUCTION

This practitioner's report describes how a team of five change agents successfully diffused a product life cycle (PLC) in a large technology company.

Diffusing IT in large human systems is a risky proposition. IT solutions commonly fail to be accepted, or are used in ways that prevent full realization of possible benefits (for an example, see Ginn 1993). Contributing factors to such failures include an emphasis on technical solutions at the expense of cultural factors, and stock solutions that are implemented without modification or in inappropriate settings or situations.

Therefore, my intent in this report is neither to champion adoption of formalized and unified PLCs, nor to provide the technical details of our solution, nor even to

Please use the following format when citing this chapter:

Ginn, Michael, L., 2006, in International Federation for Information Processing (IFIP), Volume 206, The Transfer and Diffusion of Information Technology for Organizational Resilience, eds. B. Donnellan, Larsen T., Levine L., DeGross J. (Boston: Springer), pp. 101-108.

trumpet a series of steps that will ensure diffusion success. Rather, my intention is to communicate the world as it appeared to us as we acted: what we were seeing, our motivations and hopes, choices we made and the reasoning behind them, what we think worked and why. My expectation is that this reflective reporting approach will contribute to improved diffusion success and a deepening of the theoretical basis of our work.

In this report I will briefly describe the organizational context of the diffusion project. I will then explore key success factors including change agent characteristics. Finally I'll describe my epistemologies and research methods.

2   ORGANIZATIONAL CONTEXT

In 2000, Sun Microsystems had 40,000 employees and $15 billion annual revenue mostly from server and other computing hardware sales. The company was an industry leader in innovative software (e.g., Solaris, Java), and had a dynamic CEO with a compelling vision: "The network is the computer."

Growing demand from new markets such as online services, web presencing, and digital telecom drove revenue growth, but also diverted attention from emerging issues of Sun's traditional customer base. Rapid growth was diminishing Sun's capacity to focus on the increasing complexity of new products and changing needs of their core customers. Addressing this weakness was the compelling business case for a renewed focus on PLC processes, and for a new organizational capacity to work across professional domains and business units.

At the time, a half-dozen PLCs within Sun were recognized as significant and unique standards. These various PLCs reflected post-reorganization digressions from a core hardware engineering standard, contrasting cultures of product development as seen in the formal Solaris and entrepreneurial Java software groups, or simply cultural differences between engineering and operations groups.

We foresaw significant challenges of developing and standardizing a PLC, including

- Cultural differences and even animosities
- Fear of increased bureaucracy and diminished autonomy
- Only a few narrowly adopted online tools with modest robustness
- Resources from the corporate IT group would likely not be forthcoming
- Senior management did not yet see that a single enterprise-wide PLC would address Sun's strategic business issues

However daunting these challenges, we judged that the benefits of adopting a more formal and unified PLC would far outweigh the difficulties of implementation. For example, we anticipated that group cultural differences could be confronted and resolved in service of a project that would clearly benefit Sun. We were convinced that without our PLC diffusion project requiring it, the critical cross-product coordination required to address our market challenges could not happen.

Three years later the project was completed and appeared to be successful on several levels. Sun had a single PLC and its work methods and online tools were clearly in use. The PLC had entered the everyday conversations of the company—it was not uncommon to hear people remarking on how it impacted the product on which they were working. Customization and other design choices had mitigated potential drawbacks; a PLC "process" emphasis was seen as balanced and supporting business results. Senior executives demonstrated their support with development funds, statements of personal support, and communication to media and analysts that a focus on PLCs was part of the company's plan to recover from the "dot.com collapse."

There were several significant efforts underway to resolve the remaining technical, process, and cultural "snags" that remained as barriers to getting the most value from the new unified PLC. Also, Sun's software organizations were finally able to successfully resolve a customer imperative that was given high priority by the CEO a decade earlier: to integrate all of Sun's software into a single integrated and tested quarterly release.

3 THE FOCUS OF OUR DIFFUSION EFFORT

On the surface we were trying to "install" a formally documented model that would guide the management of products from conception to retirement. The term *product life cycle* usually refers to this model and its expression in the social structures of an organization, including published guidelines of use, associated training, scheduled reviews where specific decisions are made, and the information technologies used to support its use.

We also intended to address the emotional and interpersonal capacities of the individuals who participated in the PLC's product reviews. A critical diffusion outcome was enhancing their ability to relate to and work with coworkers from different professional domains (e.g., engineering, marketing, operations) who often had different business unit loyalties. We did this by introducing language that accommodated the wide range of customs and cultures, as suggested by spiral dynamics (Beck and Cowan 1996), a developmental model of values. We also introduced formalized product reviews using facilitated, experiential role playing in workshops.

4 KEY SUCCESS FACTORS

The five change agents who conceived, created, and assisted this diffusion project would conclude that the following were key success factors for the diffusion project:

- The team members were able to secure management support to spend 50 percent of their time on this cross-enterprise effort for the several years needed to complete the project.

- An early design decision was made to build upon existing work processes and their supporting technologies whenever possible.

- Parallel emphasis on quality by Sun and the creation of a new position of Vice President of Quality, who was enrolled to sponsor our work.

- A coincidental effort to adopt GE's quality methods (six sigma) and the associated emphasis and training on organizational change to support improved business results.

- Successful use of organizational mechanisms that historically have been effective in enabling cross-functional and cross-organizational work (for example, the establishment of an executive steering committee).

- The strategic business challenges that made our work important and enhanced our ability to compellingly communicate that message.

- Outstanding reviews of our introductory training, validating our decision to outsource its design and delivery.

- Agreement by the manager of an existing online tool to expand its scope to include all of Sun's business units rather than just his own.

5   CHARACTERISTICS OF CHANGE AGENTS

Five process-oriented individual contributors from various business units and domains of work (e.g., hardware, software, operations) became committed to unifying, weaving together Sun's practices for managing products "cradle to grave." This was something that was ambitious yet realistic given their backgrounds and skills, which included

- Familiarity with the various in-use product life cycle models at Sun
- Stature in their various business units and professional domains
- Ability to conceive of work and contribution based on external strategic issues in addition to internal efficiency and political (personal) issues
- Ability to incorporate cultural and human factors into the design of an information technology or service
- A world view that could include an enterprise-wide span of business units, product types, and cultures—and a multiyear project time line
- A bias for the values and methods of action research (Bentz and Shapiro 1998; Torbert et al. 2004)
- Familiarity with the capability maturity model[1] and its SCAMPI assessment method,[2] as well as other process models and assessment methods

---

[1]*What Is the CMMI?*, Software Engineering Institute, Carnegie Mellon University, http://www.sei.cmu.edu/cmmi/general/general.htmll.

[2]*Standard CMMI® Appraisal Method for Process Improvement (SCAMPI^{SM}), Version 1.1: Method Definition Document*, Software Engineering Institute, Carnegie Mellon University, http://www.sei.cmu.edu/publications/documents/01.reports/ 01hb001.html.

- Familiarity with the Software Engineering Institute's approach to managing technological change[3] and working with change agents and sponsors,[4] as well as other approaches to organization development and change management

6 REFLECTIONS ON EPISTEMOLOGIES AND RESEARCH METHODS

My conclusions from this diffusion are that action research is a useful approach, that addressing multiple perspectives supports project success, and that both practitioners and the field of technology diffusion are well served by reflective practitioner reports.

6.1 Using Action Research to Successfully Diffuse an Information Technology

In this diffusion project we adopted the intentions, values, and steps of action research (Bentz and Shapiro 1998). Doing so contributed greatly to our success.

We followed steps typical of action research:

- Identify a problem on which to take action
- State a goal and procedure for attaining it
- Record actions taken and progress made toward the goal
- Infer generalizations between actions and progress toward the goal
- Continually test the generalizations (some of which are reported above as key success factors)

As change agents embracing action research, our intention was to change a system while providing opportunities for development and self-determination for members of impacted systems. We created occasions for learning and participation in data collection, analysis, and decision making for those who managed, used, or were impacted by the new PLC. This helped them adapt to the stresses of change, implement effectively, and grow their capacities to design, manage, and improve new systems of work in the future.

We also deliberately created occasions for our own learning. For example, we created feedback loops by early piloting of various parts of the PLC, attempted to use the PLC ourselves, and continually tested marketing messages.

---

[3]*Managing Technological Change*, Software Engineering Institute, Carnegie Mellon University, http://www.sei.cmu.edu/products/courses/mtc.html.

[4]*Consulting Skills Workshop*, Software Engineering Institute, Carnegie Mellon University, http://www.sei.cmu.edu/products/courses/cons.skills.wkshop.html.

6.2 The Value of Multiple Perspectives in Action Research

Action research is unique among cultures of inquiry in that is grounded more in intentions and values than in a particular epistemology (Bentz and Shapiro 1998). Borrowing epistemological perspectives and methodologies as appropriate can be a strength when done with informed awareness. To support the success of our diffusion project we chose to integrate four distinct perspectives, based on the integral methodological pluralism of American philosopher Ken Wilber:[5]

- Counting observable behaviors
- Acknowledging individual's inner concerns, motivations, and experience
- Establishing a "systems thinking" understanding of how things fit together and influence each other
- Being responsible for cultural differences and the inherently subjective nature of many customs, habits, and views of how the world should work

The first two of these perspectives are well represented by the natural and human sciences as described by van Manen (1990). For example, Wilhelm Dilthey (1987) distinguished between the *Naturwissenschaften* or a natural science of things and the *Geisteswissenschaften*, which we might call a human science that addresses thoughts, values, feelings, emotions, and beliefs.

A natural science addresses objects of nature and how they behave, while a human science addresses beings that have consciousness and whose purposeful actions and making of meanings are expressions of what it is to be human in the world.

Natural and human sciences are consistent with an integral methodological pluralism, although insufficient by themselves. An excellent treatment of the perspectives taken by natural and human scientists and how they can be complemented by postmodern and other perspectives is seen in Wilber's (2001) integral theory.[6]

6.3 Action Research and Reflective Writing

Reflective writing has a rich history as a research method. Reflective writing, along with human science, was part of a hermeneutic phenomenological culture of inquiry found as traditions in Germany from 1900 to 1965 and in the Netherlands from 1945 to 1970 (van Manen 1990). Sartre (1956) even suggested that writing is the primary method of research. By writing, reflecting, and rewriting one can develop a depth that does justice to the fullness and ambiguity of lived experience.

---

[5]*Excerpt A: An Integral Age at the Leading Edge*, http://wilber.shambhala.com/html/books/kosmos/excerptA/intro.cfm/.

[6]See also Wilber's *Excerpt B: The Many Ways We Touch*, http://wilber.shambhala.com/html/books/kosmos/ excerptB/intro.cfm, and *Excerpt C: The Ways We Are in This Together*, http://wilber. shambhala.com/html/books/kosmos/excerptC/intro-1.cfm/.

For me, part of the value of this practitioner report is as a structure to write reflectively. I'm finding that, as Merleau-Ponty (1973, p. 142) said, "When I speak I discover what it is that I wished to say."

7 SUMMARY

Five change agents enhanced their company's resiliency and ability to respond to strategic business issues by diffusing an enterprise-wide PLC. We found that integral and action research approaches to diffusion supported our success.

Aspects of the diffusion project most promising for adoption by practitioners are:

- Designing and implementing diffusion projects using as many perspectives as possible
- Developing yourself as a capable change agent—I continue to do this using the integral practice frameworks of Leonard and Murphy (1995) and Wilber (2006)
- Finding and partnering with other change agents
- Using action research as a method to involve everyone in learning and implementation
- Writing practitioner reports for each of your big projects

Further explorations of integral approaches to business can be engaged at the business and leadership domain of Integral University (http://integraluniversity.org). Another promising line of research into integral perspectives and leadership is being conducted by Pauchant (2006).

References

Beck, D. E., and Cowan, C. C. *Spiral Dynamics: Mastering Values, Leadership, and Change*, Oxford, England: Blackwell Publishing, 1996.

Bentz, V. M., and Shapiro, J. J. *Mindful Inquiry in Social Research*, Thousand Oaks, CA: Sage Publications, 1998.

Dilthey, W. *Introduction to Human Sciences*, Toronto: Scholarly Book Services, 1987.

Ginn, M. L. "The Transitionist as Expert Consultant: A Case Study of the Installation of a Real-Time Scheduling System in an Aerospace Factory," in *Proceedings of the IFIP TC8 Working Conference on Diffusion, Transfer and Implementation of Information Technology*, New York: Elsevier Science Inc., 1993, pp. 179-198.

Leonard, G. B., and Murphy, M. *The Life We Are Given: A Long-Term Program for Realizing the Potential of Body, Mind, Heart and Soul*, New York: Tarcher/Putnam, 1995.

Merleau-Ponty, M. *The Prose of the World*, Evanston, IL: Northwestern University Press, 1973.

Pauchant, T. C. *The Leadergraphy Research Project on Integral Development*, The 100 Book Project, Chair in Ethical Management, HEC Montreal, 2006 (available online at http://web.hec.ca/leadergraphies/dropdown/leadergraphies_series.htm#intanalysis).

Sartre, J. P. *Being and Nothingness: A Phenomenological Essay on Ontology*, Kensington, England: Citadel Press, 1956/2001.

Torbert, W. R.., Cook-Greuter, S., Fisher, D., Foldy, E., Gauthier, A., Keeley, J., Rooke, D., Ross, S., Royce, C., Rudolph, J., Taylor, S., and Tran, M. *Action Inquiry: The Secret of Timely and Transforming Leadership*, San Francisco: Barrett-Koehler Publishers, 2004.
van Manen, M. *Researching Lived Experience: Human Science for an Action Sensitive Pedagogy*, Albany, NY: State University of New York Press, 1990.
Wilber, K. *Integral Life Practice Starter Kit: The Simplest Practice You Can Do to Wake Up*, Boston: Shambhala Publications, 2006.
Wilber, K. *A Theory of Everything: An Integral Vision for Business, Politics, Science, and Spirituality*, Boston: Shambhala, 2001.

About the Author

Michael L. Ginn is a doctoral student in the Human and Organizational Systems program at Fielding Graduate University. He received a BS in Psychology from the University of Washington and a MA in Whole Systems Design from Antioch University of Seattle. His work has appeared in the *Journal of Experimental Psychology* and the *Proceedings of the IFIP TC8 Working Conference on Diffusion, Transfer and Implementation of Information Technology*. He has presented at international conferences such as the Software Engineering Process Group Meeting and the Software and Technology Conference. Mike has worked for the Boeing Airplane Company, the Software Engineering Institute, and Sun Microsystems. He is a President's Circle member of the Integral Institute. Mike can be reached by e-mail at mikeginn@bethechange.com.

8 THE DEVELOPMENT OF A KNOWLEDGE FRAMEWORK THROUGH INNOVATION BETWEEN AN SME AND A MULTINATIONAL CORPORATION

Frank Murray
Piercom Limited
Shannon, Ireland

Abstract   *Companies must continue to innovate if they are to remain resilient to changing markets and customer conditions. This is more prescriptive for mature companies where products and innovations may have peaked. World-class companies are constantly seeking new ways to innovate and change to remain relevant and competitive. This case study looks at two technology companies, a multinational and an SME, coming from different technology poles, one hardware micro-technology and one software process technology, sharing skills and knowledge to remain resilient to ever-changing challenges.*

The key attributes demonstrated by the companies during this project could be summarized as follows:

- *Be customer centric*
- *Be agile*
- *Be knowledge intensive*
- *Be responsible to worker needs*
- *Be networked*
- *Be productive*
- *Be involved*
- *Be continually learning*
- *Be proactively diverse*

Readers of this paper may identify these attributes as building blocks for resilience as they may provide insights into what a knowledge enterprise should value to remain resilient and resourceful.

Keywords   Knowledge framework development, software process improvement, zero defects, measurement

Please use the following format when citing this chapter:

Murray, Frank, 2006, in International Federation for Information Processing (IFIP), Volume 206, The Transfer and Diffusion of Information Technology for Organizational Resilience, eds. B. Donnellan, Larsen T., Levine L., DeGross J. (Boston: Springer), pp. 109-115.

1   INTRODUCTION

Automotive, biomedical, and other vertical markets are insisting on zero defects from their suppliers. Product recalls have serious effects on cost, brand, and customer satisfaction. A standard of less than 10 parts per million failure was acceptable in the past with error responsiveness measured over months and weeks as the norm. In today's market, if errors do occur, then traceability is expected from suppliers within hours of occurrence and close loop remediation cycles within 24 to 48 hours.

Analog Devices Incorporated (ADI), a mixed signal design-to-manufacturer integrated circuit provider, identified the need to extend it's chip technology test coverage compliance to include the software test programs used to test hardware parts, thereby extending their supply-chain interrogation to achieve a holistic response to customer errors. It engaged Piercom, an Irish-based software engineering SME, to apply software process improvement techniques for key performance areas (KPAs) and set up the key performance indicators (KPIs) to trace software test errors. Piercom applied the capability maturity model (1)(CMM) as a process methodology which provides measures in software best practice across people, process, and technology paradigms. The objective of this exercise was to benchmark ADI against an established software process best-practice approach model and evaluate if any gaps in software process contributed to increased errors. The project was initiated as a result of a software test coverage issue reported by an ADI customer. Using CMM, Piercom Limited performed a traceability audit to measure errors. A joint team consisting of ADI and Piercom engineers was set up to capture the information around the software test domain. This team approach resulted in the establishment of a joint innovation, the knowledge framework, that combines processes and information around the software test domain.

2   THE RESEARCH APPROACH

The knowledge framework consists of an information repository that warehouses data, information and knowledge and acts as a portal comprising of tools, techniques, procedures, and embedded learning process guidelines in software best practice.

ADI formed a collaborative research project with Piercom seeking to provide knowledge transfer of skills, competence, and software process methods from Piercom to ADI. Piercom were tasked to deliver the knowledge framework infrastructure for combining software processes for the test engineering group at ADI.

The goals for the project were identified as

1. Reduce customer errors
2. Provide a real-time process to identify and remediate problems within n days
3. Establish a framework and best practices to proactively deal with potential errors
4. Build on ADI's investment in skill and knowledge, improving company competitiveness and resilience

An example demonstrates the need for this innovation:

The automotive industry has set zero defects as a goal for parts shipped by suppliers. An automobile manufacturer has to recall a model due to an error showing in the digital dashboard of a car. The integrated circuit (IC) in the steering harness is suspected of causing the error and the hardware and software solutions are examined. It is demonstrated that the IC failed its test coverage tolerances and for the chip supplied there must be 100 percent trace ability to capture the error in 24 hours. This supply-chain reversal search must identify all tests performed on the IC, all technology tools used, the personnel (trained or otherwise used and certification) to test the devices.

In mixed engineering environments, where hardware and software overlap, audit trails through people skills, training, mentorship, technology, processes, and procedures are a critical part of remediation.

This program seeks to create the measurement dashboard and intellectual property framework that harnesses this knowledge by development of a knowledge framework best practice.

3   THE KNOWLEDGE FRAMEWORK PROJECT

Customer error metrics were gathered. These were traced through development of people, process, and technology measures or KPIs. Reviews were conducted with a cross section of engineers to ascertain the skill, support, and certification for the test-engineering faculty in the exercise of their roles. Code previews and reviews were established. The development of coding practices, code reuse methodologies, and requirement to retain information pointed to a need for an open portal or IT infrastructure to warehouse and manage the different code components, third party tools, research, and best practice process reviews.

Project Phase 1 (120 Days):   Define and implement the CMM process methodologies for a group of product lines measuring customer errors. Scope the needs for the high level architecture of the process workflows across the product test lifecycle.

Project Phase 2 (120 Days): Implement across a wider range of product lines and develop the knowledge framework portal infrastructure to manage the shared services knowledge pool.

4   THE SOLUTION

Piercom Limited selected CMM as a benchmark process to evaluate Analog Devices' level of compliance to the standards set out under CMM's levels 1 through 5.

Metrics were gathered to evaluate customer errors, time to market, and new product introduction process steps. This forms the "management dashboard" to provide control and measurement to executive management. Reviews were conducted with a cross section of engineers to ascertain the skills and support structures available to the test engineering faculty in the exercise of their roles. A central team was selected from both companies to ensure that ownership and structure were established across process, skills, technology tools, and IT infrastructure. Piercom Limited provided parallel resources to coach and guide such areas as code previews and reviews, development of coding practices, code reuse opportunity, and IT infrastructure in database design, third party tools research, and best practice process reviews. A complete rewrite of the overall testing (hardware and software) roadmap incorporating software linked steps was undertaken.

5   THE RESULTS

A business model and architecture called the knowledge framework for testing practices emerged. Customer communication became more proactive as a result of data combined in the knowledge framework infrastructure and measurement around error tracking improved. There was increased emphasis on interlinked IT networks and databases. A more concentrated effort to profile skills and training needs was a significant by-product of the project. A skills matrix for future learning was developed. Different agile coding practices and formal methods were examined and a "cookbook" developed to implement consistent coding convention. KPIs and KPAs were clearly identified and measured. There was a marked improvement in process and procedural steps in software testing.

6   KEY RECOMMENDATIONS FROM THE PROJECT

It was recommended that CMM be adopted as the benchmark process to maintain the control model for the testing lifecycle as it pertains to software. The implementation of a formal certified training and mentorship program was also identified. Training of all engineers in CMM awareness and the software lifecycle model would be a key value-added knowledge investment. Establishing a skills matrix as a key component of test project definition was also identified and recommended It was felt that there was a reduction in new product slippage due to software process improvement and it was recommended that the program be extended to 15 product lines. The development of a reusable-software database was seen as key to continuous improvement.   The institution of consistent project management procedures, coding methodologies, and naming conventions was seen as a sensible approach to reducing repetition and inefficiency.   The building of a consistent knowledge infrastructure to support a software reuse methodology and optimize the use of tools and software components was a key recommendation. The project gave ADI and Piercom the ability to track the percentage of code reuse per derivative, platform, and breakthrough new product release and was accepted by all as key to successful management of test error remediation.

Finally, the development of external linkages with other companies and academic institutions for shared learning was seen as important for insights into process innovation and learning. This had been a blind spot in benchmarking best practice. Utilizing an SME as a catalyst to focus effort in a specific knowledge domain was seen as a good first step in innovative resilience.

7　FUTURE COLLABORATION AND EXPANSION OF KNOWLEDGE FRAMEWORK

Piercom and ADI have identified the need for such a knowledge framework infrastructure and have proceeded commercially to develop this project. The opportunity to map the needs of other multinationals into such a program seems logical to benefit a wider audience. If the needs analysis and mapping was completed across a group of multinationals, then the opportunity to provide a generic knowledge framework could serve this domain across industry.

ADI and Piercom are keen to develop this initiative with partners providing the knowledge framework approach for advanced learning and skills development. The joint project team have visited other multinationals across different vertical markets to evaluate if the needs at ADI are mirrored for these other multinationals in the test practices domain. The findings are that there is similarity and opportunity for best practices through process innovation concepts to scale across vertical markets (automotive, semiconductor, and bio-medical). Indeed the development of such a best practice competency could leverage competition for all multinationals. Harnessing existing competency and building on existing platforms of knowledge can prove a decisive competitive tool in expanding existing mandates, which could be argued is a driver of resilience.

The testing arena could become a key differentiator for ADI and the raw material (resource) is in place through the test engineering resources group, whose skill and knowledge can be harnessed.

ADI and Piercom have invested significant hours in meetings and discussions with seven multinationals (IBM, Avocent, Lucent, Kostal, Boston Scientific, Nortel, and Analog Devices), presenting a proof of concept model and receiving formal support from four multinationals to progress to a cluster in this area. The seven multinationals have indicated their interest in progressing further in 2006. They believe that they could champion the case within their corporations for collaboration and shared-learning in this area.

ADI, the Atlantic Technology Corridor (an Irish association promoting the development of industry and technology along the Atlantic coast) support the cluster. All of the companies listed above have agreed to lend their names to this initiative, as have academic and government agencies.

8　APPROACH USED IN FUTURE COLLABORATION

To develop a cluster in this area, the aproach used will be similar to that outlined in ECOLEAD, a European Consortia using virtual organization partnerships to develop linkages for shared learning between companies and academia.

The associated collaborative cluster consists of multinationals, small to medium enterprises, and research groups. Value-added is through a shared knowledge model. The work could lead to the development of an international competency cluster in test best practices and leverage other research and IP creation.

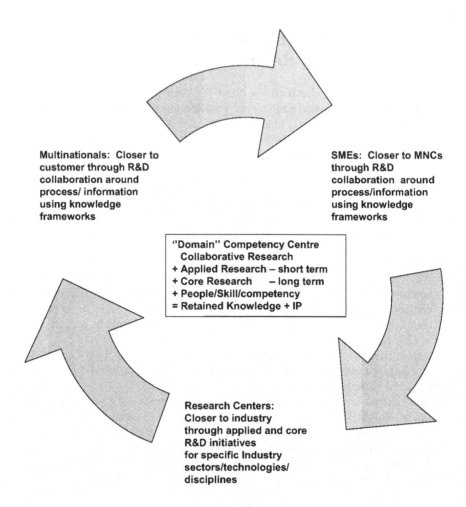

Figure 1. Collaborative Groups in Proposed Competency Cluster Supported by a Knowledge Framework. (Source: Piercom Limited & Analog Devices Corporation Project Team)

Acknowledgments

The author wishes to thank Dr. Brian Donnellan, NUIG Galway for inviting Piercom and Analog Devices to share their experiences. The author would also like to acknowledge the support of Dick Meaney, Vice President, ADI, J. J. O'Riordan, Head of Test & Measurement, ADI, Gordon Thomson, Head of Quality Test Practices, ADI, Paul Newton, Software Process Director, Piercom Limited, and Paul Ryan, Head of Process Consulting, Piercom Limited, for their significant participation in this program. The support of IDA, Ireland, Enterprise Ireland, Nortel, Boston Scientific, and Kostal GMBH is also acknowledged.

About the Author

Frank Murray has over 25 years of international software business management experience working for the multinational and SME sectors in the United States and Europe. Frank has been Managing Director of Piercom Limited from 1998 and is the majority owner. Frank held senior executive roles as European Managing Director for the Briggs & Stratton software division and as principal at DFS Associates, the Swiss-based consultancy specializing in software innovation. As European Software Business Practices Manager for Digital Equipment Corporation (later CompaQ and HP), Frank managed operations for DEC's 1Bn software enterprise. In 2004, Frank was invited by Professor David Parnas to participate on the Advisory Board for the Software Quality Reliability Laboratory at University of Limerick.

Frank was awarded a Bachelor of Science degree in Mathematics, Analytical Techniques and Instrumentation and Chemistry from NUIG in 1979. He attended the International Advanced Management Program at INSEAD, Paris; IMD, Lausanne and IFL in Sweden from 1984-1989. He serves on a number of commercial and voluntary management boards and has delivered a number of keynote addresses to international conferences and to academic institutes. Frank can be reached by e-mail at frank.murray@piercom.ie.

Affiliations: Piercom Limited

Piercom Limited are a provider of best practice process improvement innovation techniques. The research and development culture at Piercom has led to the creation of a number of innovative solutions to solve large IT integration issues across people, process, and technology. Piercom are developing the capability to deliver the knowledge infrastructure that supports software best practices.

In 2002, Piercom Limited provided the CRM solutions to the Irish government that resulted in Ireland achieving the number 1 position in e-government benchmarking across 18 countries as reported by Cap Gemini. In 1998, Piercom Limited were awarded the prestigious Washington-based Smithsonian Medal for Innovation in Technology and business-related services. Piercom's technology is showcased at the institute.

Piercom Limited are the IT partners of the Irish government and list General Electric Aviation, ADI, Dell, Banta, Johnson & Johnson, Nortel, Boston Scientific, and Kostal GMBH as part of their growing network of clients. Piercom Limited are members of LERO, the Irish Software Engineering Research Centre recently formed through Science Foundation Ireland funding. The company was founded in 1993 as a campus company at the University of Limerick and has evolved from software reengineering through IT integration and into software process.

Analog Devices, Inc. (NYSE: ADI) is a world-leading semiconductor company specializing in high performance analog, mixed-signal, and digital signal processing integrated circuits. Since ADI was founded in 1965, its focus has been to solve the engineering challenges associated with signal processing in electronic equipment. ADI's products play a fundamental role in converting real-world phenomena such as temperature, motion, pressure, light, and sound into electrical signals to be used in a wide array of applications ranging from industrial process control, factory automation, radar systems, and CAT scanners to cellular base stations and telephones, broadband networking, computers, cars, and digital cameras.

ADI currently has a worldwide workforce of approximately 8,900 employees, including over 3,000 engineers. Wafer fabrication facilities for high-performance analog products are located in Massachusetts, California, and Ireland. Product testing is conducted at facilities in the Philippines. Corporate headquarters are located in Norwood, Massachusetts.

Part 4

Strategic Perspectives

9 TEN STRATEGIES FOR SUCCESSFUL DISTRIBUTED DEVELOPMENT

Brian Lings
Björn Lundell
University of Skövde
Skövde, Sweden

Pär J. Ågerfalk
Brian Fitzgerald
University of Limerick
Limerick, Ireland

Abstract   *This paper presents an overview of the field of distributed development of software systems and applications (DD). Based on an analysis of the published literature, including its use in different industrial contexts, we provide a preliminary analysis that structures existing DD knowledge, indicating opportunities but identifying threats to communication, coordination, and control caused by temporal distance, geographical distance, and socio-cultural distance. An analysis of the case and field study literature has been used to identify strategies considered effective for countering the identified threats. The paper synthesizes from these a set of 10 general strategies for successful DD which, if adopted, should lead to increased company resilience.*

Keywords   Distributed software development, global software development, strategies, case studies, distributed development framework, development process, literature analysis

1   INTRODUCTION

Resilience—the ability to adapt to changing circumstances and recover from disruption—is an important property of organizations in today's turbulent business environment (Lengnick-Hall 2005; Riolli and Savicki 2003). In the wake of the bursting information technology bubble, many software organizations have turned toward glo-

Please use the following format when citing this chapter:

Lings, Brian, Lundell, Björn, Ågerfalk, Pär, J., Fitzgerald, Brian, 2006, in International Federation for Information Processing (IFIP), Volume 206, The Transfer and Diffusion of Information Technology for Organizational Resilience, eds. B. Donnellan, Larsen T., Levine L., DeGross J. (Boston: Springer), pp. 119-137.

bally distributed development (DD) as a way of cutting costs, gaining access to new markets, and enabling round-the-clock work (e.g., Carmel 2003). This is a trend that is likely to continue: according to the United Nations' 2004 World Investment Report, off-shoring of IT-enabled services is forecast to expand 24-fold by 2007 from a base of $1 billion in 2002. However, DD is in itself a rather disruptive innovation (Lyytinen and Rose 2003), putting new demands on both individuals and organizations. In any case, DD is certainly not the "silver bullet that slays the software productivity monster," alluding to Fred Brooks' vivid description of the software crisis (Brooks 1986, p. 1071). On the contrary, there are many issues to tackle for any organization adopting DD.

In ideal software development teams, members have rich interactions, both formal and informal; share a common organizational culture, which promotes good coordi-nation and facilitates effective control; represent a good mix of all required technical skills and relevant experience, made readily accessible to all team members; and are familiar with, and provided with, homogeneous tools and technologies appropriate for the project. DD adds new demands to the software development process by potentially threatening each of these ideal properties.

In this paper we characterize the main opportunities and threats to DD projects, and synthesize, from reported case and field studies in real industrial settings, strategies which have proven successful in practice. These form 10 general strategies for suc-cessful DD.

The paper is organized as follows. Section 2 presents the concepts used in the analysis, and outlines a framework used for characterizing opportunities and threats in DD. Section 3 presents the research approach adopted for this study. Section 4 presents 10 major strategies that together represent a synthesis of those proposed in the literature based on case and field studies. In section 5 we summarize and reflect on our findings.

2 THEORETICAL BACKGROUND

For the purpose of this research, we take the position of Ågerfalk et al. (2005) in defining DD. Here, *development* is interpreted broadly as any software development life cycle activity. This thus extends beyond "pure" development activities and includes, for example, deployment and maintenance. A development team is distributed if its team members are not collocated, but geographically spread out.

For a number of years, the international workshop on Global Software Development (GSD) has highlighted the impact of distribution on *communication, coordination*, and *control* within DD life cycle activities (see, for example, Damian et al. 2003). This view is consistent with the position taken by a number of authors who have focused on one or more of these three fundamental processes to understand DD (e.g., Carmel and Agarwal 2001; Evaristo et al. 2004; Malone and Crowston 1994; McChesney and Gallagher 2004; Nurmi et al. 2005; Sutanto et al. 2004). Coordination and control have also been identified as central to the creation of organizational resilience in an IS industry context (Riolli and Savicki 2003). Hence, understanding these processes is key also to understanding DD as a resilient response to an ever changing business environ-ment (see Lengnick-Hall 2005). In particular, the communication, coordination, and control activities are affected over a number of *dimensions*, which have been well elaborated in the literature (e.g., Battin et al. 2001; Boland and Fitzgerald 2004; DeLone et al. 2005; Espinosa and Carmel 2003; Ghosh et al. 2004; Heeks et al. 2001; Sutanto et al. 2004). These relate to temporal, geographic and socio-cultural distance. These processes and dimensions have been incorporated into a framework of issues in distributed development (Ågerfalk et al. 2005).

We will use this framework to present the results of our own study on strategies for effective DD, and so introduce it briefly here. Successful *communication* is "the exchange of complete and unambiguous information—that is, the sender and receiver can reach a common understanding" (Carmel and Agarwal 2001, p. 23). The communication process concerns the transfer of knowledge and information between actors, and the tools used to facilitate such interaction. *Coordination* is "the act of integrating each task with each organizational unit, so the unit contributes to the overall objective" (Carmel and Agarwal 2001, p. 23) The coordination process concerns how this inter-action makes actors interdependent on each other: "Two people have a coordination problem whenever they have common interests, or goals, and each person's actions depend on the actions of the other" (Clark 1996, p. 62). *Control* is "the process of adhering to goals, policies, standards, or quality levels" (Carmel and Agarwal 2001, p. 23). The control process concerns the management and reporting mechanisms put in place to make sure a development activity is progressing. *Temporal distance* is a directional measure of the dislocation in time experienced by two actors wishing to interact. Temporal distance can be caused by time zone difference or time shifting work patterns. In general, low temporal distance improves opportunities for timely synchronous communication but may reduce management options. *Geographical distance* is a directional measure of the effort required for one actor to visit another at the latter's home site. Geographical distance is best measured in ease of relocating rather than in kilometers. In general, low geographical distance offers greater scope for periods of collocated, inter-team working. *Socio-cultural distance* is a directional measure of an actor's understanding of another actor's values and normative practices. As a consequence, it is possible for actor A to be socio-culturally closer to actor B than B is to A. It is a complex dimension, involving organizational culture, national culture, language, politics, individual motivations, and work ethics. In general, low socio-cultural distance improves communication and lowers risk.

A development context is considered distributed if it exhibits significant distance in the geographical dimension. We would consider a development team comprising members in two different offices in different cities within the same country to be distributed, even if they exhibit low temporal and socio-cultural distance. The key feature is that the cost (not necessarily monetary) to bring dispersed team members together is a significant inhibitor to spontaneous face-to-face meetings. When a DD project exhibits high distance in all dimensions, it is commonly referred to as a GSD project.

The complete framework, presented as Table 1, forms a matrix in which each cell represents the impact of one dimension on one process. The table has been populated with an overview of the DD issues relating each process to each dimension (from Ågerfalk et al. 2005). This is the basis for our later analysis.

Table 1. An Overview of the Framework for Analyzing DD (adapted from Ågerfalk et al. 2005)

	Dimension		
Process	**Temporal Distance**	**Geographical Distance**	**Socio-Cultural Distance**
Communication	Reduced opportunities for synchronous communication, introducing delayed feedback. Improved record of communications.	Potential for closer proximity to market and utilization of remote skilled work forces. Increased cost and logistics of holding face to face meetings.	Potential for stimulating innovation and sharing best practice, but also for misunderstandings.
Coordination	With appropriate division of work, coordination needs can be minimized. Coordination costs typically increase with distance.	Increase in size and skills of labor pool can offer more flexible coordination planning. Reduced informal contact can lead to reduced trust and a lack of critical task awareness.	Potential for learning and access to richer skill set. Inconsistency in work practices can impinge on effective coordination, as can reduced cooperation through misunderstandings.
Control	Time zone effectiveness can be utilized for gaining efficient 24 × 7 work. Management of project artefacts may be subject to delays.	Difficult to convey vision and strategy. Communication channels often leave an audit trail, but can be threatened at key times.	Perceived threat from training low-cost rivals. Different perceptions of authority/hierarchy can undermine morale. Managers must adapt to local regulations.

3   RESEARCH METHOD

In conducting this research, our goal was to consider how companies may increase resilience through adopting effective DD practices. To this end, we have conducted a literature analysis with the aim of characterizing successful strategies for distributed development practice and relating these to the framework of Table 1.

We conducted an analysis of the published literature. For the literature analysis, systematic searches of the literature were made using keyword and author searches, and searches of tables of contents of journals and conference and workshop proceedings. Bibliographic databases were used to assist in forward and backward referencing. Papers were included if they had a core focus on DD, and were based on reported case or field studies in real industrial settings. An extensive note file was also compiled, with quoted sections from papers that contained their major import. This allowed faster filtering in the later stages of analysis, but context was always checked against the full text. The text resulting from this process was coded using a set of codes that evolved during the analysis. These codes form the resulting 10 strategies.

4   STRATEGIES USED IN SUCCESSFUL DD PROJECTS

In this section we consider the peer-reviewed literature on DD processes, specifically focusing on case studies and field studies in DD. The intention is to group and characterize the strategies proposed from real-world experience for reducing risk in DD and thereby leveraging its opportunities.

4.1 Have a Clear Distribution Rationale

When establishing a collaboration involving stakeholders with different native languages, there is a perceived increase in socio-cultural distance. For example, it has been argued that the "language factor is one of the reasons for the success of offshore IT work in countries with strong English language capabilities such as the Philippines and Singapore" (Carmel and Agarwal 2001, p. 27). An approach used by some U.S. companies is to "invest in English as a Foreign Language courses for those who are not fluent in English to improve professional communication" (Carmel and Agarwal 2001, p. 27).

In order to minimize the need for communication when identifying potentially successful development scenarios, Heeks et al. (2001) report that one should try to "focus on well-structured, stable projects"; this has "helped some case study clients push a lot of information exchange into the formal realm that IT-mediated distance can handle relatively well" (p. 59). Herbsleb and Grinter (1999b) elaborate on this idea, suggesting that, to the extent possible, one should "only split the development of well-understood products (or parts of products) where plans, processes and interfaces are established and likely to be stable" (p. 94). If stability is not achieved, the need for communication within the project will significantly increase.

Stability can be affected by socio-cultural distance regarding method usage. The issue of method transfer, even in non-distributed development contexts, has been shown to be a complex and difficult activity (Lings and Lundell 2004). Software development practice often involves improvisation and deviation from documented methods. To master the development processes used in a development project there is a need for informal communication, which for GSD implies travel and direct meetings between stakeholders (Heeks et al. 2001, p. 59).

In establishing an international project involving different sites, it is important to consider time-zone differences between sites. Minimizing time-zone differences facilitates effective synchronous communication, but eliminates the advantage of follow-the-sun type work (Carmel and Agarwal 2001, pp. 27-28). Consequently, establishing sites in a global project presents a trade-off with respect to temporal distance.

4.2 Clarify All Understandings

There are many informal agreements made between partners when setting up a distributed project, and these should be properly understood by all parties. One way in which to clarify is to document. The importance of documenting project goals is emphasized by Bass and Paulish (2004), based on studies at Siemens. They elaborate on the potential risks claiming that "in the absence of clear direction, local cultural and personal biases are going to influence decisions. The resulting choices may not be in line with the overall goals of the project" (p. 10).

Based on GSD projects in the telecommunication company Alcatel, Ebert and DeNeve (2001) recommend clearly documenting all understandings. They suggest defining "at a project's beginning which teams are involved and what they will do in each location" and ensuring that "commitments exist in written and controlled form" (Ebert and DeNeve 2001, p. 68). It is particularly important to clarify understandings between teams in interorganizational collaborations. In an empirical study, Pyysiäinen (2003) found that background information was often lacking, causing problems in building trust between sites. It was found in the study that a "useful practice in the beginning of a project was a collocated training of the development process to be used" (p. 72).

It is also important to have mechanisms for monitoring goal fulfilment. This can be handled in different ways. For example, Boland and Fitzgerald (2004) report from a case study on GSD at Analog Devices that the software manager required each developer to "submit a task report at the beginning of each week," which helped to reduce inter-site dependencies. Such delivery reports contain

> a list of their specific goals for the week and a summary of their progress for the previous week. The report also indicates if the developer intends to make any deliveries during the week (i.e., check their work into the main source tree). This reporting process enables the software manager to be aware of work progressing across all the development sites and provides the necessary information to coordinate tasks among the developers (Boland and Fitzgerald 2004, p. 5).

However, they report that the strategy of using delivery reports was combined with strategies for temporary collocation (see section 4.8) for strengthening morale and motivation.

4.3 Leverage Modularity

The importance of a well-partitioned architecture is stressed by Bass and Paulish (2004), who claim that "in order to facilitate work break down across multiple sites, the architecture needed to reflect the organizational structure of the project" (p. 10). Based on their study at Siemens, they observed that there

> needed to be well-defined components or subsystems with understood dependencies for each site. These components or subsystems also needed to take into account the technical skills of the staff at the responsible development sites (p. 10).

In applying this strategy, the project itself may be made to reflect the structure of the system to be built, to guarantee no tension in the light of Conway's Law (which says that the structure of the system mirrors the structure of the organization that designed it). Herbsleb and Grinter (1999b) use this idea to recommend, "To the extent possible, assign work to different sites according to the greatest possible architectural separation in a design that is as modular as possible" (p. 94).

At one extreme, the project may be broken down into multiple components at the start (Akmanligila and Palvia 2004). This is contrasted with an approach in which local requirements gathering is followed by collocation of representatives from each team for defining a common structure (see section 4.8).

Distributed component development brings with it the issue of system integration and the need to avoid a "big bang" integration activity within a project (Battin et al. 2001). From their case study at Motorola, they report that they "grew an incremental understanding of pair-wise network element interactions and never faced 'big bang' integration" (p. 73).

4.4 Use Cultural Mediation

Liaisons between teams have been found to be a very effective strategy for building trust in a project. For example, Battin et al. (2001) found, in a GSD project in Motorola, that liaisons were a good way for overcoming socio-cultural tensions within a project. In their own words, "The liaisons provided the key link between the architecture team and the development teams, as well as providing the US management team with a face to put with the non-US centers" (p. 74).

Herbsleb and Grinter (1999b) recommend that one creates a pool of liaisons in a project. Specifically, they recommend giving

the early travelers the explicit assignment of meeting people in a variety of groups at the other site, and learning the overall organizational structure. Try to send gregarious people who will enjoy this role. When they return, make it known they can help with cross-site issues, and free up some of their time to do so (p. 94).

Many companies have project managers or key executives who act as cultural liaisons, implying that they frequently travel between the key stakeholder sites. In so doing, the role is "to facilitate the cultural, linguistic, and organizational flow of communication and to bridge cultures, mediate conflicts, and resolve cultural miscommunications" (Carmel and Agarwal 2001, p. 27). An interesting variation of this is put forward by Ebert and DeNeve (2001), based on experience from Alcatel, a large telecommunication company. They claim that management should rotate "across locations and cultures to create the necessary awareness for cultural diversity and how to cope with it" (Ebert and DeNeve 2001, p. 69).

Cultural mediation may also be facilitated by means of "straddlers" (Heeks et al. 2001) who bridge gaps in a project by having "one foot in the client's world and one in the developer's world" (p. 59). Effectively, straddlers are adept at bridging between two different development cultures having (usually) had experience in both.

The use of an offshore-onshore bridgehead in GSD is discussed by Carmel and Agarwal (2001), labeling this as the 75/25 rule of thumb: Essentially, 75 percent of personnel work occurs offshore, while 25 percent occurs onshore (usually at the customer site—for example, in the US). This arrangement optimizes cost savings (offshore) while maintaining closeness to the customer. The individuals assigned to work onshore are typically the more experienced and culturally assimilated. They act to understand the customer's requirements specifications and translate them to the offshore programmers (p. 26).

Such an arrangement, by allowing the use of face-to-face communication, reduces miscommunication between stakeholders at different sites and has been found to be "reassuring" to customers (Carmel and Agarwal 2001, p. 26).

4.5 Facilitate Human Communication

Face-to-face communication is still acknowledged to be the best in most situations, but is clearly not always practical. Hence, a number of communication strategies have been used to maintain elements of synchronous communication. For example, Ebert and DeNeve (2001) recommend provision of "sufficient communication means, such as videoconferencing or shared workspaces and global software libraries" (p. 69) as an approach for improving human communication within distributed projects. However, current technology often brings with it the inherent "challenge of delay due to inadequate (asynchronous) communication" (Damian and Zowghi 2002, p. 10).

Battin et al. (2001) report that they met their "real-time communications needs by teleconferencing," which "became a critical component" in their communication strategy (p. 72). Interestingly, they used conference calls despite the fact that they could "report a problem by email almost instantaneously to all teams," reasoning that "resolution often required detailed discussions" (p. 72). To overcome time-zone problems in arranging such meetings they schedule discussions "during the night from the site requesting the conference call" (p. 72).

In reporting from a field study conducted in a multisite organization, distributed over five continents, Damian and Zowghi (2002) discuss strategies for improving informal human communication among team members through initial face-to-face kick-off meetings (which relates to the strategy of temporary collocation; see section 4.8), and "on-going scheduled informal meetings across sites" (p. 9). Electronically equipped rooms were provided for "drop-in" purposes "to share work artifacts as they would if they started a design discussion near someone's cubicle" (Damian and Zowghi 2002, p. 10). The usefulness of such chat between developers in problem solving situations was also identified by Paasivara (2003, p. 62). In the study, Paasivara notes that developers felt that when chatting they were able to easily post "clarifying counter questions" and that "chat session can be open all the time" (p. 62).

4.6 Manage Processes

From their study at Siemens, Bass and Paulish (2004, p. 10) note the importance of weekly teleconferences to monitor status and highlight issues. They stress the importance (but acknowledge the difficulty) of taking into account time zones and local holiday schedules when scheduling such meetings. When sites have some overlapping time, it is good to plan the work process at each site so that overlap time can be devoted to such meetings (Espinosa and Carmel 2003). Such time can be increased by modifying work patterns. Paasivara (2003) observes that weekly meetings are appropriate for information and monitoring purposes in both directions (i.e., customer to supplier and vice versa), and recommends an agenda that concentrates on "tasks done, tasks to be done, problems and open issues" (p. 62).

Leadership is important for managing software development processes, and perhaps even more so when managing distributed projects. Ebert and DeNeve (2001, p. 68) recommend that a project should have "one project leader who is fully responsible for achieving project targets," and that members of the project management team should represent "the major cultures within the project" (p. 68).

Based on a field-study, Passivara and Lassenius (2004) report that design and code reviews "seemed to be useful in distributed projects with distant sites or subcontractors" (p. 44). They note that such "reviews are early checks that the distributed teams have understood the requirements correctly and are doing what they are supposed to do" (p. 44).

4.7 Develop a Sense of "Teamness"

To strengthen the team culture, Ebert and DeNeve (2001) recommend setting up "a project homepage that summarizes project content, progress metrics, planning information, and team-specific information" (pp. 68-69). Bass and Paulish (2004) note the importance of such measures for communicating progress to team members. They report from a study in Siemens how making the URL for a test system available for all the team members boosted morale for the team: members became aware of the rapid progress being made. "The result was a much greater sense of team than would otherwise have been possible in a globally distributed project" (Bass and Paulish 2004, p. 10).

On the content of a common web site, Espinosa and Carmel (2003) recommend various awareness tactics related to time and work hours, including publishing hours and time differences for the different sites. Damian and Zowghi (2002) recommend going beyond a simple home page to the use of "collaborative Internet technologies" for synchronous testing and collaborative prototyping activities (p. 9). They suggest the use of a human facilitator and "an integrated, richer communication media that integrates data, video and audio channels, in the decision-making teleconferencing calls" (p. 10). Using such an approach in an intercontinental project, they perceived more effective requirements decision-making meetings and improved conflict management.

The issue of trust is closely related to encouragement of a team culture in a project. As noted by Pyysiäinen (2003), properly informing all stakeholders about project progress is also important for strengthening trust in a team. Instead of quantitative feedback (number of working hours etc.), it is important to provide feedback on "quality and concrete contributions of the deliverables" (p. 73). However, perceptions of trust can vary. For example, Damian and Zowghi noted clear differences between how Australian and American stakeholders perceived the importance of *trust*. In their own words, while "trust" was a word often heard in the interviews with the Australian group, for the American stakeholders trust was not an issue. While it is clear that this is due to some sort of cultural difference, one may believe that it is a matter of national or functional culture differences (p. 4).

Part of building a team culture is to reduce the socio-cultural distance between stakeholders within a firm. To this end, Carmel and Agarwal (2001) note the strategy of establishing software centers in other countries rather than outsourcing, bringing IT workers "within the corporate network—inside the firewall—with access to all knowledge-bases, calendars, Web pages, and so forth. They are also trained in the corporate methodologies, policies, and systems" (p. 26).

4.8 Encourage Temporary Collocation

When companies undertake parallel development activities, they sometimes temporarily collocate people. Such meetings are often used to synchronize activity, but may also be used to strengthen morale and lower socio-cultural distance.

Boland and Fitzgerald (2004) report on the use of quarterly sync-up meetings as a very successful strategy for maintaining morale and motivation among team members. They observed that among developers there were comments on "feeling 'energized' and highly motivated after meetings with all the team members" (p. 6) Heeks et al. (2001) report on extensive use of such meetings which "proved to be more effective at synching values and informal information, in a way that IT-mediated communication could not" (p. 56). Visits were undertaken both ways (i.e., North America to India and vice versa).

Temporary collocation is also recommended by Damian and Zowghi (2002) as an approach for improving "awareness of users' local working context" and for contributing to "better communication with sources of requirements through a more appropriate participation from field personnel" (p. 9). It can also be used to strengthen the liaison role in cultural mediation (see section 4.4). Espinosa and Carmel (2003) report, from experiences of UK, German, and Indian software teams, that it is common for Indian team members to be trained in the UK and Germany for a few months. Thereafter, they go back to India and "serve as points of contact for the UK and German developers" (p. 252).

With respect to scheduling periods of collocation, it is recommended to front load travel in a project. Pyysiäinen (2003) notes that a "common kick-off meeting" in the beginning of the project was found to be a "successful way to create initial familiarity between members" (p. 72). Herbsleb and Grinter (1999b) put it this way: "bring people who need to communicate together early on. All other means of communication will work better once developers, testers, and managers have some face-to-face time together" (p. 94).

4.9 Encompass Heterogeneity

It may be that homogeneity appears attractive within a distributed project, but heterogeneity is likely to be unavoidable and so should be carefully planned for. There may be heterogeneity in methods and/or tools and/or terminology.

Battin et al. (2001) report on the need to accommodate existing processes, to "let each team begin producing results immediately, using a process they were familiar with. If the teams had been forced into a common process, the learning curve would have impacted the delivery of the system" (p. 75).

To cater for heterogeneity in process Ebert and DeNeve (2001) recommend providing "an interactive process model based on accepted best practices that allows tailoring processes for the specific needs of a project or even team" (p. 69).

A related problem concerns notations and terminology used in a project. This was experienced in the project analyzed by Battin et al. (200, p. 75): "We understood the inconsistency in notations and terminology in the beginning of the project and came up with a set of common 'work products' and vocabulary." They emphasize the need for standardization in documentation at the project level to facilitate tracking in the shared project databases.

Although potentially advantageous, homogeneity may not be achievable in the tools chosen for a project. For example, the same version of a tool may not be marketed and supported in all locations. As experienced by Battin et al. (2001, p. 74), "Obtaining the same version of a product from multiple sales teams proved quite difficult. While the latest version of most products was readily available in the US, the vendors were often still introducing previous versions in other countries."

Given this, it might be tempting to consider shipping a common tool set to all sites. Apart from ensuing support problems, export licences may not be available. The use of tools under an Open Source licence would naturally change the nature of this problem.

4.10 Develop an Effective Tool Base

Battin et al. (2001, p. 74) recommend the adoption of a common SCM tool and problem tracking tool for all sites. With respect to tools, they note that it is "less important to focus on the particular tools" than to understanding the functions these tools support. This is also emphasized by Herbsleb and Grinter (1999a), who recommend that one invest in "tools that address the real problems" (p. 70). By this, they mean tools that "make it easier to find organizational information, to maintain awareness about the availability of people, and to have more effective cross-site meetings, especially spontaneous ad hoc sessions" (p. 70).

To handle time separation between developers in a distributed project, a number of support tools may be used. A key for achieving this is to

> make better use of asynchronous technologies, such as electronic mail, voice mail, and use of various shared databases and other repositories (groupware, knowledge management, team intranets and web sites, discussion areas, etc.) (Espinosa and Carmel 2003, p. 251).

However, Herbsleb and Grinter (1999a) point out that although "video conferencing, desktop video, electronic bulletin boards, and workflow applications might add value in some circumstances," such tools "do not directly address the core problems" (p. 70).

5 ANALYSIS OF STRATEGIES FOR DD SUCCESS

In this section, we summarize the strategies for DD success, and position them within the framework of Table 1. In so doing, the 10 strategies are related to opportunities and threats in DD. We then consider practitioner literature, as a check for congruence with the peer-reviewed research sources. The 10 strategies for DD success are first summarized and then related to the framework of Table 1.

5.1 A Summary of the Ten Strategies

S1: Have a clear distribution rationale: Not all projects and not all collaboration contexts are equally amenable to DD. From a context perspective, choose offshore teams with a language in common. It may be advantageous to select for low temporal distance, unless follow-the-sun working is relevant. In any case, guarantee regular working time overlap between sites. Rigorously enforce an acceptable capability maturity level of all partners. From a project perspective, only consider DD for well structured, well understood and stable projects, decomposable into discrete tasks.

S2: Clarify all understandings: At the start of any project agree and communicate project goals and targets, and ensure that commitments are genuinely understood. Define which teams are involved, and what will be done in each location. Further, agree and document binding interorganizational processes and stabilizing processes.

S3: Leverage modularity: A system architecture mirrors the structure of the organization that built it (Conway's law), so for software development work, plan the architecture of the system around the distributed structure of the team. This will reduce the need for intensive collaboration, and allow optimum utilization of local skills. For other life-cycle phases plan natural divisions of work in relatively small bundles.

S4: Use cultural mediation: Training in cultural issues is useful. Beyond that, use a cultural mediator, or liaison. This is a person from one team context spending time in another, and becoming a link person between the teams. Many GSD teams use liaisons, who may spend short periods relocated or may even be relocated for an entire project—effectively becoming part of a bridgehead. A more radical suggestion is to rotate management across locations (and therefore cultures) to improve awareness.

S5: Facilitate human communication: Synchronous communication is most effective face to face, but a number of strategies can address the weaknesses of remote communication. Providing rich technologies may help, but improving efficacy of standard technologies is important. A human facilitator in teleconferencing can reduce misunderstandings and smooth conflicts. Language classes can improve confidence and reduce a tendency to asynchronous forms of communication. Increasing informal communication and past face to face meetings can lead to improvements in more formal meetings.

S6: Manage processes: Having one, identified project leader with full responsibility should be supplemented with team and local project managers, even though responsibilities overlap. Regular teleconferences and regular developer reports are recommended for monitoring project status. Plan meetings to occur during overlapping working hours, which can be expanded by time-shifting. Synchronizing delivery and integration cycles between partners, and instigating design and code reviews to verify requirements, are important. Incremental development and release schedules with short cycles are also cited.

S7: Develop a sense of teamness: Common strategies include the development of a project home page, which includes team member details and important planning information such as national holidays. Also summarize project progress as well as planning and team-specific information. Record decisions and make them easily accessible. Ensure timely feedback to communications about progress, including deliverables. Real-time sharing of artefacts, including ideas, perhaps further facilitated by time-shifting.

S8: Encourage temporary collocation: Investing in periods of collocation for teams can reduce future problems in all future processes, but such relocations need planning and can be expensive. Consider collocating developers, not only managers. There may be a one-off project initiation session, where understandings are forged and strategic thinking can take place. There may also be regular (e.g., quarterly) synchronization and review meetings, but front-loading travel is considered most effective. Variation includes project phasing, with one phase distributed and another phase in-house.

S9: Encompass heterogeneity: There can be advantages in accommodating heterogeneous methods, tools, and terminology, but such accommodation needs to be planned and catered for. Tool heterogeneity may be forced because of local restrictions (export licensing, available support, etc.). Local terms and concepts need to be mapped to a common ontology to prevent project-level confusion. One suggested strategy is to provide an interactive process model that can be tailored for each team.

S10: Develop an effective tool base: A common software configuration management tool is recommended for coordination, probably replicated at each site. This can be enhanced by creative use of the comments fields as an extra form of asynchronous communication. The key thing is to invest in tools that address the real problems. Tool take-up is otherwise low.

5.2 Relating the Strategies to the Framework

The first strategy—have a clear distribution rationale—addresses primarily problems associated with temporal distance by reducing the need for communication, which in turn simplifies coordination and control. Reducing communication also reduces potential problems in the socio-cultural dimension, such as culturally induced misunderstandings.

The second strategy—clarify all understanding—is mainly a way to minimize potential misunderstandings and communication breakdowns which can result from non-overlapping socio-cultural backgrounds. Clearly documenting such things as project goals and individual partner commitments helps to remove the communication problems otherwise caused through differing interpretations of informal agreements.

The third strategy—leverage modularity—suggests that the system architecture should be designed to reflect the geographical (and competence) structure of the project. In this way, local expertise can be utilized efficiently, thus reducing potential coordination and control problems.

The fourth strategy—use cultural mediation—suggests that it is worth spending resources on reducing socio-cultural distance by means of facilitating face-to-face meetings. Different approaches can be used, but the main idea is to have at least some people at each node who have met people at peer nodes in person. This also reduces the perceived geographical distance, if not the physical.

The fifth strategy—facilitate human communication—focuses on the communication process across all three dimensions of distance. Good communication is also fundamental for successful coordination and control and so can indirectly be seen to address these processes also. The utilization of innovative IT-based solutions for real-time conversations is crucial for succeeding with this strategy.

The sixth strategy—manage processes—addresses the control and coordination structure of a project with respect to temporal distance. Basically, there need to be processes in place for harmonizing tasks between nodes at predefined points in time, so that all nodes can plan their work around these contact points.

The seventh strategy—develop a sense of teamness—aims to facilitate communication and coordination by stimulating the feeling of being a member of a team. A project is more likely to be successful when all members share a sense of belonging to the same team.

The eighth strategy—encourage temporary collocation—takes the cultural mediation strategy even further by suggesting that all developers should spend time at remote sites on a temporary basis. If a cultural liaison facilitates communication between sites, having local peers at the remote site more directly increases the team's coordination.

The ninth strategy—encompass heterogeneity—aims to prepare for problems introduced by the fact that any DD team is naturally heterogeneous. Allowing for different work practices but managing these through a common method tailoring framework is central to successful coordination and control.

The tenth and final strategy—develop an effective tool base—aims to facilitate coordination and control through the use of standardized tool support for configuration and change management.

The 10 strategies and how they map to the framework of Table 1 are shown in Table 2. Each of the 10 strategies has been positioned in Table 2 according to its main emphases.

From Table 2 we can conclude that there are indeed DD strategies that address all problem areas constituted by the nine cells of the framework. However, this does not mean that all problems are solved. It may be tempting to think of Table 2 as a tool to find an optimal minimal set of strategies that will cover all nine DD problem areas. This is not advisable since there is no guarantee that any one strategy is either necessary or sufficient to overcome problems in any particular area. Rather, the mapping should be seen as a guide to which areas may have been left out should particular strategies not have been put into practice. It is also a fact that the success of each strategy is contingent upon the particular organizational context and so must be tailored to suit each specific situation.

The fact that most of the strategies deal with the socio-cultural dimension could be interpreted in two quite different ways. On the one hand, it could mean that this dimension is particularly problematic and important, hence a lot of effort has been spent on reducing socio-cultural distance. On the other hand, it could mean that this dimension is trivial and that many obvious strategies have emerged. Judging by the many problems reported in the literature, the former is probably the most likely.

Table 2. Positioning the Strategies for DD Success Within the Framework of Table 1

Process		Dimension	
	Temporal Distance	**Geographical Distance**	**Socio-Cultural Distance**
Communication	Have a clear distribution rationale (S1) Facilitate human communication (S5)	Use cultural mediation (S4) Facilitate human communication (S5) Encourage temporary collocation (S8)	Have a clear distribution rationale (S1) Clarify all understandings (S2) Use cultural mediation (S4) Develop a sense of teamness (S7) Encourage temporary collocation (S8)
Coordination	Have a clear distribution rationale (S1) Manage processes (S6) Develop an effective tool base (S10)	Leverage modularity (S3) Encourage temporary collocation (S8) Develop an effective tool base (S10)	Clarify all understandings (S2) Develop a sense of teamness (S7) Encourage temporary collocation (S8) Encompass heterogeneity (S9)
Control	Have a clear distribution rationale (S1) Manage processes (S6) Develop an effective tool base (S10)	Leverage modularity (S3) Develop an effective tool base (S10)	Clarify all understandings (S2) Encompass heterogeneity (S9)

5.3 Congruence with Practitioner Viewpoints

The practitioner literature is largely consistent with the research literature, acknowledging the problems and dimensions of DD (see, for example, Coar 2003-2004), but also giving some pragmatic insights into experience of DD. For example, the increased risks are well recognized, including that associated with the unsettling and potentially demotivating effects of major outsourcing decisions (Goulston 2004). However, the need for CIOs to be proactively following the lead of large corporations in outsourcing is seen as a driving force for increased globalization at least over the medium term (Smith 2004). Practitioner guidelines are largely consistent with the strategies outlined above, although some detail is added. For example, Smith goes on to detail a *collocation* strategy of keeping prototyping and piloting work in-house but outsourcing production. Turnlund (2003-2004) emphasizes the importance of leveraging modularity in his "workgroup containment" rule. The general consensus seems to be that outsourcing "means trouble for the unprepared" (Grossman 2003).

6   CONCLUSIONS

In this paper we have considered how companies may become more resilient through adopting effective DD practices. Since DD could be seen both as a response to external pressures and as a disruptive innovation that may well introduce new internal turbulence, understanding the particular DD challenges and opportunities is crucial for any organization adopting DD. In order to adapt to changing circumstances brought about by DD, successful strategies for coping with the processes of coordination, control, and communication must be adopted. To understand these processes in the context of DD, we have used a framework that combines the three processes with the three distances characterizing DD: temporal distance, geographical distance and socio-cultural distance. Altogether this framework thus provides nine areas that pose challenges and opportunities for DD projects. Based on existing literature from case and field studies we have synthesized and presented ten general strategies for successful DD. These strategies have been shown to address all of the nine DD problem areas of the framework—albeit the extent to which they can be combined to synergistically solve all major DD problems remains as a future research topic. Consequently, further deep case and field studies are needed.

Although we have considered only traditional DD in this study, there are many striking examples of successful distributed development in the area of open source systems development. Some even conjecture that paradigms encompassing the successful strategies of both OSS and commercial projects are the holy grail of distributed development, enabling cross-fertilization of ideas throughout traditional distributed and OSS development. Such studies would allow further development of the strategies presented here, with a view to informing best practice throughout DD, and thereby increasing resilience in software development companies.

Acknowledgments

This research has been financially supported by the European Commission via FP6 Coordinated Action Project 004337 in priority IST-2002-2.3.2.3 CALIBRE (http://www.calibre.ie), and also by the Science Foundation Ireland Principal Investigator projects B4-STEP and Lero.

References

Ågerfalk, P., Fitzgerald, B., Holmström, H., Lings, B., Lundell, B., and Ó Conchúir, E. "Framework for Considering Opportunities and Threats in Distributed Software Development," in *Proceedings of the International Workshop on Distributed Software Engineering*, Austrian Computer Society, 2005, p. 47-61.

Akmanligil, M., and Palvia, P. C. "Strategies for Global Information Systems Development," *Information & Management* (42:1), 2004, pp. 45-59.

Bass, M., and Paulish, D. "Global Software Development Process Research at Siemens," in *Proceedings of the 3rd International Workshop on Global Software Development* (collocated with ICSE 2004, International Conference on Software Engineering), Edinburgh, Scotland, May 24, 2004, pp. 8-11 (available online at http://gsd2004.cs.uvic.ca/docs/proceedings.pdf).

Battin, R .D., Crocker, R., Kreidler, J., and Subramanian, K. "Leveraging Resources in Global Software Development," *IEEE Software* (18:2), 2001, pp. 70-77.

Boland, D., and Fitzgerald, B. "Transitioning from a Co-Located to a Globally-Distributed Software Development Team: A Case Study at Analog Devices Inc.," in *Proceedings of the 3rd International Workshop on Global Software Development*, (co-located with ICSE 2004, International Conference on Software Engineering), Edinburgh, Scotland, May 24, 2004, pp. 4-7 (available online at http://gsd2004.cs.uvic.ca/docs/proceedings.pdf).

Brooks, F. P. Jr. "No Silver Bullet: Essence and Accidents of Software Engineering," in H. J. Kugler (ed.), *Information Processing 1986*, Amsterdam: Elsevier Science Publishers B.V. (North-Holland), 1986, pp. 1069-1076.

Carmel, E. "Introduction to the Special Issue of EJISD: The Emergence of Software Exporting Industries in Dozens of Developing and Emerging Economies," *The Electronic Journal on Information Systems in Developing Countries* (13), Special Issue, May 2003, pp. 1-2 (available online at www.ejisdc.org).

Carmel, E., and Agarwal, R. "Tactical Approaches for Alleviating Distance in Global Software Development," *IEEE Software* (18:2), 2001, pp. 22-29.

Clark, H. H. *Using Language*, Cambridge, England: Cambridge University Press, 1996.

Coar, K. "The Sun Never Sets on Distributed Development," *Queue*, December/January 2003-2004, pp. 32-39.

Damian, D., Lanubile, F., and Oppenheimer, H. L. "Addressing the Challenges of Software Industry Globalization: The Workshop on Global Software Development," in *Proceedings 25th International Conference on Software Engineering*, Los Alamitos, CA: IEEE Computer Society Press, 2003, pp. 793-794.

Damian, D. E., and Zowghi, D. "The Impact of Stakeholders' Geographical Distribution on Managing Requirements in a Multisite Organization," in *Proceedings IEEE Joint International Conference on Requirements Engineering*, Los Alamitos, CA: IEEE Computer Society Press, 2002, pp. 319-328.

DeLone, W., Espinosa, J. A., Lee, G., and Carmel, E. "Bridging Global Boundaries for IS Project Success," in *Proceedings of the 38th Annual Hawaii International Conference on System Sciences (HICSS'05) - Track 1*, Los Alamitos, CA: IEEE Computer Society Press, 2005, pp. 1-10.

Ebert, C., and De Neve, P. "Surviving Global Software Development," *IEEE Software* (18:2), 2001, pp. 62-69.

Espinosa, A., and Carmel, E. "The Impact of Time Separation on Coordination in Global Software Teams: A Conceptual Foundation," *Software Process Improvement and Practice* (8), 2003, pp. 249-266.

Evaristo, J. R., Scudder, R., Desouza, K. C., and Sato, O. "A Dimensional Analysis of Geographically Distributed Project Teams: A Case Study," *Journal of Engineering and Technology Management* (21:3), 2004, pp. 175-189.

Goulston, M. "The Inner Cost of Outsourcing: When Contemplating Outsourcing, CIOs Should First Think About Their People," *CIO Magazine*, November 1, 2004 (available online at www.cio.com/archive/110104/interview.html).

Ghosh, T., Yates, J. A., and Orlikowski, W. J. "Using Communication Norms for Coordination: Evidence from a Distributed Team," in R. Agarwal, L. Kirsch, and J. I. DeGross (eds.), *Proceedings of the 25th International Conference on Information Systems*, Washington, DC, December 2005, pp. 115-127.

Grossman, E. (ed.). "New World Order," *Queue*, December/January 2003-2004, pp. 27-31.

Heeks, R., Krishna, S., Nicholson, B., and Sahay, S. "Synching or Sinking: Global Software Outsourcing Relationships," *IEEE Software* (18:2), 2001, pp. 54-60.

Herbsleb, J. D., and Grinter, R. E. "Architectures, Coordination, and Distance: Conway's Law and Beyond," *IEEE Software* (16:5), 1999a, pp. 63-70.

Herbsleb, J. D., and Grinter, R. E. "Splitting the Organization and Integrating the Code: Conway's Law Revisited," in *Proceedings of the 21tst International Conference on Software Engineering (ICSE'99)*, New York: ACM Press, 1999b, pp. 85-95.

Lengnick-Hall, C. A. "Adaptive Fit Versus Robust Transformation: How Organizations Respond to Environmental Change," *Journal of Management* (31:5), 2005, pp. 738-757.

Lings, B., and Lundell, B. "On Transferring a Method into a Usage Situation," in B. Kaplan, D. P. Truex III, D. Wastell, A. T. Wood-Harper, and J. I. DeGross (eds.), *Information Systems Research: Relevant Theory and Informed Practice*, Boston: Kluwer, 2004, pp. 535-553.

Lyytinen, K., and Rose, G. M. "The Disruptive Nature of Information Technology Innovations: The Case of Internet Computing in Systems Development Organizations," *MIS Quarterly* (27:4), 2003, pp. 557-595.

Malone, T. W., and Crowston, K. "The Interdisciplinary Study of Coordination," *ACM Computing Surveys* (26:1), 1994, pp. 87-119.

McChesney, I. R., and Gallagher, S. "Communication and Co-ordination Practices in Software Engineering Projects," *Information and Software Technology* (46:7), 2004, pp. 473-489.

Nurmi, A., Hallikainen, P., and Rossi, M. "Coordination of Outsourced Information System Development in Multiple Customer Environment: A Case Study of a Joint Information System Development Project," in *Proceedings of the 38th Hawaii International Conference on System Sciences*, Los Alamitos, CA: IEEE Computer Society Press, 2005, pp. 1-10.

Paasivaara, M. "Communication Needs, Practices and Supporting Structures in Global Inter-Organizational Software Development Projects," in *Proceedings of International Workshop on Global Software Development* (co-located with ICSE 2003, International Conference on Software Engineering), Portland, Oregon, May 9, 2003, pp. 59-63 (available online at http://gsd2003.cs.uvic.ca/gsd2003proceedings.pdf).

Paasivaara, M., and Lassenius, C. "Using Research Methodologies and Challenges in GSD," in *Proceedings of the 3rd International Workshop on Global Software Development* (co-located with ICSE 2004, International Conference on Software Engineering), Edinburgh, Scotland, May 24, 2004, pp. 42-47 (available online at http://gsd2003.cs.uvic.ca/gsd2003proceedings.pdf).

Pyysiäinen, J. "Building Trust in Global Inter-Organizational Software Development Projects: Problems and Practices," in *International Workshop on Global Software Development* (co-located with ICSE 2003, International Conference on Software Engineering), Portland, Oregon, May 9, 2003, pp. 69-74 (available online at gsd2003.cs.uvic.ca/gsd2003proceedings.pdf).

Riolli, L., and Savicki, V. "Information System Organizational Resilience," *Omega: The International Journal of Management Science* (31), 2003, pp. 227-233.

Smith, G. "You Can't Outsource Everything," *CIO Magazine*, November 1, 2004 (available online at http://www.cio.com/archive/110104/peer.html).

Sutanto, J., Kankanhalli, A., and Tan, B. C. Y. "Task Coordination in Global Virtual Teams," in R. Agarwal, L. Kirsch, and J. I. DeGross (eds.), *Proceedings of the 25th International Conference on Information Systems*, Washington, DC, December 2004, pp. 807-819.

Turnlund, M. "Distributed Development Lessons: Why Repeat the Mistakes of the past If You Don't Have To?," *Queue*, December/January 2003-2004, pp. 27-31.

United Nations. *World Investment Report 2004: The Shift Towards Services*, New York: United Nations Conference on Trade and Development, 2004.

About the Authors

Brian Lings, after a number of years at the University of Queensland, Australia, joined the Department of Computer Science at the University of Exeter, becoming its first elected head of department. He is a consultant with Certus Technology Associates and a member of the academic staff of the University of Skövde, Sweden. He chairs the steering group of the BNCOD database conference, the main forum for database researchers in the UK. His research centers on the socio-technical evaluation of tool and method support for model-based distributed development. He is a codeveloper of the *2G* method, and continues to be active in applications of the method. Brian can be reached by e-mail at brian.lings@his.se.

Björn Lundell has been a staff member at the University of Skövde since 1984. He has contributed to international standardization (ISO), established active links with a number of Swedish private and public organizations, and coleads the work package on distributed development in the EU FP6 Co-ordination Action project CALIBRE (www.calibre.ie). He is a co-developer of the *2G* method, a qualitative method evolved for use in socio-technical evaluations which has been applied to the analysis of open source software usage in organizations. Over the past 5 years, he has gained significant experience in conducting case studies for analyzing and evaluating socio-technical phenomena in organizational contexts. His research is published in a variety of international journals and conferences. He has a general interest in qualitative methods and his research centers on the issues of technology evaluation, open source and distributed development models, and theoretical and practical aspects of method transfer into real organizational usage. Björn can be reached by e-mail at bjorn.lundell@his.se.

Pär J Ågerfalk received his Ph.D. from Linköping University and is currently a postdoctoral research fellow at the University of Limerick and an assistant professor at Örebro University. He is the deputy coordinator and scientific manager of the EU FP6 project CALIBRE and also co-leader of the work package on distributed development. His current research centers on open source software development in the secondary software sector, globally distributed and flexible software development methods, and how information systems development approaches can be informed by language/action theory. His over 40 peer-reviewed publications have appeared in a variety of international journals, books, and conference proceedings, and he is currently an associate editor of *European Journal of Information Systems* and a guest editor of *Communications of the ACM* and *Software Process: Improvement and Practice*. Pär can be reached by e-mail at par.agerfalk@ul.ie.

Brian Fitzgerald works at the University of Limerick, Ireland, where he is a research fellow and Science Foundation Ireland Principal Investigator. He has a Ph.D. from the University of London and has held visiting positions in Sweden, the United Kingdom, and United States. His publications include seven books and more than 80 papers, published in leading international conferences and journals. Brian has attracted research funding in excess of 10 million euro overall on his projects. Having worked in industry prior to taking up an academic position, he has more than 20 years experience in the software field. This experience was gained in a range of sectors and in several countries including Ireland, the UK, Belgium, and Germany. Brian can be reached by e-mail at brian.fitzgerald@ul.ie.

10   IMPROVISATION AS STRATEGY: Building an Information Technology Capability

Thi Lien Pham
Ernest Jordan
Macquarie University
Sydney, Australia

Abstract   *There is substantial literature on the use of information technology for competitive advantage and organizational transformation. In the main, this literature speaks to the world of IT-capable organizations, pursuing ever more challenging goals. This paper reports on a case study of an organization that had similar aims for its use of IT, but lacked the capability. Senior management chose a strategy of improvisation with the goal of learning-by-doing so that the capability would be developed. The paper assesses the achievements to date, suggests forward paths, and offers guidelines to organizations that find themselves in a similar state.*

Keywords   Competitive advantage, business strategy, IT capability

1   INTRODUCTION

The early propositions of competitive advantage through information technology espoused by, among others, McFarlan (1984) and Porter and Millar (1985) later became concerned with the sustainability of that advantage (for example, Clemons and Row 1991; Feeny and Ives 1990). However, for the majority of organizations, this cannot be the case; they cannot all be leaders. The analysis provided by the resource-based view of IT suggests that many organizations must be satisfied with a position of *competitive parity* where information technologies are viewed as homogeneously distributed (Mata et al. 1995). This matches the position of Carr (2003), where IT is viewed as a utility that cannot deliver any sustainable advantage. However Mata et al. (1995) show that it is the management of IT, rather than the IT itself, that is able to deliver sustainable advantage. They suggest that strongly developed IT management capabilities are able

Please use the following format when citing this chapter:

Pham, Thi Lien, Jordan, Ernest, 2006, in International Federation for Information Processing (IFIP), Volume 206, The Transfer and Diffusion of Information Technology for Organizational Resilience, eds. B. Donnellan, Larsen T., Levine L., DeGross J. (Boston: Springer), pp. 139-156.

to deliver new applications that have value to the business more often, more reliably, and more effectively.

The IT-led transformation literature also addresses organizations that are IT-capable (Applegate 1994; Bjørn-Andersen and Turner 1994; Turban et al. 2004). The business process reengineering movement (Hammer and Champy 1993) lauded IT as an enabler of the radical changes in the organization. The widely quoted case studies of organizational transformation through IT have a sometimes unwritten assumption that merely choosing the correct IT, making a decision, will enable it to be implemented and the benefits achieved. This may be true for IT-capable organizations (although the stories of project failure are often ascribed to organizations that one would imagine to be generally competent) but for organizations where IT capability is underdeveloped, the achievability of project goals will be seriously in doubt.

What options then are available to the organization that is not IT capable? If a hypothetical SWOT analysis done by the board and senior management shows that, for their organization, IT is a weakness, what can be done? This is especially challenging if the board and senior management are aware that IT is an increasing basis of competition, efficiency, and product development. This paper reports on just such an example, where the senior management needed to transform the IT capability so that IT could transform the organization. Senior management took a decision of improvisation—an attempt at self-sufficiency that could be regarded as a "sink or swim" approach. This is unusual for a conservative, government-owned insurance company anywhere in the world, but perhaps more especially in a developing economy. We report on a far-sighted approach that is working and assess its achievements.

2   THEORETICAL BACKGROUND

This paper draws on two key literature themes: IT capability and improvisation. These are then combined into a framework for understanding how improvisation may be regarded as a strategy when aiming to build IT capability.

2.1 IT Capability

Information technology is generally available to all organizations; there are few purchase restrictions in force around the world. IT is not a scarce resource at its basic commodity level, as Carr (2003) convincingly argued. However, some organizations do better with their IT than others and for some this is a consistent achievement. The key discriminator is not the technology but the management of it (Bharadwaj 2000; Mata et al. 1995). Consistently superior management of IT is an overarching IT capability that enables the organization to deliver real value to the business (Dvorak et al. 1997), and achieve long-term competitiveness (Ross et al. 1996).

But what precisely are these capabilities? Bharadwaj (2000) defined IT capability as the ability to mobilize and deploy IT-based resources in combination with other resources and capabilities. Those IT-based resources are IT infrastructure, human IT resources comprising technical and managerial IT skills, and intangible IT-enabled resources such as knowledge assets, customer orientation, and synergy. Ross et al. (1996) argue that competent staff, strong relationships between business and IT, and a reusable technology base are the foundations. However this argument is still short on specifics that would guide an under-achieving organization. Peppard and Ward (2004) mentioned three interrelated attributes of IT capabilities:

- A fusion of business knowledge with IS knowledge
- A flexible and reusable IT platform
- An effective use process (with its two aspects: using the technology and working with information)

Similarly the principles espoused by Dvorak et al. (1997, p. 166), may be goals aimed at in the establishment of organizational capability and can be summarized as

- Business-driven IT
- Business funding of IT
- Flexibility and simplicity
- short term results
- Constant productivity improvements
- Reciprocal understanding between business and IT

but they are not indicators in themselves of achievement or capability. Furthermore, there is little empirical evidence offered to support these propositions.

The approach taken by Feeny and Willcocks (1998) is particularly valuable. Using outsourcing as a test case, or "winnowing" mechanism, they identify the capabilities that an organization must maintain even though its IT is outsourced. They then infer that these same capabilities are precisely those that are needed, and critical, to organizations that do not outsource. Feeny and Willcocks (pp. 357-359) list these core capabilities as

- IS/IT leadership
- Business system thinking
- Relationship building
- Architecture planning
- Making technology work
- Informed buying
- Contract facilitation
- Contract monitoring
- Vendor development

Building on the work of Feeny and Willcocks, Ward and Peppard (2002, pp. 595-596) identified eight key "inabilities" that organizations admitted. These are

- **Business strategy**: An inability to ensure that business strategy formulation identifies the most advantageous use of information, systems, and technology.
- **Benefits delivery**: An inability to monitor, measure, and evaluate the benefits delivered from IS/IT investment and use.

- **Managing change**: An inability to make the business and organizational changes required to maximize the benefits without detrimental impact on stakeholders.
- **Information governance**: An inability to define information management policies for the organization and the roles and responsibilities of general management and the IS function.
- **Benefits planning**: An inability explicitly to identify and plan to realize the benefits from IS investments.
- **Business performance improvement**: An inability to identify the knowledge and information needed to deliver strategic objectives through improved management processes.
- **Information asset management**: An inability to establish and operate the processes that ensure data, information, and knowledge-management activities meet organizational needs and satisfy corporate policies.
- **Prioritization**: An inability to ensure that the portfolio of investments in applications and technology produces the maximum return from the resources available.

This list, when viewed as *abilities* rather than *inabilities* forms one of the frameworks for this study. How organizations can make the transition from inabilities to abilities requires other models.

The work of Ciborra is significant but again often speaks of capable organizations. One view he supported for the transition from lower levels of capabilities to higher levels is that of organizational learning. Andreu and Ciborra (1996) develop a model that shows how IT can be used for the development of core capabilities in the organization, although here they are concerned with the role for IT in developing competencies elsewhere in the organization. This model involves three learning loops.

- The routinization loop, which uses resources available in the wider environment to develop work practices.
- The capability loop, which takes these work practices and, through management actions, develops capabilities.
- The strategic loop, which takes capabilities and, when guided by the business mission develops core capabilities in a competitive context (Andreu and Ciborra 1996).

This model is presented in Figure 1. It shows that the development of work practices can occur in isolation from the strategic inputs. In the routine of their work, staff build practices that, when recognized by management, can become the basis of competencies. Tuning these to the needs of the organization's goals and its competitive environment can then build core competencies.

This model can be used to examine the development of IT capability in particular in an organization.

2.2 Improvisation

Early work on improvisation drew on concepts from the world of music, jazz in particular, but over time the phenomenon of improvisation within organizations has been

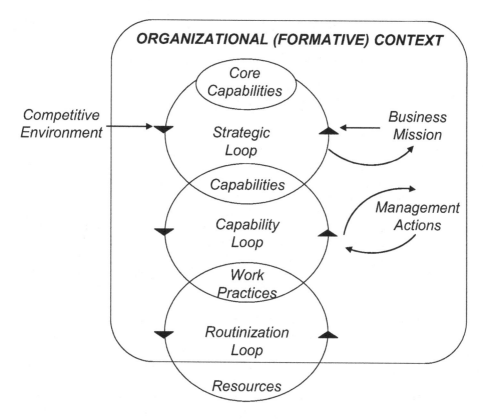

Figure 1. Basic Learning Processes (Reprinted from *Journal of Strategic Information Systems* (5), R. Andreu and C, Ciborra, "Organizational Learning and Core Capabilities Development: The Role of IT," p. 118, Copyright © 1996; used with permission from Elsevier.)

studied in its own right (Barrett 1998; Kamoche 2003). Given that planning and control play such significant roles in management research and practice, one emphasis of the improvisation literature has examined the absence of planning or the restricted time between planning and action (Barrett 1998; Cunha et al. 1999; Moorman and Miner 1998a, 1998b; Weick 1998). A second stream of research deals with spur-of-the-moment actions, such as in crisis situations (Weick 1988) or essentially intuitive, spontaneous action without planning (Ciborra 1999).

In bringing concepts of improvisation to the field of information systems, Orlikowski (1996; also Orlikowski and Hoffman 1997) drew reference to the responses to the day-to-day disasters, disruptions, and outages that are unfortunately too common.

Thus we adopt the broad definition of organizational improvisation of Cunha et al. (1999, p. 302) as "the conception of action as it unfolds, by an organization and/or its members, drawing on available material, cognitive, affective and social resources." The specific inclusion of the word *available* stresses the complementary concept of bricolage, where solutions are developed only from what is available, rather than what is best. We further note the point made by Miner et al. (2001) that improvisational action can occur and be studied at any level of analysis, including strategic improvisation by an entire firm.

2.3 Improvisation Toward IT Capability

Improvisation could happen at all levels of and in all kinds of organizations (Ciborra 1999; Miner et al. 2001), even in highly structured organizations. Ciborra (1999) reviewed the everyday activity in both emergency and routine circumstances and showed that improvisation is ubiquitous and economically relevant in both market and hierarchy structures. The fifth of the capabilities in the Feeny and Willcocks (1998) model is "rapidly achieving technical progress by one means or another," which expresses one aspect of improvisation. If that technical progress includes a reference to the other capabilities, then we can see that improvisation is compatible with their model. On the other hand, a high-level decision to improvise can be seen as strategic. Silva (2002) shows that improvisation can indeed be a strategic decision. More broadly, the strategic decision may be to improvise rather than a specific, unique improvised decision.

One of the positive outcomes of improvisation is learning, mentioned earlier. Organizations doing improvisation can learn in three ways: learn how to improvise, learn through the formalization/routinization of their improvisation, and learn about themselves and their environment through the action component of improvisation (Cunha et al. 1999). Miner et al. (2001) argued that improvisation can be seen as a special type of short-term, real-time learning itself and that improvisation not only draws on prior learning but may be a factor that influences other, long term organizational learning activities. With the view that "people continually learn and improvise while working" (Brown and Duguid 1991, cited by Ciborra 1999, p. 81), it is believed that the learning that happened in an improvising organization might be both the outcome of improvisation and the "learning in working/learning by doing" process itself. This paper tries to analyze the case of building IT capability in a developing country in relation with this improvisation phenomenon and this view will affect the way that this paper presents and analyzes its case study.

Is improvisation necessarily quick and unexpected, or is it simply the outcomes of improvisation that are unexpected? This sense of improvisation—making do with what you have and making something special out of it—is distinctly different from Silva's (2002) concept, where improvisation is expressed by "quick and unexpected solutions" (p. 129). However, Silva shows that improvisation can indeed be a strategic decision. More broadly, the strategic decision may be to improvise rather than a specific, unique improvised decision.

3   RESEARCH APPROACH

The case study presented here concerns the process of building IT capability in a Vietnamese insurance organization, Baoviet. When Baoviet needed a system for its newly created life insurance business, several factors drove it to an improvisation approach. However, the main objective was that the business units would learn about IT and the IT unit would learn about business needs, and that this learning would happen on the job. Thus IT capability would be improved. Bao Viet Life became a separate company in 2004.

A case study investigation has been conducted on site at the head office and Hanoi branch of Bao Viet Life. More than 40 managers and IT staff were involved in a study that used interviews and questionnaires. Semi-structured interviews were conducted concerning the evolving capabilities in IT. Simple questionnaires were then used to extend the coverage. The interviews were semi-structured based on the above-mentioned IT capability model and had an average duration of some 2 hours. They were not taped; instead, notes were taken. The risk in this procedure is being not completely faithful to the words used by the interviewees, but it made them feel more comfortable. The questionnaire design also drew on the Ross et al. (1996) study and the Peppard and Ward (2004) capability model. The study received ethics approval from the researchers' university. Besides the interview and questionnaire survey results, many of the company's written documents were collected for the purpose of analysis later.

The case study will be presented; analysis and discussion relating to improvisation theory will follow.

4 CASE AND ANALYSIS

Baoviet Insurance Company (Baoviet) has 45 years of experience in providing insurance services. Until 1995, however, this did not include life insurance. By 1995, the gains from economic growth after 10 years of economic reform had substantially improved the living standard of the Vietnamese people. Vietnam experienced a sustainable economic growth rate of about 6 percent during this 10 year period. The demand for life insurance emerged when those with higher incomes started thinking about their longer term living conditions and investments. Baoviet faced the decision of how to develop this potential but avoid the risks and complications of this new form of business.

The life insurance business development project on the table in 1995 included plans of joint-ventures with foreign partners. However, the tender offers were refused and Baoviet decided to develop using its own efforts. Baoviet was then a government-owned monopoly and did not want to share the potentially strong returns in that initial period and so it decided to develop a local brand of life insurance. The process of developing this new business from scratch was completely by a process of trial and error.

The major challenges for life insurance development were the lack of experience in product development, business procedures, product knowledge of agents and staff, IT development and use, and risk management. However, the life insurance business of Baoviet experienced an unexpectedly strong growth rate and all business functions and systems were under severe pressure. In 2000 Baoviet changed its business strategy for life insurance to "growth and management" with a strong emphasis on improving various aspects of management.

The business model of Baoviet was (and remains) decentralized, with all branches relatively independent in providing services to customers. The head office is responsible for product development, guiding business processes, training, and support. The branches are responsible for directly providing products and serving customers. Because of the limitations of the telecommunication infrastructure and low experience in IT development in Vietnam, online data centralization was not feasible at all until recently. That is, branches were required to maintain their own data about policyholders.

It is worth mentioning that a recent entrant (a global player) in the Vietnamese insurance business has significant IT know-how and is using this effectively to build market share.

4.1 Early Stage

In 1996, Baoviet launched its life insurance business. This was the first, and monopoly, provider doing life insurance business in the marketplace. In the period from 1996 to 1999, it was undertaken in only 20 out of the 61 branches. By 2002, all of Baoviet's 61 branches located in all provinces across the country had implemented the life insurance business.

In the early 1990s, there was no substantial Vietnamese software company in the market, let alone one that specialized in insurance. It was not easy to find programmers, and packages were not available in the Vietnamese market. In addition, Baoviet's life insurance business was still small in terms of number of customers and premium income. The first attempt at IT development in 1996 was for management of policies using FoxBase.[1] This software was developed by a business staff member rather than Baoviet's IT department, which had no knowledge of life insurance. It was first used in two branches in Hanoi and Ho Chi Minh City and then was installed in those branches with life insurance business.

Under the pressure of fast business growth and unforeseen management requirements, the software did not meet business demands and was not stable. It remained outdated even though it was continuously updated. In 1998, a replacement, more comprehensive FoxBase application was launched by the Baoviet IT department. This new system had more functionality and could work with larger volumes of data. However, the IT problems continued mounting. The most common problems were functional errors, inflexible reporting, and little support for decision making, combined with the slow speed of operation. In addition, IT problems were caused by untrained staff. Business staffs were also learning how to establish the new business processes and kept changing their business procedures, especially when launching new products. The IT staff also were exploring business procedures and enhancing their IT skills at the same time. A senior software developer in the current Bao Viet Life IT Centre said,

Baoviet IT staff hadn't got enough knowledge and experience in the life insurance business at that time. So, building in-house software was the right decision. It helped IT staff to learn more technical skills and business knowledge so that they could assess software that external partners offered later.

---

[1]A competitor product to Ashton-Tate's dBaseIV, then the market leader in PC database software. It had limited multiuser capability and was eventually purchased by Microsoft (now Visual FoxPro).

By 1999, the information technology market in Vietnam was growing with more IT companies and increasing awareness of IT's role in business. The government especially emphasized its importance as well, giving some encouragement for developing information technology in the country through initiatives such as tax exemptions for importing hardware and software and priority for Internet infrastructure development. The achievements in Vietnam's economic development had improved people's standard of living. The large population (over 80 million) combined with the gradual increase in awareness of life insurance created a large potential life insurance market for Vietnam, which attracted increasing attention from foreign companies. Some were permitted to open for business in Vietnam in 1999, ending Baoviet's monopoly in life insurance. Competition became the emerging issue with which Baoviet's executive management had to prepare to cope. In the 1999 business strategy, it was specified that one of the main principles for developing the information systems was the use of a "self-sufficiency" approach, making use of external resources. They decided that an essential step was outsourcing IT, so they called for presentations from several software application vendors, both local and foreign.

At that time, the life insurance business was still new in Vietnam. Baoviet staff had both insufficient IT skills and insufficient business knowledge. It was particularly challenging for them to assess the sophisticated "total solution" offerings from overseas. These packages seemed to be good but they were thought to be unsuitable to Baoviet's current business situation and organization structure. They would need to be significantly modified to meet the current state of business. If an overseas solution was chosen, Baoviet faced changes to its organizational structure and its business processes that would challenge personnel competence. Changing the organizational structure in a state-owned enterprise would be a difficult task, but changing people was seen to be even harder. It would not only involve major effort but also take time. In addition, the purchase of overseas software would represent a significant budgetary investment to Baoviet.

On the other hand, there were some advantages of choosing local vendors: lower costs; using the Vietnamese language, leading to better and more efficient communication; potential learning while developing software with a partner; and the partner's greater understanding of Vietnamese business culture. The disadvantages were that local vendors had little knowledge of the life insurance business. If they were chosen, Baoviet staff would have to teach them and provide that knowledge. Also they were not as experienced as foreign partners in both their business and technical knowledge.

All things considered, Baoviet's executives decided to go with one local vendor to build its life insurance software using an Oracle environment. With that choice, they could both learn from the partner as well as learn by doing and they could avoid losing a big amount of money and avoid a big mistake if the project failed because of its risks.

4.2 Local Outsourcing

Baoviet started its life insurance IT project with the local vendor in 1999 while still using the old software. Baoviet established an IT project group to cooperate with the partner. They had to work intensively to share knowledge of the life insurance business and to specify Baoviet's requirements for the partner.

In addition to the lack of understanding of the new business and the weakness in project management of Baoviet staff themselves, the Vietnamese partner was similarly inexperienced and lacking in insurance knowledge. After a pause in 2000 to evaluate the project's achievements, it was eventually terminated in 2001, with an estimated 70 percent completion.

IT staff had gained experience and knowledge from the partner, and in the process they also increased their business knowledge. So, they felt capable of continuing the project in-house. Bao Viet Life's senior management then made the decision to continue building the software in-house. The IT staff had to develop the remaining 30 percent and to modify and correct it to meet business requirements.

4.3 Insourcing

In spite of the failure of the project, Baoviet still implemented the partly developed software to all branches across the country. Even though the software was not flexible, could not meet the business demands, and had many errors, it still was much better than the old software. The initial period of in-house development was a very hard time for the IT staff. One IT Manager said,

It was a black period in user support because the incomplete software was too difficult to use and it had many mistakes. The partner did not support us because of the project cancellation. Correcting mistakes as well as developing the last 30 percent was an overload for the IT staff.

An IT center (for Bao Viet Life) was established by Baoviet in June 2001 to include personnel from the IT department and personnel from the project group. This helped a more confident continuation of the development and modification of the life insurance software in-house. The Software Development Manager reported,

The establishment of the IT center demonstrated the investment and concern of senior management. It has brought a certain efficiency. We have about 30 IT staff with more servers, better information systems, and especially improved working and development procedures.

They had software development procedures to apply which they did not have before. Thus, the systems were more accurate and robust than before.

When initially installed, the software had so many errors that IT staff had to upgrade it almost every day. It was very frustrating for both business and IT people.

Most of the upgrades (about 60 to 70 percent) stemmed from software mistakes that were written by the local partner. About 30 percent of the upgrades were to meet the business and user requirements.

In a situation of swimming or sinking, the IT staff had to learn and cope with the situation very quickly and very intensely. They strongly believe that they learned while doing their jobs.

4.4 Achievements

In a report on IT development strategy (2003) for the life insurance business, written by the Baoviet IT Center, the main principle was no longer *self-sufficiency* but it was a move to *making use of outsourcing* strategy. This was developed at the time that Bao Viet Life was about to become an independent, autonomous business.

The strategic objective of Baoviet information systems for Bao Viet Life was specified as

> *to meet the insurance and investment business requirements, to support the decision making process and management, to improve service quality and to create competitive advantage in the market for Bao Viet Life.*

By 2003, the IT staff had completed the software. The previously incomplete 30 percent was fulfilled. The software now has enough functionality and can satisfy operational requirements from the business departments. Some 45 percent of survey respondents agreed that the information systems now satisfy or fully satisfy the business requirements while another 47 percent said information systems do satisfy business requirements but need to be improved. Due to the decentralized data model and the need to transport and merge each branch's data, sometimes reports did not meet the head office management requirements, nor were they timely. Most respondents (85 percent) agreed that, although Bao Viet Life's IT capability still has some weaknesses, it has been progressing in comparison with the past several years.

Bao Viet Life staff have learned while doing their job; they have learned how to manage projects better and gained technical and management skill from the partner. More significantly, they (IT staff) have learned by doing their own modification and correction of software, and they have gained good knowledge of the life insurance business—this was agreed by 87.5 percent of both IT and business people replying to the survey. Most of the interviewees believed that the relationship between business and IT staff has been getting better over time. Most people (92.5 percent) believed that Bao Viet Life's senior management has strongly encouraged their staff in using IT applications in their job.

One of the IT management commented,

> *In the past, we had to upgrade the software almost every day. And after that the frequency was once per 5 days. Now, it is once a week (7 days). And in some weeks, there is only some small thing or nothing to upgrade.*

Various reasons for the reduced frequency of software upgrades were specified by a senior software staff,

> *Business staff have been getting a better understanding of life insurance business. Thus their requirements are much more sufficient and understandable now. They are no longer making so many changes in their business procedures. ...IT staff's technical skills and business skills are much better than before. They have also got more experience in managing and solving*

problems.....The relationship between IT and business staffs has been getting better.

In assessing the staff skills and competency, the IT manager said that

For technical problem solving, IT staffs are now really much faster than before thanks to their strong experience, knowledge, and better technology. At present, IT staff are good at Oracle. They are even better than staff of all other IT companies except FPT).[2]

Most of the interviewees agreed that if they could do it all again, they would still choose the same strategy that Baoviet had chosen but they would focus more on management and implementation.

In its SWOT analysis in 2004, one of the main strengths identified in Bao Viet Life's IT Center, was that,

Bao Viet Life IT staff are qualified and active enough to manage, to absorb, and to develop its information technology systems.

The main principle guiding the development of information systems to 2010 was

to make use of outsourcing, combining with the coordination and strictly management and synchronous proceeding in proper phases.

For Bao Viet Life, insurance software, part of the plan for the 2004-2005 period, was to improve the existing software while reevaluating the system design and determining the weaknesses of the systems and how to overcome them, It also needed to prepare for building new software systems in 2005-2006. During 2006-2007, the plan is to redesign the whole system, building web facilities and a Bao Viet Life call center.

In the 2005 final half-year plan, it was specified that the Information Center has to

prepare alternative solutions for replacing BVLIFE—the existing software— for the centralization of management direction.

Bao Viet Life has started the implementation of this strategy with several study projects. In October 2005, some vendors were called to present package solutions for the life insurance business. Bao Viet Life has found itself back in the decision situation it faced in 1999, only this time it is far better prepared and senior management are prepared to abandon the solutions so painstakingly developed over the intervening period. Bao Viet Life also faces this decision as an autonomous business unit.

---

[2]FPT is currently recognized as the leading IT company in Vietnam.

5 DISCUSSION

The discussion will first analyze the process of building the IT capability of the company, following the main sequences of the special situations in that process. Then, based on the frameworks mentioned earlier, an analysis will be done to see if the company was successful in building its IT capability as a result of improvisation.

5.1 Improvisation

The analysis approach of Silva (2002) is used to identify the situations in which key management actions took place. These are summarized in Table 1. The special/critical situations in the table are the conditions that trigger a decision or action taken which was assessed as improvisation. Bricolage is recognized when "making do" is observed.

In the first situation, insurance was a new business with relatively small revenue and few staff. One staff member in the business area developed simple software by himself, initially for only his use. This kind of situation is seen as improvisation because there was "no split between composition and performance...no split between design and production" (Weick 1993, p. 131, cited in Miner et al. 2001, p. 313). The development of software occurred during normal work.

In the second situation, Baoviet was faced with unanticipated fast growth of its business and its internal problem of lack of software. It decided to develop the software using available personnel and resources in the IT department, making do with what was available. Such development was unanticipated and had not been provided for. Although this decision action contains all of the characteristics of improvisation, it apparently features more bricolage (Cunha et al. 1999).

Table 1. Situation and Action Analysis (based on Silva 2002)

Special Situation	Organizational Situation	Action Taken	Main Feature
Newly launched business in a new emerging market	New and small insurance business	Software developed by business staff.	Improvisation and bricolage
Fast growth business	Software did not meet business demand	New comprehensive software developed by IT department	Bricolage
Information technology market growth. Competition introduced	Had to cope with business demand and competition	Local outsourcing	Improvisation
Outsourcing project failed	Better knowledge and capable staff.	Continued in house building the software.	Bricolage improvisation

The introduction of competition in the insurance market could be considered as a very critical emergent situation for a monopoly company such as Baoviet. Competition was unexpected and the way it worked was unanticipated. Baoviet did not possess any kind of preplanned course of action and fast action was required. Thus, the local outsourcing decision that took place was again improvisation.

The last situation was also unexpected and had not been planned for. It could be seen as a crisis because it "characterized by low probability/high consequence events that threaten... fundamental goals of an organization" (Weick 1988). Baoviet decided to build its software in-house with all resources available (a bricolage feature). This action also was an improvisation action itself because it "comes into being as a response to a crisis" (Weick 1993, cited in Silva 2002).

Through those four critical situations, which occurred in the process of building IT capability in Baoviet, it could be seen that improvisation has been a pattern of actions. Using the notion of strategy as "a pattern in actions over time" (Mintzberg 1994), we argue that improvisation was indeed the strategy adopted by Baoviet. This strategy is unusual itself, however, an important question is whether it was a success. The Baoviet IT capability will now be analyzed.

5.2 The Outcomes of Improvisation

The section will follow the cited frameworks to analyze Bao Viet Life's achievements in building IT capability using the evidence of the interviews and survey. Two earlier stages are used to draw a contrast with the present situation. Stage 1 represents the time (1999) at which Baoviet approached a local software company to develop its life insurance application. Stage 2 (2001) was the point at which the application was then brought in-house. The current state is based on the case study investigation in 2005. Table 2 shows the capability assessment following Feeny and Willcock's model over the three periods.

In all strategy documents and reports from Baoviet senior management and IT leaders, IT goals and directions have consistently been set. These have supported the IT staff's belief that their first priority is to contribute to meeting business demands and achieving business solutions. So, there is/IT leadership competency could be assessed as good over time using either Feeny and Willcock's model or Ward and Peppard's.

In Baoviet, the business development has been integrated with the IT capability reasonably well. Business processes were changed to meet business demands, subject to current IT ability both in staff skills and the technology itself. In the IT manager's opinion, currently IT follows business demands but in the future "technology will lead to business changes."

Due to the "culture gap between techies and users" (Feeny and Willcocks 1998, p. 13), Baoviet IT and business staff had only a basic working relationship in the beginning. They would only talk with each other if needed. Later, IT and business staff had to cooperate strongly together over the intervening period to get their job done. For mutual benefit, they had no choice but to cooperate closely with each other. Thus, their working relationship has been getting closer and better. Now, there is a mutual confidence, shared purpose, and efficient communication. The relationship building competency has improved significantly over time, from fair in the first two periods to be good now.

Table 2. Baoviet's IT Competencies Using the Feeny and Willcocks Framework

No.	Competency	Explanation	Stage 1	Stage 2	Now
1	IS/IT leadership	Integrating IS/IT effort with business purpose and activity	Good	Good	Good
2	Business system thinking	Envisioning the business processes that technology makes possible	Fair	Good	Good+
3	Relationship building	Getting the business constructively engaged in IS/IT issues	Fair	Fair	Good
4	Architecture planning	Creating a coherent blueprint for a technological platform that responds to current and future business	Not good	Not good	Not good
5	Making technology work	Rapidly achieving technical progress by one means or another	Average	Fair	Good
6	Informed buying	Managing the IS/IT sourcing strategy that meets the interests of the business	Fair	Good	Good

Stage 1: Local company develops software; Stage 2: Brought in-house

The two critical contributions of Baoviet IT staff that make technology work are that they "rapidly troubleshoot problems that are disowned by others across the technical supply chain" and they identify "how to address business needs that can not be properly satisfied by standard technical approaches" (Feeny and Willcocks 1998, p. 13). Thus, Bao Viet Life has achieved significant improvement in this capability. In its current state, Bao Viet Life has few outsourced services, so the "informed buying" has not been developed as a capability. However, with the experience from the past IT project, Bao Viet Life has improved its capability at managing the IS/IT sourcing strategy and that is upgraded to good.

One of the critical weaknesses recognized by the IT manager and IT staff is the inflexibility of the technological platform. Thus we assess Bao Viet Life's current IT infrastructure as unable to respond to future business requirements. This area is the one that needs to be focused on and improved by senior management and IT leaders.

For outsourcing related competencies (contract facilitation, contract monitoring, vendor development), insufficient evidence was collected to assess those competencies and they have been omitted from the analysis. These capabilities should have improved if Baoviet staff have been learning the experiences from past projects; however, we reserve this area for further study.

The above analysis shows that Baoviet's IT capability has also been improved substantially using the IT capability components draw from Ross et al. (1996) and Peppard and Ward (2004), IT and business knowledge and skills, and the relationship between IT and business people. The only improvement not supported by the evidence collected is in technology infrastructure.

Table 3. Selected Baoviet IT Abilities Using Ward and Peppard's Framework

	Ability	**Explanation**	**Stage 1**	**Stage 2**	**Now**
1	Business strategy	ability to ensure that business strategy formulation identifies the most advantageous uses of IS and IT	Good	Good	Good
2	Benefits delivery	ability to monitor, measure and evaluate the benefits delivered from IS/IT investment and use	Poor	Fair	Good
5	Benefits planning	an ability explicitly to identify and plan to realize the benefits from IS investments	Poor	Fair	Good

Stage 1: Local company develops software; Stage 2: Brought in-house

Additional analysis using Ward and Peppard's model (2002) is shown in Table 3. As only three out of eight abilities can be assessed with enough evidence, the remainder are omitted. In terms of business strategy, Baoviet's business strategies show that it is consistently good over time. Evidence from questionnaires, interviews, and the company's written documents demonstrate Baoviet's significant improvement in its benefits delivery and benefits planning abilities. For the other abilities, we were unable to assess any improvement as this required access to senior management, who have not yet participated.

The achievement of Bao Viet Life through its "learning by doing" process could be better understood by using Andreu and Ciborra's (1996) basic learning processes. In other words, the approach to transform from lower levels of capabilities to higher levels in Baoviet is the improvisation process itself. Through the challenging period of coping with the increasingly competitive market combined with its scarce financial and human resources, Baoviet staff have substantially developed their work practices (regularly upgrading IT systems and software and improving their knowledge, skills, and working relationships). Its IT capability has been developed from these work practices. The question of whether IT has become a core capability in Baoviet could not be answered, but this is part of the ongoing research. It is at this point, with the possibility of adopting a world-class software package, that such capability will be revealed. However, we could see that the capability development process has been effective in understanding the situation in Baoviet.

6   IMPLICATIONS

Building IT capability in this case actually is a sequence of improvisation actions. Thus, improvisation can be seen as Baoviet's strategy itself. Furthermore, it is a successful improvisation case, which might be a good example from which other companies with the same situation, especially in developing countries, might learn.

Transformation of organization through IT is usually seen as relevant to sophisticated organizations. This paper takes the transformation idea wider to include IT and shows that the IT and the organization can engage in simultaneous transformation. Two models in particular—Andreu and Ciborra (1996) and Feeny and Willcocks (1998)—

have been useful in the analysis. They have been particularly powerful in identifying the areas where development is least or unknown. This indicates that the models could usefully be applied as diagnostic tools or guidance instruments for organizations with limited IT capability.

Senior management took an unusual long-term perspective in deciding to develop capability with an in-house attempt at software development, with the certain understanding that this would be replaced when the organization had the capability to evaluate and to implement systems. They entered into that decision knowing that whatever software was developed would be written off in the near future. They retained the idea of installing best-practice systems, once their staff could understand and work them. The business was expected to make-do or simply do-its-best with the goal of learning. Such improvisation as a strategy is in itself an unexpected finding from a state-owned enterprise in a developing economy.

References

Andreu, R., and Ciborra, C. "Organizational Learning and Core Capabilities Development: the Role of IT," *Journal of Strategic Information Systems* (5), 1996, pp. 111-127.

Applegate, L. M. "Managing in an Information Age: Transforming Organizations for the 1990s," in R. Baskerville, S. Smithson, O. Ngwenyama, and J. I. DeGross (eds.), *Transforming Organizations with Information Technology*, Amsterdam: North Holland, 1994, pp. 15-94.

Barrett, F. "Coda: Creativity and Improvisation in Jazz and Organizations: Implications for Organizational Learning, *Organization Science* (9:5), 1998, pp. 605-622.

Bharadwaj, A. "A Resource-Based Perspective on Information Technology and Firm Performance: An Empirical Investigation," *MIS Quarterly* (24:1), 2000, pp. 169-196.

Bjørn-Andersen, N., and Turner, J. A. "Creating the Twenty-First Century Organization: The Metamorphosis of Oticon," in R. Baskerville, S. Smithson, O. Ngwenyama, and J. I. DeGross (eds.), *Transforming Organizations with Information Technology*, Amsterdam: North Holland, 1994, pp. 379-394.

Brown, I. S., and Duguid, P. "Organizational Learning and Communities of Practice," *Organizational Science* (2:1), 1991, pp. 40-57.

Carr, N. "IT Doesn't Matter," *Harvard Business Review*, May 2003, pp. 41-49.

Ciborra, C. "Notes on Improvisation and Time in Organizations," *Accounting Management and Information Technologies* (9), 1999, pp. 77-94.

Clemons, E. K., and Row, M. C. "Sustaining IT Advantage: The Role of Structural Differences," *MIS Quarterly* (15:4), 1991, pp. 487-505.

Cunha, M. P., Cunha, J. V., Kamoche, K. "Organizational Improvisation: What, When, How and Why," *International Journal of Management Review* (1:3), 1999, pp. 299-341.

Dvorak, R. E., Holen, E., Mark, D., and Meehan, W. F. "Six Principles of High-Performance IT," *McKinsey Quarterly* (3), 1997, pp. 164-177.

Feeny, D. F., and Ives, B. "In Search of Sustainability," *Journal of Management Information Systems* (7:1), 1990, pp. 27-46.

Feeny, D. F., and Willcocks, L. P. "Re-Designing the IS Function Around Core Capabilities," *Long Range Planning* (31), 1998, pp. 354-367.

Hammer, M., and Champy, J. *Reengineering the Corporation*, New York: HarperCollins, 1993.

Kamoche, K., Cunha, M. P., and Cunha, J. V. "Towards a Theory of Organizational Improvisation: Looking Beyond the Jazz Metaphor," *Journal of Management Studies* (40:8), 2003, pp. 2021-2051.

Mata, F. J., Fuerst, W. L., and Barney, J. "Information Technology and Sustained Competitive Advantage: A Resource-Based Analysis," *MIS Quarterly* (19:4), 1995, pp. 487-505.

McFarlan, F. W. "Information Technology Changes the Way You Compete," *Harvard Business Review*, May-June 1984, pp. 93-103.

Miner, A. S., Bassoff, P., and Moorman, C. "Organizational Improvisation and Learning: A Field Study," *Administrative Science Quarterly* (46), 2001, pp. 304-337.

Mintzberg, H. *The Rise and Fall of Strategic Planning: Reconceiving Roles for Planning, Plans, and Planners,* New York: Free Press, 1994.

Moorman, C., and Miner, A. S. "The convergence of planning and execution: improvisation in New Product Development, *Journal of Marketing* (62:3), 1998a, pp. 1-20.

Moorman, C., Miner, A.S. (1998b), Organizational improvisation and organization memory, *Academy of Management Review* (23:4), 1998b, pp. 698-723.

Orlikowski, W. J. "Improvising Organizational Transformation Over Time: A Situated Change Perspective," *Information Systems Research* (7:1), 1996, pp. 63-92.

Orlikowski, W. J., and Hoffman, J. D. "An Improvisational Model for Change Management: The Case of Groupware Technologies," *Sloan Management Review*, Winter 1997, pp. 11-21.

Peppard, J., and Ward, J. "Beyond Strategic Information Systems: Towards an IS Capability," *Journal of Strategic Information Systems* (13), 2004, pp. 167-194.

Porter, M., and Millar, V. E. "How Information Gives You Competitive Advantage" *Harvard Business Review*, July-August 1985, pp. 149-160.

Ross, J., Beath, C. M., and Goodhue, D. L. "Develop Long-Term Competitiveness through IT Assets," *Sloan Management Review* (38:1), 1996, pp. 31-42.

Silva, L. O. "Outsourcing as Improvisation: A Case Sstudy in Latin America," *The Information Society* (18), 2002, pp. 129-138.

Turban, E., Leidner, D., McLean, E., and Wetherbe, J. *Information Technology for Management: Transforming Organizations in the Digital Economy*, New York: Wiley, 2004.

Ward, J., and Peppard, J. *Strategic Planning for Information Systems* (3rd ed.), Chichester, UK: Wiley, 2002.

Weick, K. E. "Enacted Sensemaking in Crisis Situations," *Journal of Management Studies* (25:4), 1988, pp. 305-317.

Weick, K. E. "Introductory Essay: Improvisation as a Mindset for Organizational Analysis," *Organization Science* (9:5), 1998, pp. 543-592.

Weick, K.E. "Organizational Redesign as Improvisation," in G. P. Huber and W. H. Glick (eds.), *Organizational Change and Redesign: Ideas and Insights for Improving Performance*, New York: Oxford University Press, 1993, pp. 345-379,

About the Authors

Thi Lien Pham is a scholarship Ph.D. student at Macquarie Graduate School of Management, Macquarie University, Australia. This paper relates to part of her Ph.D. research. She had 5 years working experience as a management consultant and 2 years as a market researcher in Vietnam. She can be contacted by email to lienpt@hotmail.com.

Ernest Jordan is a professor of Management at Macquarie Graduate School of Management where he teaches e-business and IT management. He has published on the issues of IT strategic alignment, IT governance, and IT risk management. Ernest has extensive experience in information system development and management in major organizations overseas and in Australia. His recent research activity is concerned with matching the IT governance approach to the IT risk portfolio. He can be contacted at Ernest.Jordan@mgsm.edu.au.

11

THE CHALLENGE OF MANAGING KNOWLEDGE IN INNOVATIVE ORGANIZATIONS: Internal Versus External Knowledge Acquisition

Andrea Deverell
University of Limerick
Limerick, Ireland

Astrid Heidemann Lassen
Aalborg University
Aalborg, Denmark

Abstract   *Ideas are no longer generated solely within a firm's internal boundaries but also sourced from the external knowledge environment. Therefore, firms can no longer rely solely on internal knowledge to develop new ideas or solve problems. This paper is based on empirical research which investigates different knowledge acquisition strategies utilized by firms during the innovation process. It suggests that there is a relationship between the kind of innovative activity (cumulative or radical) and the sourcing of knowledge (i.e., the internal and/or external environment). Two hypotheses are derived from the literature and tested empirically. These hypotheses are based on the premise that cumulative type organizations focus primarily on internal knowledge or existing core competencies within the firm and are less likely to scan the external environment for ideas and knowledge, whereas radical type organizations are continually pushing out the boundaries of knowledge and replacing existing core competencies with new ideas and knowledge and are therefore predisposed toward utilizing external knowledge. The research findings confirm the hypotheses and enable the development of a third dimension based on a dual ability to focus on both cumulative and radical innovation aligned with the most appropriate knowledge acquisition strategy.*

Keywords   Knowledge acquisition, technology transfer, radical and cumulative innovation, agility and resilience

Please use the following format when citing this chapter:

Deverell, Andrea, Lassen, Astrid Heidemann, 2006, in International Federation for Information Processing (IFIP), Volume 206, The Transfer and Diffusion of Information Technology for Organizational Resilience, eds. B. Donnellan, Larsen T., Levine L., DeGross J. (Boston: Springer), pp. 157-178.

1   INTRODUCTION

Interest in knowledge management and technology transfer on the part of academics and practitioners has increased dramatically in recent years. This is evident in the growing number of publications dealing with this topic (Chesbrough 2003; Kaplan 1999; O'Connor and Ayers 2005; O'Reilly and Tushmann 2004). With the advent of the information age, the growing importance of university based scientific research, and the increasingly diffuse nature of knowledge, knowledge monopolies have effectively become a thing of the past (Chesbrough 2003). As a result, knowledge has become widely accessible and available to all, and this has directly impacted how people acquire and manage knowledge.

Continuous developments in computing and information technology have acted as catalysts to the rapid dissemination of knowledge, providing a means to reach a globally dispersed audience. This coupled with the development of organizational information systems has provided firms with the capability of storing and organizing large quantities of information. In this reality, increasing interest is being shown in the successful sourcing, use and protection of knowledge as an essential competitive variable, providing advantages to firms effectively managing this resource over those that do not (Argote and Ingram 2000; Darroch 2005; Kogut and Zander 1996).

The realization of the connection between knowledge and an organization's innovation ability has resulted in the emergence of complex models for the transfer of knowledge between firms, research institutes, inventors, entrepreneurs, universities, and other sources. In today's knowledge economy, a firm's ability to leverage knowledge in order to innovate is crucial.

The present paper is built around the perception of the existence of a strong connection between a firm's ability to leverage knowledge and its ability to innovate. This is dealt with in more detail in section 2.1 of this paper. An initial review of the literature has revealed the need for the development of a clearer understanding of the relationship between knowledge, innovation, and organizational productivity. In this paper, the authors limit the scope of research to that of the relationship between knowledge and innovation. In particular, the authors have been intrigued by the generic use of the term innovation in the context of knowledge. While the existence of varying degrees of innovation is clearly recognized in the literature, there is little recognition of this complexity in the field of knowledge management and therefore it requires further investigation.

As such, the aim of the paper is to further unfold the question: *What is the relationship between cumulative/radical innovation and internal/external knowledge acquisition respectively?*

In order to explore this relationship, the authors initially conducted a literature study on knowledge management and innovation in order to be able to discuss the existing insights into the connections between knowledge and innovation, and in this way establish a frame of reference.

Additionally, four case-studies in industrial firms involved in respectively cumulative and radical innovation have been carried out, providing evidence on the methods of knowledge acquisition used in each type of firm.

The structure of the paper is divided as follows. Section 2 provides the theoretical background to the study, which is framed around the concept of closed (section 2.3) and open (section 2.5) innovation, giving rise to the development of two hypotheses regarding the relationship between cumulative/radical innovation and internal/external knowledge acquisition. This is followed by a brief summary of the research methodology, discussing the approach applied in the construction of this paper. Four case studies are then presented, revealing characteristics on historic development, innovation strategy, and knowledge acquisition strategy fir each of them. The findings in the cases provide an empirical foundation for discussing the hypotheses developed through theory, and highlight possible extensions of theory on open versus closed innovations systems, which is presented and discussed in section 5. Section 6 outlines the major conclusions of the paper and points to areas of further research that will provide additional contributions to the understanding of the area of research, which are not covered in the present paper.

2 THEORETICAL BACKGROUND

2.1 Knowledge and Innovation

Knowledge-based assets and organizational learning capabilities are increasingly recognized in the literature as potential sources of competitive advantage. The ability to acquire and utilize knowledge effectively is argued to be critical for the firm's innovation activities and performance (Cohen and Levinthal 1990).

Modern literature on innovation emphasizes the importance of the ability to utilize external knowledge sources in innovation activities (Chesbrough 2003; Cockburn and Henderson 1998; Cohen et al. 2002; von Hippel 1988). For example, according to Chesbrough (2003), openness to using external sources of information and ideas in the firm's innovation processes, as well as interaction among different partners, is of high importance when creating value through innovation activities. Firms are increasingly dependent on their customers, suppliers, and other complementary capabilities as initiators of product and process improvement and sources of new ideas (von Hippel 1988). This perspective is also reflected in the seminal distinction made by March (1991) between exploitation and exploration, equal to and introvert versus extrovert focus on acquiring knowledge for the development of innovation.

2.2 Levels of Innovation: Cumulative to Radial Innovation

For the purpose of this paper two definitions regarding the level of organizational innovation are defined by the authors. *Cumulative innovation* is defined as the incremental improvement and introduction of existing products/technologies or services, which are perceived as low to medium risk, into existing markets usually building on a firm's core competencies. *Radical innovation* is defined as the development of significantly new ideas, which are perceived as high risk into new markets often resulting in the destruction of a firm's core competency and the creation of new competencies.

Intensive competition on global markets has effectively forced firms to be increasingly innovative in their approach but also in their product offerings. Continual improvement or cumulative innovation is no longer perceived to be enough to sustain a firm in the long-term. Hamel (1996, p. 69) eloquently states that "pursuing incremental improvements, while rivals reinvent the industry, is like fiddling while Rome burns." Firms can, therefore, no longer rely solely on internal knowledge generation in order to develop new ideas or solve complex problems, but must source knowledge from the external environment as well. The literature presents pros and cons that support both views. Darr et al. (1995) and Baum and Ingram (1998) have suggested that firms benefit most from knowledge generated within the boundaries of the firm, while, Menon and Pfeffer (2003) and Chesbrough (2003) contend that innovative firms benefit from knowledge generated from inside and outside the firm.

Whichever knowledge acquisition model is supported, the knowledge possessed by the company has, as such, become an essential factor in relation to a firm's ability to innovate. Argote et al. (2003), suggest that research should focus on establishing the conditions under which using internal versus external knowledge is more likely to improve a unit's performance. This paper suggests that an organization's innovation strategy should be aligned with its knowledge acquisition strategy.

Current research on knowledge management outlines the importance of the location of organizational boundaries and the implications this has on knowledge transfer and organizational performance (Argote et al. 2003; Chesbrough 2003). Boundaries can restrict or facilitate the flow of knowledge into and out of on organization. In this context, the open and closed innovation paradigms developed by Chesbrough are used as a means for classifying the link between organizational type and knowledge acquisition strategy. Both are discussed below.

2.3 Closed Innovation Paradigm

The closed innovation paradigm, as described by Chesbrough, is an organizational psychology that fundamentally believes that innovation can be managed. According to Cooper (2000), an organization's ability to succeed rotates around its aptitude to organize or manage innovation to achieve an expected end (i.e., market success and profitability). Others have suggested that by building on a firms' core competencies (Hamel 2000), making sufficient finances available, establishing a well-defined innovation process (Cooper 2002), and developing the ability to research, develop, and market new technologies an organization can succeed in developing a competitive edge. It is undeniable that many firms have achieved and will continue to achieve profitability through this kind of an innovation system.

What is closed innovation? The closed innovation system is based on the premise that innovation happens within a firm's boundaries (Chesbrough 2003). Traditional innovation theory suggested that firms can develop competitive advantage by building in-house research and development competencies that effectively enable the development and commercialization of new products, processes, or services. Clear organizational boundaries enable the careful protection of ideas. Business development strategy is normally based on clearly defined objectives and justifiable product/market trajectories. New ideas are screened to fit the organizational psychology and culture. The development and maintenance of core competencies is central to the firm. A closed innovation system's organizational boundaries are represented by solid lines, which signify an impermeable barrier to the outside world.

2.4 Closed Innovation Systems and Cumulative Innovation

Closed innovation characteristics are based on the above premise that organizations can manage innovation. Chesbrough (2003) and Bessant (2003a) contended that closed innovation systems are fundamentally focused on the continuous improvement of existing products/processes and services, and are critical to sustaining and enhancing shares of mainstream markets (Baden-Fuller and Pitt 1996) and meeting ever more demanding requirements from existing customers (Bessant 2003b). This focus on improvement of the existing consequently leads to a certain degree of path dependency and lack of ability to accommodate or initiate change. Business opportunities are carefully selected to fit organizational strategy or current technology trajectories. Innovation operating routines are refined and stable. There are normally strong links and knowledge flows along clear channels within the organization's boundaries.

Dosi (1982) argued that while a firm's experience is important, it can often greatly reduce its ability to spot opportunities and move into areas outside what it considers core competencies. There is a dichotomy between a firm's need to innovate in order to compete in today's global economy and its learned inability to be agile and responsive to emergent challenges. Current management literature suggests that organizations should build strategy around their key resources: financial, human, and capital (Fahy 2000; Prahalad and Hamel 1994). The resource based view of the firm suggests that competitive advantage can be gained through the identification and deployment of key capabilities possessed by a firm into the marketplace. Some researchers (Barney 1991; Grant 1991) have suggested that competitive advantage can be sustained by organizations as they are difficult to duplicate. Resources are generally buried within the organization. It is not surprising, therefore, that when presented with the need to change, most firms are unable to alter the inertial forces driving a firm down a particular path (Garcia and Calantone 2002).

Based on this understanding the authors develop the following hypothesis regarding the relationship between cumulative/radical innovation and internal/external knowledge acquisition:

H1) Organizations implementing a cumulative innovation strategy are more likely to implement internal knowledge acquisition strategies.

2.5 The Open Innovation Paradigm

As mentioned above, there have been other attempts at identifying the role played by the external knowledge environment in the development of new innovations. These include the idea of networked or distributed innovation involving end-users in innovation (Herstatt and von Hippel 1992) and the triple helix model which suggests that there are a number of players central to successful innovation: companies; research institutes, and the public sector (Etzkowitz 2002).

Kusunoki's (1997) assertion that radical innovation requires change at a variety of organizational levels furthers the argument that it is necessary to address radical innovation with a different set of organizational capabilities. These capabilities must be build to support open innovation (Chesbrough 2003), tolerate a level of chaos and emergence or at least the ability to adapt to circumstances that are continuously changing (Vidgen 2004) and break path dependency and over reliance on best practices (Bessant 2003a).

> Besides technological capabilities, introducing radical product changes tech-
> nological capabilities, introducing radical product change to a market often
> requires a new set of organizational capabilities embedded in structures, com-
> munication channels, and information processing procedures of organizations,
> and it is usually quite difficult for established firms to adjust the organization's
> capabilities for developing innovative products (Kusunoki 1997, p. 32).

What is open innovation? Open innovation is described as distinct from closed innovation insofar as innovations are not only developed internally using an organization's own capability but also externally. Chesbrough (2003) suggested that organizations with open innovation systems have boundaries that are porous. Open innovation systems work like the process of osmosis: knowledge is passed in both directions between the internal organization and the external environment and it crosses organizational boundaries, enabling the internal organ to grow and develop. In accordance with the dynamic capability view of the firm (Teece et al. 1997; Zott 2003), an open innovation system considers the firm essentially a knowledge processing and utilizing entity, focusing on interfirm performance differences mainly from dissimilar abilities among firms in order to exploit existing assets and to explore and build up new capabilities. As such, the organizational capabilities of sensing weak signals and seizing opportunities (Teece 2000) essentially contribute to innovative performance and long-term competitiveness. Ideas that originate internally can often be researched or developed externally (e.g., in a research laboratory, university or other relevant organization). Ideas can also be sourced externally and researched internally or externally.

2.6 Open Innovation Characteristics and Radical Innovation

Open innovation characteristics are built around the premise that there are a variety of sources that assist in the development of innovations. These sources exist both internally and externally to the organization. Open innovation views innovation as a process that effectively gets an idea to market, but it is by no means a linear static process. Organizations implementing an open innovation strategy do not operate within clear mental frameworks but rather these models emerge over time and are subject to continual change. They are path independent and generally involve a probing or learning type environment. They are risk taking and often run with multiple parallel bets. They tolerate a level of ambiguity and chaos and inevitably except a level of failure. Operating patterns are emergent and often poorly documented. Finally knowledge flows are less structured and peripheral vision is important. Intellectual property is developed internally or sourced externally and ownership is generally shared. Drawing comparison to the distinction between cumulative and radical innovation, open innovation systems seem to provide circumstances that favor the development of radical innovation. Radical innovation is, in contrast to cumulative, characterized by its emergent and nonlinear nature, its path independency, and the creative combination and use of several sources of knowledge (Christensen 1997; Leifer et al. 2000).

Based on this understanding, the authors develop a second hypothesis regarding the relationship between cumulative/radical innovation and internal/external knowledge acquisition.

> *H2) Organizations implementing a radical innovation strategy are more likely to implement external knowledge acquisition strategies.*

3 RESEARCH METHODS

This paper draws on the perception that there is a strong connection between the knowledge acquired by a company and its ability to innovate. However, the authors found it interesting to open up both the terms *innovation* and *knowledge* even further and explore the relationship between the degree of innovation and the source of knowledge empirically.

The empirical investigation was carried out in four industrial organizations (two Irish and two Danish) over a period of 3 months in 2005. The cases were developed based on qualitative semi-structured interviews with senior managers, middle managers, and developers to examine their perception of innovative capabilities and knowledge acquisition and the factors that contribute to development and integration. In the following analysis of the cases, citations to these interviews will be used in order to illustrate and validate the conclusions drawn. As such, the citations referred to do not reflect the number of informants in each case, but are selected expressions made by key informants that underline central points particularly well.

The four case companies were all involved in high-end technological innovation and were selected based on their variability in order to ensure a qualitative insight into cumulative, radical, and ambidextrous innovation. This insight was aimed at providing answers to the stated research question. The reliability of the results as well as the validity of the differences emerging was ensured by applying a protocol on innovation strategy and knowledge acquisition strategy to all cases.

While no two innovation projects in the study are the same, the authors observed patterns in relation to process characteristics and conditioning factors. Despite the fact that the research was conducted in two different countries, the analysis of the four cases gives no reason to suspect a bias due to national differences. As such, the authors have not found it necessary to add a comparative analysis based on national characteristics, but have evaluated the cases on the same grounds in connection to the topic of research.

Table 1. Company Profiles: Case Studies

Company Profiles	Case Study 1	Case Study 2	Case Study 3	Case Study 4
Established	1989 2000 (Reengineered)	2003	1976 1993 (Reengineered)	1999
Industrial Sector	Industrial Printing	Editing and Television	Audio products	Power Conversion Technology
Number of Employees	1989 – 45 2005 – 24	6 (3 Internal, 3 External)	185	35
Ownership	VC and Private	Shared Ownership, OM, Director, VC.	Shared Ownership, OM	Shared Ownership, OM
Intellectual Property	Developed Internally 100% Ownership	Developed Externally Shared Ownership	Developed Internally and Externally Shared Ownership	Developed Internally and Externally Shared Ownership

4 EMPIRICAL FOUNDATION

The following section provides a brief introduction to each case study, followed by a description of each firm's innovation and knowledge acquisition strategy, with particular focus on the existence of organizational boundaries. The concluding subsection focuses on the links between the two elements. In this way, the exploratory research provides an empirical frame for analyzing hypotheses 1 and 2 developed above.

4.1 Case Study One: Print Inspection Ltd.

4.1.1 Background

Print Inspection Ltd. was established in 1989. The company's core product is printing inspection equipment and it is focused mainly on the industrial printing sector. The firm currently employ 25 people. In 2000, the company was reengineered and its core business refocused. According to John, CEO, "*This was necessary, as the firm was doing a little bit of everything but nothing particularly well.*" The reengineering process effectively resulted in the identification of a number of core competencies and the realization of the central role played by the knowledge or experience gained by the firm over time. As a result, the firm is now very focused on the management of internal knowledge and the only links to the external environment are through sales representatives to end customers. Intellectual property is developed internally and owned 100 percent by the company. The company does not hold any patents.

4.1.2 Innovation Strategy

Print Inspection implements a cumulative innovation strategy. This is evident by the description of the organization. The company has been in existence for the last 16 years and its core technology remains the same. The product roadmap that guides the organization over 6 month periods is based on re-releases that involve incremental improvements normally requested by the customer or suggested by the engineering team. The company builds on previous innovation in an incremental fashion. As John stated, *"We are doing the actual development on features for 4.1 but we are also doing prototyping and feasibility for features for 4.2....cumulative innovation is probably a lot to do with our roadmap and our steady incremental forward movement."*

The reengineering process that took place in the organization in 2000 establishes the organization's commitment to core competencies or existing knowledge and reinforces the view that the firm is clearly focused on cumulative innovation. When questioned on the reasoning behind the reengineering process, John pointed out that *"core competencies have been developed over a 10 year period in Print Inspection Ltd., and we are not about to destroy them, rather leveraging them to their true potential."*

4.1.3 Knowledge Acquisition Strategy

The recognition of the existence of a number of core competencies has enabled the firm to focus on its own capability to innovate. However, John suggests that he has concerns that this focus may impede them from spotting other opportunities and cause the organization to suffer from what he termed limited thinking: *"Breaking out of our roles and thinking beyond the current state is difficult."* Knowledge is acquired on a need to know basis, driven mainly by product improvements and customer requirements. John revealed that, *"as the product is based on our key expertise we normally have the solution internally."*

Learning mainly takes place in the internal organization: *"A lot of learning gets done within the organization....its not nice and neat and formalized."* John felt that people predominately learn from interacting with each other. The only mention of external learning was trade shows but he felt that *"they are soon enough going to be dead"* as they are merely social occasions. Learning is mainly web-based now. A key learning activity for Print Inspection is to encourage exchanges between the technical knowledge gained through research and the experience gained in the field with customers.

Print Inspection's intellectual property is developed in-house. Certain components are bought off the shelf. The company does not currently have any licence agreements or hold any patents. Intellectual property is kept secret through nondisclosure agreements. John stated that intellectual property is *"our own but not through patents."* Key intellectual property includes mechanical design of product, software development, and lighting systems.

4.1.4   Conclusions

Core competencies are an integral part of Print Inspection Ltd. The company's policy of moving from a broad to a narrow competency base has enabled them to focus on key niche markets while continually improving performance. The organization is firmly focused on cumulative innovation and driven by internal knowledge. As such, Print Inspection's innovation strategy is aligned with its knowledge acquisition strategy. However, there is evidence of an awareness of the existence of limited thinking as expressed by John which he believes is a concern (Dosi 1982; Stalk et al. 1992).

4.2 Case Study Two: Picture Sounds Ltd.

4.2.1   Background

Picture Sounds Ltd. was established in 2003. The business core product is a software music composer, aimed at the editing and television industry. The firm currently employs three internal staff and subcontracts work to three external staff (university based researchers). The company was started by an entrepreneur who came up with the initial idea but was uncertain if it was technically possible. Having clarified that the idea was indeed possible and identifying the relevant expertise within a university, the entrepreneur recruited a partner who was to provide the balance between entrepreneurial ambiguity and financial and business strategy. The company, in collaboration with the university, has developed the product to prototype stage and will take the product to market in the next 6 to 8 month period.

Intellectual property (IP) is developed in collaboration. This involves both internal and external knowledge sources. IP ownership is shared between key stakeholders.

4.2.2   Innovation Strategy

Picture Sounds implements a radical innovation strategy. The organization had to seek and create completely new competencies. The innovation pattern can be described as creative destruction: *"It's now technically possible to create relationships between pictures and sound that were never technically possible before....I think it is going to result in a series of art forms for the 21st century which have no parameters in anything we understand at the moment."* When questioned by the researcher if there were identifiable core competencies within the organization, he replied *"that while there were definable skill sets within the organization, it was too early to suggest that there were clear core competencies."* As Richard, the owner pointed out *"they haven't blended yet....It's kind of like a group of musicians."* Some of the key skills that are identifiable are clearly based on product requirements and include music (composition and editing skills), finance (management and control), software (development), and unique research ability (within the college). He felt that keeping all of these diverse abilities playing in harmony is the complicated task.

4.2.3   Knowledge Acquisition Strategy: Original or Unique Competencies

Identifying the technical ability to bring the initial idea to reality was crucial. According to Richard, *"engineers particularly look at me and say you're mad, you can't do this....the senior researcher is absolutely the key to all this, because he said yeah we can do that, you are right."* Before meeting the researcher people felt that this is not how the world works, and the arguments were ontological rather than technical. Identifying the expert in the college was a turning point for the fledgling company.

There is a fluid boundary between the internal and external organization. Knowledge is passed between both entities. Richard reveals *"it would be inconceivable not to go out and look."* Picture Sounds also has in place a formal advice structure which involves various experts from the public and private sector. Picture Sounds is a virtual knowledge organization.

Intellectual property was the biggest challenge facing Picture Sounds Ltd. Richard stated, *"There is a lack of understanding of IP....in many cases the starting point for negotiation was absurd....If you are a traditional company you won't get researchers like the ones we have got."* He also suggested that *"if you don't get the researchers you wont get the venture capital as it is intellectual property that they invest in."* Managing the interaction between the venture capitalists and the college was very challenging: *"The college's due diligence process is very understandable, they need to guarantee intellectual flexibility."*

Richard reveals that *"ownership had to be discussed at all levels....no researcher is going to get involved if the company wants to own everything....somebody else makes a fortune and you can be sure that it is not the academic."* Picture Sounds worked with the college and venture capitalist to find middle ground that was acceptable to each partner. Richard also pointed out that *"finding middle ground was difficult....I have no issues with sharing, I don't think people own ideas, it's the other way round, the ideas own the people....just as the aborigines suggest that the land owns them."*

4.2.4   Conclusions

External knowledge plays a central part in Picture Sounds Ltd. The entrepreneur was initially driven on by his passionate belief that his idea was a good one, without the knowledge of its technical feasibility. The competencies required for developing the innovation are unique and were only found by chance. Organizational knowledge boundaries can be described as porous, enabling knowledge to pass freely in both directions (Chesbrough 2003). Finally the intellectual property model in Picture Sounds Ltd. is one of shared ownership (O'Reilly and Tushmann 2004). Richard *"by the time this gets any sense of reality it will not be mine any more than it will be anyone else's."*

4.3 Case Study Three: TC Electronic Ltd.

4.3.1   Background

TC Electronic (TC) was founded in 1976 by two brothers; KR and JR, as a true entrepreneurial firm where one brother (JR) took care of the finances, the organization and the business, and the other (KR) dealt with the development of products and was a visionary on the technological area. From the beginning, TC was very much influenced by the two brothers' personal interest in optimizing the quality of guitar pedal effects. Thus, the firm from the outset had the prime focus of creating extremely high quality audio products. Especially KR's interest in and flair for technology and his ability to create new ideas meant that the company was able to do so, and this soon gave the firm a strong brand name in the industry.

In 1985, TC, as one of the first in the world, moved from analogue into digital signal processing, inspired by the development in other electronic industries, and had thus spotted a worldwide tendency ahead of all competitors. In this sense, TC developed a *disruptive innovation* (Christensen 1997) and was able to take over large amounts of market share.

Up through the 1980s, the turnover increased and sales expanded to several countries. Managing director MPL explains, *"In the '80s we usually produced one fantastic product for one marked, and when we then discovered that the technology could be used in another market, we just went ahead and produced a product for this marked."* In this sense, the company was very influenced by external input, even though the actual development remained a primarily internal activity.

In 1993, with 25 employees, the organization underwent a major reengineering process including a partial change of ownership. New competencies in the form of management skills were attracted from the outside and the company limited the market focus to professional audio products. During the next one and a half years, a radically new technology was developed which aimed at offering unique sound effects to these environments. This resulted in high growth for a number of years (40 percent annually).

The firm now employs 185 people. New products are still developed on the basis of the existing technology, but the organization continuously seeks out new opportunities on its own and in cooperation with academia as well as a large network of companies within different areas of sound processing.

4.3.2 Innovation Strategy

TC implements a radical innovation strategy, which is suggested by the very large number of technology/product developers employed in the firm. Of the 185 employees, 40 are developers. MPL explains that the personality profiles he asks for in his employees combine the ability to work in teams, be self-reliant and very highly skilled. *"The TC people all have to be able to work with other people and see the quality in other people's work. However, being innovative means that people also have to be unique, and we hire the very best."* The structure of TC is very organic and non-hierarchic. The high level of responsibility that most employees have is a key element to the success and a driving factor for both personal and technological development. Therefore, formalities are very limited in the company and a casual and light-hearted ambience is encouraged and nurtured. MPL believes that *"all these elements create an atmosphere of being a part of something important and groundbreaking."*

In addition to employing innovative individuals internally, TC is also engaged in cooperation with research institutions and other companies in order to be a part of the development of new knowledge even though this might not be directly applicable in TC products at the present time.

It is the explicit strategy of TC to continuously be engaged in front-end innovation as well as creating cumulative innovation based on existing technology. MPL recognizes the difficulty of striking the right balance: *"We had this 4-year-old space acoustic and launched it on the German computer market. All reviews and all home pages praise it to the sky stressing that it's the most innovative thing that has happened to the market for a long time. In here, people just shake their heads, because it's old and dusty to them. So they haven't been able to see the opportunity in the market—they don't understand what business is, but are so caught up in exploring all aspects of the technology."*

4.3.3   Knowledge Acquisition Strategy

MPL very explicitly emphasizes the importance of external knowledge sources for the success of TC Electronic. To him, the technological capabilities of the firm are developed based on a long tradition of research in acoustics in Denmark. The skills his employees have are due to this, and the continued development of knowledge in the field advances as fast as it does because it is pushed forward by several different companies and research institutions. *"In the 1950s, Brüel & Kjær were world leaders within the world of precision instrumentation for acoustics and vibration measurement. They played a major role in the development of acoustics and vibration sciences themselves. DTU and AAU today have leading research centers within acoustics and the Aalborg region is cluster for extensive development of the mobile industry. In addition, there is Oticon and GN producing digital hearing aids, B&O working with digital sound processing in TVs and loudspeakers, and several loudspeaker producing companies such as Jamo and Dali. All this involves focus on and research in digital sound processing and has created a great ambiance for world leading development of front-end technology"*

MPL explains that he spends much of his time networking with a wide range of different actors in order to both stay close to the progress of competitors and get inspiration from sources outside his normal scope. By doing so, he wishes to create a balance between inspiration for radical and cumulative innovation. *"Our R&D department is extremely visionary, skilled and creative, and can create products of the future continuously. However, without being market-oriented these products are in danger of being ahead of the market, thus not generating sales. On the other hand, in a high-technology company all development cannot be based on market analysis, as this will lead to a short termed vision, creating 'me-too' products and not innovative products."*

4.3.4   Conclusion

The innovation strategy of TC Electronic emphasizes the balance between internal and external knowledge generation. Internal developers are often leading within their fields and able to generate radical inventions. However, in order to transform these inventions into real opportunities in the market, MPL encourages interaction externally as this will create the needed market understanding as well as enhance the technological understanding. This is emphasized at all levels of the organization, as all are expected to contribute to continued development. On several technological developments, TC has shared ownership with external partners, such as research institutions or other industrial companies.

4.4 Case Study Four: B&O ICEpower Ltd.

4.4.1   Background

The company started in 1994 when B&O discussed the possibility of basic research within audio power transition with an associate professor at the Technical University of Denmark (DTU), with the purpose of increasing the energy efficiency and the quality of audio equipment. A Ph.D. project was initiated jointly between the company and the research institution, giving the employed Ph.D. researcher (KN) access to both worlds.

By 1996, KN had achieved the first groundbreaking results on what was to become the ICEpower technology. He explains that it was made possible primarily due to three factors: a systematic approach, determination, and the ability and possibility to combine several sources of knowledge available in the company and the research institution.

By 1997, B&O decided to start the implementation of the technology in their products. However, KN saw wider perspectives in the technology and introduced the idea of creating a spin-off company. This was done in 1999 as a joint ownership between KN and B&O. KN explains how the knowledge from B&O this way remained a continuous source of knowledge and competencies. Today ICEpower employs 35 individuals and has a customer base including many well-known brands such as Sony, Bose, and Sanyo.

4.4.2   Innovation Strategy

The initiation of the development of the ICEpower technology was a result of a radical innovation strategy, where two sources of existing knowledge realized the benefits both could gain from cooperating. By establishing such cooperation, a very fluid border was created between the two, creating room for KN to exploit the knowledge of both.

This radical approach to innovation, however, becomes even clearer when looking at how KN continues the development of ICEpower today. KN's vision for ICEpower is *"technological leadership within audio power conversion in a wide/broad sense—from the power plug to the acoustic output. The most intelligent solutions to any power transition function in audio relations."* This he wants to achieve by creating an organization aimed at interacting with external sources, such as competitors, research institutions, and the founding company.

4.4.3   Knowledge Acquisition Strategy

The radical innovation strategy of ICEpower also reflected the knowledge acquisition strategy of the company. KN has deliberately placed the physical setting of the company very close to the research institution that participated in the original project, as this gives him the opportunity to interact with students and researchers on a frequent basis. KN explains that he continuously has a handful of Master's students working on ICEpower-specific projects as their Master's thesis. This gives him the opportunity to explore new areas at very low costs, as well as stay closely connected to the ideas developed at the research institutions. He refers to this as "*the playground of ICEpower, creating grounds for new radical breakthroughs, performed in an integrated cooperation with DTU.*"

Also from a market perspective KN is focused on developing the company through the use of external knowledge. He explains that through establishing partnerships within areas that ICEpower neither possesses nor wants to develop internally, he is able to reach new markets and increase the implementation potential of the technology. These partnerships will also enable him to learn about new venues.

4.4.4 Conclusion

The creation of ICEpower itself was a result of cooperation between an industrial company and a research institution. This founding openness toward use of external knowledge sources is also reflected in ICEpower today, as close cooperation with research institutions is part of the strategy on how to be able to continuously generate radical breakthroughs in spite of a limited internal research capacity due to its small size. In addition, ICEpower is also, to a high degree, focused on cooperation with industrial relationships, and draws benefits in particular from the continued mutual partnership with B&O. The intellectual property model is, for this reason, also based on shared ownership. As such, the innovation strategy and the knowledge acquisition strategy are closely connected, aimed at interacting with external knowledge resources in order to explore new opportunities.

5 DISCUSSION

Through the development of an understanding of the concepts of open/closed innovation systems and cumulative/radical innovation strategies, the authors have arrived at two hypotheses regarding the relationship between innovation strategy and knowledge acquisition strategies. In the following, these hypotheses are discussed in light of the empirical findings, giving grounds for their rejection or validation. The findings are discussed below under the hypothesis headings established in sections 2.3 and 2.4. The following offers an overview of each hypothesis and provides a brief summary of the evidence drawn from the case studies. Each hypothesis is illustrated in the conceptual model (Figure 1). Section 5.3 puts forward a new proposition which suggests that it is necessary to extend the understanding of innovation and knowledge acquisition strategies into a third dimension.

5.1 Hypothesis One

Organizations implementing a cumulative innovation strategy are more likely to implement internal knowledge acquisition strategies.

Case study one demonstrates a clearly focused innovation strategy of cumulative innovation, evidence of which is provided in the following: products are continually improved, formally catered for in the company roadmap; there is a definite focus on core competencies, which have remained mainly unaltered over time; there are clear organizational boundaries; and the internal research and development team play a central role in innovation, with little evidence of external knowledge linkages. This case study suggests that, as an internally focused organization, they are less likely to look to the external knowledge environment for opportunities, ideas, and knowledge. The owner-manager himself suggests that he is fearful that they are blinded by their own abilities and cannot move outside their own areas of speciality to explore new, novel ideas or radically different applications of their own technology.

This provides evidence that cumulative innovation is indeed dependent on internal knowledge that is developed and improved over time. It also suggests that organizational boundaries are as suggested by Chesbrough (2003), an impermeable barrier to the outside knowledge environment. It identifies a clear link between organizational innovation strategy which in this case is one of continual improvement in line with the requirements of existing customers and knowledge acquisition strategy which is based on building and harnessing core competencies. The empirical findings hence provide a validation of the first hypothesis.

5.2 Hypothesis Two

Organizations implementing a radical innovation strategy are more likely to implement external knowledge acquisition strategies.

Case study two has built its existence around external knowledge. The knowledge acquisition model is based on a direct collaboration with the research institution or university. The company is completely reliant on external knowledge without which it would not be in existence. The organizational boundaries are extremely porous and knowledge passes in both directions, continuously enabling the internal organization to absorb knowledge produced externally. The organization implements a radical innovation strategy which has literally forced them to search for knowledge in the external environment. This suggests that if radical innovation requires new knowledge, an organization is more likely to scan all available knowledge sources. This provides evidence of hypothesis two: that organizations implementing a radical innovation strategy are more likely to implement external knowledge acquisition strategies. This case study suggests that organizations following this strategy often do not possess the knowledge required for radical innovation internally as it is dramatically new. The knowledge that needs to be created for a radical innovation is often highly research intensive; most organizations do not have the in-house expertise to carry out blue sky research. There are many knowledge sources external to the organization that are skilled to do the necessary research required to bring a radical idea into fruition.

The empirical findings thereby also support the second hypothesis.

It should, therefore, be noted that hypotheses one and two are both identifiable in the selected case studies. There is evidence to support both hypotheses. Case study one suggests that organizations implementing a cumulative innovation strategy are more likely to implement internal knowledge acquisition strategies, while case study two demonstrates that organizations implementing a primarily radical innovation strategy are more likely to implement an external knowledge acquisition strategy. Both these assertions are in line with current theory and practice.

5.3 Extending the Understanding of Innovation and Knowledge Acquisition Strategy into a Third Dimension

Based on the empirical findings, the authors argue that there is indeed a need to extend even further the understanding of the relationship between cumulative/radical innovation and internal/external knowledge acquisition.

Case studies three and four fit elements of an open innovation system. However, they demonstrate not only the competency to source knowledge from the internal and external environments but also a dual ability to manage both radical and cumulative innovation at a strategic level. The literature suggests that these kinds of organizations are rare (O'Connor, and Ayers 2005) but do exist (O'Reilly and Tushman 2004). O'Reilly and Tushman suggested that some organizations have successfully developed radical innovations while at the same time protecting their traditional businesses. In order to achieve this, companies have set up organizationally distinct units that are tightly integrated at the top management level. Hence, this exploratory research provides evidence of a new proposition that calls for further empirical research. The proposition is built on the evidence of a limited but existent ability to manage a dual strategy of cumulative and radical innovation supported by relevant internal and external knowledge acquisition strategies.

The proposition suggested by the authors is aimed at effectively establishing a continuous focus on both cumulative and radical innovation, referred to as ambidextrous innovation, and is formulated as the following:

(P) Organizations implementing a dual innovation strategy (cumulative and radical) are more likely develop the abilities to acquire knowledge both internally and externally.

The authors suggest that this is the ability to integrate an internally focused iterative innovation strategy and an externally focused radical innovation strategy that will place new demands on both the organizational structure and the individuals concerned. This new proposition is not based on an easily definable entity but rather an organic, learning organization with a dual ability. The individuals and the organization must grow and build on past experience while at the same time pushing out the boundaries of knowledge into exciting new areas. This will require the development of new organizational and individual mindset: the ability to move across industry boundaries, source knowledge from diverse locations, and develop creative intellectual property models while at the same time enabling the individual within the organization an element of intellectual freedom.

This proposition has a number of preliminary implications:

(1) Individuals and organizations will need to sidestep their own cognitive limitations.

(2) Developing core competencies is central, but the ability to move outside these competencies is also important.

(3) Organizations need to move toward a ubiquitous state where location is not as central as access to groundbreaking research.

Integrating the two validated hypotheses and the proposition of an extended understanding of the relationship between cumulative/radical innovation and internal/external knowledge acquisition into one visual frame, the conceptual model emerges (see Figure 1).

6   CONCLUSIONS AND FURTHER RESEARCH

The aim of the paper has been to unfold the question: *What is the relationship between cumulative/radical innovation and internal/external knowledge acquisition respectively?*

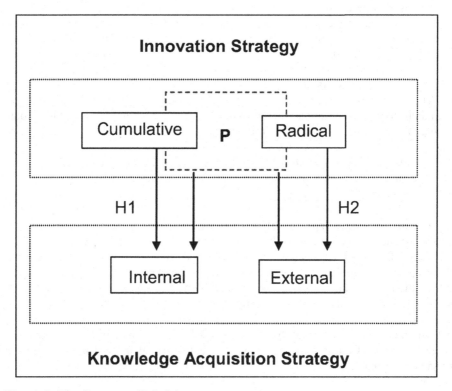

Figure 1. The Conceptual Model

This was achieved by the development of two hypotheses through theory and by testing with four case studies. The case studies gave rise to a validation of the two hypotheses, showing a relationship between cumulative innovation and the implementation of an internal knowledge acquisition strategy and a radical innovations strategy and an external knowledge acquisition strategy.

The case studies, however, also revealed a need for extending the understanding of the relationship between innovation strategy and knowledge acquisition strategy even further. As a result, the authors developed a proposition built around the need for the development of best practice for dual innovation strategy involving a clear focus on both cumulative and radical innovation and internal and external knowledge acquisition.

An interpretation of these results is that cumulative innovation requires well-organized, clearly focused, competency-based knowledge whereas radical innovation requires a firm to move out of its comfort zones, breaking down organizational boundaries to locate and transfer in and out new knowledge and capabilities. This creates a clear dichotomy with the potential of driving the firm in two opposing directions (internal and external). However, proof does exist that firms can successfully combine a number of knowledge acquisition strategies and evidence of this is presented in the case studies (2, 3, and 4). This new breed of firm manages to transfer knowledge across fluid boundaries, and to locate value proposition on knowledge that is purchased or developed in collaboration with a third party, thereby enabling them to develop organizational agility. However, this tends to be on a project by project basis rather than at an organizational strategic level.

This indicates that in order to successfully drive both cumulative and radical innovation, companies must align innovation strategy with knowledge acquisition strategy. Otherwise, they are likely to fail at both kinds of innovation. The inability to manage current knowledge and competencies can be as fatal as being blinkered to external knowledge.

To conclude, therefore, agility and the ability to move between cumulative and radical innovation is central. In order to do this, firms must manage to leverage their current competencies but at the same time move outside their traditional knowledge boundaries and create porous, living learning organizations. From the evidence presented in this paper, the authors concur with prior research (Chesbrough 2003; Cockburn and Henderson 1998; Cohen et al. 2002; von Hippel 1988) that the ability to utilize external knowledge sources in radical innovation activities is crucial.

However, while there is recognizable evidence to suggest that firms are successfully acquiring knowledge from both the internal and external knowledge environment, there is still a sizable distance to go before firms can successfully develop ambidextrous capability enabling focused radical and cumulative innovation (O'Connor and Ayers 2005; O'Reilly and Tushman 2004). Finally, further research in the space between knowledge management and innovation is necessary in order to clarify the most effective models for knowledge acquisition to actively support diversity in innovation at both the organizational and individual level.

This empirical research project has opened up a number of interesting opportunities for further research. The case studies were focused on the acquisition of knowledge from the internal and external environment. While not in the scope of this study, an important first step toward building an ambidextrous or dual ability to support innovation strategy and knowledge acquisition is to identify a set of metrics to measure effects on productivity and profitability. The case studies revealed interesting and new intellectual property models, which are increasingly complex in nature and continue to evolve rapidly to support novel knowledge acquisition strategies. There is a need for further research to establish the most effective methods to support novel knowledge acquisitions strategies. Other areas of interest include the importance of physical location versus virtual location on knowledge acquisition.

There are also a number of limitations to this research project that need to be addressed in further research. First, case studies, while probably the most appropriate research method for this kind of research, are often criticized as a "less desirable form of inquiry than either experiments or surveys" (Yin 1989, p. 24). Many of the arguments made concern the ability to generalize from the research findings. However, case studies do permit generalization of a theoretical nature (i.e., generalizing from data to theory; Yin 1989). While concerns remain on the external validity of research findings generated by case studies, the method appears to be gaining acceptance as a means of generating new insights into complex organizational phenomena (Slappendel 1996). Second, this study was limited to in-depth case studies in Ireland and Denmark and it would be interesting to see if the findings of this study are applicable to a broader audience of firms drawn from a number of other countries and diverse industrial settings.

References

Argote, L., and Ingram, P. "Knowledge Transfer: A Basis for Competitive Advantage in Firms," *Organizational Behavior and Human Decision Process* (82:1), 2000, pp. 150-169.

Argote, L., Mc Evily, B., and Reagans, R. "Managing Knowledge in Organizations: An Intergrative Framework and Review of Emerging Themes," *Management Science* (49:4), 2003, pp. 571-582.

Baden-Fuller, C., and Pitt, M. *Strategic Innovation*, London: Routledge, 1996.

Barney, J. "Firm Resources and Sustained Competitive Advantage," *Journal of Management* (17:1), 1991, pp. 99-120.

Baum, J., and Ingram, P. "Survival-Enhancing Learning in the Manhattan Hotel Industry," *Management Science* (36:7), 1998, pp. 140-154.

Bessant, J. *Challenges in Innovation Management: The International Handbook on Innovation*, Amsterdam: Elsevier Science Ltd., 2003a, pp. 761-774.

Bessant, J. *High-Involvement Innovation: Building and Sustaining Competitive Advantage Through Continuous Change*, New York: Wiley , 2003b.

Chesbrough, H. *Open Innovation: The New Imperative for Creating and Profiting from Technology*, Boston: Harvard Business School Press, 2003.

Christensen, C. M. *The Innovators Dilemma: When New Technologies Cause Great Firms to Fail*, Boston: Harvard Business School Press, 1997.

Cockburn, I. M., and Henderson, R. M. "Absorptive Capacity, Coauthoring Behavior, and the Organization of Research in Drug Discovery," *Journal of Industrial Economics* (46:2), 1998, pp. 157-182.

Cohen, W. M., and Levinthal, D. A. "Absorptive Capacity: A New Perspective on Learning and Innovation," *Administrative Science Quarterly* (35:1), 1990, pp. 128-152.

Cohen, W. M., Nelson, R. R., and Walsh, J. P. "Links and Impacts: The Influence of Public Research on Industrial R&D," *Management Science* (48:1), 1990, pp. 1-23.

Cooper, R. "Doing it Right: Winning at New Products" *Ivey Business Journal* (64:6), 2000, pp. 54-60.

Darr, E, Argote, D., and Epple, D. "The Acquisition, Transfer and Depreciation of Knowledge in Service Organizations: Productivity in Franchises," *Management Science* (41:11), 1995, pp. 1750-1762.

Darroch, J. "Knowledge Management, Innovation and Firm Performance," *Journal of Knowledge Management* (9:3), 2005, pp. 101-115

Dosi, G. "Technological Paradigms and Technological Trajectories," *Research Policy* (11), 1982, pp. 147-162.

Etzkowitz, H. "Networks of Innovation: Science, Technology and Development in the Triple Helix Era," *International Journal of Technology Management and Sustainable Development* (1:1), 2002, pp. 7-20.

Fahy, J. "The Resource-Based View of the Firm: Some Stumbling-Blocks on the Road to Understanding Sustainable Competitive Advantage," *Journal of European Industrial Training* (24:2-4), 2000, pp. 94-104.

Garcia, R., and Calantone, R. "A Critical Look at Technological Innovation Typology and Innovativeness Terminology: A Literature Review," *The Journal of Product Innovation Management* (19:2), 2002, pp. 112-132.

Grant, R. "The Resource-Based Theory of Competitive Advantage: Implications for Strategy Formation," *California Management Review* (33:3), 1991, pp. 114-35.

Hamel, G. *Leading the Revolution*, Boston: Harvard Business School Press, 2000.

Hamel, G. "Strategy as Revolution," *Harvard Business Review* (74:4), July-August 1996, pp. 69-82.

Herstatt, C., and von Hippel, E. "From Experience: Developing New Product Concepts Via the Lead User Method: A Case Study in a 'Low Tech' Field," *Journal of Product Innovation Management* (9), 1992, pp. 213-221.

Kaplan, S. M. "Discontinuous Innovation and the Growth Paradox," *Strategy and Leadership*, March/April 1999, pp. 16-21.

Kogut, B., and Zander, U. "What Firms Do? Coordination, Identity and Learning," *Organization Science* (7:5), 1996, pp. 502-519.

Kusunoki, K. "Incapability of Technological Capability: a Case Study on Product Innovation in the Japanese Facsimile Machine Industry," *Journal of Product Innovation Management* (14:5), 1997, pp. 368-382.

Leifer R., MdDermott, C. M., O'Connor, G. C., Peters, L. S., Rice, M. P., and Veryzer, R. W.*Radical Innovation: How Mature Companies Can Outsmart Upstarts*, Boston: Harvard Business School Press, 2000.

March, J. G. "Exploration and Exploitation in Organizational Learning," *Organization Science* (2:1), 1991, pp. 71-87.

Menon, T., and Pfeffer, J. "Valuing Internal Versus External Knowledge," *Management Science* (49:4), 2003, pp. 497-513.

O'Connor, G., and Ayers, A. D. "Building a Radical Innovation Competency," *Journal of Research and Technology Management* (48:1), 1005, pp. 309-334.

O'Reilly, C., and Tushman, M. "The Ambidextrous Organization," *Harvard Business Review* (82:4), 2004, pp. 74-81.

Prahalad, C., and Hamel, G. "The Core Competencies of the Corporation," *Harvard Business Review*, May/June 1994, pp. 79-91.

Slappendel, C. "Perspectives on Innovation in Organizations," *Organizational Studies* (17:1), 1997, pp. 107-129.

Stalk, G., Evans, P., and Shulan, L. "Competing on Capabilities: The New Rules of Corporate Strategy," *Harvard Business Review*, March/April, 1992, pp. 57-69.

Teece D. J "Strategies for Managing Knowledge Assets: The Role of Firm Structure and Industrial Context," *Long Range Planning* (33:1), 2000, pp. 35-54.

Teece, D. J., Pisano, G., and Shuen, A. "Dynamic Capabilities and Strategic Management," *Strategic Management Journal* (18:7), 1997, pp. 509-533.

Vidgen, R. "Adaptive Information Systems Development," in *Proceedings of the IFIP WG 8.6 Working Conference on IT Innovation for Adaptability and Competitiveness,* Leixlip, Ireland, May 31–June 2, 2004, pp. 1-16.

von Hippel, E. *The Sources of Innovation*, New York: Oxford University Press, 1988.

Yin, R. K. *Case Study Research: Design and Methods* (rev. ed.), Newbury Park, CA: Sage Publications, 1989.

Zott, C. "Dynamic Capabilities and the Emergence of Intra-industry Differential Firm Performance: Insights from a Simulation Study," *Strategic Management Journal* (24:2), 2003, pp. 97-125.

About the Authors

Andrea Deverell is pursuing a Ph.D. investigating novel knowledge acquisition strategies as a means for increasing innovation and creativity in organizational contexts. She has over a decade of experience in higher education, both as lecturer and administrator, and her work has focused on effective collaboration and knowledge transfer between academia and industry. From 1999 to 2003, Andrea served as Technology Transfer Officer based in the Office of the Vice-President of Research, University of Limerick. In this role she facilitated over 35 collaborative research projects between academia and industry. Andrea is an active member of the Global Continuous Innovation Network (CINET). She is author of a number of papers in the field of Innovation and coauthor of "Assessing the Role of Open Source Software in the European Secondary Software Sector: A Voice from Industry," which received a Best Paper award at The International Conference on Open Source System, Genova, Italy, 2005. Andrea can be reached at andrea.deverell@ul.ie.

Astrid Heidemann Lassen is currently in the process of completing her Ph.D. at the Center for Industrial Production, Aalborg University, Denmark. Her research interests lie within the fields of corporate entrepreneurship and radical innovation. Astrid can be reached at ahl@iprod.aau.dk.

Part 5

Resilience and Competitive Advantage

12 RESILIENCE AS A SOURCE OF COMPETITIVE ADVANTAGE FOR SMALL INFORMATION TECHNOLOGY COMPANIES

Brian Webb
Frank Schlemmer
Queen's University of Belfast
Belfast, N. Ireland

Abstract   *Resilience, defined as the capacity for continuous reconstruction, is based on Hamel's earlier work on core competencies. We deploy the resilience concept to explain the performance differentials of small information technology companies. Our interviews with owner-managers suggest that the resilience concept is insufficient to account for competitive advantage and suggest that a sole focus on core competencies can even create competitive disadvantage. In particular, those managers that focused too much on their own core competencies and ignored market developments and other stakeholders created competitive disadvantages. We therefore suggest that resilience can only be a source of competitive advantage if it is extended with the option of replacing core competencies. In addition, core competencies frequently have to be supplemented by competencies of partners or customers in order to achieve competitive advantage.*

Keywords   Core competence, core rigidity, resilience, SMEs, IT

1   INTRODUCTION

Resilience, defined as "the capacity for continuous reconstruction" (Hamel and Valikangas 2003, p. 55), is based on Hamel's earlier work on core competencies (Prahalad and Hamel 1990). However, it has been suggested that core competencies also have a dysfunctional flipside—the core rigidities that impede change (Leonard-Barton 1992). We argue that this critique also applies to Hamel and Valikangas' understanding of resilience and that their concept can be enhanced by going beyond the core competencies. Furthermore, the original concept of resilience was designed for

Please use the following format when citing this chapter:

Webb, Brian, Schlemmer, Frank, 2006, in International Federation for Information Processing (IFIP), Volume 206, The Transfer and Diffusion of Information Technology for Organizational Resilience, eds. B. Donnellan, Larsen T., Levine L., DeGross J. (Boston: Springer), pp. 181-197.

large multi-business companies and focuses, for example, on the allocation of resources to different strategic business units, political conflicts in large companies, and bureaucracy. Yet, small companies also face the challenge of continuous reconstruction or resilience. Dean et al. (1998) even suggested that flexibility and change is more important for small companies than for their larger competitors. But small companies differ in many ways from large ones, for example, in their structure (Hannan and Freeman 1984), management (Feindt et al. 2002; Schlenker and Crocker 2003), and behavior (Hitt et al. 1991; Woo 1987).

We conducted interviews with owner-managers in order to explore how resilience can be a source of competitive advantage for small IT companies. We grounded our work in the dynamic capabilities concept (Eisenhardt and Martin 1997; Teece et al. 1997) and found that continuous reconstruction of human resources, customer relationships, and IT resources is a source of competitive advantage in high velocity markets. This paper contributes to the literature in three ways. First, it suggests that including external resources and stakeholders in the resilience concept increases its explanatory power. Second, it empirically demonstrates that continuous reconstruction is a source of competitive advantage. Third, the resilience concept is applied to small instead of large companies.

The remainder of the paper is structured as follows. In the next section, the literature on core competencies, core rigidities, and resilience is briefly reviewed. Furthermore, some differences between small and large companies are highlighted. Our focus on small IT companies is then discussed. In the research method section, the data collection and sampling process are explained. Then the results are presented; the discussion and conclusions follow.

2   LITERATURE REVIEW

In their quest for resilience, Hamel and Valikangas (2003) develop the core competencies concept (Prahalad and Hamel 1990) which suggests that companies should aim at developing leadership in selected areas—the so called core competencies. The core competencies can be a source of competitive advantage if they fulfil the following three criteria. First, they have to provide potential access to a wide variety of markets. Second, they should make a significant contribution to the perceived customer benefits of the end product. Third, they should be difficult for competitors to imitate. Prahalad and Hamel further argue that companies should focus only on a few (maximum of 5 or 6) core competencies, and then transfer the core competencies to core products. They describe Honda as an example that had the core competence to build high-revving, smooth-running, lightweight engines for motorcycles and then exploited this core competence for other markets, for example cars, four-wheel off-road buggies, and boat motors.

Prahalad and Hamel (1990), among others, laid the fundament for the resource-based view of the firm (RBV), which is based on the assumption that a firm can be seen as a bundle of resources and capabilities (Penrose 1959) that can lead to competitive advantage and superior rents. It has been argued that the traditional resource-based view has not adequately explained how and why certain firms have competitive advantage in situations of rapid and unpredictable changing markets. The dynamic capabilities framework (Teece et al. 1997) analyzed the sources and methods of wealth creation and capture by firms operating in environments of rapid and unpredictable market change. In such conditions, the mere existence of appropriate bundles of specific resources and capabilities is not sufficient to sustain competitive advantage. Instead, a firm must constantly reconfigure, gain and dispose of their resources and capabilities to meet the demands of a shifting market.

Whereas the resource-based view was developed in strategic management research it has also been deployed in information technology and information systems research. For example, Wade and Hulland (2004) suggested that the RBV can be used as a framework to evaluate the value of strategic IS assets and for comparing IS resources with non-IS resources.

Many of the early studies deploying the resource-based view to IS research identified and defined IS resources. Ross et al. (1996) identified the following three IT assets: human assets (for example, problem solving orientation, business understanding, and technical skills), technology assets (for example, physical IT assets, technical platforms, and databases), and relationship assets (for example, partnerships with other divisions, client relationships, and shared risks and responsibility). Feeny and Willcocks (1998) identified nine IS core capabilities: IS leadership, business systems thinking, relationship building, architecture planning, making technology work, informed buying, contract facilitation, contract monitoring, and vendor development. Bharadwaj (2000) defined IT infrastructure, human–IT resources, and IT-enabled intangibles as IT resources. She argues that the capability to deploy these IT resources synergistic with other organizational resources and capabilities can lead to competitive advantage. She found that firms with high IT capability tend to outperform a control sample of firms on a variety of profit and cost-based performance measures. Santhanam and Hartono (2003) extended this study with a more sophisticated methodology and came to very similar results. Zhang and Lado (2001) argue that the potential contributions of information systems to competitive advantage can be understood in terms of their impact on the development and utilization of distinctive organizational competencies (input-based competencies, transformation-based competencies, and output-based competencies). Tippins and Sohi (2003) divide IT competency into IT knowledge, IT operations, and IT objects and show that it affects organizational learning, which then affects firm performance.

Definitions for resources, dynamic capabilities, core competencies and rigidities are provided in Table 1.

A combination of the core competencies concept and the dynamic capabilities framework was developed by Hamel and Valinkangas (2003) and labeled resilience. Resilience is the ability to dynamically invent business models and strategies as circumstances change, and defined as "the capacity for continuous reconstruction" (p. 55). Hamel and Valikangas' main argument is that companies should focus on their existing resources, but that the continuously changing environment, customer preferences, markets, and competition force them to continuously reconstruct them.

Whereas the resource-based view in general, and the core competencies and resilience concepts in particular, have been extensively discussed in the literature, they

Table 1. Definitions

	Authors	**Definition**
Resources	Amit and Schoemaker (1993)	Stocks of available factors that are owned or controlled by the firm.
Dynamic capabilities	Teece et al. (1997)	The firm's ability to integrate, build, and reconfigure internal and external resources.
Core competencies	Leonard-Barton (1992)	A knowledge set that distinguishes and provides a competitive advantage.
Core rigidities	Leonard-Barton (1992)	Inappropriate sets of knowledge that actively create problems.

were mainly developed for large companies. The articles on core competencies (Prahalad and Hamel 1990) and resilience (Hamel and Valikangas 2003) are illustrated with many examples of companies like NEC, Honda, Sony, IBM, Toyota, and Motorola, all of them large companies. However, we believe that the basic resilience concept also applies to small companies because they also face the challenge of continuous reconstruction or resilience. It has even been argued that flexibility and change is more important for small companies than for large ones (Dean et al. 1998).

Small companies differ in their structures from their larger competitors. For example, SMEs tend to be structured more simply than larger enterprises and they lack structural inertia (Hannan and Freeman 1984). They are often governed by owner-managers, and the vast majority of strategic decisions are usually made by one person (Feindt et al. 2002; Schlenker and Crocker 2003), who often has an entrepreneurial oriented and risk seeking leadership style (Hitt et al. 1991; Woo 1987). In addition, small companies challenge competitors more actively and are faster than large companies in reacting to challenges and they are often very effective by focusing their strategic moves (Chen and Hambrick 1995) and innovation (Hameresh et al. 1978) in a narrow domain.

This suggests that many issues that were raised about core competencies (Prahalad and Hamel 1990) and resilience (Hamel and Valikangas 2003) do not apply to small companies, for example, bureaucracy and political conflicts within large organizations or the allocation of resource to different strategic business units. We believe that the simple structures and the focused strategies of small companies are a promising research setting because this simplifies the analysis and enables us to better explore the concept of resilience.

Another difference between small and large companies is that they control different resources and capabilities. For example, small companies frequently suffer from resource poverty (Welsh and White 1981), which often affects business strategy development and the perceptual and physical barriers to growth (Fillis et al. 2004). They usually have fewer financial and human resources (Caldeira and Ward 2003; Chow et al. 1997; Gribbins and King 2004; Ihlstrom and Nilsson 2003). Thus the process of allocating and managing resources differs between small and large companies mainly because small ones have fewer resources and simpler structures.

Hamel and his colleagues (Hamel and Valikangas 2003; Prahalad and Hamel 1990) believe that large companies take unnecessary risks by diversification and by approaching markets in which they can't exploit their core competencies, which often undermines their competitive advantage. The reverse conclusion would be that small companies, which tend to focus their strategy in a narrow domain (Chen and Hambrick 1995) or niche (Porter 1980) can create competitive advantage by focusing on their core competencies, which then leads to resilience.

The focus of this paper is small IT companies but our larger study is of e-SMEs. Research on e-SMEs is still very rare and is often limited to small firm's adoption and usage of the Internet (see Kula and Tatoglu 2003; Tiessen et al. 2001) and frequently lacks grounding in academic theory (Griffin 2000). However, there are more rigorous SME studies in the IS area. For example, Thong (2001) developed a resource-based model to analyze resource constraints and information systems implementation in Singaporean small businesses and found that external technical expertise is a very important factor of IS implementation success. Duhan et al. (2001) analyze the role of property-based and knowledge-based resources for IS strategies of a not-for-profit organization. Caldeira and Ward (2003) found that management perspectives and attitudes toward IT adoption and use, and the development of internal IT competence, are success factors for the adoption of IT.

Some researchers have examined how small e-businesses differ from large ones. For example, Duhan et al. (2001) suggested that small firms could create competitive advantage online because they are more flexible, they can conduct changes more quickly, and they work more closely with customers. In addition, SMEs are usually more entrepreneurial and willing to experiment and innovate in business models than their larger competitors with established hierarchies (Jutla et al. 2002). On the other hand small companies are restricted by their limited resources (Jutla et al. 2002), which can have more restraint on marketing options compared to larger companies (Jones 2004). Saban and Rau (2005) found that resource and knowledge limitations hamper the usage of websites of SMEs. Furthermore, SMEs use the Internet less strategically (Webb and Sayer 1998) and less for marketing purposes (BarNir et al. 2003) than their larger competitors.

3   RESEARCH METHOD

Resilience, defined as continuous reconstruction, will be evaluated in terms of reconstructing resources (Hamel and Valikangas 2003). According to the dynamic capabilities framework (Teece et al. 1997), firms have to build, integrate, and reconfigure resources in order to match them to the changing environment. For this research, the Powell and Dent-Micallef (1997) framework, which consists of human resources, business resources, and IT resources, was combined with the dynamic capabilities framework, which consists of building, integrating, and reconfiguring resources (Teece et al. 1997). The research framework is shown in Figure 1. (Examples of dynamic capabilities and their enablers are shown in Appendix A.)

Given their importance to the success of the firm (Gans and Quiggin 2003; Lins 1998), the primary sources of data were semi-structured interviews with the owner-

Resources Dynamic Capabilities	Human Resources	Customers*	IT Resources
Building			
Integration			
Reconfiguration			

*In our research, we focused specifically on customers as a business resource because all managers highlighted the importance of customers in the interviews.

Figure 1. Framework

managers. The interviews were conducted at the work place of the managers. This enabled the researcher to develop a level of detail about the individual and place and to be highly involved in actual experiences of the participants (Rossman and Rallis 1998). A literature search was conducted in tandem with data collection and analysis in order to ground the analysis theoretically. Interview data were triangulated through a qualitative content analysis of the companies' websites. These data were primarily used to verify company interview data, and thus increase the validity of the findings (Silverman 1993). The interview transcripts were analyzed through the categorization and analysis of emergent concepts and ideas and constant comparison of these concepts to identify common themes (Miles and Huberman 1984).

As suggested by Miles and Huberman (1984), codes were created before the fieldwork. As shown in Table 2, dynamic capabilities were divided in the three subcategories—building (bui), integrating (int), and reconfiguration (rec) of resources—and the examined resources were human resources (hr), customers (cu), and IT resource (it). The coded transcripts of the high, average, and low-performers were analyzed by searching these codes and then directly contrasting them in order to find out how they differ (Strauss and Corbin 1990). (An example of a coded interview is given in Appendix B.)

Table 2. The Codes

Dynamic Capability		Resources	Codes
Building		human resources.	bui-hr
		customer relationships.	bui-cu
		IT resources.	bui-it
Integration	of	human resources.	int-hr
		customers relationships.	int-cu
		IT resources.	int-it
Reconfiguration		human resources.	rec-hr
		customer relationships.	rec-cu
		IT resources.	rec-it

Since this paper is part of a larger research project, we used data from a postal survey measuring resources and capabilities as performance drivers of e-business SMEs (we defined e-business SMEs as companies with less than 250 employees that are selling online). The 106 companies surveyed were ranked according to their financial performance. In this paper, we only focus on the 13 IT companies that replied to our survey. However, three of the companies went out of business; therefore, the sample size was 10. Two were used for a pilot study and thus eight IT companies remained. Two managers didn't want to participate and therefore six interviews (two high performers, one low performer, and three average performers) were conducted. Table 3 provides an overview of the six companies.

According to Hamel and Valikangas (2003, p. 63), resilience is "the ultimate advantage." Competitive advantage is typically measured in terms of financial performance (Hawawini et al. 2003). Managers were asked if their performance over the last 3 years was outstanding and if they had exceeded their competitors. We used the financial performance data of the postal survey for identifying high, average, and low performers (Rouse and Daellenbach 2002). Financial performance was measured in terms of revenues, sales growth, and return on assets, by six questions, each of them with a five-point Likert scale (Powell and Dent-Micallef 1997). Therefore, the theoretical minimum performance was 6 (6 questions × 1 point) and the maximum performance was 30 (6 questions × 5 points). The company with the lowest financial performance had 6 points and the best performing company had 29 points; the mean was 17.47 (standard deviation = 4.99). The companies were divided into the following three groups: low performers (6 to 13 points), medium performers (14 to 21 points), and high performers (22 to 29 points).

- **High IT 1** was an Internet solutions provider with eight employees. They had the exclusive rights to distribute Internet connectivity of the international Internet backbone provider MCI for Northern Ireland. The relationship with MCI enabled the company to offer customers a fast and reliable Internet connection. Furthermore High IT 1 offered a range of additional products and services such as hosting, virtual private networks, connectivity, network support and maintenance, and specialized software products. High IT 1 won an innovation award for the development of networked services for combining voice and data services without the necessity of managing procurement and provisioning of the facilities. High IT 1 purchased 70 percent of their products and services online.

Table 3. The Companies

	Financial Performance	Difference to Mean	Number of Employees	Turnover
High-IT 1	23	+5.5	8	£ 600,000
High-IT 2	24	+6.5	6	£ 350,000
Average IT 1	21	+3.5	13	unknown
Average IT 2	14	-3.5	9	£500.000
Average IT 3	14	-3.5	3	unknown
Low-IT	11	-6.5	10	unknown

- **High IT 2** specialized in local government and compliance consultancy and software solutions. They were the market leader in the provision of browser-based applications for the public sector in Northern Ireland. They purchased 80 percent of their products and services online and because, all of their products are online, 100 percent of their sales are in e-business.

- **Average IT 1** specialized in video streaming and the design and development of highly interactive web applications. They had 13 employees, offering a wide variety of services including video streaming, software development, and the design of web applications, consulting (for example, in content management, broadband applications, and video on the web), and video archiving. In addition, they offered software products such as security and surveillance, content management, and video archiving and presentation software. Average IT 1 purchased 80 percent of their products and services online and created all their revenues online.

- **Average IT 2** specialized in new media and advertising design. In the new media area, they designed websites and online games; in the advertising area, they designed billboards, annual reports, brochures, etc. They had nine employees and they were the first design agency to acclaim Investors in People.[1] Average IT 2 purchased only 1 percent of their products and services and created only 5 percent of their turnover online.

- **Average IT 3** was a web and multimedia design company that targeted small businesses as customers. They offered a large variety of services including web design, hosting, maintenance, and training. They had three employees, supplied 75 percent online, and created 50 percent of their turnover online.

- Low IT, the low performer in the IT industry, had 10 employees and supplied IT-solutions for membership management and accounting, access, and stock control to sports clubs. With the integrated system, the members' smartcard allowed them to gain access to the clubhouse and make purchases at the bar, restaurant, or shop. Low IT created 5 percent of their revenues online and purchased 70 percent of their products and services online.

4   RESULTS

This research aimed at examining resilience, defined as the continuous reconstruction of resources. The results are summarized in Table 4. The matrix includes human resources, customers, and IT resources, and how they were reconstructed. It shows a set of characteristics (bullet points) of resilience. Each characteristic represents a difference that was identified. These differences include the managers' commitment

---

[1]Investors in People is an initiative founded by the UK government to develop companies through building training and development activity in their business strategy.

Table 4. Results

Resources DC	Human Resources	Customers	IT Resources
Building	• Training programs for managers • Training programs for employees	• Experimentation • Employees understand markets	• Cooperation with other companies
Integration	• Team building • New employees	Integrate customer feedback	• Integrate external IT
Reconfiguration	• Structure • Processes	• Tailor offers to customer needs • Additional services	• Matching of IT and business processes

to resilience, their activity in developing resilience, and their beliefs as to whether their companies created competitive advantage in that area. If the managers' answers indicate positive resilience and competitive advantage, the characteristic is categorized as positive resilience (+1), and if it indicates negative resilience and competitive disadvantage, it is categorized as negative resilience (-1). If the managers' answers are inconclusive or if that specific characteristic doesn't apply to a specific company, it is categorized as inconclusive (0).

Table 4 was developed by directly contrasting high with low performers as suggested by Rouse and Daellenbach (1999). Each of the bullet points is a characteristic in which they differed. For example, managers of both high performers were involved in training programs and offered training programs for their employees, and the low performer did not. The manager of High IT 1 said, "We do believe in ongoing training [and] updating our skill sets….we acquire the skills that are necessary to serve the clients." Furthermore, the high performers regularly engaged in team building activities and took a more active role in integrating new employees in the team than the low performer. The high performers also constantly reconfigured the firm's structure and processes and the low performers did not. For example, the managers of both high performing IT companies continuously asked questions such as "How can we mold things to actually make them operate better" (High IT 1). The manager of High IT 1 also believed that "if you cannot accept change and you cannot work with change then there is no point in being in this business and you can go home and close the door immediately."

Similarly, the manager of High IT 2 was committed to find out "how we can improve the process" and they continuously asked themselves the questions: "Is the process that we are following for this project successful? Are we failing anywhere? Is it going more slowly or quickly than expected?" In contrast, the manager of Low IT showed a high resistance to change. Not only did he avoid any changes at the organizational level, he even resisted any changes at the product level. He said, "We try to avoid changes to the product." In contrast, High IT 1 offered a variety of standardized product packages, and also tailored the products especially to the customer needs. The manager said, "Nothing is set in stone...we are able to take each customer's requirements and individualize." Similarly, the manager of High IT 2 stated that rather than expecting the customers to adapt to their product, they would modify their products and services to the customer requirements.

In terms of customer relationships, the high performers engaged heavily in experimenting and they made sure that their employees had a solid knowledge of the markets for better understanding customer needs. That helped them to acquire new customers and to enhance existing relationships. In contrast, the low performer was not active in that area and said, "We don't want to put too many resources in it." The high performers also had an open ear and integrated customer feedback in the company. The low performing manager tried to "avoid changes to the product [because] we like selling our product as it is." In contrast, the high performers tailored services to customer needs and offered a wider range of services than the low performer.

The main difference in managing IT was that the high performers worked much closer with their customers. They integrated their own IT systems better with those of their customers, and tailored IT according to the customers' business processes. For example, the manger of High IT 1 said, "We are able to take each customer's requirements and individualize them and bring together all the necessary parts that they are looking for and then put it together as a package for what they are looking for." In contrast, the manager of Low IT said, "We try to avoid if they want a particular system for themselves."

As suggested by Levitas and Chi (2002), we also compared average performing companies to the high and low performers. In contrast to the high and low performers, the average performers had a mixed bag. They created competitive advantages on some characteristics (bullet points) and disadvantages on others. The net effect of the advantages and disadvantages caused average financial performance.

5   DISCUSSION AND CONCLUSIONS

This paper applied the resilience concept (Hamel and Valikangas 2003) to small IT companies. We focused on the technology sector because it is typically characterized by rapid market changes which are the actual cause for continuously reconstructing a firm's resources (Teece et al. 1997). The results suggest that even though the concept has been developed for large companies, it can also be applied to small ones. We believe that the simple structures and the focused strategies of small companies are an adequate research setting for exploring the resilience concept.

Resilience was defined as continuous reconstruction of resources (Hamel and Valikangas 2003). The reconstruction process was divided in the subcategories of building, integrating, and reconfiguring resources. Interviews with owner-managers indicate that high performing companies create competitive advantage by resilience, average performing companies create a combination of advantages and disadvantages, and low performers create competitive disadvantages.

However, our data suggests that Hamel and Valikangas resilience concept, which is based on the Hamel's earlier work on core competencies and existing resources, may be too narrow. Whereas the concept of core competencies has attracted huge interest by practitioners, it has also been heavily criticized by researchers because core competencies can also become competency traps (Levitt and March 1988) or core rigidities (Leonard-Barton 1992). Leonard-Barton discovered a paradox by showing that core competencies facilitated the development of projects closely aligned with the core business, but that they also inhibit innovation, lacking alignment with the core business. She called these core rigidities, the dysfunctional flip-side of core competencies. Thus managers face the dilemma of both utilizing and maintaining their core competencies, and yet avoiding their dysfunctional flip side by renewing and replacing them.

This paradox is supported by further research. For example, Dougherty (1995) discovered that core incompetences grow around a firm's core competencies. This was supported by Henderson's (1993) research, which suggested that organizational skills were hampered by incumbents' previous experience. Similarly, Sorenson and Stuart (2000) suggested that greater reliance on prior developments is associated with more innovation (at semiconductor and biotechnology companies) but that this innovation (which relies on own developments) is less relevant, and is therefore a hallmark of obsolescence. In the same vein, Rosenkopf and Nerkar (2001, p. 303) found that "firms that focus inward on their core competencies run the risk of developing innovations that wind up being peripheral to the aggregate path of technological development." Furthermore, they discovered a trade-off between the impact of innovation on the domain of the core business and the overall impact beyond that domain. They argued that innovations based on core competencies tend to create domain impacts and subsequently short term gains; innovations beyond the core competencies tend to create overall impacts and subsequently long term gains. They believed that the reason for the higher impact of innovations outside their core competencies could be the usage of external expertise. In particular, including external expertise increases the number of choices between different technologies and thus the likelihood of choosing well-regarded technology. In contrast, building on internal expertise restricts that choice.

In conclusion, the literature supports Leonard-Barton's suggestion that core competencies have to be renewed *and replaced*. But the resilience concept as suggested by Hamel and Valikangas only focuses on renewing and not on replacing. Our data suggests that a too-strong internal focus and ignoring stakeholders such as customers and partners can be a source of competitive disadvantage. For example, the low performer continuously ignored customer feedback, was not capable of integrating his own IT with the customers' systems, focused only on a single core product without offering modifications or additional services, and subsequently created competitive disadvantages. In contrast, the integration of customer feedback, cooperation with other companies, integrating new employees in the company, and training courses with external trainers helped the high and average performers to create competitive advantages.

The paper contributes to the literature in three ways. First, the resilience concept is relatively new and has attracted little attention by researchers. Our results suggest that the resilience concept (Hamel and Valikangas' 2003) is incomplete, mainly because it doesn't address Leonard-Barton's suggestion that core competencies may have to be replaced as well, otherwise they could become core rigidities. Second, it empirically demonstrates that continuous reconstruction is a source of competitive advantage. Third, the resilience concept is applied to small instead of large companies.

The main implication for managers is that they should not exclusively focus on core competencies. Our results suggest that it is a very thin line between a core competence and a core rigidity. Obviously, continuous reconstruction of human resources, customer relationships, and IT resources is a source of competitive advantage. But managers should also seek to strengthen the resources they control by including external expertise, as Leonard-Barton suggested. They have to renew *and* replace them, if necessary.

The key limitation of this study is that it followed a middle road between rich insights and number of organizations from which the data was collected. In particular, the main data sources were the interviews with owner-managers. However, this bears the risks of interviewee bias and memory failure, but the analysis was supplemented by contrasting the findings to the information that was offered on the company website and this information confirmed the results. Furthermore, the findings in this study are based on the examination of six firms. However, the findings presented above have a strong intuitive and conceptual appeal, and are amenable to quantitative verification. Another limitation of the study is the focus on the IT industry and generalizability to other industries is questionable. Furthermore, this paper examined small companies that were managed by a single person. Therefore, the findings can probably not been applied to manager teams or boards of directors.

This study is explorative and can thus only be a first step in analyzing the relationship between resilience and competitive advantage at small companies, which can be supplemented by further empirical verification. Furthermore, as little is known about the effective management of the trade-off between core competencies and core rigidities, this could be addressed either by long-term in-depth qualitative studies or by large scale quantitative work.

References

Amit, R., and Schoemaker, P. J. H. "Strategic Assets and Organizational Rent," *Strategic Management Journal* (14:1), 1993, pp. 33-46.

BarNir, A., Gallaugher, J. M., and Auger, P. "Business Process Digitization, Strategy, and the Impact of Firm Age and Size: The Case of the Magazine Publishing Industry," *Journal of Business Venturing* (18), 2003, pp. 789-814.

Bharadwaj, A. S. "A Resource-Based Perspective on Information Technology Capability and Firm Performance: An Empirical Investigation," *MIS Quarterly* (24:1), 2000, pp. 169-196.

Caldeira, M. M., and Ward, J. M. "Using Resource-Based Theory to Interpret the Successful Adoption and Use of Information Systems and Technology in Manufacturing Small and Medium-Sized Enterprises," *European Journal of Information Systems* (12), 2003, pp. 127-141.

Chen, M., and Hambrick, D. C. "Speed, Stealth, and Selective Attack: How Small Firms Differ from Large Firms in Competitive Behavior," *Academy of Management Journal* (38:2), 1995, pp. 453-482.

Chow, C. W., Haddad, K. M., and Williamson, J. E. "Applying the Balanced Scorecard to Small Companies," *Strategic Finance* (79:2), 1997, pp. 21-28.

Dean, T. J., Brown, R. L., and Bamford, C. E. "Differences in Large and Small Firm Responses to Environmental Context: Strategic Implications from a Comparative Analysis of Business Formations," *Strategic Management Journal* (19), 1998, pp. 709-728.

Dougherty, D. "Managing Your Core Incompetences for Corporate Venturing," *Entrepreneurship Theory and Practice* (19:3), 19995, pp. 113-135.

Duhan, S., Levy, M., and Powell, P. "Information Systems Strategies in Knowledge-Based SMEs: The Role of Core Competencies," *European Journal of Information Systems* (10), 2001, pp. 25-40.

Eisenhardt, K. M., and Martin, J. A. "Dynamic Capabilities: What Are They?," *Strategic Management Journal* (21), 2000, pp. 1105-1121.

Feeny, D., and Willcocks, L. "Re-design the IS Function Around Core Capabilities," *Long Range Planning* (31:3), 1998, pp. 354-367.

Feindt, S., Jeffcoate, J., and Chappel, C. "Identifying Success Factors for Rapid Growth in SME E-Commerce," *Small Business Economics* (19), 2002, pp. 51-62.

Fillis, I., Johansson, U., and Wagner, B. "A Qualitative Investigation of Smaller Firm E-Business Development," *Journal of Small Business and Enterprise Development* (11:3), 2004, pp. 349-361.

Gans, J. S., and Quiggin, J. "A Technological and Organizational Explanation for the Size Distribution of Firms," *Small Business Economics* (21:3), 2003, pp. 243-256.

Gribbins, M. L., and King, R. C. "Electronic Retailing Strategies: A Case Study of Small Businesses in the Gifts and Collectibles Industry," *Electronic Markets* (14:2), 2004, pp. 138-152.

Griffin, A. "From the Editor," *Journal of Product Innovation Management* (17), 2000, pp. 97-98.

Hamel, G., and Valikangas, L. "The Quest for Resilience," *Harvard Business Review* (68:3), September 2003, pp. 52-63.

Hameresh, R. G., Anderson, M. J., and Harris, J. E. "Strategies for Low Market Share Business," *Harvard Business Review* (56:3), 1978, pp. 95-102.

Hannan, M. T., and Freeman, J. H. "Structural Inertia and Organizational Change," *American Journal of Sociology* (89), 1984, pp. 149-164.

Hawawini, G., Subramanian, V., and Verdin, P. "Is Performance Driven by Industry- or Firm-Specific Factors? New Look at the Old Evidence," *Strategic Management Journal* (24:1), 2003, pp. 1-16.

Henderson, R. "Underinvestment and Incompetence as Responses to Radical Innovation: Evidence from the Photolithographic Alignment Equipment Industry," *Rand Journal of Economics* (24:2), 1993, pp. 248-270.

Hitt, M. A., Hoskisson, R. E., and Harrison, J. S. "Strategic Competitiveness in the 1990s: Challenges and Opportunities for U.S. Executives," *Academy of Management Executive* (5:2), 1991, pp. 7-22.

Ihlstrom, C., and Nilsson, M. "E-Business Adoption by SMEs: Prerequisites and Attitudes of SMEs in a Swedish Network," *Journal of Organizational Computing and Electronic Commerce* (13:3/4), 2003, pp. 211-223.

Jones, C. "An Alternative View of Small Firm Adoption," *Journal of Small Business and Enterprise Development* (11:3), 2004, pp. 362-370.

Jutla, D., Bodoril, P., and Dhaliwal, J. "Supporting the E-Business Readiness of Small and Medium-Sized Enterprises: Approaches and Metrics," *Internet Research: Electronic Networking Applications and Policy* (12:2), 2002, pp. 139-164.

Kula, V., and Tatoglu, E. "An Exploratory Study of Internet Adoption by SMEs in an Emerging Market Economy," *European Business Review* (15:5), 2003, pp. 324-333.

Leonard-Barton, D. "Core Capabilities and Core Rigidities: A Paradox in Managing Product Development," *Strategic Management Journal* (13), 1992, pp. 111-125.

Levitas, E., and Chi, T. "Rethinking Rouse and Daellenbach's Rethinking: Isolating vs. Testing for Sources of Sustainable Competitive Advantage," *Strategic Management Journal* (23:10), 2002, pp. 957-962.

Levitt, B., and March, J. G. "Organizational Learning," *Annual Review of Sociology* (14), 1988, pp. 319-340.

Lin, C. Y. "Success Factors of Small and Medium-Sized Enterprises in Taiwan: An Analysis of Cases," *Journal of Small Business Management* (36:4), 1998, pp. 43-56.

Miles, M. B., and Huberman, A. M. *Qualitative Data Analysis: A Sourcebook of New Methods*, London: Sage Publicatoins, 1984.

Penrose, E. *The Theory of Growth of the Firm*, London: Basil Blackwell, 1959.

Porter, M. E. *Competitive Strategy: Techniques for Analyzing Industries and Competitors*, New York: Free Press, 1980.

Powell, T. C., and Dent-Micallef, A. "Information Technology as Competitive Advantage: The Role of Human, Business and Technology Resources," *Strategic Management Journal* (18:5), 1997, pp. 357-387.

Prahalad, C., and Hamel, G. "The Core Competencies of the Corporation," *Harvard Business Review* (68:3), 1990, pp. 79-91.

Ravasi, D., and Verona, G. "Organizing the Process of Knowledge Integration: The Benefits of Structural Ambiguity," *Scandinavian Journal of Management* (17), 2001, pp. 41-66.

Rosenkopf, L., and Nerkar, A. "Beyond Local Search: Boundary Spanning, Exploitation, and Impact in the Optical Disk Industry," *Strategic Management Journal* (22:4), 2001, pp. 287-306.

Ross, J. W., Beath, C. M., and Goodhue, D. L. "Develop Long-Term Competitiveness Through IT Assets," *MIT Sloan Management Review* (38:1), 1996, pp. 31-42.

Rossman, G. B., and Rallis, S. F. *Learning in the Field: An Introduction into Qualitative Research*, Thousand Oaks, CA: Sage Publications, 1998.

Rouse, M. J., and Daellenbach, U. S. "More Thinking on Research Methods for the Resource-Based Perspective," *Strategic Management Journal* (23:10), 2002, pp. 963-967.

Saban, K. A., and Rau, S. E. "The Functionality of Websites as Export Marketing Channels for Small and Medium Enterprises," *Electronic Markets* (15:2), 2005, pp. 128-135.

Santhanam, R., and Hartono, E. "Issues in Linking Information Technology Capability to Firm Performance," *MIS Quarterly* (27:1), 2003, pp. 125-153.

Schlenker, L., and Crocker, N. "Building an E-Business Scenario for Small Businesses: The IBM SME Gateway Project," *Qualitative Market Research: An International Journal* (6:1), 2003, pp. 7-17.

Silverman, D. *Interpreting Qualitative Data*, London: Sage Publications, 1993.

Smith, A. J., Boocock, G., Loan-Clarke, J., and Whittacker, J. "IIP and SMES: Awareness, Benefits, and Barriers," *Personnel Review* (31:1/2), 2002, pp. 62-85.

Sorenson, J. B., and Stuart, T. E. "Aging, Obsolescence and Organizational Innovation," *Administrative Science Quarterly* (45), 2000, pp. 81-112.

Strauss, A. L., and Corbin, J. *Basics of Qualitative Research: Grounded Theory Procedures and Techniques*, Newbury Park, CA: Sage Publications, 1990.

Teece, D. J., Pisano, G., and Shuen, A. "Dynamic Capabilities and Strategic Management," *Strategic Management Journal* (18:7), 1997, pp. 509-533.

Thong, J. Y. L. "Resource Constraints and Information Systems Implementation in Singaporean Small Businesses," *Omega* (29), 2001, pp. 143-156.

Tippins, M. J., and Sohi, R. "IT Competency and Firm Performance: Is Organizational Learning the Missing Link?," *Strategic Management Journal* (24), 2003, pp. 745-761.

Tiessen, J. H., Wright, R. W., and Turner, I. "A Model of E-Commerce Use by Internationalizing SMEs," *Journal of International Management* (7:2), 2001, pp. 211-233.

Wade, M., and Hulland, J. "*Review*: The Resource-Based View and Information Systems Research: Review, Extension, and Suggestions for Future Research," *MIS Quarterly* (28:1), 2004, pp. 107-142.

Webb, B., and Sayer, R. "Benchmarking Small Companies on the Internet," *Long Range Planning* (19:6), 1998, pp. 815-827.

Welsh, J. A., and White, J. F. "A Small Business Is Not a Little Big Business," *Harvard Business Review* (59:4), 1981, pp. 18-32.

Wernerfelt, B. "A Resource-based View of the Firm," *Strategic Management Journal* (5:2), 1984, pp. 171-180.

Woo, C. Y. "Path Analysis of the Relationship between Market Share, Business-Level Conduct and Ris," *Strategic Management Journal* (8:2), 1987, pp. 149-168.

Zhang, M. J., and Lado, A. A. "Information Systems and Competitive Advantage: A Competency-Based View," *Technovation* (21), 2001, pp. 147-156.

Zollo, M., and Winter, S. "Deliberate Learning and the Evolution of Dynamic Capabilities." *Organization Science* (13:3), 2002, pp. 339-351.

About the Authors

Brian Webb is a senior lecturer in Information Systems, School of Management and Economics, Queen's University of Belfast, N. Ireland. He is a former Distinguished Erskine Fellow in the Department of Accounting, Finance, and Information Systems, Faculty of Commerce, University of Canterbury, New Zealand. He holds a Bachelor's degree from Queen's, an MBA from the University of Ulster and a Ph.D. from University College London. In 1999 he was visiting scholar in the Department of Computer Science, University of British Columbia, Canada. Prior to becoming an academic, Brian worked as a systems analyst in both the UK and the United States. He is currently on secondment as a Senior Researcher at the Centre for Competitiveness, Belfast. He may be contacted at b.webb@qub.ac.uk.

Frank Schlemmer is the owner-manager of a small independent retailer based in Nuernberg, Germany. He is also currently in the final stages of completing his doctoral studies at the Queen's University of Belfast. He has written a number of papers on the impact of IT and small firms and has previously published a book on performance management. He may be contacted at frank.schlemmer@gmx.de.

Appendix A. Examples of Dynamic Capabilities and Their Enablers

Dynamic Capability (Teece et al., 1997)	Of (= Examples)	By (= Enablers)
Learning is a process by which repetition and experimentation enable tasks to be performed better or quicker. It also enables new production opportunities to be identified. The organizational knowledge generated by such activity resides in new patterns of activity, in "routines" or a new logic of organization.	Zollo and Winter (2002): • Operating routines	Teece et al. (1997) and Eisenhardt and Martin (2000): • Experimentation • Collaborations and partnerships • Developing individual and organizational skills • Joint contributions of employees

Dynamic Capability (Teece et al., 1997)	Of (= Examples)	By (= Enablers)
Integration is the coordination of internal and external activities and technologies.	Teece et al. (1997) and Eisenhardt and Martin (2000): • Customer feedback on different stages of the value chain • New technologies in organizational processes • Stakeholders (for example alliancing and partnering with suppliers or other companies) • New knowledge in the organization	Ravasi and Verona (2001): • Fluid project-based organization • Interaction between experts of different professional areas • Cross-functional teams • Reduction of physical and structural barriers
Reconfiguration of the firm's asset structure and the accomplishment of the necessary internal and external transformation.	Teece et al. (1997) and Eisenhardt and Martin (2000): • Resources • Capabilities	Ravasi and Verona (2001): • Open and informal culture • Openness to individual proposals and creativity • Broad involvement in strategic process Teece et al. (1997) and Eisenhardt and Martin (2000): • Reduction of costs for change • Exit routines

Appendix B: Extract of Coded Interview

This section of the interview was mainly about learning and building strategic assets and about reconfiguration. I stands for interviewer (the researcher) and R for the respondent (the managing director). The left column shows the codes that emerged during data collection and the right column the codes that were created before data collection.

Manager's Activity and Commitment	Question and Answer	Dynamic Capabilities
[A]Com-bui: The manager appears to be committed toward learning. [B]Act-buy: Saying that she couldn't stop learning indicates that she already learns.	I: Does your company learn easy? R: Yes, but I think in this competitive market, you have to keep learning all of the time.[A] I mean if you stop learning then you become complacent and someone else tips you to the post and I think it's what makes us hungry for the industry. [B]You must always be a step ahead and try and find out what is next to come aboard and learn that if need be so yes, I do think so.[1]	[1]Bui-hr: The manager believed that she created competitive advantage by learning and developing human resources.

Manager's Activity and Commitment	Question and Answer	Dynamic Capabilities
[C]and [D]Act-bui: More indicators for her active role in building human resources. [E]Another indicator for her commitment toward learning.	I: Are you involved in any training programs? R: Well, as an employer I do appraisals so I do individual appraisals with them and I have nominated one of the top members of staff, she does a unique training program, an individual training program for each one of them so, also if there are areas if they would be weak on she would take them on different times one-to-one and strengthen their, build up whatever they need trained on. [C]We also do outside training where we would go to product knowledge training or we also go to the UK.[2] We would go to it once a year so we try and keep up where budget is possible,[3] as much training as we can. I think it is very important. I am from an ex-training background myself. I was a teacher for seven years so it's kind of naturally in me anyway to keep the training going, you know but keeping learning going keeps the brain going, keeps you stimulated. It prevents boredom. It does, definitely.[E]	[2]Bui-hr: Participation in training programs was an indicator for building human resources, because only the high performers did that. [3]Bui-cr: Understanding of market trends was an indicator for building customer relationships.
[F]Com-bui: More indicators for activity and commitment toward learning	I: Did you have a lot of change inside your company in the last years? R: Well we have had extreme growth and due to that then a lot of change. We have expanded, there has been a lot of growth[4] and I would also be involved in training the London guys so I go over every three months to make sure, to give them a training plan, make sure they are implementing what I have done prior and make sure the managers are managing and training the staff properly but we do all of that so the growth has been huge that way, you know.[F]	[4]Rec-hr: The company structure and the business processes were changed.

13 ANALYSIS OF OUTSOURCING AND THE IMPACT ON BUSINESS RESILIENCE

Pati Milligan
Baylor University
Waco, TX U.S.A.

Donna Hutcheson
XR Group, Inc.
Dallas, TX U.S.A.

Abstract   *Business and corporate resiliency rely on information technology and information systems organizations to outsource the tasks, **not** the responsibility for adequate service or adequate controls. A key success factor is to outsource procedures and processes that are not "broken" or ineffective. As management examines the viability to outsource all or part of the IT services, a successful plan will always prioritize and assess risks associated with **what** to outsource, then **where** (required location of service delivery), then **who** will provide delivery of the service. Successful IT outsourcing must be carefully managed. Therefore, to help control outsource application project costs, make change control a critical component of the project to be managed with the same cost benefit analysis used to decide on a new process in the beginning. This paper analyzes the risks of outsourcing, trends in outsourcing domestically and offshore, approaches for managing outsourcing, and the legal and regulatory consequences of outsourcing. Each component impacts business and corporation resilience.*

Keywords   IT outsourcing, outsourcing services, off-shore, managing outsourcing, business resilience

1 INTRODUCTION

Business and corporate resiliency rely on information technology to outsource tasks, **not** responsibility for adequate service or controls. A key success factor is to outsource procedures and processes that are not "broken" or ineffective. As management

Please use the following format when citing this chapter:

Milligan, Pati, Hutcheson, Donna, 2006, in International Federation for Information Processing (IFIP), Volume 206, The Transfer and Diffusion of Information Technology for Organizational Resilience, eds. B. Donnellan, Larsen T., Levine L., DeGross J. (Boston: Springer), pp. 199-208.

examines the viability to outsource all or part of IT services, a plan should be built that will always keep in mind determining *what* to outsource, *where* (location of service delivery), then *who* will provide delivery service.

The issues, concerns, and impact on business resiliency in the era of outsourced services and offshore service delivery are basically the same as before. Evolution of corporate and economic globalization in recent years has mandated a comprehensive analysis of the relationship between resilience in a given geographical location and overall organizational resilience.

2   RESEARCH CASES

Six research cases are specifically noted in this report.

1. Company B, a large global petroleum company headquartered in the UK with operations in Europe, the Middle East, Far East, Africa, Australia, and the United States.

2. Company E, a global communications company, headquartered in the Baltics, that develops and supplies advanced systems, products, and services for mobile and fixed-line communications to network operators, with operations in Europe, the Middle East, Africa, Asia Pacific, North America, and Latin America

3. Company F, a consumer products company based in Texas with international operations in Europe, South and Central America, the Caribbean, Canada, the Far East, Australia, and the Middle East.

4. Company H, a large U.S.-based hospital with multiple branch locations.

5. Company O, a U.S.-based private company with multiple business lines,

6. Company U, a premier U.S.-based REIT (real estate investment trust) corporation with large assets and revenue.

3   REASONS FOR OUTSOURCING

Headcount reduction: Company U determined computers and IT were not critical to their operation. Their core competency was buying and leasing real estate or mortgages. So, Company U reduced the internal IT head count to one and outsourced all IT services. IT audits revealed significant problems and control issues. In 2005, Company U was absorbed by another REIT that had a large internal IT service department.

Lack of internal expertise: Company B outsources IT to achieve standardization of IT Technologies wherever possible. Company B has acquired several large petroleum companies whose IT systems used shared services, domestic outsourcing, and near-shore outsourcing. Company B's IT strategy has been to retain the existing IT structure for a period of 12 to 18 months, study the service delivery methods that were successful and those that would not fit Company B's overall IT strategy. A team of Company B employees and domestic providers in the acquired corporation's country restructured the IT technology used and the delivery of service. If the acquired company did not have sufficient expertise to convert to the new, common technology, those projects were outsourced. This technique has proven successful from the corporate standpoint, but not from the subsidiary standpoint.

Company F outsources multiple services to multiple providers. Shared services are used for all IT operations (except security) for European and Asian locations. Shared services for ERP applications, networking, and application security for all locations are provided internally at the corporate offices. Internal IT audit services are outsourced domestically or nearshore, depending on availability of qualified audit providers. Company F examines each task and service needed to support international IT operations, determines where the task or service should be provided, then who should provide the service or complete the task. The resiliency of Company F has been proven strong over the past 5 years. Stock price and dividends have financial analysts advising to buy or hold.

Emerging technologies: Emerging technologies were always implemented into the corporation through a combination of contingency staffing and domestic providers. Depending on the complexity of the emerging technology and the level of associated training, outsourcing has roughly equal success and failure histories.

Network outsourcing: Company E outsources all IT services—some effectively, others fraught with problems. Company E outsources all telecommunications to other network operators, both global and domestic to office locations. They also provide hosting services to global network providers. The theory is that Company E's core competencies are the advanced solution design and operation of switches and routers. Company E is a leader in this hosting service.

ERP applications: Company E uses IBM as the sole provider for ERP application implementation globally. Because IBM has outsourced a major portion of Company E's application tailoring and implementation, the hybrid form of provider services has added a complexity resulting in many problems for the North America division of Company E. First-level application support is provided globally by HP, thus adding another layer of complexity and opportunity for miscommunication.

Company E's North America division conducted an IT application audit. Segregation of duties issues were numerous. Finding and correcting the profile security problems was outsourced to a third-party provider (one specializing in IT audits). A problem was identified and corrected in the developer instance of the ERP software. The other respective service providers were notified of the requirement to migrate. Migration failed. The resulting research took three days to locate and correct the cause of the migration failure; it should have taken less than an hour. The design and flow of code from development to test to production was the cause. This situation is common at Company E. Red tape, communication across time zones, finger pointing, and lack of total picture by any one provider severely impacts the resilience of IT. However, corporate executives state that it has no impact on the resilience of the business. Many outside consultants and auditors view Company E's outsourced operations as a massive hemorrhage.

DBMS: Company B stores the master data for all enterprise systems at headquarters IT. Local data and replicas of enterprise data are stored at domestic provider locations. All DBMS support is provided by domestic providers.

Company E relies on HP to manage storage and location for all data and DBMS support.

Company F stores enterprise data at headquarters. All local data is provided by the shared services groups. All DBMS support is provided by headquarters IT staff.

All three companies view the outsourced DBMS as a success story.

Web presence: All small to medium U.S. companies outsourced design and hosting of websites to domestic providers. Content was provided and/or approved by corporate headquarters. Corporate IT groups did not participate. A total of 75 percent of medium to large global companies provided design and hosting of the website in-house; the other 25 percent outsourced to domestic providers. This is a successful service with minimal costs.

Business transformation or change in business strategies: As management reviews short and long term business and IT strategies, new requirements emerge. Most often noted is the requirement to provide 24/7 monitoring of IT infrastructure, and 24/7 call centers to cover global time zones. Monitoring IT 24/7 by offshore or domestic providers is reported to be most satisfactory with minimum problems. Call centers tend to have a dichotomy: high success is reported by providers and inadequate success is reported by internal users and external clients. How does this different perspective affect the resilience of the business?

Disaster recovery/business continuity planning: Standardization across borders is essential to maintaining business resilience in the face of natural disaster or political unrest. Disaster recovery can be instant and seamless if business processes can be done at any location. The major impact of natural disasters can be avoided by moving services before the disaster hits. A recent example is the short downtime of companies in New Orleans with comprehensive disaster recovery plans for hot recovery sites in various parts of the world. Likewise, companies that had outsourcing agreements with providers in other areas had minimal downtime. Businesses with neither plan have a resilience factor of 0, affecting company survival.

Internal political issues: Upper management is disappointed with previous IT solutions, so the CIO upgrades or replaces a legacy system with new systems or new technology. Often the decision is made to outsource selection, tailoring, and implementation before determining why the legacy system did not meet executive needs and whether a new system or technology will succeed where the legacy system failed. Was it the system and technology or was it the design and procedures?

4   PROS, CONS, AND RISKS

Multisourcing allows companies to select "best of breed" providers in a competitive market. Best of breed involves using the best provider for a particular IT service category or subcategory. A disadvantage is the compound management of multiple service relationships.

Single source outsourcing results in communication with a single management contact for accountability. It also limits the "blame game." A caveat for single source is that too often the buyer requests a service from the provider that is not in the provider's core competence area.

Total IT services outsourcing (one or more providers) plans for the arrangement to last from 8 to 10 years. Total IT outsourcing was one of the major reasons for collapse of Company U above. Conversely, if a company has no cutting edge technology or special IT requirements, total outsourcing can work.

Selective sourcing allows companies to choose subtasks rather than an entire business process as in total sourcing. A key consideration when deciding is what the buyer does best versus what can be done better by outsourcing. Companies B, E, F, and H achieved high success in outsourcing desktop maintenance and support for hardware and software. All buyers' management teams state that this strategy has improved response time, cost, and business staff productivity. Internal help desk support for ERP applications outsourced offshore achieved less than satisfactory results for Company B and Company E. First-level business management at Company B and Company E report that staff productivity has negatively impacted their productivity.

Frequently in business, past "war stories" negatively affect our decisions regarding outsourcing opportunities. For example, a failure in outsourcing the internal help desk colors our judgment about outsourcing desktop maintenance. Each company experience improves the ability to positively contribute to the resiliency of the business through outsourcing appropriate tasks. Not every company benefits from outsourcing. Out-sourcing decisions are interlinked with individual business cases and often it is better to retain the process in-house. The CIO of Company O, states he is against outsourcing for IT. He believes benefits initially gained from outsourcing IT services are lost within 2 years and that it takes twice as long to recover from the negative impact to the business.

To ensure resilience of the service relations, the management team should (1) complete due diligence to discover the capabilities of each party in the final set of providers, (2) establish baseline documents of current performance, and (3) research benchmark studies to measure expected performance against industry norms.

If buyers need global service delivery, then it is essential that the chosen provider have global infrastructure and business continuity to support the buyer's requirements.

Successful outsource agreements result when companies have well-defined outsource strategies with specific contracting and negotiation plans. These plans should include both market and business impact analysis.

If internal user dissatisfaction with outsourced services is severe enough, internal departments will find ways to circumvent some portion of the outsourced service. Example: Company E has several departments that believe the procedures associated with server, application, and data security operations prohibit them from doing their jobs efficiently. Departments purchase servers, charge them as expense line-items, install appropriate applications, store the department data, and run department business totally outside the outsource process. What happens to business resiliency when a problem occurs with the server, application, or data?

Table 1. Pros and Risks to Business Resiliency

Pro	Risks to Business Resiliency
Logical Security	
• Provider cost and maintenance fee distributed among clients • Rapid updates with live monitoring • Dedicated staff with up to date knowledge	• Loss or unauthorized access of data • Data integrity • Failure to fully design, develop and implement enterprise security architecture • Rely primarily on the firewall • Failure to understand the relationship security has with the organization
Specialized Service	
• No in-house training	• Inability to support service during ongoing operation
Desktop and Server Maintenance	
• Remote control • Consistent version control • 45% reduction in IT costs per employee	• Inaccurate/corrupted data and process integrity • Inadequate built-in controls • Few written procedures • Inadequate unauthorized access protection • Unapproved change implementation • Failure to maintain the application • Intellectual property theft • Customer information lost, manipulated or stolen • Delayed service
Disaster Recovery	
• Frequently outsourced IT service • Well established outsource service • Service costs: low maintenance and does not require dedicated full-time staff • Reduces risk of destroying company business	• Hot/cold recovery • Data access and integrity • Business/customer service disruption • Financial/external report misstatement • Lack of staff to support recovery • Access to recent back-up
Voice and Data Telecommunications	
• Well established outsource service	• Illegal/malicious hacking • Denial of service attacks • Data corruption • Bottlenecks • Slow response times
Infrastructure Operations	
• No need for land or building to house equipment/personnel	• Inadequate buyer risk assessment • Inadequate provider controls and ineffective monitoring • Lack of strategic planning to meet buyer's needs • Failure to maintain the system

Pro	Risks to Business Resiliency
Application Development and Maintenance	
• Does not pay provider during downtime • No need to interview, hire, train team members • No direct management of team members	• Inefficiencies in the business process supported by the application • Inadequate contingency strategies for delayed projects • Average outsourced projects are completed successfully and effectively 63% of the time
Help Desk: Internal/Customer	
• Less knowledgeable technicians can resolve 80% of all help desk calls	• Information may not be shared among buyer departments and providers • Conflicting behavior or solutions from the provider team • Difficulty in identifying performance trends or problems • Inability to respond quickly to changing market conditions • Loss of revenue from customer dissatisfaction • Customer requirements may be misunderstood • Provider staff may not be trained to meet customer needs effectively • Inaccurate reporting • Provider employees may breach organization standards related to security and confidentiality • Incomplete/inaccurate recording and communication of problem— common or critical • Cultural differences may interfere with escalation of problems to appropriate buyer staff • Key decision-makers may not be aligned with day-to-day operations

5 COSTS OF OUTSOURCING

Outsourced customer service operations can cost almost a third more than those retained in-house. Of organizations that outsource customer management operations purely to cut costs, 80 percent will fail to do so, while 60 percent of those who outsource parts of the customer facing process will have to deal with customer defections and hidden costs that outweigh any potential savings offered by outsourcing.

Providers may not be financially viable resulting in premature termination of the service the number of buyers prematurely terminating an outsourcing relationship has doubled to 51 percent while the number of buyers satisfied with their off-shoring providers has plummeted from 79 to 62 percent. Outsourcing of any strategic or ineffective process is doomed to failure.

Total costs, including functional interdependencies of outsourced functions are critical to understanding the additional costs of indirectly related functions. The following costs are among those often overlooked in the cost analysis:

- Feasibility study costs.
- Travel expenses to oversee projects or audit.
- More frequent, extensive audits.
- Different auditing practices among countries.
- Theft and piracy.
- Shipping losses.
- Additional administration and paperwork.
- Training and turnover—retraining in the buyer's business goals and processes.
- Cultural and communication difficulties.
- Hidden costs—companies absorbed cost assumed to be the responsibility of the provider resulting in the net effect of no savings from the outsourcing. To maximize the positive impact on company resilience, selection criteria must also prioritize experience; cultural fit, similar work ethics and vision will assure a more effective outsourcing relationship.
- Legal services.
- Offshore practice of state-owned equipment financing.
- Initial cost reductions may be lost as economies supplying cheaper skills are inflated by the influx of business.
- Longer process path from initiation to completion.
- Stronger controls increase costs.
- Salaries of other IT and business support personnel directly related to the service.
- Offshore facilitation and cultural-related costs for offshore outsourcing (under the table payments to receive priority state-controlled services).
- Country-specific risks—stability of political or economic environment, utility and transportation infrastructure

6   OUTSOURCED SERVICES REALITY

Outsourcing agreements impact more than the touch point between buyer and provider. Network connections, including those to other buyer IT resources, other provider IT resources, and the Internet, must be secured at all connecting points, regardless of location, to ensure that access is controlled. If buyer management does not monitor network points, buyer resources are vulnerable to attack and penetration. Reporting should include a chart showing the IT services, all locations where they are delivered (buyer side and provider side), and the type and level of controls and security in place.

Performance metrics design, frequency, and breadth can determine outsourcing success or failure. To be effective, performance metrics should be specific, measurable, time or value based, and relevant to the provider and service being outsourced. A com-

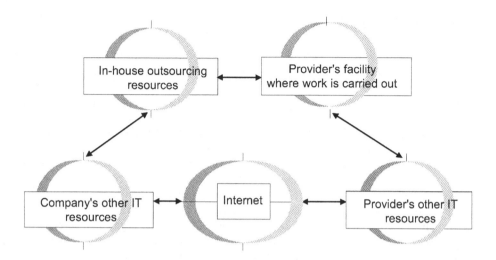

Figure 1. Outsourcing Connection Points

mon example in help desk services: A performance metric may be that 75 percent of all problems are resolved in the first contact. Providers may close problems as resolved when in fact the client is not satisfied. Specific examples of poor metrics: Company U included in the service agreement that provider would supply support as requested by the IT administrator. How is the quality of the provider performance measured? Company E included performance measures in the service agreement for workstation acquisition, installation, and maintenance. The following data is collected and reported on a rolling 13 month basis: the number of planned workstations by division, department, and location; the number of actual workstations by division, department, and location. Another example: 95 percent of all workstation equipment repairs will be completed and returned to the employee within 1 business day. Routine reviews of the contract helps ensure support of business resiliency. Between 30 and 50 percent of IT outsource contracts need to be substantially renegotiated.

7 CONCLUSION

Outsource providers will no longer be able to compete on price alone. Providers must proactively add value. Reduced cost does not always result in retained or created value. Offshore cost benefits will gravitate toward the level of home territory options.

Buyers will focus more on what service is outsourced, where the service is delivered, and who provides that service. To help ensure business resiliency, buyers will contract with providers they know will respect controls, performance, and growth with the buyers. Change and relationships will continue to be primary factors in the future of IT outsourcing. For the complete paper, please contact the authors.

About the Authors

Pati Milligan is an associate professor of Information Systems at Baylor University. She received her Ph.D. from University of North Texas and master's degrees from Texas A&M University and Texas A&M Commerce. Her research interests include electronic commerce and IT auditing. Pati teaches client/server applications and VB programming courses at the graduate and undergraduate level in the business school. Prior to joining the faculty at Baylor in 1983, Pati spent 3 years in the insurance industry. Pati can be reached at pati_milligan@baylor.edu.

Donna Hutcheson is Principal and CEO of XR Group, Inc., responsible for executive IT consulting and IT auditing at global and domestic USA corporations. Her goal is to ensure that clients' technology foundations are cost effective, meet the client corporations' business goals, and provide for transacting business in a global economy, one which is increasingly influenced by the Internet. Donna began her career by teaching computer science at the graduate and undergraduate level. She moved to industry with the Atlantic Richfield Company (ARCO) where she spent more than 20 years serving in a wide variety of management roles, including training, client services, operations, operations support, planning, groupware and artificial intelligence, international office technology implementations, and international IT auditing. She currently serves on the executive board of the North Texas Chapter of the Information Systems Audit and Control Association, and on the Industry Advisory Board of the Audit Programs at University of North Texas, University of Texas at Dallas, Texas A&M Commerce, and Tarrant County College. She can be reached by e-mail at dhutch@ xrgroup.com.

14 THE WIZARD OF OZ: Instilling a Resilient Heart into Self-Service Business Applications

Gabriel J. Costello
Galway-Mayo Institute of Technology
Galway, Ireland

Abstract   *Speech enabled business applications are characterized by complex imple-mentations that bring together language processing technologies, applications development, and end-user psychology. Resilience is critical to maintaining business to customer relationships when implementing these self-service solutions. The Wizard-of-Oz experiment is a valuable technique for simu-lating and building human–machine prototypes to ensure successful deploy-ment of the completed service. This paper proposes the simplification and diffusion of the methodology to facilitate the growth in demand for automated e-business transactions.*

Keywords   Wizard-of-Oz (WOZ) experiments, self-service technology (SST), automatic speech recognition (ASR)

1 INTRODUCTION

The growth of self-service technology (SST) in business to customer (B2C) transactions is being driven by the diffusion of information and communications technology (ICT) and the demand to move from high-cost manual transactions to low-cost automated self-service in enterprises and the public service. The Gartner Group have forecast that 70 percent of customer service contacts for information and remote transactions will be automated by the end of 2005 with an associated increase in investment in Web SST (Pujari 2004). These services are becoming increasingly critical for enterprises challenged with providing e-commerce solutions and building relationships in a world where customer and vendor do not meet face-to-face (Singh 2002). Among STT interfaces, the use of speech is regarded as ideal because it is the most "natural, flexible, efficient and economic form of human-machine communication"

Please use the following format when citing this chapter:

Costello, Gabriel, J., 2006, in International Federation for Information Processing (IFIP), Volume 206, The Transfer and Diffusion of Information Technology for Organizational Resilience, eds. B. Donnellan, Larsen T., Levine L., DeGross J. (Boston: Springer), pp. 209-216.

(Koumpis 1998). However, creating conversational automated agents with responsibility for service levels and maintaining customer relationships is a complex challenge. Providing speech-enabled services requires capability in speech communication technologies, applications programming, and professional services developed in the environment of customer psychology and culture. Consequently, implementation of such solutions brings together many features crucial for resilience—cognitive, emotional, relational, and structural—as outlined in the conference theme. This paper takes a practitioner's perspective based on the author's experience of product lifecycle management of interactive voice response (IVR) and speech technologies in the e-business product portfolio of a telecommunications company. During this period, there was an industry realization that the main challenge was not the maturity of the underlying speech and language processing technologies but the development and deployment of robust customer solutions.

The first section of the paper presented an overview of the self-service business environment and introduced one innovation in the area: speech-enabled automated systems. The paper now proceeds as follows. Section 2 provides a technical description of speech and language processing, treated as a primary innovation in the area of SST. The subsequent section describes the testing of speech-enabled systems that are critical to the deployment of resilient applications. In particular, the focus is on a test methodology called Wizard-of-Oz experiments, viewed as a secondary innovation. Section 4 reviews the diffusion of the technique in areas outside of speech-enabled B2C solutions. The discussion in section 5 argues that the growth of business critical SST calls for the wider dissemination of knowledge and expertise in WOZ experiments and the need for research to address limitations with the technique. Finally, suggestions for future work and the conclusions are presented.

2   SPEECH AND LANGUAGE PROCESSING

Speech communication brings together a number of fields including language processing, computational linguistics, psycholinguistics, voice technologies, grammar checking, and information retrieval (Jurafsky and Martin 2000). Development of applications involve dialog design, integration testing, data collection, tuning, and performance analysis, which results in expensive implementations. Gartner's researchers have included speech recognition as one of the top 10 technologies that will have the biggest impact on enterprises in the period 2002 to 2007. Speech solution providers are citing high profile implementations including a UK bank that is handling millions of calls per week and a U.S. healthcare service with two million customers that has patients and physicians using its speech-enabled appointments facility (Nortel 2005). However, it is worth noting that speech recognition has remained on the Gartner "Emerging Technologies Hype Cycle" for the last 10 years (Gartner 2005). Speech technologies include speech recognition, text-to-speech (TTS) synthesis, and speaker verification (authentication), a branch of biometrics. Recognition has evolved from initial basic discrete (isolated word) recognition to large vocabulary continuous speech recognition (LVCSR) and natural language understanding (NLU). These systems can be speaker dependent, as in the case of dictation products, or speaker independent, in the case of customer service applications with a large number of callers (Childers 2000).

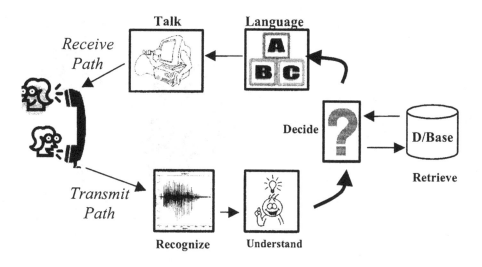

Figure 1. A Generalized Typology of a Speech-Enabled System

The move to provide speech services via the Web is being facilitated by VXML (Voice eXtensible Mark-up Language), a standard of the World Wide Web Consortium (W3C 2005), which allows conventional telephony interfaces such as IVR to evolve using voice gateways linked to a Web server.

Figure 1 shows the main components of a typical conversational system (Zue and Glass 2000) used for B2C information retrieval. First, the customer's spoken input is transmitted to a speech recognizer and the signal is processed. In the next step, the system produces a meaningful (semantic) representation of the signal. Then the system decides what information to retrieve from the database. This decision-making process may take a number of iterations if the dialogue manager seeks clarification from the customer when the input is deemed inadequate or ambiguous. The receive path generally delivers the required information to the customer in a spoken format using language generation and speech synthesis.

3   WIZARD-OF-OZ EXPERIMENTS

Three design principles have been proposed for designing dialogue systems and can be summarized as follows (Gould and Lewis [1985] in Jurafsky and Martin 2000):

- early focus on user and task
- simulations and prototypes
- iteratively test them on the user and fix the problems

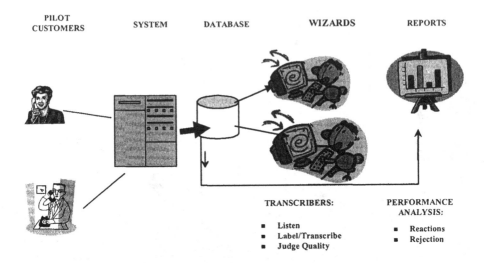

Figure 2. Typical Architecture of a WOZ Speech Application Experiment

A number of test methods are used to tune a speech-enabled system, including usability testing at various stages of the development process, focus groups, and piloting the service in a population of "friendly" users. One technique developed to simulate human-computer dialogue systems is called a Wizard-of-Oz (WOZ) experiment, where a hidden human operator replaces the automated agent in order to experimentally investigate the usability of the system before being deployed in the field (McInnes et al. 1997). The Wizard-of-Oz is also known as a PNAMBIC (**P**ay **N**o **A**ttention to the **M**an **B**eh**I**nd the **C**urtain) system, where the human operator (the wizard) is disguised behind some interface software and the caller thinks that they are interacting with an automated application. The concept originated from the 1899 book by Frank Baum and the 1939 MGM film where Dorothy, the Tin Man, the Lion, and the Scarecrow follow the yellow brick road to Oz in order to make their requests to the awesome Wizard. In the end, the awe-inspiring ruler of Oz turns out to be just a simulation controlled by a very ordinary human (Biberman et al. 1999). In WOZ experiments, the function of the Wizard is played by a human but the user believes it is a computer. Figure 2 shows the typical architecture of a WOZ experiment designed to simulate a speech recognition application.

The technique can provide data on the interaction, acoustic performance, language model, and semantics. It has the advantage of being able to test the proposed solution at an early stage of the development cycle as only the interface software and the databases are required. Other advantages include rapid iterations and the ability to compare a number of design solutions. However, as it is very difficult to cover all of the errors, limitations and constraints of the live application, the conclusions from WOZ experiments can to be rather idealised and even provide false positive results (Jurafsky and Martin 2000). In many cases, WOZ experiments are outsourced to specialist consultants.

4 DIFFUSION OF WOZ

In the previous sections, this paper has described the relationship between a primary innovation (speech-enabled self-service) and a secondary innovation (WOZ experiments) during the design and testing of B2C applications. However, there have been a number of research projects aimed at applying the methodology to other areas. Yang et al. (2000) applied WOZ to the development of a learning interface agent in order to make the system more natural, intelligent, and even emotional. In another context, a WOZ experiment has been extended to involve a robotic interface that is capable of simulating a number of different social behaviours (de Ruyter et *al.* 2005). The procedure has shown that the development of an artificial intelligence interface to provide "active help" has benefitted system users (Davis 1998). Wider applications of the method include collection of empirical data on mathematics tutorials in German (Benzmüller et al. 2003). One of the most novel implementations was the Neimo project, which extended the WOZ technique to the study of multimodal systems and provides evidence that the methodology can be broadened to designing, building, and evaluating services that allow the use of combined input media (Salber and Coutaz 1993). Another area of research has focused on simplifying both the data collection function and the model building that presently makes implementation of the methodology time consuming and expensive (Munteanu and Boldea 2000). A system called DiaWoZ has been designed to collect data in the complex domain of tutorial dialogues between university students and a mathematical tutoring system. The architecture places emphasis on modularity and clear interface requirements that allow for the progressive refinement of consecutive WOZ experiments (Fiedler and Gabsdil 2002). However, in spite of the implementation of the above applications, the evidence from the literature is that the technique is still very much in the realm of the innovator.

5 DISCUSSION

Business analysts are predicting the continued rapid growth in automated ICT applications and deployment of SST. These services bring together leading-edge technologies, the psychology of human-machine interaction, business processes, and the management of customer contacts. The resilience of the solution is critical in an environment where customer relationship management is being entrusted to a computer application and network. The focus on end-user driven development is posing questions on how to overcome traditional barriers between the user and the developer (Pettersson 2003). All of these challenges are presently being encountered in the deployment of speech-enabled business applications, which are currently limited to expensive implementations in verticals such as financial services, telecommunications and healthcare. Wizard-of-Oz experiments provide an effective early prototype environment to test interactions between humans and voice applications. The methodology requires a multidisciplinary approach, bringing together psychology, culture and technology as well as fields such as synthetic computer characters that attempt to make humanoid agents lifelike (Thorisson and Cassell 1996) . However, the technique needs to be diffused to a larger community especially through education, currently only being addressed on a

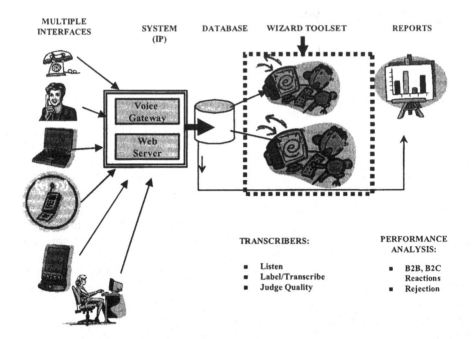

Figure 3. Future Work on Multiple Input WOZ Toolset

small scale, for example, by Henry Lieberman in the MIT Media Lab (2005). Future cross-disciplinary research is required to simplify WOZ experiments and address the weaknesses outlined above to enable the diffusion of the methodology to the wider area of SST and automated Web services. Challenges include ethical considerations of using people in usability testing, language and cultural localization, cost-effective implementation, and accessibility. Figure 3 presents the concept of multiple interfaces to a WOZ environment that is Internet protocol enabled and supported by a flexible development toolset—a "wizard" for wizards. The proposed topology also includes the generation of statistical data for performance analysis of the design.

6 CONCLUSIONS

This paper has provided a practitioner's perspective on the requirement for resilient self-service speech-enabled applications. The business factors driving the growth in automated e-business solutions were described. An overview was given of the complexity of speech and language processing and the skills required to deploy voice-enabled B2C services while managing customer relationships. The important part played by Wizard-of-Oz experiments for the early simulation and testing of such systems was illustrated. Examples were provided of research into the dissemination of the methodology beyond the present, expensive, customer contact solutions. It was argued that the increasing demand for resilient automated e-business and the associated capability to integrate end-user psychology with technology calls for the wider diffusion of WOZ techniques. Future work was then proposed to simplify and automate the method to bring it to a wider audience and address concerns with the validity and reliability of results. B2C self-service applications of the future will, like the Tin Man, need to have a heart.

References

Benzmüller, C., Fiedler, A., Gabsdil, M., Horacek, H., Kruijff-Korbayová, I., Pinkal, M., Siekmann, J., Tsovaltzi, D., Vo, B. Q., and Wolska, M. "A Wizard-of-Oz Experiment for Tutorial Dialogues in Mathematics," in V. Aleven, U. Hoppe, J. Kay, R. Mizoguchi,H. Pain, F. Verdejo, and K. Yacef (eds.), *Proceedings of the AI in Education (AIED) Workshop on Advanced Technologies for Mathematics Education*, Sydney, Australia, 2003, pp. 471-481.

Biberman, J., Whitty, M., and Robins, L. "Lessons from Oz: Balance and Wholeness in Organizations." *Journal of Organizational Change* (12:3), 1999, pp. 243-254.

Childers, D. G. *Speech Processing and Synthesis Toolboxes*, New York: John Wiley & Sons, 2000.

Davis, J. S. "Active Help Found Beneficial in Wizard of Oz Study," *Information and Software Technology* (40), 1998, pp. 93-103.

deRuyter, B., Saini, P., Markopoulos, P., and Breemen, A. v. "Assessing the Effects of Building Social Intelligence in a Robotic Interface for the Home," *Interacting with Computers* (17:5), 2005, pp. 522-541.

Fiedler, A., and Gabsdil, M. "Supporting Progressive Refinements of Wizard-of-Oz Experiments," in C. P. Rose and V. Aleven (eds.), *Proceedings of the ITS2002 — Workshop on Empirical Methods for Tutorial Dialogue Systems*, San Sebastian, Spain, 2002, pp. 62-69.

Gartner. "Gartner Highlights Key Emerging Technologies in 2005 Hype Cycle," Group, Boston, 2005 (available online through www.gartner.com).

Gould, J. D., and Lewis, C. "Designing for Usability: Key Principles and What Designers Think," *Communications of the ACM* (28:3), March 1985, pp. 300-311.

Jurafsky, D., and Martin, J. H. *Speech and Language Processing: An Introduction to Natural Language Processing, Computational Linguistics, and Speech Recognition*, Upper Saddle River, NJ: Prentice-Hall, Inc., 2000.

Koumpis, K. "Corporate Technological Positioning in Automatic Speech Recognition and Natural Language Processing," Master of Science Dissertation, Science and Technology Policy Research (SPRU), University of Sussex, 1998.

Lieberman, H. "The 'Wizard of Oz' Agent Experiment," unpublished paper, 2005 (available online at http://www.media.mit.edu/~lieber/Teaching/Collaboration/Turvy/Turvy.html).

McInnes, F. E., Jack, M. A., Carraro, F., and Foster, J. C. "User Responses to Prompt Wording Styles in an Automated Banking Service with a Wizard of Oz Simulation of Word-Spotting," *IEE Colloquium on Advances in Interactive Response Technologies for Telecommunications Services* (Digest No: 1997/147), June 12, 1997, pp. 7/1-7/6.

Munteanu,C., and Boldea, M. "MDWOZ: A Wizard of Oz Environment for Dialog Systems Development," in *Proceedings of the Second International Conference on Language Resources and Evaluation*, Athens, Greece, 2000, pp. 1579-1582.

Nortel. "Position Paper: The Power of Speech," 2005 (available online through www.nortel.com).

Pettersson, J. S. "Prototyping Interactivity before Programming," in *Proceedings of the Workshop on End User Development, Conference on Human Factors in Computing Systems* (CHI 2003), Fort Lauderdale, FL, April 6, 2003, pp. 73-75.

Pujari, D. "Self-Service with a Smile? Self-Service Technology (SST) Encounters among Canadian Business-to-Business," *International Journal of Service Industry Management* (15:2), 2004, pp. 202-209.

Salber, D., and Coutaz, J. "Applying the Wizard of Oz Technique to the Study of Multimodal Systems," in L. J. Bass, J. Gornostaev, and C. Unger (eds.), *Human-Computer Interaction Selected Papers*, Berlin: Springer-Verlag, 1993, pp. 219-230.

Singh, M. "E-Services and Their Role in B2C E-Commerce." *Managing Service Quality* (12:6), 2002, pp. 434-446.

Thorisson, K., and Cassell, J. "Why Put an Agent in a Body: The Importance of Communicative Feedback in Human-Humanoid Dialogue" (Abstract) in *Proceedings of Lifeline Computer Characters '96,* Snowbird, UT, October 5-9, 1996, pp. 44-45.

W3C. World Wide Web Consortium (W3C): Voice Extensible Markup Language (VoiceXML) Version 2.0, 2005 (available online through http://www.w3.org/).

Yang, Y., Okamoto, M., and Ishida, T. "Applying Wizard of Oz Method to Learning Interface Agent," *IEICE Workshop on Software Agent and its Applications (SAA2000) and Special Issue on Software Agent and its Applications Transactions of IEICE*, 2000, pp. 223-230.

Zue, V. W., and Glass, J. R. "Conversational Interfaces: Advances and Challenges," in *Proceedings of the IEEE* (88:8), Special Issue on Spoken Language Processsing, 2000, pp. 1166-1180.

About the Author

Gabriel J. Costello is a lecturer in Engineering at the Galway-Mayo Institute of Technology, Galway, Ireland. Prior to this he worked in the telecommunications industry with Nortel where he held new product introduction and product line management positions in the IVR, Self-Service and Customer Contact Center business units. Gabriel can be reached by e-mail at gabrielj.costello@gmit.ie.

Part 6

Innovation Studies

15 CONFERENCEXP: An Enabling Technology for Organizational Resilience

Murray Scott
National University of Ireland, Galway
Galway, Ireland

Gino Sorcinelli
Peter Gutierrez
University of Massachusetts, Amherst
Amherst, MA U.S.A.

Chris Moffatt
Philip DesAutels
Microsoft Corporation

Abstract
In order to respond to dynamic challenges, this paper argues that companies can develop a resilient capacity through the development of virtual teams and use of enabling technologies such as video-conferencing. The ability to respond to change creates pressure for proactive responses and the development of organizational flexibility and structural agility. Virtual teams and the use of technology such as video-conferencing can help organizations meet the evolving challenges of the business world and enable organizations to adapt better. This technology enables workers to increase their productive capacity and take advantage of expert collaborations. As a result, managers are looking to video-conferencing technology to help implement initiatives on the development of organizational resilience.

This practitioner report relates experiences from a project designed to give students experience of virtual teams in which the skills necessary to become effective members of a resilient organization can be acquired. This practitioner report also attempts to relate the tactics management uses to build resilient organizations and the supporting role video-conferencing can play. A new video-conferencing technology—ConferenceXP—is also described as a platform for the creation of flexible, distributed and virtual teams.

Keywords   Video-conferencing, virtual teams, organizational resilience

Please use the following format when citing this chapter:

Scott, Murray, Sorcinelli, Gino, Gutierrez, Peter, Moffatt, Chris, DesAutels, Philip, 2006, in International Federation for Information Processing (IFIP), Volume 206, The Transfer and Diffusion of Information Technology for Organizational Resilience, eds. B. Donnellan, Larsen T., Levine L., DeGross J. (Boston: Springer), pp. 219-227.

1   INTRODUCTION

Competitive pressures constantly force organizations to reevaluate their business strategies (Porter 2001; Venkatraman 1994). Indeed, in the current business environment, the attainment of success is due more to the continuous capacity for change rather than relying on traditional advantages (Hamel and Valikangas 2003). The ability to respond to change creates pressure for proactive responses and the development of organizational flexibility and structural agility (Paul et al. 2004). Virtual teams and the use of technology such as video-conferencing can help organizations meet the evolving challenges of the business world and enable organizations to adapt better (Townsend et al. 1998).

This practitioner report describes a project underway to create a virtual problem-based learning project, where students develop the socio-technical skills necessary to become effective members of globally distributed virtual teams.

2   THEORETICAL BACKGROUND

In order to respond to dynamic challenges, this paper argues that companies can develop a resilient capacity through the development of virtual teams and use of enabling technologies such as video-conferencing. Virtual teams are commonly described as a group of geographically dispersed individuals, formed to complete a specific project, that communicate using information and communications technology (Sarker and Sahay 2003).

Recent trends such as globalization, distributed teams, and market pressures for new product development have increasingly led to the development of cross-functional virtual teams (Paul et al. 2004). With the increasing shift from the production of material goods to information-based products, virtual teams not only have increased in economic importance but also provide important benefits such as increased utilization of employee time and availability and the ability to leverage expert knowledge regardless of location (Quinn 1992).

The effective utilization of human skill is an important factor not only in achieving resilience (Hamel and Valikangas 2005) but also in the fostering of innovation in virtual teams. Virtual teams have frequently been cited as suitable environments for innovative potential given their focus on problem solving and the resultant need for expert knowledge and creativity (Vissers and Dankbaar 2002). The scarce availability of such expert knowledge coupled with other competitive factors such as travel and cost have created a significant demand for companies to explore technological platforms to facilitate the work of virtual teams (Press 1998). One of the most promising of these communications technologies is video-conferencing (Fish et al. 1993).

2.1 Communication: Supporting Innovation
      in Virtual Teams

Innovation capacity is influenced by communication levels in an organization. For example, in large organizations, the connection between external market opportunities and internal organizational resources may appear, on the surface, to be somewhat *ad hoc*. This linkage between internal and external actors depends on communication channels to facilitate the routing of information about new market opportunities. In practice, innovative capacity is dependant on informal social networks of professional acquaintances who make the linkages needed to form the appropriate project teams and realize the potential of new ideas. Proponents of this view emphasize three aspects of communication: first, the importance of context, second, the role of narrative, and third, the so-called "small world network" phenomenon. These three concepts will be expanded upon in this section.

2.1.1 Context

Researchers in knowledge management have drawn attention to the importance of context in knowledge creation. Nonaka and Konno (1998) see knowledge as being embedded in *ba* (shared places), where it is then acquired through one's own experience or reflections on the experiences of others. Snowdon (2000) describes a somewhat similar concept that he calls *cynefin*—a Welsh word that represents the link between a community and its shared history "in a way that paradoxically both limits the perception of that community while enabling an instinctive and intuitive ability to adopt to conditions of profound uncertainty" (p. 10). Snowdon uses the concept to emphasize that people never start from a zero base when a knowledge management system is being designed because all members of the system come with baggage, positive and negative, derived from multiple histories.

2.1.2 Narrative

Denning (2004) emphasizes the importance of narratives in innovation processes. In his view, narratives capture context whereas abstractions decontextualize knowledge. Narratives also communicate tacit knowledge. Through narrative, people tell more than they know whereas abstractions only convey explicit knowledge.

Bolin et al. (2004) show how some common organizational initiatives like business process reengineering and total quality management tend to fail in motivating and engaging people sufficiently and outlined an alternative method for driving change management through narrative. They view narrative as a vehicle for change and organizational development and propose the use of myths, tales, and stories as triggers in change projects in order to develop a creative and dynamic atmosphere in which change can be achieved.

2.1.3 Small World Networks

Freeman (1991), in his review of the literature, noted that empirical studies of innovation since the 1950s had demonstrated "the importance of both formal and informal networks, even if the expression *network* was less frequently used" (p. 502), and that "multiple sources of information and pluralistic patterns of collaboration were the rule rather than the exception" (p. 503) Indeed, Allen et al. (1983) contend that "the overwhelming dominance of personal contact in technology transfer has been replicated in study after study, yet it is consistently ignored by policy-makers" (p. 201).

In order to describe the transition from a regular lattice to a random graph, Watts and Strogatz (1998) introduced the concept of small-world network. It is notable that the small-world phenomenon is indeed very common. Another interesting manifestation of the "small-world effect" is Milgram's (1967) so-called "six degrees of separation" principle, suggested by a social psychologist.

The research by Watts and Strogatz on small world networks and by Barabási and Albert (1999) on "scale-free" networks has enlarged our concept of what actually constitutes a network. The key contribution of this new small world network view is that it should be possible to configure links in a social network in a manner so as to get a small-world network effect (where information can flow across the network in a relatively few hops), but also retain the benefits of high clustering (where closely knit groups focus on their specific goals and deliverables). The key to the approach is the identification of social connectors. "Sprinkled among every walk of life…are a handful of people with a truly extraordinary knack of making friends and acquaintances. They are connectors" (Gladwell 2000, p. 20).

2.2 Video-Conferencing and Resilience

Video-conferencing provides the technical platform to facilitate the interaction of virtual team members and offers better communication opportunities than other computer-mediated tools due to enhanced social presence and the potential for high levels of media richness (Townsend et al. 2001). As a result, this technology enables workers to increase their productive capacity and take advantage of expert collaborations (Kettinger and Grover 1997). Managers are looking to video-conferencing technology to help implement initiatives on the development of organizational resilience (see Table 1).

In order to achieve the benefits of virtual teams and develop organizational resilience, the successful diffusion and implementation of this technology is critical. From a study of video-conferencing in virtual workgroups, Townsend et al (2001) argue that there is a clear imperative for organizations to teach employees how to interact effectively in a virtual environment. It is also noted that perceptions of the technology are moderated by the social experiences of the users and that the subsequent evaluation of its usefulness is determined by a complex set of cultural beliefs and expectations (Sarker and Sahay 2003; Townsend et al. 2001). Valikangas (2004, p. 2) identifies four steps to corporate resilience and points out that the first and fundamental step is the development of a "greater willingness to access information from multiple sources for richer content ….so that cross-functional decision making gets better results."

Table 1. Resilience and ICT to Support Virtual Teams (adapted from "Putting Organizational Resilience to Work," L. Mallak, *Industrial Management* (40:6), 1998)

Tactics Used by Managers to Build a Resilient Organization	How Can Video-Conferencing Can Play a Supporting Role
Use positive reinforcement to increase the frequency and intensity of desired behaviors.	Provide platform for regular feedback, public recognition and encouragement.
Provide constructive feedback when individuals fail so they can see what went wrong and walk away from the experience with a positive mental framework.	Facilitate "after-action reviews" of what went wrong so that staff walk away from the experience with a positive mental state.
Gradually expand decision-making boundaries.	Promote the flow of information across the team so that the quality of decision-making is enhanced.
Break down organizational structures that act as barriers against resilience.	Enable inputs to be gathered and participation to be nurtured from all levels and locations of the organization.
Develop bricolage skills.	By stressing the need to design and implement solutions on the fly in a problem-based learning environment, staff become more comfortable about taking the necessary steps and calculated risks to solve problems and satisfy customers.

3 PRACTICE REPORT: IMPLEMENTING CONFERENCEXP IN A MULTICULTURAL, COLLABORATIVE, PROBLEM-BASED LEARNING ENVIRONMENT

During the 2005 academic year, students from the University of Massachusetts, Amherst (UMass) participated in a cross-cultural, collaborative project with the National University of Ireland, Galway. The Business Information Systems (BIS) program at NUI Galway and the Isenberg School revised their curriculum so students learn to manage, share, and use information technology more effectively in collaborative work-group settings. Connecting the workplace and the classroom to enhance the educational experiences of management students and prepare them to become future business leaders who can survive and thrive in an environment that mandates organizational resilience is the driving force behind this cross-cultural educational effort. This project made use of ConferenceXP, a conferencing platform developed by Microsoft Research (MSR), to connect students in a virtual transatlantic classroom.

3.1 Project Objectives

In line with the characteristics of virtual team work and the imperative to provide instruction in the use of video-conferencing, faculty members from BIS and UMass derived two main project objectives: (1) to provide students with experience of the technology so they can align communication and decision making for problem solving and in doing so use video-conferencing to evaluate alternatives, and (2) to provide experience of working in virtual teams in a cross-cultural environment. The focus on problem-solving in this environment is further supported by Mallak (1998), who identifies members of the resilient organization as sharing decision-making power which in turn enables timely and effective responses to unexpected change.

Faculty members in both programs have identified the following learning objectives for the students:

- To master problem-solving skills through searching for, retrieving, analyzing, synthesizing, and integrating information and ideas
- To distill information into manageable categories and translate that information into effective business decisions
- To collaborate and work productively with others in multicultural work environments

3.2 Project Design

There are two key components to this project's pedagogical design. The first is the design of IT-related exercises and group projects that (1) build on the strengths of a cross-cultural educational environment, (2) foster interdependence among students, (3) are relevant to student learning goals, and (4) fit student skill sets and abilities. The second is a facilitation methodology for cross-cultural learning groups that builds on the best practices of effective teaching, but also adapts them to account for environmental and cultural differences.

4   THE CONFERENCEXP PROJECT

The UMass/BIS project made use of ConferenceXP as the video-conferencing platform. The ConferenceXP project was initiated at Microsoft Research in 2002. The main goal of this project was to provide a platform that would enable and support the creation of flexible, distributed, and virtual teams. To date, research and investigation around ConferenceXP has been directed toward exploring its effectiveness in distributed learning and collaborative learning environments in higher education.   The ConferenceXP project also attempts to take advantage of the availability of increased bandwidth and computing power to create a low cost, highly scalable platform of high fidelity conferencing and collaboration over the Internet. ConferenceXP provides a unique implementation of video-conferencing as it makes use of new technologies and platforms such as multicasting and Internet 2.

4.1 ConferenceXP Services and Applications

ConferenceXP provides three services that enhance and extend its functionality. The ConferenceXP venue service manages venues which are virtual spaces where users can participate in real-time collaboration activities. The ConferenceXP archive service enables recording and playback ConferenceXP sessions.

These core services provide the platform for researchers who can design and prototype collaborative and innovative applications that take advantage of the ConferenceXP platform.

4.2 ConferenceXP Platform and Architecture

The foundation of the ConferenceXP project is the ConferenceXP research platform, which enables researchers and developers to deploy distributed applications that incorporate support for high-quality, low-latency audio and video conferencing over broadband networks, as well as collaborative applications like shared presentation, ink-enabled annotations using Tablet PC's, and shared video.

The ConferenceXP client provides built-in support for high-quality, multi-point conferencing over high-bandwidth, multicast-enabled networks. The multi-point conferencing capability supports full-screen, real-time video at 30 frames per second, as well as collaborative applications like chat, shared presentation, and shared video. Presentation and ink-enabled annotations are integrated with Microsoft OneNote.

5 CONCLUSION

The importance of video conferencing lies in the ability of the technology to provide an enabling environment for creativity and flexibility and hence to support resilience. This paper has highlighted the need for companies to possess the ability to respond to environmental pressures in order to remain competitive. Developing a resilient capacity, therefore, requires management to ensure that employees have the necessary skills to become effective members of a resilient organization. Such tactics include positive reinforcement of desired behaviors, providing constructive feedback, encouraging the expansion of decision-making boundaries, removing organizational barriers to resilience and the development of bricolage skills. Video-conferencing is an important enabling technology in this context as it provides a platform for feedback, facilitates experiential reviews, promotes the gathering and flow of information, and provides a supportive problem-based learning environment.

This practitioner report describes a project undertaken by UMass and NUIG to develop a course that provides such an environment for students to learn these skills and in doing so enable students to become more effective employees in the future. The key features of the course design were to create assignments that promoted a problem-based learning approach, encouraged students to access and synthesize information from multiple sources, enabled a sharing of decision-making power, and exposed students to the communication challenges inherent in cross-cultural virtual teams.

This project was made possible through the use of ConferenceXP, the product of a three year research project from Microsoft Research. This technology was specifically designed to provide organizations with a platform to enable the creation of virtual teams and was further motivated by the recent increase in bandwidth to provide high quality video-conferencing facilitates.

References

Allen, T., Hyman, D., and Pickney, D. L. "Transferring Technology to the Small Manufacturing Firm: A Study of Technology Transfer in Three Countries," *Research Policy* (1242), 1983, pp. 199-211.

Barabási, A-L., and Albert, R. "Emergence of Scaling in Random Networks," *Science* (286), 1999, pp. 509-512.

Bolin, M., Ljungberg, J., and Bergquist, M. "A Narrative Approach to Change Management," Fifth European Conference on Organizational Knowledge, Learning and Capabilities, Innsbruck, Austria, 2004.

Denning, P. "The Social Life of Innovation," *Communications of the ACM* (47:4), 2004, pp. 15-20.

Fish, R. S., Kraut, R. E., Root, R. W., and Rice, R. E. "Video as a Technology for Informal Communication," *Communications of the ACM* (36:1), 1993, pp. 48-61.

Freeman, C. "Networks of Innovators: A Synthesis of Research Issues," *Research Policy* (20:5), 1991, pp. 499-514.

Gladwell, M. *The Tipping Point*, London: Abacus, 2000.

Hamel, G., and Valikangas, L. "The Quest for Resilience," *Harvard Business Review* (81:9), 2003, pp. 52-63.

Hamel, G., and Valikangas, L. "In Search of Resilience," The Woodside Institute, Woodside, CA, 2005 (available online through http://www.woodsideinstitute.org/pubslist.php).

Kettinger, W. J., and Grover, V. "The Use of Computer-Mediated Communication in an Inter-organizational Context," *Decision Sciences* (28:3 1997, pp. 513-556.

Mallak, L. "Putting Organizational Resilience to Work," *Industrial Management* (40:6), 1998, p. 8-13.

Milgram, S. "The Small Wworld Problem," *Psychology Today* (2:60), 1967.

Nonaka, I., and Konno, N. "The Concept of '*Ba*': Building a Foundation for Knowledge Creation," *California Management Review* (40:3), 1998, pp. 40-53.

Paul, S., Seetharaman, P., Samarah, I., and Mykytyn, P. P. "Impact of Heterogeneity and Collaborative Conflict Management Style on the Performance of Synchronous Global Virtual Teams," *Information & Management* (41:3), 2004, pp. 303-321.

Porter, M. "Strategy and the Internet," *Harvard Business Review* (79:3), 2001, pp. 62-78.

Press, L. "Low Cost Estimation of Travel Trade-Offs," *Communications of the ACM* (41:6), 1998, pp. 17-20.

Quinn, J. B. *Intelligent Enterprise: A Knowledge and Service Based Paradigm for Industry*, New York: Free Press, 1992.

Sarker, S., and Sahay, S. "Understanding Virtual Team Development: An Interpretive Study," *Journal of the Association for Information Systems* (4), 2003, Article 4.

Snowdon, D. "Complex Acts of Knowing: Paradox and Descriptive Self-Awareness," *Journal of Knowledge Management*, Spring 2002.

Townsend, A., M., S. Demarie, M., and Henderson, A. R. "Desktop Video Conferencing in Virtual Workgroups: Anticipation, System Evaluation and Performance," *Information Systems Journal* (11:3), 2001, pp. 213-227.

Townsend, A., M., S. Demarie, M., and Henderson, A. R. "Virtual Teams: Technology and the Workplace of the Future," *Academy of Management Executive* (12:3), 1998, pp. 17-29.

Valikangas, L. "Four Steps to Corporate Resilience," *Strategy and Business News*, May 24, 2005.

Venkatraman, V. "IT-Enabled Business Transformation: From Automation to Business Scope Redefinition," *Sloan Management Review* (35:2), 1994, pp. 73-87.

Vissers, G., and Dankbaar, B. "Creativity in Multidisciplinary New Product Development Teams," *Creativity and Innovation Management* (11:1), 2002, pp. 31-42.

Watts, D. J., and Strogatz, S. H. "Collective Dynamics of 'Small-World' Networks," *Nature* (393), 1998, pp. 440-442.

About the Authors

Murray Scott is a lecturer in Information Systems at the National University of Ireland, Galway. He is currently pursuing a Ph.D. in electronic government at the National University of Ireland, Galway. His research interests include electronic government, stakeholder management theory and e-learning technologies. His research on electronic government has been published in leading international IS conferences, in *Journal of Electronic Commerce in Organizations, Business Process Management Journal,* and *International Journal of Services and Standards*. Murray can be reached by e-mail at Murray.scott@nuigalway.ie.

Gino Sorcinelli joined the Isenberg School of Management, University of Massachusetts Amherst, for fall semester 1994 as a member of the Accounting and Information Systems Department, and the Director of Computer Resources. Since assuming this position, he has been responsible for teaching courses about business information systems as well as managing the computer and network resources within the Isenberg School. Gino can be reached by e-mail at gino@som.umass.edu.

Peter Gutierrez is a network analyst at the University of Massachusetts, Amherst, where he works on the campus network and the connection to the Internet and Internet2. He has been there for 15 years, since the network was expanded from science and engineering schools to the entire campus. Peter can be reached by e-mail at peterg@nic.umass.edu.

Chris Moffatt is a senior program manager in the External Research and Programs group at Microsoft Research. He is a member of the Research Applications and Frameworks Team that builds research platforms and collaborates with universities to advance the state of the art of computing, and facilitates the development of innovative approaches to education that prepare students for the challenges of the future. Chris can be reached by e-mail at chrismof@ microsoft.com.

Philip DesAutels is the Academic Developer Evangelist for Microsoft Corporation supporting New England. His research interests include distributed applications, loosely coupled system and semantic tagging as means of enabling collaborative learning and working environments. He has applied these research areas in the past at Excite@Home, Ereo, PrivaSeek and the World Wide Web Consortium (W3C). Philip can be reached by e-mail at philipda@ microsoft.com.

16 ASPECTS ON INFORMATION SYSTEMS CURRICULUM: A Study Program in Business Informatics

Markus Helfert
Howard Duncan
Dublin City University
Dublin, Ireland

Abstract   *Despite the variety of traditional study programs related to Information Systems and the formation of combinations between computing, business, and management studies, at present universities seem to be not well prepared to equip graduates with the valuable knowledge and skills required for organizational transformation. Consequently, traditional study programs and career paths for Information Systems graduates might have to be revised and new programs established. Addressing the need for an innovative and cross-disciplinary study model to equip graduates with transformation skills, in 2003 we started to develop a master's program in Business Informatics. This paper outlines the core elements of this program and explores how we equip students with capabilities required for transformation processes. We provide experiences from the interdisciplinary accreditation process of the program and outline our future plans.*

Keywords   Transformation, business informatics, curriculum development, change management

1   INTRODUCTION

Driven by technological innovations, organizations periodically face radical and dramatic transformation, in which well-established structures, successful for decades, have started to change rapidly. Consequently organizations are frequently required to realign their structures. The need for transformation has accelerated the introduction of new methods, processes, and structures (Evans and Wurster 1999). However, many organizations fail to design technological solutions that provide a sustainable compe-

Please use the following format when citing this chapter:

Helfert, Markus, Duncan, Howard, 2006, in International Federation for Information Processing (IFIP), Volume 206, The Transfer and Diffusion of Information Technology for Organizational Resilience, eds. B. Donnellan, Larsen T., Levine L., DeGross J. (Boston: Springer), pp. 229-237.

titive advantage. In this context, organizational resilience is seen as one of the core capabilities for organizations and individuals to absorb strain and recover from untoward events through continuous reconstruction (Mallak 1998). Using Holling's (1973, p. 17) definition of resilience—"the capacity of a system to absorb and utilize or even benefit from perturbations and changes that attain it, and so to persist without a qualitative change in the system's structure"— the resilient organization designs and implements the structures effectively, as positive adaptive behaviors that are quickly matched to the immediate situations (Mallak 1998). However, individuals often face these situations without adequate training or preparation.

In general, information system graduates should be equipped with the capability to analyze organizational processes and solve business problems. Considering the difficulties noted above, they also require capabilities to initiate and lead transformation as well as understanding the wider social, economic, and cultural implications of proposed transformations. The interdisciplinary character will increase as claims that IT is no longer a source of strategic advantage have generated a growing concern over the loss of pure technology-oriented jobs (Carr 2003) and increased the demand for business-oriented IT jobs (Benamati and Mahanney 2004). It is expected that demand will increase for integration, enterprise architecture, information management, and business process management. The demand for graduates capable of coordinating complex information and supply chain networks and project mangers coordinating global IT projects is expected to increase. Young professionals may need to understand how to manage project teams and lead change, especially in geographically and ethnically diverse teams.

However, despite the fact that computing departments are forming valuable relationships with business and management studies, at present universities are often challenged to equip graduates with the required transformation skills. A recent exploratory study by Helfert and Duncan (2005) illustrates the variety of traditional Information Systems related study programs. Universities offer a variety of courses for many years. Nonetheless, the dynamics and rapid changes in recent years demand education programs that equip graduates with the capability to manage transformation. This is the core field of interest in this article, in which we provide some aspects on information system curriculum and outline a Master's program that is intended to equip graduates with the capabilities for organizational transformation.

As a thematic framework, we use the concept of "business informatics," which seems to be suitable to offer core capabilities related to managing IT-related transformations. Section three provides a summary of the experience made during the accreditation process and describes some characteristics of the program. We conclude our work with further directions and suggestions.

2   BUSINESS INFORMATICS

Over the past few decades, Business Informatics has matured as a stream of research and study within the field of Information Systems, with a growing number of universities offering study programs in Business Informatics. In contrast to *informatics*, which primarily concerns the technology of information and communication systems, and business, which focuses on management functions, *Business Informatics* centers on business information systems as socio-technical systems comprising both machines and humans (e.g., Ferstl and Sinz 2001; Gesellschaft für Informatik 2003; Heinrich 2001; Mertens 1998; Scheer 1998; Wissenschaftliche Kommission der Wirtschaftsinformatik 1994).

The success of the subject derives from a coherent methodological approach. Similar to the business engineering approach (Winter 2002), business informatics requires a holistic and interdisciplinary view of transformation, which not only considers technical and business aspects, but also cultural, political, and social issues that are crucial for successful transformation. Business informaticians must be capable of applying technical and managerial competence to envision, design, communicate, lead, and implement transformation projects. Guided by engineering principles, the transformation process is implemented through a methodological approach. Indeed the holistic and methodological approach based on engineering principles is central to business informatics, which can be summarized as a socio-technological and business oriented subject with *engineering* penetration (Disterer et al. 2003). Business informatics centers on information systems architectures and takes an active role in aligning business strategy, business processes, and information technology.

In order to construct a basic framework for business informatics study programs in our previous work (Helfert and Duncan 2005), we synthesized the MSIS 2000/IS 2002 model curriculum framework (Gorgone et al. 2000, 2002) and the recommendation for business informatics at universities (Gesellschaft für Informatik 2003). Our final framework is presented in the appendices. The structure follows basically the proposed curriculum building blocks in the MSIS curriculum. However, in order to accommodate the particular subjects related to business informatics, we added subject blocks of mathematics and logic, structural science, legislation, economics, and business engineering. We also included often-taught business subjects like logistics, procurement, and supply chain management. The list of career electives and domain-specific subjects presented here illustrates just some of the possible topics.

3   A MASTER OF SCIENCE IN BUSINESS INFORMATICS

3.1 Diversity of Information Systems

The curriculum for a Master's program in Business Informatics was developed over the last 2 to years, with the valuable support of an international accreditation board. The board included four international experts in the field of Business Informatics from Ireland, UK, and Austria. Representing the interdisciplinary character of the program, we aimed to include members from different backgrounds representing a thematically well-balanced accreditation board. Members of the board presented particular expertise in

- knowledge and data engineering and process modeling
- strategic information systems
- information systems management
- practical approaches in the banking sector

Table 1. Framework for Information Systems' Viewpoints

		Perspective		
		Informatics/ Computing	Information Systems	Business and Management
Aspect	Subjects/Topics to be included			
	Teaching mode			

Between the first proposal for the program in 2004 and the final recommendation for accreditation in May 2005, the accreditation board met and discussed the curriculum three times. During the meetings the diversity of particular expertise was reflected within the discussions and recommendations, which led to changes for the program. The diversity of different viewpoints made it difficult to maintain the characteristics of business informatics throughout the program. It seems the curriculum should include many related subjects ranging from business and information system strategy to mathematics, statistics and programming.

The discussions indicated that the controversy is often due to two complementary but fundamentally different streams in Information Systems, with on the one hand a technology, engineering, and method oriented perspective and, on the other, a business- and management-orientated focus. A different emphasis in Information Systems related degrees was observed, with an emphasis on management aspects on the one hand, and the business informatics and information systems engineering perspective on the other. In order to structure the different backgrounds and viewpoints we propose a framework that is illustrated in Table 1. This framework will be used in our further research to structure the diversity of Information Systems degrees.

3.2 Program Layout

The central focus of the proposed curriculum for business informatics is to qualify individuals to lead IS-related transformations, enabling them to apply technological solutions and develop information system architectures to solve business problems of organizations. With this goal in mind, the curriculum focuses on an engineering perspective and the integration of cultural studies. The program is intended for students who have achieved a primary degree in Computing, Computer Science, Software Engineering, or a comparable discipline. The program is designed to be completed in one calendar year of full-time study and consists of two taught semesters followed by a practical project.

3.2.1 Curriculum Structure

The curriculum emphasizes engineering principles and includes a module on structural science, which encompasses management science, data engineering, and data mining. It also has a strong modeling component, and includes modules on IS architec-

Table 2. Curriculum Overview

Semester 1	• Research Skills/Seminar Topics • Information System Architecture • Structural Science	• Business Process Management • Strategic Management of Information Technology • Business Studies
Semester 2	• Supply Chain Management • Managing and Working in an Intercultural Environment • Managing Change	• Sectoral applications of Information Systems • Regulation in Information Systems • Project Management
Summer	• Dissertation/Practicum	

ture and business process management. The integrative perspective is provided by the supply chain management module. The program also covers the more traditional Information Systems disciplines such as strategic management of information technology. An overview of the general program structure is provided in Table 2. Three complementary strands can be identified in the program, which can be related to our business informatics framework: business and consulting skills, information technology/information systems in business, and informatics in action. These are illustrated in the appendix.

3.2.2 Transferable Skills

In addition to the emphasis on engineering principles and core subjects of business informatics, the study program also supports the building of capabilities for managing transformations by aiming to expand transferable skills. In essence, transferable skills are those skills which, having been learned in one context, can then be applied in another. A summary of transferable skills by module is provided in the appendix. Typically these skills are based on modern teaching, learning, and assessment methods, that include

- guided independent study and activity, with specialist input when appropriate
- recent or current case studies
- essay and report writing
- collaborative group work and discussions
- presentation of findings to the group as a whole

3.2.3 Practicum

In the final semester, from May to August, students work on a *practicum* or major project of a practical nature. The general objective of the practicum is to allow students to draw on the theoretical knowledge gained over the taught element and to apply it in a practical setting in a European environment. The practicum gives students the opportunity to demonstrate their ability to analyze problems in the field of Business Informatics and draw conclusions according to scientific methods within a given time frame.

4 CONCLUSION AND FUTURE DIRECTIONS

This paper presented aspects on an Information Systems related curriculum and summarized some experiences gained during the accreditation process. The final curriculum as outlined above comprises a balanced and interdisciplinary structure, which centered on engineering principles and focuses on transformation, models, and methods. The engineering penetration throughout the program is seen as one important characteristic, which differentiates this program from management oriented information systems degrees. Therefore, the business informatics approach appears to us not only to be innovative with regard to its interdisciplinary character, but moreover the engineering perspective and the integration of cultural studies and practical experiences in an international setting equip graduates with required transformation capabilities. The program will be launched in September 2006, and further evaluation and adjustments to the curriculum might be required. In our further research we intend to analyze the differences to other information system programs. Also, an evaluation of the gained capabilities in the form of transformation skills would be interesting.

References

Benamati, S., and Mahaney, R. "The Future Job Market for Information System Graduates," in *Proceedings of the 10th Americas Conference on Information Systems*, New York, 2004, pp. 2925-2928.

Carr, N. G. "IT Doesn't Matter," *Harvard Business Review* (85:5), 2003, pp. 41-49.

Disterer, G., Fels, F., and Hausotter, A.(eds). *Taschenbuch der Wirtschaftsinformatik* (2nd ed.), Munich: Carl Hanser Verlag, 2003.

Evans, P., and Wurster, T. S. *Blown to Bits: How the New Economics of Information Transforms Strategy*, Boston: Harvard Business School Press, 1999.

Ferstl, O. K., and Sinz, E. J. *Grundlagen der Wirtschaftsinformatik* (4th ed.), Munich: Oldenbourg, 2001.

Gesellschaft für Informatik. "Rahmenempfehlung für die Universitätsausbildung in Wirtschaftsinformatik," *Informatik Spektrum* (25:2), 2003, pp. 108-113.

Gorgone, J., Feinstein, D., Longenecker, H. E., Topi, H., Valacich, J. S., and Davis, G. B. "Undergraduate Information Systems Model Curriculum Update–IS 2002," in R. Ramsower and J. Windsor (eds.), *Proceedings of the Eighth Americas Conference on Information Systems*, Dallas, TX, 2002, pp. 808-815.

Gorgone, J., Gray, P., Feinstein, D., Kasper, G. M., Luftman, J. N., Stohr, E. A., Valacich, J. S., Wigand R. T. "Model Curriculum and Guidelines for Graduate Degree Programs in Information Systems," *Communication of the Association for Information Systems* (3:1), 2000, pp. 1-51.

Heinrich L. J. *Wirtschaftsinformatik—Einführung und Grundlegung* (2nd ed.), Munich: Oldenbourg, 2001.

Helfert, M., and Duncan, H. "Business Informatics and Information Systems—Some Indications of Differences in Study Programs," in D. Wainwright (ed.), *Proceedings of UKAIS Conference*, Northumbria University, Newcastle upon Tyne, March 24, 2005.

Holling, C. S. "Resilience and Stability of Ecological Systems," *Annual Review of Ecology and Systematics* (4), 1973, pp. 1-23.

Mallak, L. A, "Putting Organizational Resilience to Work," *Industrial Management* (40:6), 1998, pp. 8-13.

Mertens, P. "Geschichte und ausgewählte Gegenwartsprobleme der Wirtschaftsinformatik," *WiSt Wirtschaftswissenschaftliches Studium* (24:4), 1998, pp. 170-175.

Scheer, A.-W. *Wirtschaftsinformatik—Referenzmodelle für industrielle Geschäftsprozesse (Studienausgabe)* (2nd ed.), Berlin: Springer, 1998.

Wissenschaftliche Kommission der Wirtschaftsinformatik. "Profil der Wirtschaftsinformatik," *Wirtschaftsinformatik* (35:1), 1994, pp. 80-81.

Winter, R. "An Executive MBA Program in Business Engineering: A Curriculum Focusing on Change," *Journal of Information Technology Education* (1:4), 2002, pp. 279-288.

About the Authors

Markus Helfert is a lecturer in Information Systems at the School of Computing, Dublin City University (Ireland). His research centers on information quality management and includes research areas such as data warehousing, healthcare information systems, supply chain management, and information system architectures. He is program chair for the European Master of Science in Business Informatics. Markus can be reached by e-mail at markus.helfert@computing.dcu.ie.

Howard Duncan is a lecturer at the School of Computing, Dublin City University (Ireland). His research interests are in business process management, software engineering, and project management. He teaches courses in business organization, application programming, and business process management. Howard can be reached by e-mail at howard@computing.dcu.ie.

Appendix A: Thematic Division of the Business Informatics Framework and Coverage of Topics

Informatics and Fundamentals in Engineering	Business and Economics	Information Systems	Integration and Enterprise Engineering	Informatics in Action (representative)
Information and Communication Technology (Hardware, Software, Networks and Communication Technology) (a) *Programming and Algorithms, Data and Object Structures* (a) *Mathematics and Logic* (Analysis, linear Algebra, Numeric, Logic) (a) *Structural Science* (Decision theory and methods for strategic decision making (e.g. risk analysis), statistics and quantitative models and methods, operations research, computational modeling and simulation) (c)	*Accounting and Financing* (b) *Marketing, Production, Procurement, Logistics* (b) *Organization, human resources and corporate management* (b) *Legislation and Economics* (b)	*Fundamentals of Information Systems* (Types of IS, IS Industry, IS relevant legal frameworks, Management and IS) (c) *Principles of Business Information Systems* (Principles of functional and process orientation and industry solutions) (c) *Data Engineering* (Data modeling and management, knowledge engineering and business intelligence) (c) *System and Software Engineering* (analysis, modeling and design) (a) *Managing Data Communication and Networking* (a) *Information Management* (Information, Knowledge and People, Project and Change Management, IS/IT Policy and Strategy, Ethics and Privacy) (c)	*Business Engineering and Information System Architecture* (c) *Integrating Information System Functions, Processes and Data* (c) *Integrating Information System Technologies and Systems* (a)	Academia and Research (b) Academic and Research) Libraries (b) Biochemistry and Molecular Biology Consulting Consumer Health Information (d) Customer Relationship Management (d) Data Warehousing (d) Decision Making E-Government Information Electronic Commerce Electronic Publishing Environmental management Financing and Banking (d) Healthcare Information (d) Human Factors Insurance Management Knowledge Management Library Services Logistics Multimedia Technologies Project Management (d) Techniques of IT-consulting (d) Technology Management (d)

Notes: a.   Prerequisite (knowledge gained in previous degree)   c.   Information Technology/Information Systems in Business
             b.   Business and Consulting Skills   d.   Informatics in Action

Appendix B. Summary of Transferable Skills by Module

Module	Critical Thinking	Problem Management and Solving	Research Skills and Methods	Communication	Group-Work and Interpersonal Skills	Intercultural, Social and Community Awareness	Planning, Organizing and Resource Management
Research Skills/Seminar Topics	●	○	●	◑			◑
Information System Architecture	○	○					
Structural Science	○	●					◑
Business Process Management	○	●	◑				◑
Regulation in IS	○	○				◑	◑
Business Studies	○			○		◑	◑
Strategic Management of Information Technology	○	◑		●	◑		●
Supply Chain Management	○	●		◑	○		◑
Sectoral applications of Information Systems	○	◑			◑	○	◑
Project Management	◑	◑	●	◑	◑	○	●
Managing Change	○	◑		●	●		
Managing and Working in an Intercultural Environment	○	○		●	●	●	
Practicum	●	●	●	●	●	●	●

Legend:
● Considerable development
◑ Moderate development
○ Some development
  Negligible development

17 THE RISE OF THE PHOENIX: Methodological Innovation as a Discourse of Renewal

David Wastell
Nottingham University Business School
Nottingham, UK

Tom McMaster
Information Systems Institute, University of Salford
Greater Manchester, UK

Peter Kawalek
Manchester Business School
Manchester, UK

Abstract   *The imperatives on contemporary organizations to adapt to an uncertain and turbulent environment are intense. Resilience refers to the ability to cope with change through a continuous process of renewal. The pace of change is at least as great in the public as the private sector, with technology being integral to the UK government's modernization agenda. This represents a stiff challenge for the traditional, technically oriented IT department. Here we recount the history of one such department in a local government institution as it sought to reinvent itself to respond to these new demands. The development of an IS methodology, embodying a business and customer-centered approach, was seen as key to generating the required capacity to support strategic change in the wider organization. Although methodological innovation can be problematic, here it was brought off successfully. This was attributed to several factors, including the adoption of a participative action research approach and the commitment of senior IT management. Above all, the sense of crisis prevailing at the outset of the initiative was decisive. Crises present a major challenge to organizational sense-making; here the impending threat was interpreted positively as a proactive opportunity to develop a new strategic identity. A resilient "discourse of renewal" was kindled, with the need to build new technical capabilities through methodological innovation playing a central part.*

Please use the following format when citing this chapter:

Wastell, David, McMaster, Tom, Kawalek, Peter, 2006, in International Federation for Information Processing (IFIP), Volume 206, The Transfer and Diffusion of Information Technology for Organizational Resilience, eds. B. Donnellan, Larsen T., Levine L., DeGross J. (Boston: Springer), pp. 239-256.

Keywords   Organizational resilience, public sector, modernization, methodological innovation, action research, discourse of renewal, organizational crisis, micropolitics

1 INTRODUCTION

Every 500 years (or 540, 1,000, 1,461, even 12,994, depending on the cultural context!), the legendary and beautifully plumaged Phoenix[1] self-cremates in its nest of cinnamon twigs, rising again to embalm the ashes of the old Phoenix in an egg of myrrh. Something of a Jungian archetype symbolizing the universal cycle of birth, death, and rebirth, the Phoenix figures widely as a cultural motif in religious ritual and imagery, classical and popular culture, flags and other symbolic artefacts. Renewal is the theme of this paper, in the more prosaic context of organizational resilience, which refers to the internal processes of equilibration that ensure the continuity of systems in the face of destabilizing events, shocks, and disturbances (i.e., stressful environmental challenges that threaten viability). Faced with such threats, a variety of reactions are possible, but of interest here is the potential for renewal, reinvention, or reconstruction to better meet the exigencies of a changing world. Through a "discourse of renewal," organizational entities, like the Phoenix, may rise again from their metaphorical ashes. Here we tell the story of how one such group, the IT department in a large public sector bureaucracy, undertook its quest for self-renewal. The case is of particular relevance in the context of IFIP WG8.6, as the development of an innovative IS methodology was the key to survival and prosperity. While the fortunes of the IT group provide the main narrative interest, its transformation has afforded new capacities which have augmented the resilience of the organization as a whole. Indeed, this was the key to the department's regeneration strategy.

In general, these are certainly interesting times for the IS/IT function. As organizations come to rely more and more on technology to deliver strategy and drive performance, the pressures on IT departments have steadily intensified (Fitzgerald et al. 2002). The threat of outsourcing looms large, serving to encourage those who might falter or fail. A challenging world indeed for the traditional IT department, immured in the basement of the organization. The imperatives for organizational change are at least as pressing in today's public sector as in the commercial sphere. The injunctions to reform and modernize public services are strident and ubiquitous, encapsulated in the global mantras of the new public management (Wastell 2006). Technology is integral to this change agenda. The vocabulary of eGovernment depicts information and communication technology (ICT), in language bordering on the evangelical, as the

---

[1]Firebird, Benu, Fenghuang, Ho-oo, or Yel according to ancient Russian, Egyptian, Chinese, Japanese, and Native Americans, respectively. As a symbol of renewal, examples are easily found, including the flags of Atlanta and San Francisco, both depicting the Phoenix surmounting a wreath of flames, symbolizing renaissance from human and natural disaster. This paper itself is a Phoenix, a palimpsest resurrected from the ruins of so many earlier versions!

talismanic enabler of transformation (Kawalek and Wastell 2005).[2] Here, the IT/IS function in a metropolitan local authority recognized that it was becoming increasingly marginal to the operations of the organization as a whole. It did not provide the capability required to support an ambitious program of strategic change that had been articulated in the authority's business strategy, or to respond to the ever-pressing injunctions of the external modernization agenda. Faced with this crisis, rather than adopting a defensive stance, they embarked upon a proactive process of internal reforms in order to reposition themselves in the strategic vanguard of the organization. At the heart of this was a new methodological approach to the development of information systems embodying a more business and customer-oriented ethos.

Innovation in IS practice is a problematic endeavor. Research on the implementation of new software tools evidences substantial resistance and frequent rejection (Iivari 1996; Orlikowski 1993), and much greater resistance is to be expected for complete methodologies given the scale of change involved (Hardgrave et al. 2003). Methodologies are more embracing than individual tools, requiring substantial restructuring rather than more localized changes. Huisman and Iivari (2006) report that methodologies tend to be more favored by managers than developers. Nandhakumar and Avison (1999) describe methodologies as a "necessary fiction" of symbolic status but too mechanistic to be of practical use. The critical studies of Kautz and McMaster (1994) and Wastell (1996) also narrate the vicissitudes of implementing structured methods. Fitzgerald et al. (2002) comment generally on the widely reported low level of method use, especially among experienced developers, echoing the general scepticism found in earlier studies (e.g., Fitzgerald 1998). These authors provide a useful framework for understanding the technical and political rationalities of "methods-in-action" and of the barriers that militate against the adoption of formalized approaches (e.g., the messiness and contingencies of real-world practice). Significantly, they highlight the political role played by formalized methods in professionalizing and legitimizing IS practice, paving the way for a more proactive role of IS in strategy formulation. The comfort/confidence factor is also emphasized, recalling the tendency of developers to "fetishize" methods, as recounted in Wastell (1996).

The dominant theoretical approach for the study of innovation in our field draws on the classical diffusionist framework of Rogers (1995), which has spawned the influential technology adoption model (Davis et al. 1989). Recent papers applying TAM to methodological change include Templeton and Byrd (2003) and Hardgrave et al. (2003). In essence, Rogers portrays innovation as a decision-making process in which individual adopters decide whether to embrace a new technology or not. The limitations of Rogers for understanding organizational innovation have been addressed by Van de Ven (1995), who highlights the step-change in complexity of organizational processes as opposed to individual adoption decisions. A more recent critique in an organizational context is provided by Lundblad (2003). The limitations of technology focused accounts and the need to examine the broader social context of IS innovations has also been emphasized by Kautz and Nielsen (2004). In this paper, we develop this discourse further by

---

[2]The recently published National IT Strategy, for instance, is emblematically entitled "Transformational Government Enabled by Technology" (Cabinet Office 2005). eGovernment (in the UK) is seemingly passé; tGovernment's the thing!

reframing methodological innovation as predominantly an issue of organizational change, rather than technology adoption. This reframing brings to bear fresh theory from organizational science to cast new light on the problematics of innovation, in particular on the key role of organizational crises as the drivers of change.

The role of crises as instigators of change is hardly novel. Gersick's (1991) concept of punctuated equilibrium reflects the idea that the *status quo* will prevail in organizations unless there is a perceived need for change. Shocks are required to overcome this organizational inertia; "only when people reach a threshold of sufficient dissatisfaction with existing conditions, [will] they initiate action to resolve their dissatisfaction" (Van de Ven 1995, p. 275). The concept of organizational crisis is a nuanced one, going beyond the stereotypical notion of a seismic event, arising out of the blue. Such crises may arise from many sources (Kovoor-Misra et al. 2001): from technological disasters, from declining performance, but equally from growth too (developmental crises). While they may often be abrupt, unexpected and infrequent, equally they may be slow-moving, predictable, and recurrent. Common to all usages is the presence of a serious existential threat to the organization, arising from some exogenous or endogenous source, together with a degree of time pressure to respond (Kovoor-Misra et al. 2001). Crises may evoke a range of organizational responses from passivity to active coping. Defensive reactions all too often occur (Wastell 1999) when severe threats are confronted, including a state of paralysis described as "threat-rigidity" (Barnett and Pratt 2000). But crises may provide innovatory opportunities too: to deal with problems, to unfreeze old behaviors, to develop new ways of understanding and acting (Kovoor-Misra et al. 2001). Seeger et al. (2005) refer to this positive, post-crisis orientation as a *discourse of renewal*, its hallmark being a practical, prospective orientation to the future rather than an exculpatory and defensive attitude to the past.

Here we advance the general argument that methodological innovation should be understood as organizational change. The outcome of the initiative will be contingent on a range of nontechnical, organizational factors, which are more fundamental than the technological features of the innovation itself. In particular, there must be a potent sense of purpose, a crisis, driving the change, with the methodological innovation seen as a developmental opportunity, a progressive solution to the impending threat (Kovoor-Misra et al. 2001). Without this clarity of purpose and the keenly felt need to change, the attempt to innovate is likely to founder. The paper will cover the following broad areas. It will first describe the local context and the change process within the field setting before moving on to outline the results of this process. We will conclude by reflecting on what has been learned regarding the practical accomplishment of resilience and the nature of methodological innovation as a process of organizational change.

2   ANTECEDENT CONTEXT AND METHODOLOGY

The setting for the project is Salford City Council (SCC), a local government institution in the North West of England. Salford is a medium-sized city of around 250,000 inhabitants, and one of 10 local authorities making up the Greater Manchester conurbation. Like most local authorities in Britain, SCC is organized around key service areas, such as housing, social services, education, etc. There is a central IT services department (ITSD) staffed (at the outset of the story) by around 20 professionals organized in a number of specialist teams (e.g., software development, PC support).

The story begins in the summer of 1999, shortly after the "failure" of ITSD to implement a CASE tool in a project (CAPELLA) supported by European funding. This antecedent failure is significant and will be returned to in the "Discussion." More details of CAPELLA may be found in Kautz et al. (1999), with a recent analysis of its miscarriage appearing in McMaster and Wastell (2004). In short, CAPELLA foundered because key stakeholders (practitioners especially) were uncommitted to the use of the CASE tool, which became increasingly seen as marginal to the urgent, practical problems facing ITSD (e.g., Y2K, legacy system maintenance). Of particular salience here was the clarion call in CAPELLA's final report for "strong alignment of the introduction of new technologies [with] short term demands [and] long term business goals" (Williams and Willetts 1999, p. 3). The report went on to recommend the adoption of a new systems development methodology. The need for a more business-oriented approach had also been articulated in the City's Information Society Strategy, published earlier that year. The Strategy's aim was to harness the potential of IT to improve the social and economic well-being of the people of Salford. It was recognized that a business process reengineering (BPR) approach was required to implement the strategy, focusing on the innovative use of IT to realize radical business change. Quoting again from the CAPELLA report:

> Externally, requirements from Central Government to improve services and provide greater value for money, involving constant re-engineering of business processes, has placed Information Technology in a position of increasing expectations to aid such transformations...not only in delvering improved products, but in strengthening its capacity in coping with changes arising for new demands and expectations. (Williams and Willetts 1999, pp. 5-6)

The miscarriage of CAPELLA and the publication of the Information Society Strategy form key antecedent features of the local context. It is also important to consider change events in the wider environment of the sector as a whole (Meyer et al. 1995). Here the most potent forces relate to the emergence of eGovernment in the UK, which may be traced back to the publication of the central government's 1999 white paper, "Modernising Government" (Cabinet Office 1999). This challenged all public sector organizations (including local government) to deliver efficient and responsive citizen-centered services, and IT was seen as critical to achieving these aims. The ambitiousness of the agenda was reflected in the target to electronically enable 100 percent of relevant services, initially by 2008 but subsequently accelerated to 2005. Various national initiatives lent force to the modernization program. A so-called "Pathfinder" initiative was launched in 2001, whereby significant new funding was set aside for local authorities able to demonstrate a leading position in relation to some aspect of eGovernment.

Rather than adopting an external methodology, ITSD took the decision to develop its own (to be known as SPRINT) and the approach taken was action research (AR). Greenwood and Levin (1998) define AR as research carried out by a team of professional researchers in collaboration with members of an organization or community, the aim being to support action leading to a more just or satisfying situation for the stakeholders. Given its highly applied nature, the discipline of IS has long been seen as a natural application domain for action research (Baskerville and Wood-Harper

1998), the typical usage being to develop new systems (e.g., Davison 2001; Simon 2000). It is unusual to use AR as a tool for constructing new methodological approaches. Of note is a study by Mathiassen (2002) in which an AR-like approach was used to support and improve IS development practices in four organizations. Mathiassen refers to his mode of enquiry as *collaborative practice research.*

Work commenced in July 1999, spearheaded by a small AR team led by the head of ITSD, and also comprising two local academics (who had worked with SCC before, during CAPELLA) and several developers, including one section leader. The remit of the academics was to bring to bear their prior knowledge of IS methodology, to support the use of the emerging framework in practice, and to facilitate its further development. The academics also took prime responsibility for recording ideas and experiences, and acted as custodians of the evolving documentation of the methodology as it took shape. The role of the practitioners was to codevelop the emerging framework, contributing to its progressive refinement, applying it in practice, and reflecting on its strengths and weaknesses. The practical means of developing the framework was that of collaborative working and reflection, with all members of the team working closely together on a series of projects, using this shared experience as the basis for developing and refining the methodology. Much of this reflection was embedded in the work itself, during project meetings, informal discussions, etc., supplemented by *ad hoc* brainstorming sessions to capture key ideas and experiences. More formal workshops were also held off-site to discuss major developments to the methodology.

The following section will describe the history of the project. Table 1 provides a project time-line to support the narrative. It summarizes the main events that took place, in terms of internal developments and in the external environment (locally and nationally) that materially impinged on the work. The account has been constructed from the collective reflections of the AR team, corroborated where possible by contemporaneous documentation (e.g., workshop minutes, internal reports, policy documents). Formal interviews with key practitioners were carried out in the summer of 2004 to provide further reflection and corroboration, and to fill in any lacunae. Unless indicated otherwise, quotations in the text below were extracted from these interviews.

3   THE SPRINT CHRONICLES

As noted, the project was formally launched in July 1999, as one of the key work programs of the City's Information Society Strategy. BPR was seen as vital to delivering the Strategy's visionary aims: "to improve cost effectiveness, service responsiveness and co-operation across the City, joining-up service delivery across agencies" (City of Salford 1999, p 1). Interviewed in 2004, the head of ITSD reflected on the original motivation for the project:

> We were largely a traditional, technically orientated IT department; our people were predominantly technology people. We did try to understand the Council's strategic agenda but our alignment was vague. We were seen as people who built software, put PCs on desks and installed networks rather than adding strategic value.

Another senior officer in ITSD, subsequently to head up the BPR team, described the situation in very bleak terms:

> We went through a strange phase in the olden days. Departments increasingly thought they could do things for themselves, they could buy their own system and didn't need ITSD. This was leading us to stagnation in the way we were moving; we had no role or identity. Y2K also diverted us. We were hardly involved in the SAP procurement; we were too busy on Y2K. We were feeling very marginal at the time.

In the eyes of the head, the aim of the project was bold and radical, nothing less than to reposition IT as a "true enabler of business transformation." Work began based on prior BPR work by the academics, largely in the commercial sector (Wastell et al. 1994). This was reviewed by the AR team and a draft methodology produced in early October 1999, which was christened SPRINT (Salford Process Reengineering Involving New Technology). In mid-October, a paper was presented by the head of ITSD to SCC's senior management team recommending adoption of SPRINT and its deployment on a comprehensive program of BPR projects. Significantly, no additional resource was requested in order to carry out this ambitious initiative; it would be done within the existing IT budget. The recommendation was accepted and an internal BPR team was constituted to carry forward the work, in conjunction with the academics. In effect, this formalized the AR team. The first project carried out was crucial in proving and refining the methodology. It focused on the administrative team supporting the committee-based decision-making structures operational within the Council at that time. Work began in late October, and concluded in January 2000 with the production of a set of radical proposals. Far from mere office automation of the clerical function (as had been originally envisaged), the proposals focused on the need to support the role of elected representatives in decision-making through the creation of a new information management function. More details of this inaugural project, including its evaluation, may be found in Kawalek and Wastell (2005).

Two further projects were quickly instigated early in 2000, in the Housing and Treasury departments respectively. The second of these was a notable success. A key problem facing Treasury was the high number of unanswered telephone queries, identified in a report the previous autumn. The department had also performed very poorly in an external audit of its housing benefits process, having been awarded the bottom grade by the Housing Benefits fraud inspectorate. Users participated fully and vigorously in the BPR process, including carrying out a comprehensive process mapping exercise, largely unaided by the BPR experts. Workshops were held on a regular basis, and the work was enthusiastically led by a senior user. The main reengineering recommendation was to create a dedicated customer contact center for Treasury, which went live in October 2000. The transformation in Treasury's housing benefit service effected by the center was ultimately reflected in the award of a four-star rating (Table 1). Two further BPR projects were launched over the summer of 2000 and adaptations made to SPRINT to add new tools, including tailoring its use for customer-centered analysis and contact center design.

Table 1. Project Time Line

Dates	Internal Event (to BPR Team)	External Event
July 1999	SPRINT project commences.	
October 1999	Draft SPRINT framework published. BPR program and team given formal approval, initial pilot project launched.	Analysis of calls to treasury reveals 90% unanswered.
Jan/Feb 2000	SPRINT report produced for pilot project. Projects in Housing and Treasury launched.	Benefits Fraud Inspectorate review awards Treasury 0 grading for benefits process.
April/May 2000	Treasury project completes with detailed analysis and reengineering proposals. Contact Center main recommendation.	Customer Services (CS) dept. created with corporate role.
June/July 2000	Revision of SPRINT to address call center requirements. Housing report delivered.	Outsourcing threat comes to fore. Think-tank set up to consider options.
Aug–Oct 2000	Planning for second wave of BPR projects as part of rolling BPR program. Contact Center brought into full operation.	
Jan/Feb 2001	Work on further SPRINT projects (Registrar and Job applications) commences.	National eGovernment Pathfinder scheme announced, £25 new funding. Salford Pathfinder bid successful.
July 2001	Completion of the above projects. First formal SPRINT workshop.	Creation of Salford Advance.
Sept–Dec 2001	Detailed mapping of all customer transactions commences, part of eGovernment compliance & planned expansion of Contact Center.	MBS report published in December Outsourcing finally recedes as threat.
Mar–Jun 2001	Projects in Education and Social Services complete.	Stall at national Pathfinder conference in London to disseminate outputs of work.
July 2002	Second SPRINT workshop, and review of BPR program.	
September 2002	Projects completed in Licensing and Economic Development. Transaction mapping completes.	
Oct–Dec 2002	Review of SPRINT instigated. Licensing project completes.	National Strategy for local eGovernment published.
Jan/Feb 2003	Fully revised version (3.0) of SPRINT produced .	Benefits service awarded a 4-star rating and Charter Mark for excellence.

Three external developments were influential over the ensuing 12 months. First was the appearance of a serious threat to outsource the IT function. To forestall this, ITSD proposed setting up a think-tank to examine the implications fully, and an independent assessment was also commissioned from Manchester Business School (MBS). SPRINT itself was important in deflecting the threat. The head of ITSD commented: "SPRINT allowed me to say to senior management that we're repositioning ourselves, we're addressing our weaknesses, that he should trust the in-house service" (Slatcher 2002). Although the outsourcing threat persisted for over a year, ITSD's dogged resistance prevailed and by the time the MBS report was published the threat had receded. The second important development was the announcement of the national Pathfinder initiative (see above) in early 2001. SCC was one of the successful contenders, with SPRINT featuring centrally in their bid. Substantial funding (£0.5m) was obtained to accelerate SCC's BPR program to "commodify" the SPRINT methodology into a resource for the local government community as a whole, and to mentor other local authorities in IT-enabled business change. The final development was the success of the embryonic contact Center which came to be seen as a model for SCC as a whole to improve its customer relations. It was established as a corporate facility, with plans to extend the range of services to be transferred into the center.

A formal workshop was held in July 2001 to review these early experiences with SPRINT, to update and refine the methodology accordingly, and to plan the Pathfinder activities in detail. It was attended by all of the AR team, as well as several other IT staff. The meeting was positive and constructive. Many aspects of SPRINT were felt to be particularly valuable (e.g., the emphasis on process mapping and the value of direct observation—"light ethnography"—in actual work settings). Several action points resulted, including the need to develop some new components. The mood had lifted. The head of the BPR team reflected:

> Things came together nicely. SPRINT arrived at the right time, and there were also areas in the authority that needed major change. We saw the situation as an opportunity to flex our muscles. SPRINT helped to crystallize our new role. We were lucky that we decided to do BPR, and then the crises came in Council Tax and Housing Benefits, and then eGovernment. There was a lot of change going on at the time... *we were needed.*

A radical reorganization of IT services was instituted in the summer of 2001. The more routine activities of legacy system maintenance and PC support were split off into separate sections, and a new organizational entity was created, emblematically christened "Salford Advance" to emphasize its progressive role. Salford Advance subsumed the BPR team, a small research and development group, and training. It was a clear step toward realizing the head's vision of a more strategic role for IT, and also helped in creating focus and dedicated resource for the Pathfinder work.

Over the following year, SPRINT was internally deployed on a further 12 projects and most of the enhancements identified at the first workshop were implemented. Externally, over 40 other local authorities were mentored as part of the Pathfinder work. A second SPRINT workshop was held in July 2002, to review progress and identify areas for development. The full AR team was again present, supplemented by other

ITSD staff who had been involved in BPR project work. Several major new SPRINT features were proposed, by *both* practitioners and academics. The relationships between SPRINT, eGovernment, and other change initiatives, such as "best value" (Boyne et al. 2002), were also much discussed. An independent evaluation was subsequently instigated of all on-going and completed projects. Fourteen projects had been completed or were in progress. All projects had produced SPRINT outputs, and four had reached implementation in full or in part. Three of these had resolved into call center implementations, reflecting alignment with the emergent corporate plan alluded to above. Four projects were still in progress; six had reached the end of phase 1, with useful analysis having been produced, but no decision to move into implementation. In part, the evaluation report attributed these areas of blockage to the presence of a complex and fluid agenda of change within SCC, with a range of initiatives (best value, eGovernment) competing for resources and attention.

Regarding SPRINT itself, the report commented favorably as follows:

> The BPR team followed the methodology closely and deeply. The mapping of business processes was seen as a useful way of engaging the users and checking whether the BPR team had understood the process as it existed. The methodology does offer a series of tasks and tools that are valued by those who use them. By being "road-tested" within an actual organisation, the methodology has gone beyond its academic origins. If it has been found wanting it is mainly in its larger ambitions. The "real world" of organisations puts very strict limits on how a methodology can create change—it is competing with too many other things that are not easily factored into methodological design.

The report made several recommendations for the further development of SPRINT including reorganizing the material in a user-friendly way, simplifying the language, and explicitly relating SPRINT to parallel initiatives. As a result, SPRINT was thoroughly revised, with the new version (SPRINT3) completed in January 2003. It was rewritten to be more accessible, and it was given an explicit eGovernment cast. A number of new features were introduced and phase 3 replaced by a "hand-over step" at the end of phase 2. At this point in time, the action research project had largely completed its work. The prime purpose had been to generate an effective BPR methodology and SPRINT, representing the collaborative efforts of practitioners and academics alike, was the product of this work. Appendix 1 provides a brief overview of SPRINT, including its underlying philosophy; further details and a full description are publicly available on various web-sites (see below).

The detailed history thus closes here and we will end with a brief summary of how matters have moved on since. A steady stream of new BPR projects has flowed, and by the summer of 2004, a cumulative total of 22 projects had been carried out. A further review of the methodology was carried out in mid-2004, strengthening its customer-orientation and enhancing the visual appeal of the documentation; this new version was published later that year on a dedicated "gov.uk" web-site.[3] External interest in

---

[3]See www.sprint.gov.uk. Earlier versions may be inspected on www.wastell.org/SPRINT1 and www.wastell.org/SPRINT3.

SPRINT, inspired by the Pathfinder work, has continued to grow, and a user group has been formed, which held its inaugural meeting in April 2004. The group is chaired by a senior practitioner. At the time of writing, there are around 200 individual members, representing over 70 different organizations. The interview with the head of ITSD in 2004 eloquently expressed how the fortunes of ITSD had turned around since the dark days of 1999. The Head commented on the role of SPRINT within this transformation as follows:

> SPRINT helped profoundly to reposition IT as a *true enabler of business transformation.* We're now on the top table. The chief wxec now recognizes that BPR is key to achieving strategic aims and objectives. It has put us on the strategic change management map. As an example, we were central in developing a new business model for council services, called "Think Customer." It's all about joined up service delivery. We're even on the treasurer's radar now. The Council is constantly seeking substantial budget savings and we're seen as the "ghost-busters," the ones that can fill the hole. We now make a real difference to delivering the Council's agenda.

4   DISCUSSION

Let us begin by reinvoking our archetype, in the guise of Robert Aldrich's 1965 movie *The Flight of the Phoenix.* At the height of the drama, the following dialogue takes place in the blistering desert sun, as the cast come to terms with the receding possibility of rescue. They contemplate an improbable plan to save themselves, by cannibalizing a new plane from the wreckage of the old, to bring off an audacious escape:

Towns: Your theory's fine. But you get this: that engine's rated 2000 horsepower, and if I was ever fool enough to let it get started, it'd shake your pile of junk into a 1000 pieces and cut us up into mincemeat with the propeller....

Towns: I've lost five men Lew....are you asking me to kill the rest of them trying to get that death-trap off the ground. I can't do it Lew, it won't work, it just can't work!

Lew: All right, it can't. Maybe it can't and we'll all be killed. But if there's just one chance in thousand that he's got something, boy I'd rather take it than just sit around here, waiting to die.

Just as these maroons took fate into their own hands, so too did a "discourse of renewal" take hold in ITSD, equally beleaguered at the outset of our narrative; they also chose not to "sit around here, waiting to die." SPRINT was the department's Phoenix, fashioned from the ashes of CAPELLA, and compared to the limited innovation achieved in that ill-starred project (McMaster and Wastell 2004), the methodology provided the vehicle for a fundamental reinvention of ITSD's role and identity. SPRINT has been enthusiastically adopted and a dedicated BPR team now spearheads its deployment on a large portfolio of projects, and has done so for more than 5 years. The seat at the organization's "top table" has at last been secured.

The aim of this paper was to introduce briefly the SPRINT methodology, emphasizing the process of its production, and to use the case to reflect on the much-bruited troubles of methodological innovation from an organizational change perspective. How, then, may we account for the transformation in ITSD, its accomplishment of successful innovation against the usual grain? Two familiar success factors immediately stand out. We know only too well from the sad litany of failed IS projects (Laudon and Laudon 2005) that two ingredients are vital to the success of any change initiative: the commitment of senior managers and the willing participation of staff. Both of these key conditions were clearly met here. The project was led passionately by the head of ITSD, who operated throughout as a "transformational leader," fully committed to bringing off the required changes (Bass 1985). The adoption of an action research approach is also significant. It has been argued that public sector organizations are more conservative than their private sector counterparts (MacIntosh 2003). Given its intrinsically participative nature, AR would seem particularly appropriate as a change methodology in such a context where there is a long-established culture of consensus and collegiality. Mustonen-Ollila and Lyytinen (2003) have found that the majority of IS process innovations originate from within the organization. Here, a core group of practitioners were engaged throughout SPRINT's development; the methodology was not imposed from without, but developed endogenously by the practitioners and the academics working in close collaboration. The AR methodology, with all key actants involved in the cyclical learning process that drove its development, meant all internal stakeholders were naturally drawn into the innovation process and held in place, with SPRINT at the center of this strengthening network. Over time and a sustained series of deployments, this led to its ultimate congealment as a "black box" (Latour 1987), a fully accepted, organic part of the life of the department.

But this analysis is only part of the story. Other key factors were clearly at work. We argued in the "Introduction" that the turning point of any organizational innovation process is the presence of a threatening stimulus. Without such a sense of crisis, inertia will tend to prevail and any mobilization for change (at whatever level) will quickly peter out. Such organizational crises need not be abrupt, cataclysmic events; they may emerge slowly, with growing force, as the adaptive relationship between the organization and its environment steadily breaks down over a period of time (Kovoor-Misra et al. 2001). Moreover, crises may not necessarily represent direct, imminent threats. Barnett and Pratt (2000) introduce the concept of an autogenic crisis to refer to a latent threat, created or amplified by managers in order to concentrate minds, to develop solidarity and engender motivation for change.

In contrast to CAPELLA, there was a much stronger sense of the need for radical change at the outset of the SPRINT era. The Information Society Strategy and the broader eGovernment imperatives presented a powerful challenge to ITSD to develop its role, to take a more central place in the City's strategic agenda. This was later combined with a sustained outsourcing threat, against which the development of new capacities (not easily replicated by an external agency) was a convenient tactical counter. In many ways, the crisis facing ITSD at the end of the 1990s was an autogenic one; there were clear symptoms but at that point the crisis was implicit, the threat of outsourcing was yet to come, and the eGovernment agenda still embryonic. Nonetheless, times were clearly a-changing, with the traditional technology-focused paradigm seemingly ill-fitted for the brave new world of modernized public services. A challenging new role for IT at the center of the business was slowly taking shape, in prospect at least. New organizational competencies were needed to respond effectively to the pressures to reform services, and ITSD saw itself as central to this agenda. The impending crisis, still theoretical at that time, could have been resisted. There was no necessity to embrace the need for change: a defensive process of denial could have set in, with ITSD ignoring the emerging imperatives. Alternatively, the challenges could be viewed positively, as a developmental opportunity (Kovoor-Misra et al. 2001; Seeger et al. 2005).

Here the latter response prevailed; a proactive opportunity for growth and an expanded role was perceived. The sense of latent crisis prevailing at the project's outset produced a decisive alignment of all key internal actors within ITSD, both management and staff, around the need for change, and held them in place over a sustained period of transition, during which the latent threats translated into real ones, and waxed in their power. Within the initial "problematization" (Latour 1987), a discourse of renewal took shape, operationalized in the development of a new methodology. Seeger et al. (2005) identify several characteristic features of such discourse: a positive orientation to the future rather than defensive rumination; a focus on constructing new technical faculties, methods, and procedures; and an improvisational pragmatism emphasizing expediency and flexibility, rather than rational, top-down planning. The role of the leader is critical. Organizational change is *par excellence* an act of sense making (Weick 1995): basic assumptions about role and identity must be reframed and reinterpreted. The leader's prerogative is to provide this new interpretive schema, not only to inspire through passion, but to create new meaning during times of uncertainty, to make sense of the world for those in doubt and confusion. The clear vision of the head of ITSD around the need for change and for the development of a BPR capability was decisive. He was the prime orator of the renewal rhetoric.

Improvisation and resourcefulness are also critical ingredients of renewal discourse, the determination to persevere and to succeed, expediently using whatever is to hand. How vividly Aldrich's film depicts human ingenuity in the chutzpah to extemporize an entirely new plane from the shattered remnants of the old, a plane that flew against all odds and due scepticism. Much innovation, as in ITSD, is un-mandated, arising spontaneously from the middle and lower levels of organizations (Borins 2002). Change at the meso-level requires special leadership characteristics, captured well in Weick's (1990) notion of bricolage, which offers a refreshing counterpoint to the conventional view of change as top-down, rational, and planned. For mid-level innovation, where resources are scarce and formal authority limited (Borins 2002), leadership is as much about improvisation and expediency as inspiration and vision: "the main function of any leader is to draw organization out of the raw materials of life by using ingeniously whatever is at hand" (Weick 1995, p. 352). The middle manager who would be innovator, rather than apparatchik, must have something of the subtlety and agility of the trickster about him (Hyde 1998). Examples abound here of opportunism and improvisation in the leadership provided by the head of ITSD, at least matching his visionary rhetoric. These include his shrewdness in exploiting crises (for both external and internal effect), the tactical alignment of SPRINT with the emergent customer contact center, the artful deflection of the outsourcing threat, and the audacity to conjure from thin air both a BPR capacity and a major change program.

5   CODA

In this paper, we have linked two phenomena not at first sight correlated, organizational resilience and methodological innovation, through the common concept of organizational crisis. We have seen how renewal discourse is integral to resilience; how the survival of ITSD depended on the determination of its staff to reinvent themselves, to take up the challenge of a new and enlarged role, a role only they foresaw with any clarity. As a result, the organization as a whole has acquired a new capacity (for BPR) which in turn has enhanced its resilience, as the turnaround in Treasury neatly demonstrates. But the degree to which resiliency can be designed or enhanced by external intervention is a moot point. The limits are certainly clear from the present story. To a large extent, the development of Salford's BPR capability sprang from a unique configuration of chance, historical contingency, and human virtuosity. The emergence of SPRINT exemplifies innovation thriving on hardship, and the resilience of ITSD is the product of this same adversity. Had there been a conscious, top-down initiative to build capacity, the outcome might well have been very different, with additional bureaucracy and a surfeit of resources stifling, rather than stimulating, entrepreneurship, engendering sclerosis not resiliency. SPRINT itself is not a portable commodity: its efflorescence in Salford is inseparable from the unique historical processes of its development there; simply transplanting it would not, in itself, replicate the same capability (McMaster and Wastell 2005).

In general, we have noted that IS innovations often fail to take root, rapidly falling into desuetude if indeed they are ever used in earnest. Through our direct engagement in a project running against the normal trend, we have been able to construct the micropolitical causal narrative underpinning one instance of successful innovation. Lacking ethnographic grounding, such granularity of detail and understanding is necessarily absent in the high level conceptual models that typify much theory in our discipline. Generalizing with caution, we contend that a cogent sense of crisis is a necessary condition for any successful organizational change, of which methodological innovation represents but a specialized instance. The outcome of such efforts will critically depend on the degree of alignment between the innovation and the resolution of some impending threat, real or indeed latent. Where the methodology forms part of a discourse of renewal, the prospects are auspicious; otherwise, the prognosis is less hopeful. In contrast to CAPELLA, the success of SPRINT shows that radical IS innovation is feasible where there is a strong sense of solidarity and common purpose, with the innovation addressing an acknowledged crisis and the change propelled by the practitioners themselves, with resourceful and determined leadership.

References

Avison, D., Wood-Harper, A., Vidgen R. T., and Wood, J. R. G. "A Further Exploration in to Information Systems Development: The Evolution of Multiview 2," *Information Technology & People* (11), 2998, pp. 124-139

Barnett, C. K., and Pratt, M. "From Threat-Rigidity to Flexibility: Toward a Learning Model of Autogenic Crisis on Organizations," *Journal of Organizational Change* (13), 2000, pp. 74-88.

Baskerville, R., and Wood-Harper, A. T. "Diversity of Information Systems Action Research Methods," *European Journal of Information Systems* (7), 1998, pp. 90-107.

Bass, B. M. *Leadership and Performance Beyond Expectations*, New York: Free Press, 1985.

Boyne, G., Day P., and Walker R. "The Evaluation of Public Service Inspection: A Theoretical Framework," *Urban Studies* (39), 2002, pp. 1197-1212.

Borins, S. "Leadership and Innovation in the Public Sector," *Learning and Organizational Development Journal* (23), 2002, pp. 467-476

Cabinet Office. "Modernising Government," Stationary Office, Great Britain, 1999.

Cabinet Office. "Transformation Government Enabled by Technology," Norwich, UK: HMSO, 2005.

City of Salford. "People Not Technology," Internal Policy Paper, Salford City Council, 1999.

Davenport, T. *Process Innovation: Reengineering Work Through Information Technology*, Cambridge, MA: Harvard Business School Press, 1992.

Davis, F. D., Bagozzi, R., and Warshaw, P. "User Acceptance of Technology: A Comparison of Two Theoretical Models," *Management Science* (35), 1989, pp. 35, 982-1003.

Davison, R. "GSS and Action Research in the Hong Kong Police," *Information Technology & People* (14), 2001, pp. 60-77.

Fitzgerald, B. "An Empirical Investigation into the Adoption of Systems Development Methodologies," *Information and Management* (34), 1998, pp. 317-328.

Fitzgerald, B., Russo, N., and Stolterman, E. *Information Systems Development: Methods in Action*, New York: McGraw-Hill, 2002.

Gersick, C. "Revolutionary Change Theories: A Multi-Level Exploration of the Punctuated Equilibrium Paradigm," *Academy of Management Review* (16), 1991, pp. 10-36.

Greenwood, D. J., and Levin, M. *Introduction to Action Research: Social Research for Social Change*, London: Sage Publications, 1998.

Hammer, M. "Reengineering Work: Don't Automate, Obliterate," *Harvard Business Review*, July-August 1990, pp. 104-112.

Hardgrave, B. C., Davis, F., and Riemenschneider, C. K. "Investigating Determinants of Software Developers' Intentions to Follow Methodologies," *Journal of Management Information Systems* (20), 2003, pp. 123-151.

Huisman, M., and Iivari, J. "Deployment of Systems Development Methodologies: Perceptual Congruence between IS Managers and Systems Developers," *Information and Management* (43), 2006, pp. 29-49.

Hyde, L. *Trickster Makes this World*, New York: North Point Press, 1998.

Iivari, J. "Why Are CASE Tools Not Used?," *Communications of the ACM* (39), 1996, pp. 94-103.

Kautz, K., Kawalek, P., Willets, M., McMaster, T. Wastell, D., and Williams, C. "Using CASE to Enhance Service Performance in a Local Authority: The CAPELLA Project," in *Proceedings of the of International Conference on Product Focused Software Process, Improvement* (PROFES99), Oulu, Finland, 1999.

Kautz, K., and McMaster, T. "the Failure to Introduce System Development Methods: A Factor-Based Analysis," in L. Levine (ed.), *Diffusion, Transfer and Implementation of Information Technology*, Amsterdam: Elsevier/North-Holland, 1994, pp. 275-287.

Kautz, K., and Nielsen, P. A. "Understanding the Implementation of Software Process Improvement Innovations in Software Organizations," *Information Systems Journal* (14), 2004, pp. 14, 3-22.

Kawalek, P., and Wastell, D. "Pursuing Radical Transformation in Information Age Government: Case Studies Using the SPRINT Methodology," *Journal of Global Information Management* (13), 2005, pp. 79-101.

Kovoor-Misra, S., Clair, J. A., and Bettenhausen, K. L. "Clarifying the Attributes of Organizational Crises," *Technology Forecasting and Social Change* (7), 2001, pp. 77-91.

Latour, B. *Science in Action*, Boston: Harvard Press, 1987.

Laudon, J., and Laudon, K. *Management Information Systems*, Upper Saddle River, NJ: Prentice-Hall, 2005.

Lunblad, J. "A Review and Critique of Rogers' Diffusion of Innovation Theory as it Applies to Organizations," *Organizational Development Journal* (21), 2003, pp. 50-64.

MacIntosh, R. "BPR: Alive and Well in the Public Sector," *International Journal of Operations and Production Management* (23), 2003, pp. 327-344.

Mathiassen, L. "Collaborative Practice Research," *Information Technology & People* (15), 2002, pp. 321-345.

McMaster, T., and Wastell, D. G. "Diffusion or Delusion? Challenging an IS Research Tradition," *Information Technology & People* (18), 2005, pp. 383-404.

McMaster, T., and Wastell, D. G. "Success and Failure Revisited in the Implementation of New Technology: Some Reflections on the CAPELLA Project," in B. Fitzgerald and E. H. Wynn (eds.), *Innovation for Adaptability and Competitiveness*, Boston: Kluwer, 2004, pp. 313-334.

Meyer, A. D., Goes, J., and Brooks, G. R. "Organizations Reacting to Hyperturbulence," in G. Huber and W. Glick (eds.), *Organizational Change and Redesign*, Oxford, UK: Oxford University Press, 1995, pp. 66-111.

Mustonen-Ollila, E., and Lyytinen, K. "How Organizations Adopt Information System Process Innovations: A Longitudinal Analysis," *European Journal of Information Systems* (13), 2003, pp. 35-51.

Nandhakumar, J., and Avison, D. "The Fiction of Methodological Development: A Field Study of Information Systems Development," *Information Technology & People* (12), 1999, pp. 176-191.

Orlikowski, W. "CASE Tools as Organizational Change: Investigating Incremental and Radical Changes in System Development," *MIS Quarterly* (17), 1993, pp. 309-340.

Rogers, E. M. *The Diffusion of Innovations*, New York: Free Press, 1995.

Seeger, M. W., Ulmer, R. R., Novak, J. M., and Sellnow, T. "Post-Crisis Discourse and Organizational Change, Failure and Renewal," *Journal of Organizational Change* (18), 2005, pp. 78-95.

Simon, S. J. "The Reorganization of the Information Systems of the US Naval Construction Forces: An Action Research Project," *European Journal of Information Systems* (9), 2000, pp. 148-162.

Slatcher, A. "Redeveloping SPRING," Internal Report, Salford City Council, 2002.

Sullivan, H., and Skelcher, C. *Working Across Boundaries: Collaboration in the Public Services*, Basingstoke, UK: Palgrave Macmillan, 2002.

Templeton, G. F., and Byrd, T. A. "Determinants of the Relative Advantage of a Structured SDM during the Adoption Stage of Implementation," *Information Technology and Management* (4), 2003, pp. 409-428.

Van der Ven, A. H. "Managing the Process of Organizational Innovation," in G. Huber and W. Glick (eds.), *Organizational Change and Redesign*, Oxford, UK: Oxford University Press, 1995, pp. 269-294.

Wastell, D. G. "The Fetish of Technique: Methodology as a Social Defense," *Information Systems Journal* (6), 1996, pp. 25-40.

Wastell, D. G. "Information Systems and Evidence-Based Policy in Multi-Agency Networks: The Micro-Political Contingencies of Situated Innovation," *Journal of Strategic Information Systems* (15), 2006 (in press).

Wastell, D. G. "Learning Dysfunctions in Information Systems Development: Overcoming the Social Defenses with Transitional Objects," *MIS Quarterly* (23), 1999, pp. 581-600.

Wastell, D. G., and White, P. "Using Process Technology to Support Cooperative Work: Prospects and Design Issues," in D. Diaper and C. Sanger (eds), *CSCW in Practice*, Berlin: Springer-Verlag, 1993, pp. 105-126.

Wastell, D. G., White, P., and Kawalek, P. "A Methodology for Business Process Redesign: Experiences and Issues," *Journal of Strategic Information Systems* (3:1), 1994, pp. 23-40.

Weick, K. E. "Oganizational Redesign as Improvisation," in G. Huber and W. Glick, *Organizational Change and Redesign*, New York: Oford University Press, 1995, pp. 346-379..

Williams, C., and Willetts, M. "CAPELLA: CASE Tools for Process Enhancement in Local Authorities," Final Report to the European Systems and Software Initiative (ESSI), Project Number 23832, 1999.

About the Authors

David Wastell is Professor of Information Systems at Nottingham University Business School. His current research interests are in public sector reform, design and innovation, strategic alignment, and the cognitive ergonomics of complex systems. He has published widely in Information Systems, human factors, and health informatics, after an early research career in cognitive and clinical neurophysiology. He recently served on the board of *European Journal of Information Systems* and is currently a member of *Information and Management's* editorial team. David has co-organized two previous IFIP conferences (WG8.6 and WG8.2) and is program cochair for the upcoming 2007 meeting of IFIP WG8.6. He has extensive consultancy experience, especially in the public sector. He can be reached by e-mail at dave_wastell@hotmail.com.

Tom McMaster is a lecturer and researcher in the Informatics Research Centre at the University of Salford, one of the UK's leading information systems research institutes. With a variety of research interests (including technology transfer), Tom is a founding member of IFIP WG8.6, and a member of IFIP WG8.2, the UK Association for Information Systems (UKAIS), and the IRIS Association (Information Systems Research in Scandinavia). He co-organized the WG8.6 Ambleside conference in 1997, and is program cochair for the forthcoming WG8.6 conference in the UK in 2007. In 1993 Tom represented the UK at the International Conference on Inforamtion Systems' Doctoral Consortium held in Orlando, and has presented his work widely in Scandinavia, the United States, Canada, Mexico, Australia, and elsewhere. He currently serves on the editorial boards of *Information Technology & People* and *Journal of Information Systems Education*. Tom can be reached by e-mail at T.McMaster@salford.ac.uk.

Peter Kawalek is a reader in Information Systems at Manchester Business School. He has published two books and numerous papers. Peter has considerable experience in the public sector, working with a number of cities and local councils, as well as the National Health Service and other agencies. He is a board member of the Tacit Knowledge project run by the Office of the Deputy Prime Minister in the UK. He teaches on the MBA and MSc programs in Manchester, as well as the all-Ireland MSc in Public Sector Innovation run jointly by Letterkenny Institute of Technology and the University of Ulster. Peter's extensive private sector experience includes BT, Chubb Insurance, Fujitsu, Hoverspeed, and Great North Eastern Railway.

Appendix: SPRINT Headlines

SPRINT attempts to bring together elements of good practice, from the authors' previous experience and the research literature, within a single framework. Key precepts are shown below. There are three main phases, each defined in terms of a set of aims and tasks. Phase 1 is essentially one of analysis, aimed at fully understanding the business context by considering all relevant perspectives, and analyzing the effectiveness of current processes. The emphasis on context is crucial, forcing the SPRINT team to "zoom out" from the original remit, which may focus too narrowly on a particular process. Two tasks are key: building formal process models using *role activity diagraming,* and *critical goal analysis.* All strands of enquiry are focused on two pivotal questions: what are the relevant business goals and how well are they supported? The aim of phase two is to devise a set of re-engineering proposals, based on a panoramic "business vision," which guides subsequent design work in which innovative reengineering opportunities are sought. The third phase of SPRINT is concerned with implementation, through training, detailed process design and development of any new IT.

SPRINT recommends two levels of governance: a **steering group** and the **BPR team**. Senior management commitment is critical, and the former should therefore include representation at director level or similar. The BPR team should comprise a senior user as project manager, together with BPR consultants, other experts, and representative end-users.

SPRINT Precepts	Comments, Rationale
Breadth of vision	The methodology seeks to identify the full range of stakeholders in a BPR project. SPRINT has been influenced by other methodologies, most notably Multiview (Avison et al. 1998) which acknowledge the complexity of organizational contexts and the presence of multiple perspectives.
Depth of understanding	The development of a detailed understanding of processes through rigorous empirical study (including ethnography) is vital. Accounts of work given away from the scene embodied in manuals typically afford idealized representations, problematically related to actual practice (Wastell and White 1993).
Radicalism	SPRINT fully embraces Hammer's (1990) injunction to exploit the potential of IT to enable radical innovation. Although radical in vision, SPRINT is incremental in implementation, recognizing the inherent conservatism and colleagiality of public sector organizations.
Rigorous Assessment	Evaluation is important to assess benefits and facilitate organizational learning. It should follow the principles of theory-based evaluation (Sullivan and Skelcher, 2002), involving the collection of quantitative and qualitative data, complemented by appropriate contextual detail, to build a causal narrative.
Flexibility	To avoid ritualistic behavior, SPRINT is neither detailed nor prescriptive; it is best described as a tool-kit providing a semi-structured learning environment, or "transitional space" (Wastell 1999). Case studies are provided rather than detailed step-by-step prescriptions. Users are strongly encouraged to adapt the framework, including the addition of new tools.
Socio-technical philosophy	Despite the opprobrious reputation since acquired, socio-technical thinking informed early BPR approaches (e.g., Davenport, 1990). SPRINT embodies this same human-centered outlook, emphasizing the non-Tayloristic use of technology to empower and augment the role of humans, not to automate and replace them.

Part 7

Organizational Impact of IS

18 THE IMPACT OF ENTERPRISE SYSTEMS ON ORGANIZATIONAL RESILIENCE

Ioannis Ignatiadis
Joe Nandhakumar
University of Bath, UK

Abstract   *Enterprise systems are used to facilitate the seamless integration and data exchange between the various departments within an organization. In order to achieve this, rigidly defined control mechanisms must be in place in the system, which safeguard the company's data and protect from unauthorized and unintended uses of the system. This ideal for total control, however, is only achieved to a certain extent. Because of organizational necessities, the configuration of controls in the enterprise system may have unintended organizational implications. The purpose of this paper is to present the findings from a company case study, where an enterprise system is installed. We suggest that the introduction of an enterprise system creates power differentials, which serve to increase control in the organization. This results in increased rigidity, and a possible decrease in organizational flexibility and resilience. On the other hand, enterprise systems can cause drift, from the unexpected consequences of these power differentials, and the role of perceptions of people in solving a problem within the enterprise system. This reduction in control may serve in some circumstances as an enabler to organizational resilience.*

Keywords   Enterprise system, resilience, embedding, disembedding, power, control, drift

1   INTRODUCTION

Enterprise systems are used by most large and also by some small and medium enterprises as the method to reorganize and streamline internal and external operations. One particular type of enterprise system examined in this paper is that of the enterprise resource planning (ERP) system. Installation of an ERP system usually entails major

Please use the following format when citing this chapter:

Ignatiadis, Ioannis, Nandhakumar, Joe, 2006, in International Federation for Information Processing (IFIP), Volume 206, The Transfer and Diffusion of Information Technology for Organizational Resilience, eds. B. Donnellan, Larsen T., Levine L., DeGross J. (Boston: Springer), pp. 259-274.

business process reengineering issues (Al-Mashari and Al-Mudimigh 2003; Boudreau and Robey 1999), as companies often have to adapt their work practices to the ERP system. Consequently, new forms of controls need to be in place in order to ascertain the prescribed and efficient working of employees within the ERP system.

The main purpose of this paper is to conceptualize the way that organizational control in a company is aided with the use of an enterprise system, and when drift can arise from the use of such a system. The relation between control and organizational resilience is also proposed. The outcome of this research is twofold. On one hand, results from this research contribute to a better theoretical understanding of the impact of enterprise systems on control and resilience in a company. As research on enterprise systems tends to move away from initial implementation concerns and success factors, the paper offers an important dimension by presenting more critical reflections on the actual use of enterprise systems and their impact on a company. On the other hand, the findings also help companies to become more aware of the impact of enterprise systems within their organizations, highlighting areas where the system can have unintended consequences, and can function contrary to the company's expectations.

In the following section, we briefly review the previous research on the issues of power and control, and their relevance to Information Systems. We then present the theoretical underpinnings of this study, followed by a presentation of the research approach employed. We follow this with the presentation of the impacts of the enterprise system in the case study company. We then discuss and categorize the results of our research, and develop the theoretical conceptualization that arises from this discussion. We conclude this paper with the theoretical and practical implications of our study.

2   INFORMATION SYSTEMS, POWER, AND CONTROL

For Finnegan and Longaigh (2002), information is seen to be at the core of both control and coordination processes. They define control as the process by which one entity influences to varying degrees the behavior and output of another entity, through the use of power authority and a wide range of bureaucratic, cultural, and informal mechanisms. Finnegan and Longaigh mention that technology facilitates control in three ways: changing decision-making structures, formalization of behavior, and monitoring activities.

Markus's (1983) work focuses on the link between power, politics, and the implementation of a management information system. She argues that as many MISs are designed to distribute information to individuals in a certain way, MISs can alter the bases of power. In addition, Coombs, Knights, and Willmott (1992) mention that control is used to draw attention to the intended and unintended consequences of the exercise of power and the use of knowledge in social and organizational relations. They note that some people may willingly identify and subjugate themselves to the control effects of power relations, whereas others may wilfully resist them. In that sense, IT is seen as the response to competitive pressures to enhance control over processes of production and distribution (see also Bruns and McFarlan 1987).

In similar lines, Bloomfield, Coombs, and Owen (1994) argue that, paradoxically, while IT is seen to increase decentralization of decision-making, at the same time it makes possible a centralization of control (see also Bloomfield and Coombs 1992). This premise is also acknowledged by Orlikowski (1991), who states that "[information technology] facilitates decentralization and flexible operations on the one hand, while increasing dependence and centralized knowledge and power on the other" (p. 10). From her field study of a large multinational software consulting firm, Orlikowski concluded that IT tends to reinforce the existing structures of power and domination. Clegg and Wilson (1991) also mention that managerial control can be increased through technological change. In this case, the individual's opportunities for resistance can be reduced or eliminated when the technology makes redundant discretion, decision-making, and judgment. Clegg and Wilson, however, argue that technology is not the sole source of control: Controls can be embedded in the physical structure of the labor process, producing *technical* control, or can be found in the social structure, producing *bureaucratic* control.

In relation to enterprise resource planning systems, Sia et al. (2002) have examined the issues of empowerment and panoptic control (Foucault 1977) of ERP systems in the case of a restructured public hospital in Singapore. Their findings tend to indicate that although an ERP implementation has the potential for both employee empowerment and managerial control, management power seems to be perpetuated through an ERP implementation. In addition to Sia et al., Hanseth et al. (2001) argue that ERP systems, with their emphasis on integrating business processes, streamlining, and standardization, are an ideal control technology. More generally, they argue that IT is a control technology, and the IT revolution is a control revolution. In that sense, Robinson and Wilson (2001) see three ways in which the work regime within an ERP system is enforced.

• First, the integrated approach to control within an ERP model allows for its automation in a way that replaces traditional forms of hierarchical supervision.

• Second, ERPs can strengthen corporate cultures so that employees are encouraged to identify themselves with the organization's products and values.

• Third, ERPs also specify the ways in which work is to be carried out, by defining the business processes, and hence the job content of one's work.

Boudreau and Robey (2005) claim that when looking at organizational change arising from the use of IT, an agency perspective may mean limited possibilities for radical IT-induced change. An agency perspective of IT in this case takes the position that IT is socially constructed and open to a variety of social meanings and potential uses. Boudreau and Robey argue that certain technologies allow for a greater degree of human agency and others to a lesser degree. Their research looked at ERP systems, which are seen as inflexible software packages constraining user-inspired action (human agency). Their results, however, indicate that although ERP systems are seen as rigid control mechanisms, there is still scope for human agency to take place within such systems. Their findings agree with Orlikowski (2000), who acknowledges that while users can and do use technologies as they were designed, they also can and do circumvent the intended uses of technology, either by ignoring certain properties, working around them, or inventing new ones. The concept of agency is also applicable to the current research. Agency in the current research refers to the appropriation of the enterprise system by end users, and their use of it. The meanings that users attach to the workings of the enterprise system in this case, and their interpretation of it, can cause drift in the company, or can reinforce the controls imposed by the system.

In summary, the impact of power and control aspects of information systems has been investigated quite extensively in the literature. We build on the literature described above, as well as the theoretical lenses described in the following section, in order to enhance our understanding of how power and control impacts organizational resilience.

3 THEORETICAL LENSES: EMBEDDING–DISEMBEDDING AND CONTROL DETERMINANTS

This study draws on Giddens's (1990) notion of embedding and disembedding. These two constructs fall within the larger concept of modernity. Giddens defines disembedding as "the lifting out of social relations from local contexts of interaction and their restructuring across indefinite spans of time-space" (p. 21). Conversely, embedding (or reembedding) is, according to Giddens, "the reappropriation or recasting of disembedded social relations so as to pin them down (however partially or transitorily) to local conditions of time and place" (pp. 79-80). In the current context of Information Systems, the social relations that are being disembedded and reembedded are the power differentials that arise from the use of information provided by the information system, and the access to this information that is provided to disparate individuals by the control mechanisms in the information system (in this case the ERP system).

Hanseth and Braa (2000) use the analysis by Giddens to claim that even more knowledge (in the current study arising from the use of information in the information system) can in some cases decrease control. This paradox can occur because knowledge is filtered, amongst others, by the following factors:

- Differential power. Knowledge in this case is more available to those in positions of power.

- Role of values. Different perceptions and values of different settings in this case imply a different approach to knowledge and, consequently, on ways to solve a problem.

- Impact of unintended consequences. This refers to the case where no amount of accumulated knowledge can include all circumstances of its implementation, leading to unintended outcomes.

We will use the above determinants as sensitizing devices (Walsham 1993) in our research.

Because of the uncertainty and possible decreased control of modernity, Giddens likens it to a juggernaut, a runaway engine of enormous power that humanity can collectively drive to a certain extent, but which can easily get out of control and rend itself asunder. Hanseth et al. (2001) use Giddens's concept of juggernaut to parallel it with ERP installations in global organizations. Although ERPs are seen as extended control mechanisms in this case, their size and complexity can threaten an organization if they are not managed correctly and are allowed to get out of control. The following section discusses the research approach adopted for examination of a company where such an ERP system is installed.

4 RESEARCH APPROACH

This research adopts the interpretive case study approach (Walsham 1993). Interpretive approaches assume that the reality is socially constructed by human agents (Walsham 1995). According to Yin (2003), "case studies are the preferred strategy when how or why questions are being posed, when the investigator has little control over events, and when the focus is on a contemporary phenomenon within some real-life context" (p. 1). As this research examines the question of *how* enterprise systems affect the control and resilience aspects in a company, case study research is an appropriate method. The investigator in the current research was an outsider to the company, had no consultancy or other financial interests in it, and could not influence the events studied, as he did not take part in them. The focus of the research is a contemporary one, and the real-life context is the use of an enterprise system within a company.

The case study company is TransCom (a pseudonym). TransCom employs more than 74,000 people in over 70 countries worldwide. It has more than 100 years of experience in its sector. Four offices of TransCom in the UK were visited. The ERP system installed at TransCom is SAP R/3, and it was fully installed in January 2002. It is currently implemented in the UK, France, Spain, Romania, Sweden, Chile, and the United States, with an emphasis on global deployment in the future. Prior to installation of the SAP system, another ERP system (BAAN) was used, as well as a standalone finance system.

Data collection for the research was carried out between February and August 2005 (i.e., post-ERP implementation), using semi-structured interviews and nonparticipant observation. For the semi-structured interviews, a list of topics was prepared for discussion with the interviewees (office-level staff and managers), but the interviewees were free to elaborate on their own understandings, and digress when it was necessary. All the interviews were recorded and transcribed verbatim. For the nonparticipant (passive) observations, the researcher observed the subjects' daily interaction with the ERP system and the problems encountered. In addition, notes were kept after informal discussions with participants, as well as writing down observations from the field. Semi-structured interviews and nonparticipant observation are positioned by Nandhakumar and Jones (1997) in the middle of the spectrum analyzing distance and engagement of data-gathering methods. This means that in the current research, data collection didn't involve full engagement with the company as a consultant, but on the other hand there was a fair amount of interaction with it, in order to fully appreciate the context of ERP use. Table 1 shows the positions of the people that were interviewed, and the number of interviews carried out.

Data analysis for this research was carried out using techniques from grounded theory (Strauss and Corbin 1998). Certain levels of coding (open, axial) were performed on the collected data in order to categorize them and develop categories. The codes and categories emerged from the data, keeping in mind the theoretical lenses of embedding–

Table 1. Interviews Carried Out

Positions Interviewed	Number of Interviews	Area
Assistant Accountant Accounting Reports Manager Billing Clerk Accounts Payable Clerk	6	Finance
Materials Controller Materials Planner	4	Materials Management
SAP Facilitator Flow Repairable Controller Head of Production Maintenance Policy Leader Production Planner	9	Service Management
Purchasing Manager	1	Purchasing
Logistics Director Business Improvement Coordinator Inventory Planner	5	Warehouse and Distribution
Business Process and Global Information Systems Director IT Manager	4	IT Management
Total Interviews	**29**	

Table 2. Indicative Codes and Categories in Analysis

Category	Indicative Codes
Differential Power	Authorization levels Expertise Monitoring capabilities
Drift	Role of values in problem solving Impact of unintended consequences
Control	System control points System control failures
Embedding	System attributes Input information
Disembedding	System configuration and deployment Output information

disembedding and control determinants, which were described previously. Some indicative codes and higher level categories that were developed in the analysis phase are shown in Table 2.

In order to assist our coding, the interview transcripts were imported into NVivo, a computer-aided qualitative data analysis software package. NVivo was used simply as a tool for organizing, structuring, and familiarizing with the data, and the analysis was primarily done by the researchers. The codes and categories were conceptually linked with each other, with the use of mind-maps that explored their interrelationships. Although resilience did not appear in the codification per se, it was involved in the analysis on the understanding that excessive control can inhibit resilience. The following section describes the case study company, including some level of analysis.

5 CASE DESCRIPTION AND ANALYSIS: IMPACTS OF ENTERPRISE SYSTEM IN TRANSCOM

Use of an enterprise system entails definition of authorization levels, or access control mechanisms, that specify who has access to different types of data and screens in the system. As people are given different access levels depending on their needs, certain people are given more authority to carry out tasks in the system, and hence gain power. Other people are given less authority, and hence their power is diminished. In addition, these access control mechanisms were configured at a global level in TransCom, at a central location that had the responsibility for the overall configuration of the system, including the assignment of authorization levels.

However, the fact that controls in the system can be enabled doesn't mean that they are automatically put in place. The system must be appropriately configured to correctly implement these controls, which is not always the case. The way that the system is actually configured depends on the organizational necessities, as well as the perspective of the company regarding the assignment of access rights to individuals. As one interviewee mentioned,

> *I think, at the moment, I would say, the controls are very sort of lax, are very easy, because people have got authorizations to do nearly everything in some cases. It would help if the authorizations were limited to the actual trans-actions that people were meant to be doing, rather than giving them an awful lot in case they might ever need it.* (Business Improvement Coordinator)

From an organizational perspective, as a result of the assignment of authorization profiles, people at local company offices could abuse these authorizations and carry out work they shouldn't be doing.

Training was given when the system was first installed in TransCom. However, the system users considered most training that was given as incomplete, and they required more thorough and continuous training on the system. In some cases, training was not organized at all, but depended on people picking up things as they worked with the system.

> *I didn't have any formal training. I started in 1999, when we first introduced SAP to the business, and I sat with the consultants, learning the system, saying, right, if I do this, how does that happen, how do I do this, and things like that.*

One thing led to another, and I became one of the, sort of, SAP experts within the business. (Business Improvement Coordinator)

As a result of technical knowledge, certain people within the business (the Business Improvement Coordinator in this case) seemed to gain authority, even though this person's main business role was in Logistics and not in SAP consulting. Other employees in the company regarded the Business Improvement Coordinator as an ERP expert, and his help was sought whenever possible. Although there was a dedicated help desk to help users having problems in the system, people still tended to bypass this help desk, and seek the help of the perceived expert instead.

We have a UK SAP team, that is basically the help desk, but the people within the offices here tend to come to me first, because more often than not I can give them a quick solution or answer to solve their problem, rather than them logging it to the help desk, and the help desk then trying to identify what the problem is. (Business Improvement Coordinator)

The organizational consequence of this increase in authority was that certain business rules were not observed, and people tended to overlook the prescribed ways of solving a problem. This bypassing of business rules had the additional organizational consequence that people from nontechnical backgrounds had difficulty in understanding the technical jargon of the ERP system.

Power in the system can also arise because of the monitoring capabilities of an enterprise system. In this sense, people that have the authorization to monitor other peoples' work in the system, have power over the latter. From a personal perspective, some interviewees expressed their discontent about the panoptic features of enterprise systems, and the possible consequences of these features.

I think people can use [monitoring] to their own advantage. Sometimes there's too much information there, if you make a mistake or whatever, it can be used to the wrong advantage, which I am not too happy about....It's there; it can be done. That's the worrying thing. (Shift Planning Coordinator)

During the interviews, various workarounds in the system were also mentioned. Those were employed in order to achieve something that could not be done in the prescribed way, and the workings of the system had to be reinvented, or the system had to be used in other than the usual ways. In most of these cases, the intended and established controls in the system (as implemented with the relevant authorization levels) were bypassed.

There are other screens, like for example, the stores people don't actually amend the material master. But there are certain fields where you actually go through on SAP, which the stores have access to, which if you follow through the fields, it'll actually take you to the material master, which you can actually go and change it....You can actually go through the back door and change things. (Materials Controller)

Another example is that we put a block in the system to stop us using source list, basically so that we can't really amend a source list and buy stuff from other suppliers. But it doesn't really work, because all you do is still go in and create a new source list yourself. (Materials Controller)

Using the system in those unintended ways had certain side effects in some cases. From an organizational perspective, this could result in data inconsistencies, which would impact various departments in the organization. From a personal perspective, people expressed their discontent about the impacts of those side effects.

I can sit here and create orders from my site. But I can also sit here and create orders for any other sites. There's nothing stopping me in the system that says, this is not your site, you need some permission or something other to do work in their plant. Somebody from the other sites went and built some transaction on my site the other day, which messed up my stock basically....[The impact of this transaction would be] financial, because the figures wouldn't have matched. (Materials Controller)

Although these unintended consequences can and do occur, in some cases there is a business rationale behind the configuration of the system that allows these consequences to occur. However, the need for increased control is also present in these cases as well.

There are benefits to being able to do it, like for example, if say, the person who places the order in another site is off sick, and there's only say, somebody here who can place the order, then that means that he can carry out the transaction. But what he should have there is that he ought to be able to go through some authority steps to do it. (Materials Controller)

In the next section, we use the case description and analysis presented above in order to categorize the results and develop our theoretical conceptualization of the impact of enterprise systems on organizational resilience.

6 DISCUSSION AND THEORY DEVELOPMENT: EMBEDDING AND DISEMBEDDING ASPECTS OF ENTERPRISE SYSTEMS AND THEIR IMPACT ON RESILIENCE

In this section we draw on the three determinants (differential power, role of values in problem solving, impact of unintended consequences) outlined before as theoretical lenses in order to interpret the results from the case study and to develop our theoretical conceptualization.

6.1 Sources of Power

The case description of TransCom illustrates that people are given decreased or increased authority, as a result of assignments of different authorization levels to carry out tasks in the system. In addition, people with increased knowledge of the system seem to gain authority as more people depend on their expertise in order to carry out their functions. Monitoring is another source of power, where the person carrying out the monitoring is seen to control what the subordinate is doing in the system. Monitoring in this case depends on the correct assignment of authorization levels to the right individuals.

It was also mentioned in the previous section that the assignment of authorization levels is carried out centrally, at a location where global configuration of the system is implemented. Training can be done globally or locally; however, training that produces expertise in multiple areas of the system has to be carried out as a lengthy process requiring continuous interaction with the system at various levels. In the observed company, such training was self-administered and carried out by interaction with the system at a global level while the system was being rolled out to the offices. This in turn equipped the relevant person with advanced knowledge of the system, and consequently he gained authority because of his expertise.

In summary, the creation of authorization level profiles in the system, together with the monitoring capabilities of the system and the creation of expertise by various actors, resulted in the creation of power differentials. These power differentials then served to increase the control in the company by empowering different users with different levels of capabilities.

6.2 Impacts of Power

In the case presentation, the impact of certain aspects of power arising from the configuration of authorization levels, the generation of expertise, as well as the monitoring capabilities was mentioned. The configuration of authorization levels in some cases encompassed more authority than was necessary, either because of organizational requirements or because the system was too strict to allow intermediate levels of authorizations. As a result, there were unintended consequences of these configurations, which had a business impact on the company. The way to overcome those consequences was by specifying extra business rules, outside the ERP system, which defined acceptable behavior of users in the system in the case where they were allowed to carry out tasks beyond their responsibilities in the system. However, these business rules were not always followed and they were rather informal, as a consensus between peers, thereby decreasing the expected control offered by the ERP system.

Also, the perception of power differentials caused different people to see different ways in which to solve a problem. In the case where people were allocated increased authorization levels, and hence increased power, they tended to try and solve any issues in the system themselves, rather than talking to the experts who had more knowledge. Similarly, people regarded the perceived expert in SAP as their first point of call when encountering difficulties in the ERP system. This was quite informal, however, and the business rules clearly indicated that in cases of problems with the system the help desk should be the first point of call. The role of values in this case was important in bypassing the business rules, as people had different perceptions on what is the best way to get help with solving a problem in the system.

In summary, the creation of power differentials resulted in unintended consequences in the company. In addition, people saw different ways of solving a problem according to their perception of those power differentials. Both those reasons served to decrease control in the company.

6.3 Disembedding in Enterprise Systems

An enterprise system can disembed, or lift out social relations from local contexts of interaction, and restructure them across time-space. This is achieved with the global nature of the enterprise system, which is configured in a central location. The social relations in this case, that are the outcome of the enterprise system, are power differentials that result from the global nature of the system and the distribution of various pieces of information (of differing importance) to disparate actors. The disembedding process then results in increased control, caused by the centrality of the configuration of the enterprise system, and the concentration of power in the hands of selected individuals. As control increases, rigid mechanisms are put into place to make the organization more rigid and robust. As such, the processes and procedures in the company are solidified, and strict rules apply regarding access to and manipulation of company data. Depending on the degree of this rigidity in rules (enforced by the enterprise system), the company may become too inflexible to respond efficiently to conditions of change and stress, and therefore become less resilient. Manipulation or relaxing of those rules may, however, lead to more flexibility (with the cost of partial loss of control), and hence resilience can actually increase.

6.4 Reembedding in Enterprise Systems

On the other hand, an enterprise system can also be seen to reembed, or reappropriate or recast, the disembedded social relations so as to pin them down to local conditions. This is achieved with the distributed nature of enterprise systems, which can be deployed in many locations across time-space. The social relations that are reembedded in this case are the same power differentials (resulting from distribution of information in the enterprise system) that were the outcome of the disembedding process. As a result of the reembedding of these power relations, there may be drift because of the impact of unintended consequences of the system and the role of values of people in solving a problem. This reduction in control may serve to increase the resilience of the company because the employees appropriate the system for their own use and are, therefore, more able to respond to change when this occurs. On the other hand, when the employees fully follow the processes and procedures dictated by the system, then there is less or no drift, and the control structures imposed by the system are reenacted. In this case, as mentioned above and depending on the degree of rigidity imposed by the enterprise system, resilience may actually decrease.

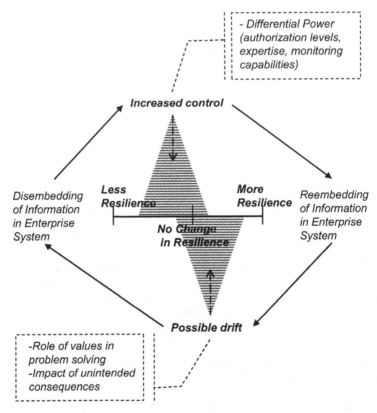

Figure 1. Embedding and Disembedding Aspects of Enterprise Systems and Their Impact on Control and Resilience

6.5 Conceptualization of Disembedding and Reembedding in Enterprise Systems

Figure 1 depicts our theoretical conceptualization of the disembedding and (re)embedding aspects of enterprise systems and their impact on control and resilience. Development of this conceptualization employs the embedding-disembedding concepts presented previously and uses as sensitizing devices the three determinants on the ways knowledge (in this case information in the enterprise system) can impact control. The development of the framework in Figure 1 is based on data gathered during examination of the case study company, as well as the understanding generated on the impact of enterprise systems on organizational resilience.

Disembedding, as shown in the figure, occurs as part of the global nature of an enterprise system with a centralized configuration. What is disembedded in this case is various pieces of informational data in the system which are made available to authorized users. This leads to increased control as a result of the creation of power differentials. Reembedding then occurs as part of the distributed nature of an enterprise system, which can be deployed across time-space. What is reembedded in this case is the information that was disembedded previously, which can now be used and processed by authorized users. This may lead to drift, stemming from unintended consequences of the system, and the perception of users regarding their use of the system.

Too much control in this case can make the organization too inflexible to absorb strain and recover from untoward events that may occur. As a result, the organization may become less resilient. On the other hand, if control is appropriately implemented to match the organizational needs, the company may become more resilient to change. This may come together with some possible drift from the original company goals and objectives, but in the end this drift, if managed correctly, may serve to make the company more flexible and resilient to future events that it may encounter.

7 CONCLUSIONS AND IMPLICATIONS

The purpose of this paper has been to present the findings of a study on the impact of enterprise systems on organizational resilience through processes of embedding and disembedding and the creation of control and drift. Our conceptualization offers a way of examining changes in resilience offered by the use of an enterprise system. Although the focus of this study was an ERP system, the results can similarly be generalized for other enterprise-wide information systems.

The results of this research shed new light on the way that enterprise systems can impact the organizational resilience of a company. Our findings agree with the literature (e.g., Hanseth et al. 2001) that enterprise systems can get out of control if not managed correctly. The contribution of this research has been to refine and conceptualize the ways in which this can occur, through the embedding and disembedding of information, and the creation of power differentials. We agree with the view of Coombs et al. (1992), whereby control is used to draw attention to the intended and unintended consequences of the exercise of power and the use of knowledge in social and organizational relations. We further refine their concepts to argue that the exercise of power within an enterprise system happens as part of a disembedding process, whereas unintended consequences happen as part of the consequent reembedding process. The disembedding process can lead to increased control, which if done excessively can stifle resilience. On the other hand, the consequent embedding process can lead to drift, which, if not left to get out of control, can serve to increase organizational resilience.

Our results here also complement those by Bloomfield and Coombs (1992), Bloomfield et al. (1994), and Orlikowski (1991), who argue that while IT can facilitate decentralization, at the same time it can make possible a centralization of control and knowledge. We argue that decentralization may offer the opportunity to increase the resilience of a company by relaxing centralized control and rigidity. On the other hand, centralization of control and knowledge, if not managed correctly and done excessively, can decrease organizational resilience.

The implications of the findings from the current research for managers and practitioners are an increased awareness of the ways that definitions of control in an enterprise system can increase or decrease organizational resilience. This implies that increased attention should be paid to the levels of authority given to individuals in the system, according to organizational needs. Too much control can serve to streamline the operations of the company, but at the same time can decrease the resilience of the company to respond to future changes. Too little control can cause excessive drift, which can be harmful to the company. The middle and best way is to allow for the required controls to be implemented, but at the same not stifle the ability of the company to respond to future challenges.

The implication of this research for designers and developers of enterprise systems is that they should work closely with managers and end users of the system to make sure that the appropriate levels of authorizations and access profiles are built in and available in the system. In the opposite case, users may be given too much or too little authority through those access profiles, which can respectively lead to either the users abusing the system, or them not being able to carry out all of their functions in the system. In the first case control is lost; in the second case, the company underperforms. In neither case, however, does resilience increase.

A limitation of the current research is that only one instance of enterprise-wide Information Systems has been examined, that of an ERP. Future research may investigate other (intra- or interorganizational) systems such as the customer relationship management or supplier relationship management systems. Although the boundaries between the latter and that of an ERP start to blur, it would be beneficial to examine the degree to which those systems strengthen or weaken the potential for organizational control and flexibility.

References

Al-Mashari, M., and Al-Mudimigh, A. "ERP Implementation: Lessons from a Case Study," *Information Technology & People* (16:1), 2003, pp. 21-33.

Bloomfield, B. P., and Coombs, R. "Information Technology, Control and Power: The Centralization and Decentralization Debate Revisited," *Journal of Management Studies* (29:4), 1992, pp. 459-484.

Bloomfield, B. P., Coombs, R., and Owen, J. "The Social Construction of Information Systems: The Implications for Management Control," in R. Mansell (ed.), *Management of Information and Communication Technologies: Emerging Patterns of Control*, London: Aslib, 1994, pp. 143-157.

Boudreau, M.-C., and Robey, D. "Enacting Integrated Information Technology: A Human Agency Perspective," *Organization Science* (16:1), 2005, pp. 3-18.

Boudreau, M.-C., and Robey, D. "Organizational Transition to Enterprise Resource Planning Systems: Theoretical Choices for Process Research," in P. De and J. I. DeGross (eds.), *Proceedings of the 20th International Conference on Information Systems*, Charlotte, NC, 1999, pp. 291-299.

Bruns Jr., W. J., and McFarlan, F. W. "Information Technology Puts Power in Control Systems," *Harvard Business Review* (65:5), 1987, pp. 89-94.

Clegg, S., and Wilson, F. "Power, Technology and Flexibility in Organizations," in J. Law (ed.), *Sociology of Monsters: Essays on Power, Technology and Domination*, London: Routledge, 1991, pp. 223-273.

Coombs, R., Knights, D., and Willmott, H. C. "Culture, Control and Competition: Towards a Conceptual Framework for the Study of Information Technology in Organizations," *Organization Studies* (13:1), 1992, pp. 51-72.

Finnegan, P., and Longaigh, S. N. "Examining the Effects of Information Technology on Control and Coordination Relationships: An Exploratory Study in Subsidiaries of Pan-National Corporations," *Journal of Information Technology* (17:3), 2002, pp. 149-163.

Foucault, M. *Discipline and Punish: The Birth of the Prison*, London: Lane, 1977.

Giddens, A. *The Consequences of Modernity*, Cambridge, England: Polity Press, 1990.

Hanseth, O., and Braa, K. "Globalization and 'Risk Society,'" in C. U. Ciborra, K. Braa, A. Cordella, B. Dahlbom, A. Failla, O. Hanseth, V. Hepso, J. Ljungberg, E. Monteiro, and K. A. Simon (eds.), *From Control to Drift: The Dynamics of Corporate Information Infrastructures*, Oxford, England: Oxford University Press, 2000, pp. 41-55.

Hanseth, O., Ciborra, C. U., and Braa, K. "The Control Devolution: EPR and the Side Effects of Globalization," *The Data Base for Advances in Information Systems* (32:4), 2001, pp. 34-46.

Markus, M. L. "Power, Politics, and MIS Implementation," *Communications of the ACM* (26:6), 1983, pp. 430-444.

Nandhakumar, J., and Jones, M. R. "Too Close for Comfort? Distance and Engagement in Interpretive Innformation Systems Research," *Information Systems Journal* (7:2), 1997, pp. 109-131.

Orlikowski, W. J. "Integrated Information Environment or Matrix of Control? The Contra-dictory Implications of Information Technology," *Accounting, Management and Information Technologies* (1:1), 1991, pp. 9-42.

Orlikowski, W. "Using Technology and Constituting Structures: A Practice Lens for Studying Technology in Organizations," *Organization Science* (11:4), 2000, pp. 404-428.

Robinson, B., and Wilson, F. "Planning for the Market? Enterprise Resource Planning Systems and the Contradictions of Capital," *The Data base for Advances in Information Systems* (32:4), 2001, pp. 21-33.

Sia, S. K., Tang, M., Soh, C., and Boh, W. F. "Enterprise Resource Planning (ERP) Systems as a Technology of Power: Empowerment or Panoptic Control," *The Data base for Advances in Information Systems* (33:1), 2002, pp. 23-37.

Strauss, A., and Corbin, J. *Basics of Qualitative Research: Techniques and Procedures for Developing Grounded Theory*, Thousand Oaks, CA: Sage Publications, 1998.

Walsham, G. "The Emergence of Interpretivism in IS Research," *Information Systems Research* (6:4), 1995, pp. 376-394.

Walsham, G. *Interpreting Information Systems in Organizations*, Chichester, England: John Wiley & Sons, 1993.

Yin, R. K. *Case Study Research-design and Methods*, Thousand Oaks, CA: Sage Publications, 2003.

About the Authors

Ioannis Ignatiadis is a research and teaching associate at the University of Bath, School of Management, England. He received his Master's degree in Technology Management from UMIST, England. He also holds a Master's degree in Information Technology from Imperial College, England, and a Bachelor's degree in Computer Science from the same university. He worked in industry as a software consultant in information technology projects for big multinational companies in the UK, Germany, and Greece, covering the pharmaceutical, logistics, energy, and IT services sectors. He also worked as a project manager/analyst in the imple-mentation of European Union-sponsored Information Society Technologies (IST) projects. His research interests evolve around the selection, implementation and use of enterprise systems within an organization. Ioannis can be reached by e-mail at I.Ignatiadis@bath.ac.uk.

Joe Nandhakumar is a reader (associate professor) in Information Systems and the Director of the Centre for Information Management in the School of Management at the University of Bath, England. He has wide-ranging experience in industry and gained his Ph.D. from the Department of Engineering, University of Cambridge, England. Joe's research focuses on the human and organizational aspects of information systems development, organizational consequences of information technology use, and theoretical and methodological issues in information systems research. He has widely published in these areas. Joe can be reached by e-mail at J.Nandhakumar @bath.ac.uk.

19 THE RISE AND DESCENT OF VISIONS FOR E-GOVERNMENT

Helle Zinner Henriksen
Jan Damsgaard
Copenhagen Business School
Frederiksberg, Denmark

Abstract   *Most nations have defined strategies for e-government. The objectives for implementing e-government are often defined but the means for fueling the adoption and diffusion of e-government are typically less clear in policy statements. The present study assesses the impact of the Danish eDay initiative. The eDay initiative simply yet powerfully states that one governmental authority has the right to demand that its communication with another authority must be in electronic format. The eDay initiative represents a drastic change in the former policy statements concerning IT adoption and diffusion in Danish government. Policy statements had previously been based on voluntary adoption based on indirect and pedagogical intervention in governmental agencies, but eDay marked a departure and the carrot has been exchanged by the stick and the voice is imperative.*

Keywords   e-Government, business process reengineering, information society

1   INTRODUCTION

The advent of digital government or electronic government (e-government) has rapidly spread throughout the world leading to a constant stream of policy documents on e-government visions from national and supranational agencies. Representing the supranational agencies, the European Union and the Organisation for Economic Cooperation and Development are among those which have launched visions for e-government (EU 2003; OECD 2003). Canada and the United States are often claimed to be among the most salient examples of nations that have gone beyond visions and actually implemented effective e-government (Holden et al. 2003; Kaylor et al. 2003). Asian countries such as Malaysia and Singapore have also proven to be in the lead with respect to effective implementation of e-government agendas (Tan and Pan 2003).

Please use the following format when citing this chapter:

Henriksen, Helle Zinner, Damsgaard, Jan, 2006, in International Federation for Information Processing (IFIP), Volume 206, The Transfer and Diffusion of Information Technology for Organizational Resilience, eds. B. Donnellan, Larsen T., Levine L., DeGross J. (Boston: Springer), pp. 275-289.

However, in a number of international rankings, the Scandinavian countries are among the forerunners in e-government (Accenture 2005; Cap Gemini 2005; UN 2004). This paper provides a description and analysis of the visions and strategies in one of the Scandinavian countries (Denmark) which may serve as a measure of which strategy yields what effects.

A common characteristic of the above-mentioned agendas and rankings is the citizen centric approach. It is an approach focusing on how governments have or are supposed to adopt IT-tools in order to provide better and faster services to citizens and businesses. A number of maturity models for e-government have been developed in the slipstream of this discourse (Kaylor et al. 2000; Layne and Lee 2001; Moon 2002). The maturity models work on the assumption that there are different levels of interaction with users and different degrees of integration of data that can be benchmarked. A high score is then a surrogate of a high level of sophistication in e-government.

A much less evaluated aspect and less visible aspect of e-government is the internal facet of the governments' own use and reuse of data generated, handled, and stored with IT. Scholl (2005) claims that e-government research is subject to an iceberg phenomenon. The top of the iceberg represents the government to citizen and business interaction whereas the governments' internal effectiveness and efficiency is largely disregarded because it is below the surface and therefore much less visible. We concur with his observation and add that only with an effective internal processing of information can the citizen and business be better serviced. Also in line with *business process reengineering* (BPR), in the *public process reengineering* (PPR) model formulated by Andersen (2004) it is suggested that public sector institutions should reorganize their internal activities in order to achieve effectiveness and efficiency by keeping their focus on the benefits for the users of the services. However, these two contributions—Andersen (2004) and Scholl (2005)—are exceptions from the rule of the citizen-centric approach dominating e-government research at present.

Our focus in this paper is on the internal aspect of e-government. Inspired by the recently launched government-wide eDay initiative, a review of one decade's worth of Danish policy statements is presented. The eDay initiative aimed at strengthening the intra- and interorganizational interaction through electronic means among all government departments and at all levels of government. Hence the objective of this paper is to present the impact of the strategy the Danish government has applied to strengthen the diffusion of e-government in and among public sector institutions in Denmark. Based on the figures from the years 2002, 2003, and 2004 on digital interaction, the internal digital handling of data, and finally uptake of technology supporting the digital handling, we discuss whether the agenda for diffusion of e-government has proven to be successful. When referring to e-government, the definition developed by Layne and Lee (2001) is applied. Layne and Lee suggested that e-government is

> government's use of technology, particularly web-based Internet applications to enhance the access to and delivery of government information and service to citizens, business partners, employees, other agencies, and government entities (p. 123).

By using this particular definition the external customers of the public sector as well as the public sector are seen as beneficiaries of e-government adoption and diffusion.

The remainder of the paper is as follows. Section 2 provides an overview of Danish government initiatives used to fuel the diffusion of e-government during the period from 1994 through 2003. Section 3 presents the stream of literature focusing on intervention and its use for fueling the diffusion of IS innovations. Section 4 outlines our data and discusses the impact of the eDay. Section 5 provides some concluding remarks.

2   THE HISTORY OF INSTITUTIONAL INTERVENTION LEADING TO THE eDAY INITIATIVE

In the Danish context, the history of institutional intervention for the support of the diffusion of IT-innovations in government dates back to 1994. In the following, excerpts of the policy statements are presented in chronological order starting with year 1994 and ending with year 2003 when the eDay initiative was launched. Not all initiatives have exclusively focused on IT adoption in the public sector. However, a particular focus on those sections concerning the public sector and its role in technology diffusion are emphasized in the presentation. We review and characterize the main initiatives and discuss their focus areas in terms of citizen-centric or focus on internal processes. All policy statements can be found at the web-site of the Ministry of Science, Technology and Innovation (www.fsk.dk under the link Publications).

2.1   1994: "Info-Society 2000"

In 1994 the Ministry of Research published the report "Info-Society 2000." The report was a consequence of the Bangemann report (1994) prepared by the EU. The Info-Society 2000 report led to a continuous stream of initiatives all suggesting how IT should be utilized in the public sector and how proper utilization would lead to benefits for the public sector, businesses, and society as a whole.

2.2 1995: "From Vision to Action—Info-Society 2000"

The first statement "From Vision to Action—Info-Society 2000" was published in 1995. The statement was used as a lever to create awareness of the great significance of the digital revolution. It was stated that this movement toward the Info-Society was a movement involving everybody. In a true Danish spirit, it was argued that if Grundtvig had been alive he would probably be connected to the Internet. Grundtvig (1783 to 1872) was a Danish poet, statesman, and church father. He was the driving force behind the establishment of the first Danish folk high schools. The folk high schools played a significant role in the education of rural youth until the 1950s when the governmental education system took over. This rather strong symbol illustrates the expectations for the move toward the information society, which was seen as the means for everybody to get involved in democratic processes and education. The strategy should thus be based on a Danish model where market forces should not, similar to initiatives in Italy (Kumar et al. 1998) and Hong Kong (Damsgaard and Lyytinen 1998), be allowed to be the only forces determining development.

Although the statement primarily focused on building a strong infrastructure, the responsibility of the public sector to engage in the movement was stressed. The role of the public sector in the digitization of the Danish society was emphasized in statements such as

Public administration (central, county and municipal levels) is to be connected in a comprehensive electronic service network, providing: better service to citizens, better service to trade and industry and support of their own use of IT, rationalisation gains, and more open decision-making processes.

By implementing these electronic service networks it was expected that

Concurrently with the replacement of IT systems, public institutions are to change gradually from paper-based archives to electronic processing and filing over the coming years.

2.3 1996: "The Info-Society for All"

In 1996, the next IT policy statement was published. The statement focused on EDI as the means to digitize the Danish society. The statement was named "The Info-Society for All—The Danish Model." In the 1996 statement, it was announced that

this new technology [EDI] presents a number of opportunities and problems, which demand political consideration and action. A cohesive, aggressive strategy for how we wish to further the developments in Denmark is necessary.

Included in this "aggressive strategy" was the 1996 action plan for electronic commerce. It was found that *"the importance of a fast, effective and consistent implementation of, e.g., EDI could hardly be overestimated."* First and foremost it was claimed that technological landmarks such as EDI could give Denmark an international lead along with improvement in efficiency of working procedures and development of new products and production processes. The goal of the 1996 action plan was thus to provide the necessary conditions for companies, the public sector, and, not least, the consumers to reap the gains resulting from EDI.

The plan is to provide dynamism and accelerate growth. This will be achieved through the public sector joining forces with a large number of commercial organizations to create joint solutions. Thereby we will avoid a state in which everyone waits for everyone else, or in which the approaches chosen are not coherent.

In order to create the necessary dynamics and consistency, seven initiatives were formulated. The initiatives primarily aimed at supporting the diffusion of EDIFACT based EDI communication, thereby supporting electronic data transactions between private companies and the public sector. The expectations regarding the ability of the public sector in relation to development and implementation were high. It was found that the public sector had to take the lead and show an example.

It was acknowledged in the introduction to the 1996 action plan that the project was ambitious and that it required involvement from several business sectors and institutions. One means to meet this end was to make the necessary arrangements to be able to execute public procurement via EDI. It was, however, the adopters that carried the main responsibility for acting according to the recommendations in the action plan.

> *One decisive feature of "the Danish model" is that, without grandiose plans, but precisely through dialogue and effective action, we are in a position to implement the necessary infrastructure quickly and to remove the barriers to it.*

This attitude was further explained by former experiences with the long Danish tradition of the establishment of the cooperative dairies and abattoirs, which successfully took place at the end of the 19th century and which led to a social and economic lift for a large number of small and often impoverished farmers. Again, strong national symbols were taken in use to promote the diffusion of IT in the Danish society. Again, a vision was created and the actors were expected to act accordingly, but no concrete actions were taken to ensure the implementation.

2.4 1999: "Focus on e-Commerce"

The outcome of the 1996 action plan was less successful than expected and in 1999—one year before the planned expiration of the action plan—a new initiative was launched. This initiative was named "Focus on e-Commerce." Focus on e-Commerce was organized to meet the conditions imposed by the information society and the Internet. The aim was to initiate concrete activities, which could promote the development of electronic commerce in Denmark. The initiative consisted of seven points for action, mostly focusing on creating safe and optimal conditions for e-commerce, which peaked at that time. One of the seven points explicitly focused on "electronic commerce in the public sector."

2.5 2000: "Digital Denmark—Conversion to the Network Society"

In year 2000, the next initiative, "Digital Denmark—Conversion to the Network Society," was announced. Five objectives were highlighted as important to digitize Denmark. Among these five objectives was "More Effective and Cheaper Service via Digital Administration," it was argued that

> *Efficient digital administration means, among other things, ensuring optimal internal procedures. IT should contribute to the public administration by optimising its organisation and working procedures to produce results in the form of measurable rationalisation gains. These gains will also contribute significantly to the public sector, solving the demographic problem which will mean that in a few years it will have to function with a smaller workforce.*

Similar to the previous initiatives the means for achieving the benefits were based on voluntariness. It was admitted that to reap the benefits of IT investments, it was necessary to face the organizational consequences of the technological investments.

2.6 2002: "IT for All—Denmark's Future"

"IT for All—Denmark's Future," an IT and telecommunications policy statement and action plan from 2002, was the next initiative. The preamble stressed that IT should be the means for promoting a reform of the public sector in Denmark. It emphasized that development should still be driven by private initiative and on market terms. One outcome of this strategy was the launch of the public procurement portal (doip.dk), which was privately owned and run. Again, seven areas of importance to strengthen Denmark as an IT nation were outlined. Among these was "an IT-based public sector."

The recommendations to strengthen an IT based public sector were

(1) The public sector to work digitally both internally and in contact with citizens and companies; (2) Public service delivery to be coherent and user-centred, with greater re-use of public data and an increasing number of general portals being means to this end; (3) Focus to be intensified including organisational upgrading of IT; and, (4) Public-sector e-commerce to be initiated and substantially increased.

Some resources were granted to implement the initiatives but it was emphasized that the policy statement should be seen as an invitation to dialogue. Furthermore, a new body was introduced: the Digital Taskforce. The role of this Digital Taskforce was (and is) to ensure coordination and progress of the move toward e-government. It is a joint board including top managers from central and local government administration. One tangible outcome of the Digital Taskforce was the eDay.

2.7 2003: "eDay 1"

The first of September 2003 was announced by the Danish government to be a special "eDay." From that day, all Danish state, regional, and local governmental authorities has the right to demand that communication with other authorities to be exchanged electronically. The practical implication of this initiative is that authorities from that day can refuse paper-based communication. The eDay initiative can be seen as a milestone in the Danish IT policy. It is the first time in the 10 years of IT policies that direct intervention is used as a means for fueling the diffusion process by creating a network effect. The eDay initiative explicitly states that public sector institutions have the right to demand that other units communicate electronically with them. Throughout the history of Danish IT policies, it has been claimed that digital communication would be beneficial for public institutions and that a shift should take place to make the Danish public sector efficient. There has been an implicit expectation that the diffusion of the necessary technologies would take place based on the recommendations but no direct control or enforcement has been used to make diffusion and implementation happen. Another remarkable shift in the policy is the introduction of the digital taskforce as an active change agency, stimulating the diffusion process. Section 5 analyzes if the eDay initiative actually has led to a strengthening of e-government.

This section presented the odyssey of Danish IT policy through one decade. The presentation focused on the content and also to some extent on the means for implementing the content of the policy statements. The next section focuses on the impact of policy statements as observed in previous studies.

3   INTERVENTION AS A LEVER FOR DIFFUSION

There are different opinions regarding the effectiveness of regulation and intervention as the means for directing action related to IT adoption. This raises the question of whether regulatory initiatives can possibly result in voluntary changes in organizational behavior leading to adoption and diffusion, or if incentives for adoption are to be found in mechanisms solely driven by economic and strategic interests. In the following, a number of considerations related to regulation are discussed. It should be emphasized that the initiatives presented above, in a legal sense, are categorized as soft law. Soft law concerns rules of conduct that are on a legally nonbinding level (Nielsen 1999). An analogy is, however, made to considerations related to explicit rules and regulation in general.

Inherent in a set of rules is the means of regulatory intervention. Three types of regulatory intervention, the pedagogical, the economic, and the normative (Eckhoff 1983) have been described as means for regulating organizational and human behavior. Prohibition and commands characterize normative interventions. Normative interventions are means for enforcing the objective of the regulation. One example of this type of intervention in relation to IT adoption is to define standards (Andersen et al. 2000). Economic interventions are characterized by influencing what people find it advantageous to do. Through economic interventions, organizations are rewarded for performing certain acts or punished for certain other types of behavior. Direct subsidy of projects can be considered an example of an economic intervention (Andersen et al. 2000). The pedagogical intervention is characterized by information campaigns initiated by governmental units and larger associations where the aim is to influence the opinion of a given group of potential adopters. Eckhoff (1983) argues that information is a must in most cases where the economic and normative regulatory interventions are brought into play, but information in itself can be used as a means of intervention.

Through information, it is possible to influence opinions and values, thus making individuals more motivated for certain types of actions wished for by the governmental units or associations. Knowledge building hence becomes an important aspect in pedagogical intervention (Andersen et al. 2000). However, governments can also effectively employ institutional measures to obtain a desired change in behavior. Institutional measures are usually classified into influential or regulatory ones (King et al. 1994). Influential initiatives aim to change the behavior of those under the institution's sway.

This is achieved without direct reference to force, or the exercise of command, but mainly through an incentive structure. Regulatory actions, on the other hand, are expected to affect directly the behaviors of entities under formal government jurisdiction. This can take the form of directives or through limiting the choice of options. Overall, regulatory measures allow conflicting decentralized decisions to be compatible without the necessity of either centralized institutions or "key" individuals to comprehend the whole system (Boyer 1988). This is sometimes necessary as, for example, the use of common standards may yield more work for each node in a system but the overall benefits clearly outweigh the sum of each node's additional work.

Within the domain of IS research, the impact of intervention is often subject to discussion. The writings of Lai and Guynes (1997), Gregor and Johnston (2001), Johnston and Gregor (2000), and King et al. (1994) uncover a discrepancy in relation to the effects of coordinated efforts made by industry and trade associations or governmental units in relation to diffusion of IT (Damsgaard and Lyytinen 2001). It has been stated that institutional (especially governmental unit) interventions (Lai and Guynes 1997) and change in the environment (e.g., regulation) (Gregor and Johnston 2001) are among the most powerful causes for IT adoption and diffusion. Deliberate institutional interventions or refraining from interventions are thus found to play a vital role in technology diffusion (King et al. 1994). The opposite point of view has, however, also been stated recently by Johnston and Gregor (2000), who argue that "deliberative coordinated action by an industry as a whole, or units purporting to represent such a group position, may be severely limited in effectiveness." Different parties can address the building of electronic infrastructures, which are a necessity for IT diffusion (Damsgaard and Lyytinen 1998).

Two of the most well-known governmental initiatives related to IT adoption and diffusion are the TEDIS project, launched by the European Commission, and TradeNet, launched by the government in Singapore. The Singaporean TradeNet was, contrary to the TEDIS project, launched as a mandatory initiative from a governmental agency, the National Computer Board. The companies involved in the export sector were obliged to implement EDI for the exchange of export documents with the public authorities. The electronic infrastructure was launched in 1989. TradeNet is the first nation-wide EDI ever implemented (Teo et al. 1997). TradeNet processed nearly all trade declaration documents by the end of 1994. The Singapore experiment can be viewed as a success in relation to diffusion of EDI in a business community, where it has achieved or even surpassed its goals (Thong 1999). Hong Kong launched a similar initiative named Tradelink but, typical for Hong Kong, Tradelink was owned by both private and public companies. Once Tradelink was operational and proved its systems worked, the government decided to shut down the counter for manual submission of trade declarations and export/import licenses. The two Asian initiatives represent examples of normative intervention.

In the Danish context, the indirect pedagogical intervention has been the sole strategy pursued in the policy statements up to the eDay initiative where more direct intervention is taken into use (Henriksen and Andersen 2004). The following section examines if the eDay initiative has gained the same success as, for example, Singapore's TradeNet.

4 ANALYSIS AND DISCUSSION OF THE IMPACT THE eDAY 1

To analyze the impact of eDay 1, statistical data were retrieved from Statistics Denmark.[1] The analysis and discussion includes the annual accounts of the public sector's use of IT in years 2002, 2003, and 2004. The reason for using this particular sample is that consistent and comparative data were available from that time span. Given that eDay was launched in 2003, it is found suitable to use these data as the source. We believe that this data is the best option available. Another possibility would be to obtain data based on a survey instrument specifically developed for the purpose of analyzing the impact of eDay in the diffusion and deployment of IT internally in the public sector in Denmark but this approach would capture intentions and impressions only. The actual use forms a concrete measure on which the impact of eDay1 can be observed.

The series of data from years 2002, 2003, and 2004 show that there has been a growth in the exchange of data electronically between governmental units whereas the exchange of documents between citizens and businesses and that the public sector has remained more or less constant. The growth in governmental units receiving documents electronically at the 25 percent level is statistically significant (p is less than or equal to 0.001). The growth is depicted in Figure 1.

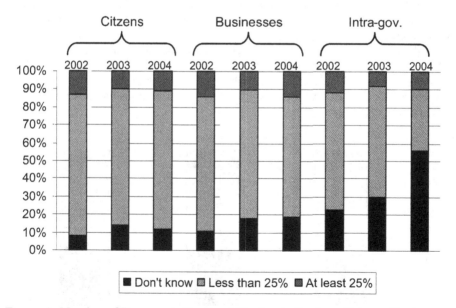

Figure 1. Number of Documents Received Electronically from Citizens, Businesses, and Other Governmental Units, 2002-2004

---

[1]"Den offtenlige sektors brug af IT 2002, 2003, 2004 [Usage of IT in the Public Sector]," Statistics Denmark, www.dst.dk.

This indicates that the eDay has had an impact on the diffusion of e-government. Public sector institutions have increased their digital interaction. Recalling that the definition used for e-government was "government's use of technology, particularly web-based Internet applications to enhance the access to and delivery of government information and service to citizens, business partners, employees, other agencies, and government entities," the implementation of e-government should also have an impact on internal working procedures. To analyze a possible impact of the growth in the number of documents being received electronically, internal electronic document handling was analyzed. Figure 2 depicts the growth in electronic document handling in the governmental units.

Figure 2 illustrates that there has only been a small growth in the number of governmental units where at least 50 percent of the cases are handled electronically. Taking into consideration that there has been a substantial growth in number of cases actually exchanged electronically intra-governmentally (see Figure 1) which is not reflected in the statistics on electronic case handling, this could indicate that the public sector institutions do not have the IT-tools necessary for handling the cases electronically. In order to analyze this closer, the uptake of case- and document-handling systems in public intuitions was analyzed.

Figure 3 depicts that the degree of sophistication on handling of electronic documents is rather low. There is a high level of deployment of electronic log-systems at all levels—and especially at the county level where the level has been 100 percent all years reported. When it comes to full electronic case handling, the deployment is rather low at the state and municipal levels. It is crucial to ask if this is due to issues related to standards.

Although there has been a significant growth in communication with other agencies in XML format during the period 2002–2004, the overall adoption rate is still low (see Figure 4). This could indicate that the Danish public sector faces a classical problem. The good will is there to adopt technology but technological infrastructures, particularly standards, are not in place.

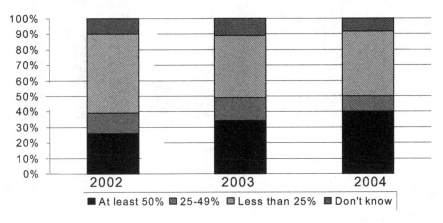

Figure 2. Number of Governmental Units Using Electronic Document Handling Systems

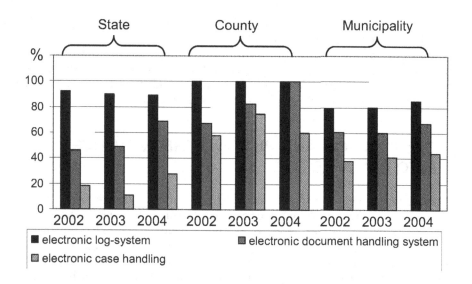

Figure 3. Deployment of Electronic Log-Systems, Electronic Document Handling Systems, and Electronic Case Handling

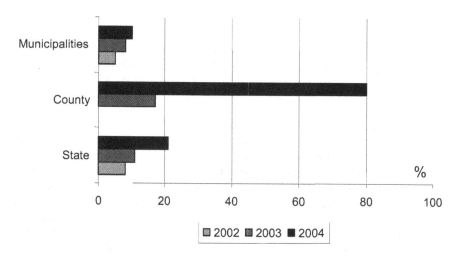

Figure 4. Communication with Other Agencies in XML Format (2002–2004)

To illustrate, the Danish Customs and Tax department introduced EDI as part of their service concept, which is to be technologically ahead of the companies they service. As a consequence, relations with the trading community improved and the image of the Customs and Tax department as a slow and dull government department shifted toward an image of a modern and progressive service organization. However, one of the main problems for the department is that, from the beginning, it allowed multiple standards, and multiple entries to the system, and having done that, it is now impossible for the department to reduce the number of entries and endorse only one standard. Instead, new versions are issued and new implementation guidelines are published at a high rate. So it is a tragedy that instead of helping setting a standard for EDI for the benefit of Danish companies, the customs and tax authorities add to the confusion by endorsing several standards and versions thereof.

5   CONCLUSION AND PUTTING THE INITIATIVES INTO PERSPECTIVE

One of the unifying principles of Danish IT policy in the domain of e-government has been to reduce the paper-based case handling in favor of electronic processing and filing. In each of the initiatives presented in section 2, there are more or less pronounced expectations for savings and efficiency gains if the public sector changes its routines from manual paper-handling to electronic procedures. In a Social Democratic spirit, adoption and diffusion of the ideas exhibited in the policy statements have been fueled by pedagogical intervention rather than more direct means such as legislation or economic rewards for changing behavior. This path has not, so far, proven to be fruitful if conclusions are made based on the figures on IT adoption in the public sector published by Statistics Denmark.

One overall challenge in relation to assessment of the outcome of coordinated initiatives is the level of analysis when measuring the outcome. One way to evaluate the success or failure of a project is based on the project's rate of adoption among potential users. As observed by Kumar et al. (1998), this might be a less fruitful path since some or all adopters at a later state might reject the innovation. To denote adoption rate as the dependent variable for success thus has to be seen in relation to time (DeLone and McLean 1992). This approach, however, is not easy to apply to the eDay initiative at this point in time given the relatively recent inception.

Our analysis suggests that the initiative so far has led to mixed results. When looking at the intra-governmental exchange of electronic messages in isolation (see Figure 1), there has been a remarkable growth. This indicates that the eDay initiative has had a positive impact on the diffusion of e-government. But a closer examination of the further deployment of the electronic messages provides a different picture. There has only been a slight increase in the number of government agencies using electronic document handling systems, which is a prerequisite for paper-less document handling as envisioned in the policy statements. This suggests that more traditional procedures are still the norm in governmental agencies. One problem appears to be the lack of basic systems supporting electronic document and case handling (see Figure 3). Ultimately, this indicates that Danish government agencies face what the business community has suffered from for decades: lack of common standards. One future challenge for the Danish public sector in order to be able to implement e-government is, therefore, to agree on a common standard for communication and interaction to make sure that the access to and delivery of government information and service to citizens, business partners, employees, other agencies, and government entities can be enhanced.

References

Accenture. *Leadership in Customer Service: New Expectations, New Experiences*, 2005 (available through http://www.accenture.com/).

Andersen, K. V. *E-Government and Public Sector Process Rebuilding (PPR): Dilettantes, Wheelbarrows, and Diamonds*, Boston: Kluwer Adademic Publishers, 2004.

Andersen, K. V., Juul, N. C., Henriksen, H. Z., Bjørn-Andersen, N., and Bunker, D. *Business-to-Business E-Commerce, Enterprises Facing a Turbulent World*, Copenhagen: DJØF Publishers (Association of Danish Lawyers and Economists), 2000.

Bangemann, M. *Europe and the Global Information Society*, Brussels: European Commission, 1994 (available online at http://www.medicif.org/Dig_library/ECdocs/reports/Bangemann.htm).

Boyer, R. "Technical Change and the Role of Regulation," in G. Dosi, C. Freeman, R. Nelson, G. Silverberg, and L. Soete (eds.), *Technical Change and Economic Theory*, London: Pinter Publishers, 1988, pp. 67-94.

Cap Gemini. *Online Availability of Public Services: How Is Europe Progressing?*, EU: DG Information and Media, March 3, 2005 (available online at http://europa.eu.int/information_society/soccul/egov/egov_benchmarking_2005.pdf.

Damsgaard, J., and Lyytinen, K. "International Trade at the Speed of Light: Building an Electronic Trading Infrastructure in Denmark, Finland, and Hong Kong," in T. J. Larsen, L. Levine, and J. I. DeGross (eds.), *Information Systems: Current Issues and Future Changes*, Laxenburg, Austria: IFIP, 1998, pp. 417-438.

Damsgaard, J., and Lyytinen, K. "The Role of Intermediating Institutions in Diffusion of Electronic Data Interchange (EDI): How Industry Associations in the Grocery Sector Intervened in Hong Kong, Finland, and Denmark," *The Information Society* (17:3), 2001, pp. 195-210.

DeLone, H. W., and McLean, E. R. "Information Systems Success: The Quest for the Dependent Variable," *Information Systems Research* (3:1), 1992, pp. 60-95.

Eckhoff, T. *Statens styringsmuligheter*, Oslo: TANUM-NORLI, 1983.

European Union. *The Role of E-Government for Europe's Future*, Brussels: European Commission, 2003.

Gregor, S., and Johnston, R. B. "Theory of Interorganizational Systems: Industry Structure and Processes of Change," in R. Sprague (ed.), *Proceedings of the 34th Hawaii International Conference on Systems Sciences*, 2001, pp. 159-170.

Henriksen, H. Z., and Andersen, K. V. "Diffusion of E-Commerce in Denmark: An Analysis of Institutional Intervention," *Knowledge, Technology, and Policy* (17:2), 2004, pp. 63-81.

Holden, S. H., Norris, D. F., and Fletcher, P. D. "Electronic Government at the Local Level: Progress to Date and Future Issues," *Public Performance and Management Review* (26:4), 2003, pp. 325-344.

Johnston, R. B., and Gregor, S. "A Theory of Industry-Level Activity for Understanding the Adoption of Interorganizational Systems," *European Journal of Information Systems* (9:4), 2000, pp. 243-251.

Kaylor, C., Deshazo, R., and Van Eck, D. "Gauging E-Government: A Report on Implementing Services among American Cities," *Government Information Quarterly* (18:4), 2001, pp. 293-307.

King, J. L., Gurbaxani, V., Kraemer, K. L., McFarlan, F. W., Raman, K. S., and Yap, C. S. "Institutional Factors in Information Technology Innovation," *Information Systems Research* (5:2), 1994, pp. 139-169.

Kumar, K., van Dissel, H. G., and Bielli, P. "The Merchant of Prato Revisited: Toward a Third Rationality of Information Systems," *MIS Quarterly* (22:2), 1998, pp. 199-225.

Lai, V. S., and Guynes, J. L. "An Assessment of the Influence of Organizational Characteristics on Information Technology Adoption Decision: A Discriminative Approach," *IEEE Transactions on Engineering Management* (44:2), 1997, pp. 146-157.

Layne, K., and Lee, J. W. "Developing Fully Functional E-Government: A Four Stage Model," *Government Information Quarterly* (18:2), 2001, pp. 122-136.

Moon, M. J. "The Evolution of E-Government among Municipalities: Rhetoric or Reality?," *Public Administration Review* (62:4), 2002, pp. 424-433.

Nielsen, R. *Retskilderne*, Copenhagen: Jurist- og Økonomforbundets forlag, 1999.

OECD. *World Public Sector Report 2003: E-Government at the Crossroads*, New York: United Nations, 2003 (available online at http://unpan1.un.org/intradoc/groups/public/documents/UN/UNPAN012733.pdf).

Scholl, H. J. "Organizational Transformation through E-Government: Myth or Reality?," in M. A. Wimmer, R. Traunmüller, Å. Grönlund, and K. V. Andersen (eds.), *Electronic Government, 4th International Conference (EGOV 2005)*, Berlin: Springer, 2005, pp. 1-11.

Tan, C. W., and Pan, S. L. "Managing E-Transformation in the Public Sector: An E-Government Study of the Inland Revenue Authority of Singapore (IRAS)," *European Journal of Information Systems* (12:4), 2003, pp. 269-281.

Teo, H. H., Tan, B. C. Y., and Wei, K. K. "Organizational Transformation Using Electronic Data Interchange: The Case of TradeNet in Singapore" *Journal of Management Information Systems* (13:4), 1997, pp. 139-165.

Thong, J. Y. L. "An Integrated Model for Information Systems Adoption in Small Businesses," *Journal of Management Information Systems* (15:4), 1999, pp. 187-214.

United Nations. *UN Global E-government Readiness Report*, New York: United Nations, 2004 (available online at http://unpan1.un.org/intradoc/groups/public/documents/un/unpan021888.pdf).

About the Authors

Helle Zinner Henriksen is assistant professor at the Department of Informatics, Copenhagen Business School. She has a M.Sc. in law from University of Copenhagen and a Ph.D. from the Department of Informatics, Copenhagen Business School. Her Ph.D. is in the field of Management of Information Systems with particular interest on the implications of institutional intervention with respect to interorganizational adoption and diffusion. Her research interests include adoption and diffusion of IT in the private and the public sector. She has presented her work at international conferences including DEXA eGov, eChallenges, ECIS, HICSS, and IFIP 8.6 and in international journals such as *Communication of the AIS, Knowledge, Technology, and Policy, Scandinavian Journal of Information Systems*, and *International Journal of Electronic Government Research*. More details on research activities and publications can be found at www.HelleZinnerHenriksen.info. Helle can be reached at hzh.inf@cbs.dk.

Jan Damsgaard is professor at the Department of Informatics, Copenhagen Business School, Denmark. He holds a Master's degree in Computer Science and Psychology and a Ph.D. in Computer Science (1996). JD is the study director of a graduate program in e-business. His research focuses on the diffusion and implementation of networked and standard-based technologies such as intranet, extranet, Internet portals, EDI, and advanced mobile services (GSM/GPRS/EDGE, UMTS, WiFi, and WiMax). In much of his research, JD seeks to explain technology diffusion using network economics and technology characteristics. He is the research director of the Mobiconomy and DREAMS projects that focus on diffusion and implementation of advanced mobile services. He has presented his work at international conferences (ICIS, ECIS, PACIS, HICSS, IFIP 8.2., and IFIP 8.6) and in international journals (*European Journal of*

Information Systems, Information Systems Journal, Journal of Strategic Information Systems, Information Society, Journal of Global Information Management, Journal of Organizational Computing and Electronic Commerce, Information Technology and People, and *Journal of the Association for Information Systems*). JD can be reached at damsgaard@cbs.dk or at http://www.cbs.dk/staff/damsgaard/.

20 THE ROLE OF EXTREME PROGRAMMING IN A PLAN-DRIVEN ORGANIZATION

Helene Dahlberg
Volvo Technology Corporation
Gothenburg, Sweden

Francisco Solano Ruiz
Elanders AB
Gothenburg, Sweden

Carl Magnus Olsson
University of Limerick
Limerick, Ireland

Abstract   *The difficulties and even lack of commitment to follow plans within plan-based organizations is a well known phenomenon (see Ciborra et al. 2000; Suchman 1987). For software development companies, this problem has become an increasing dilemma, as typically plan-driven software development assessment standards like the capability maturity model (CMM) or ISO/IEC 15504 have not always been easy to conform processes against. Particularly, in environments where requirements are rapidly changing, more agile approaches such as Scrum and extreme programming (XP) have caught on. In this work, we are reporting from a case study of an organization looking to not move completely from their plan-based processes (as they are but a part of a larger organization operating in a plan-based way), but rather adapt their overarching processes in a way that allows them to use XP to support their everyday work precluded by their current processes. To this end, we present four perspectives that organizations may take when they desire or consider becoming more agile in their development. We use the Nerur et al. (2005) key issues for moving from plan-based to agile software development to compare and analyze our findings. In doing this, we highlight a set of likely criteria necessary to successfully create a combination of the plan-driven and agile approaches.*

Please use the following format when citing this chapter:

Dahlberg, Helene, Solano Ruiz, Francisco, Magnus Olsson, Carl, 2006, in International Federation for Information Processing (IFIP), Volume 206, The Transfer and Diffusion of Information Technology for Organizational Resilience, eds. B. Donnellan, Larsen T., Levine L., DeGross J. (Boston: Springer), pp. 291-312.

Keywords   Agile software development, extreme programming (XP), plan-driven
software development, Scrum

1   INTRODUCTION

Retaining control within an organization may be an elusive objective when it comes
to software development. Ad hoc development tends to yield unpredictable quality,
costs, and time to delivery. In an effort to address this, software development companies
have been looking to define processes through which software quality, costs, and
deliveries could be projected at an early stage, monitored throughout design and development, and insured prior to release to the customer. Through continuously improving
such processes, organizations hope to find ways of working that guarantee software
quality. Agile and plan-driven are two approaches to describe processes for software
development. They are referred to as different approaches (understood as perspectives)
when mentioned in general terms. Using the concept *processes* refers to an organizational point of view, where a series of actions to create software are described, while the
term *method* defines a detailed level. Some of the most well-known agile approaches
are XP and Scrum. Examples of plan-driven approaches are the Waterfall Model and
CMM-based methods. Today, although plan-driven software development remains the
most common approach, organizations are often drifting into ad hoc adaptations of these
plan-driven processes, using quick-and-dirty solutions and behind-the-scenes improvi-
sations that are far from what the official process prescribes. Frequently, management
is not unaware of this, but simply elects to officially not be aware of such development
habits. On the one hand, you have customers and managers demanding quick deliveries
of excellent quality, using the latest and most appropriate technology, software
development languages, and techniques. On the other hand, you are expected to strictly
follow processes that demand a great deal of documentation, meetings, consideration,
and decision makers to come together and make informed calls for what to do.

Research within Information Systems has recognized this tendency to drift (see
Ciborra et al. 2000; Suchman 1987). While Suchman (1987) focuses on how plans,
although not strictly followed, may still serve as a protective umbrella under which
whatever action needed may be taken without anyone the wiser, Ciborra et al. (2000)
describe how the natural tendency of plan-driven organizations is to drift more and more
away from their initial plans, often resulting in a perceived need to plan even better the
next time, with the same failing result. Through embracing and cultivation of the
bricolage of actual work habits, Ciborra et al. argue that organizations stand a better
chance of coping with change. It is not hard to see the similarities between these two
examples with the elusive nature of plan-driven software development, as one of the
fundamental problems it has is in coping with environments that change rapidly (Boehm
2002).

Agile approaches typically focus on simplicity and speed (Abrahamsson et al. 2003;
Beck 1999a). The change from a plan-driven to an agile approach often involves
refining the processes to identify the most appropriate ones for the organization. Even
when the organization uses an agile approach, the process refinement is an ongoing
work (Williams and Cockburn 2003). Although still required in agile approaches, the

need for continuous software process improvement is less demanding than in plan-driven approaches. While agile approaches have captured widespread interest, they are still not established as a mainstream development approach, and a reason for this may lie in the cultural heritage organizations have from plan-driven development processes. Another reason is that many organizations feel that being a certified CMM or ISO user increases their customers' confidence in them, while adopting agile methods could jeopardize relations.

For the purpose of this paper, we report on how Volvo Technology Corporation (VTEC), operating in a plan-driven organization with roots in assembly line production, is approaching agile software development methods *within* plan-driven setting. This represents a promising direction for how organizations may gain the credibility often perceived as needed from operating within a plan-driven and control-oriented organization, while still being able to use more flexible work patterns that better respond to changes in the development process. VTEC is an innovation company that develops new technologies and concepts for products and processes in the transportation and vehicle industry. Upon an initiative from VTEC to challenge the plan-driven model for development that they were prescribing but not seriously subscribing to in their everyday work, the study was initiated to help make an assessment of the current work habits and leave informed recommendations for if and how an agile model for development could be incorporated to support the work inside their plan-driven process framework. In particular, this interest was born from a desire (including customer requests) to become assessed according to ISO/IEC 15504 while also adapting an agile approach, in which they could gain the day-to-day support and use that they currently perceived as missing.

The study has been conducted using a seven-phase approach (section 3), where on-site observation over 3 months, informal and formal interviews, repertory grid sessions (Kelly 1955; Tan and Hunter 2002), workshops, and literature review (section 2 and further in section 4), have served as input to our analysis. Our findings are categorized and discussed in section 4. Representing the main contribution of this paper, the categorization and discussion is an expanded overview of the four key areas when considering a move from plan-driven to agile software development processes, identified by Nerur et al. (2005). Finally, section 5 summarizes the study and reiterates the contribution of this paper.

2 RELATED RESEARCH

Below, agile and plan-driven software methods are presented and compared. These are later used in section 4 to discuss our empirical findings. Plan-driven methods may be characterized as those in which work begins with the elicitation and documentation of a "complete" set of requirements, followed by architectural and high level-design development and inspection. Agile methods, on the other hand, often argue for incremental requirement specification, a minimal amount of documentation, and—importantly—reliance on individuals and interaction (including customer collaboration) rather than processes and tools.

2.1 Plan-Driven Approaches

Plan-driven approaches generally look to reduce risk by investing in life-cycle architectures and making long-term plans. Although taking steps in the process to reduce the problem, they accept that rapid change may make plans obsolete or costly to change on a frequent basis, both in terms of time and money.

Plan-driven approaches are best suited when developers can determine the requirements in advance—including via prototyping—and when the requirements remain relatively stable, with change rates on the order of 1 percent per month (Bohem 2002). When requirements change more often than on a monthly basis, it becomes increasingly difficult to keep requirements complete, consistent, testable, and traceable. It is still vital to have good documentation when developing safety-critical embedded software. Plan-driven approaches scale well to large, stable projects, but a bureaucratic, plan-driven organization that requires an average of one person-month just to get a project approved and started might not be considered efficient on smaller projects (Bohem 2002).

The capability maturity model has been widely adopted in the software community (see Mathiassen et al. 2002; Paulk 2001; Paulk et al. 1995). CMM is a method for evaluating the maturity of the software development process of organizations. The Software Engineering Institute, responsible for the CMM, argue that predictability, effectiveness, and control of an organization's software processes lead to software quality improvements as the organization moves up the five levels that comprise the standard.

- Level 1: Initial (processes are usually ad hoc and chaotic and products and services that work frequently exceed the budget and schedule of their projects).

- Level 2: Repeatable (software development success is repeatable, focusing more on project management to track cost and schedule).

- Level 3: Defined (engineering processes are described in standards, procedures, tools, and methods, while the organization's set of standard processes are established and improved over time).

- Level 4: Managed (product and process quality is controlled using statistical and quantitative techniques to find ideal management measurements for the software development).

- Level 5: Optimizing (process performance is continuously improved using innovative technology).

ISO/IEC 15504, sometimes referred to as SPICE (www.sqi.gu.edu.au/spice), is a suite of standards for software process assessment. ISO/IEC 15504 is similar to CMM, relying on levels of process development, use, and improvement to categorize an organization's increasing capability to follow software development processes that strive to increase product or service quality. ISO/IEC 15504 defines a measurement framework for the assessment of process capability on six levels.

- Level 0: Incomplete process (there is a general failure to achieve the purpose of the processes).

- Level 1: Performed process (the purpose of the process is generally achieved, but may not be strictly planned and tracked; products conform to specified standards and requirements).

- Level 2: Managed process (the performed process is planned, tracked, and adapted).

- Level 3: Established process (the process is performed and managed using a defined process based on good software engineering principles).

- Level 4: Predictable process (the defined process consistently operates within defied control limits to achieve its defined process goals).

- Level 5: Optimizing process (the process is optimized to meet current and future business goals).

At the time of the study, VTEC was preparing for an assessment of their processes toward ISO/IEC 15504, which had also triggered their interest in possibly incorporating an agile software development process such as XP into their defined process framework.

2.2 Agile Approaches

In the beginning of the 1990s, practitioners were starting to find the heavy initial requirements documentation, as well as architecture and design development steps, of plan-driven methods frustrating and even impossible (Williams and Cockburn 2003). Several alternative development methods were gaining public attention. Each of these had a different mixture of new ideas, old ideas and transformed old ideas, and where brought together under the "Manifesto for Agile Software Development" (www.agilemanifesto.org).

These agile methods were developed in various places at different times, but agile proponents agree that the central aspects of agile methods are simplicity and speed (Abrahamsson et al. 2003). The agile method Scrum was developed for managing the software development process in an unstable environment (Schwaber and Beedle 2001). Scrum leaves open to the developers the choice of specific software development techniques, methods, and practices for the implementation process. Less time is spent trying to plan and define tasks, and less time is spent on management reports. More time is spent with the project team. Another widely known agile method is Extreme Programming (XP) (see Beck 1999b, 2000). XP is based on four principles: simplicity, communication, feedback, and courage. XP is designed for use with small teams who need to develop software quickly in an environment of rapidly changing requirements. It is in XP that our case study organization has particular interest, as they are interested in likely consequences from an introduction of XP within their plan-driven framework. There are 12 key practices in XP, listed in Table 1.

Table 1. The Twelve Key Practices in XP (from *Extreme Programming Explained*, K. Beck, 1999)

The Planning Process	Pair Programming
Small Releases	Collective Ownership
Metaphor	Continuous Integration
Simple	Forty-hour Week
Refactoring	On-site Customer
Testing before coding	Coding

Since it has been argued that XP sometimes suffers from weak management control (Vriens 2003), a blend of Scrum and XP known as XP@Scrum has gained in popularity. This approach employs the management principles of Scrum and uses them together with the engineering principles of XP. Several critical people factors are emphasized for agile methods: amicability, talent, skill, and communication (Cockburn and Highsmith 2001). This is not to say that agile methods require uniformly high-capability people. Many agile projects have succeeded with people of mixed experience, as have plan-driven projects. The main difference is that agile methods achieve much of their agility by relying on the tacit knowledge embodied in the team, rather than always striving to collect and document the knowledge (Boehm 2002). There are risks involved in relying on this tacit knowledge, as unrecognized shortfalls may lead to irrecoverable architectural mistakes. Nevertheless, the effectiveness achieved when running smoothly is hard to deny. Agile methods require customers that are committed, collaborative, knowledgeable, representative, and operate with dedication to the development team in order to reach full potential. When little documentation is produced, formally reviewed, and agreed upon by all parties, the involvement of the customer is something that can not be ignored or allowed to slip.

2.3 Combining the Agile Approach in a Plan-Driven Context

Paulk et al. (1995) identify some interesting questions on agile- and plan-driven methods within software development. Can we combine selected agile practices with our traditional plan-oriented practices? How much change is necessary when transitioning to and using agile methods? How can agile practices improve the quality of our products? As the pace in the introduction of technology, tools, and techniques has picked up over the last decade, many CMM and ISO 9000 organizations are now reviewing how their process framework can be adapted to better suit a more frequently changing environment. One way of doing this has been to adopt some agile practices, looking to increase their efficiencies without having to abandon their plan-oriented strategies and (importantly) putting their plan-oriented certifications in jeopardy. Boehm (2002) argues that both agile and plan-driven have a home ground of project characteristics in which each works best, and the other will have difficulties. Further, he argues that hybrid approaches that combine both methods are feasible, and even necessary for projects that combine a mix of agile and plan-driven home ground characteristics. The project leader behind the development of the CMM for software regards agile methods like XP to be compatible with CMM up to level three (Paulk 2001). Vriens (2003) describe a successful move from a plan-driven software development process to XP@Scrum, while still becoming approved for CMM level two. Another example of how agile thinking can come into a plan-driven context is illustrated by Mathiassen et al. (2002) and their in-depth exploration of how software process improvement (SPI) can become more agile, while retaining a plan-driven perspective. Using four case studies as an empirical foundation for their arguments, they identify several critical success factors for improving plan-driven software processes to better cope with rapidly changing environments. Key among these is the involvement of management in the continuous SPI efforts and the organizational determination to go through with them. Furthermore, the goals for improving the software development process must be in line with business goals in order to be implemented fruitfully. As our host organization VTEC are operating from a process designed to be assessed toward the ISO/IEC 15504 standard, we are, in this paper, assisting them in exploring how ISO/IEC 15504 can be used together with XP.

Before starting any move from a plan-driven to an agile approach there are many factors to consider, and organizations must carefully assess their readiness when doing so. Nerur et al. (2005) present key issues in making such decisions and we present an adapted and expanded version of these key issues in our discussion of the findings from the VTEC case study. Nerur et al., as does Boehm, advise caution when moving from a plan-driven to an agile development approach. "While the opportunities and benefits that agile methodologies afford make them attractive, organizations should be circumspect in embracing them or in integrating them with existing practices" (Nerur at al. 2005, p. 77). Organizations not heeding this warning risk making ill-judged decisions regarding the changes this might bring, how to proceed in implementing them, and what the overall cost versus benefit might be.

3 RESEARCH APPROACH

The intent of this study is to assess the current state of process use within VTEC with the specific purpose of identifying the effect that a combination of plan-driven and agile approaches would have on the organization. On a general level, this corresponds to the growing interest from industry to follow certified software development processes such as ISO and CMM, but at the same time retain the high level of flexibility that is perceived as vital in rapidly changing environments. To answer this, we have collected a wide array of data, ranging from on-site observation and field notes, to formal repertory grid sessions, informal interviews, and workshops. As the use of repertory grids has been seminal to our work, we spend section 3.1 on outlining the basic elements and assumptions of the technique, before we present our seven-phase approach in section 3.2.

3.1 Personal Construct Theory and the Repertory Grid Technique

Members of organizations attempt to make sense of their environment by inter-preting events, actions, and objects through their personal view of the world. In IS research, this process has previously been explored through, for instance, *Weltan-schauung* (Churchman 1971), cognitive maps (Weick and Bougon 2001), technological frames (Orlikowski and Gash 1994), and mental models (Daniels et al. 1995). In this work, we have addressed this through exploring the perceptions held by key personnel in the software development process at VTEC, using the notion of personal constructs. In his work on personal construct theory, Kelly (1955) argues that individuals strive to make sense out of the world by constantly testing their experiences against an evolving network of hypotheses.

> Constructs are used for predictions of things to come, and the world keeps on rolling on and revealing these predictions to be either correct or misleading. This fact provides the basis for the revision of constructs, and, eventually of whole construct systems (Kelly 1955, p. 14).

Kelly emphasizes that we use our own personal constructs to understand and interpret events taking place around us. By organizing these experiences into a personal construct system, we make sense of the present situation and try to anticipate future states. In essence, Kelly argues that it is natural for us as humans to consider the nature of our surroundings through personal constructs that are bipolar (i.e., that we define experiences in dualities such as *<Tall—Short>* or *<Nice—Rude>* if we are describing someone). The repertory grid technique is a structured yet highly flexible and partici-pant-driven way to identify and assess our personal constructs (Olsson and Russo 2004).

The main components in repertory grids are elements, constructs, the links between them, and the sense-making process of analyzing them.

- Elements are entities within the domain of investigation and could be different things depending on the character of the domain. For instance, if the targeted domain is the general perception of different car brands, the choice of elements could be known brands like Volvo, Toyota and Ford.

- Constructs describe the character of the elements from the research participant's perspective. There are four alternative approaches in eliciting constructs (Tan and Hunter 2002). The approach used here is considered the classical way, and is known as the triadic sort form.

- Having obtained elements and constructs, the respondents are then asked to rate each of the elements using the elicited (in our case, but otherwise supplied) constructs.

- Techniques for analyzing the grids created include content analysis (Moynihan 1996), rearranging (Bell 1990), transforming (Shaw and Thomas 1978), and the original analysis of content and structure (Kelly 1955). However, in this paper, we have chosen to focus on how the repertory grid technique also can be used as an efficient tool for eliciting and presenting personal constructs that, in our case, enabled us to perform in-depth group workshops as well as individual discussions with the respondents to identify the actual links between de facto development and the intended (plan-driven) software development process. These links represent the bricolage of perceptions, tools, and techniques used at VTEC to cope with the changing environment and projects of varying size and nature (some incorporating both software and hardware development).

As an example, we present the display grid of Respondent C, showing his percep-tions on the various stages of their current process (Requirement, Formal Review, etc., on the bottom). On the left and right side of the figure are the constructs, and in between them are the rankings that Respondent C gave for their current development stages. For instance, looking at the construct *<Stimulating – Boring>*, Respondent C finds *Imple-mentation* and *Formal Review* stimulating (a rating of one) while the *Documentation* and *Quality Assurance* stages are perceived as *Boring* (rating 5).

For the sake of completeness, we have included the display grids of all our respondents in the appendix.

3.2 Data Collection

We approached the study by defining clear phases for data collection and analysis. The data needed for this study was first an assessment of the actual (i.e., the enacted rather than prescribed) development process used at VTEC. Having obtained an under-standing of this plan-driven process, we wanted to compare the actual process with the prescribed plan-driven process and XP practices to outline likely conclusions about how using XP would affect the organization. Continuously through the phases, we reviewed related literature from the adoption of agile processes, in particular focusing on XP.

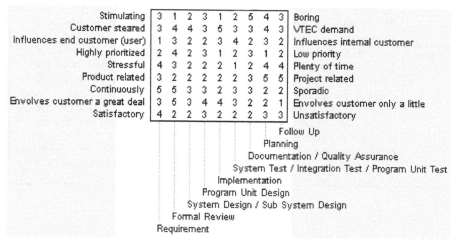

Figure 1. Display Grid for Respondent C

Table 2. The Six Phases of Our Research Approach

Phase A	**Contacting people for participating in interviews, planning the interviews, and choosing elements.** VTEC was asked to provide us with access to a group of representative users of VTEC's development process being considered as experienced developers or project leaders. We asked that this reference group have experience with various types and sizes of projects. The group formed as our reference group consisted of four people, which we refer to as respondents A, B, C, and D. Respondents A, B, and C are project leaders with a background as software developers; respondent D is a software developer.
Phase B	**Performing recorded interviews.** These recorded interview sessions were performed individually with the participants in the reference group. Prior to the interviews, we grouped the elements from Phase A into triads for eight different settings in such a way that every element would be reviewed at least twice.
Phase C	**Eliciting constructs and rating the elements.** To be able to compare the grid results between the participants of the reference group, and also to secure the quality of the constructs, we decided to adapt the use of the repertory grid technique in one aspect. The practiced method describes how the constructs are elicited during the interview sessions and further how this elicitation is immediately followed by the respondent's rating (Tan and Hunter 2002). Our adaptation was to separate the interview sessions from the rating and to identify the constructs from the interview data after having conducted all interviews. A few days after the interviews, the participants received a matrix to fill in their ratings, using the full set of constructs elicited.
Phase D	**Analyzing grids and interviews about VTEC's current development process.** As we have relatively few respondents, we choose to do an interpretative content analysis of the grids rather than rely on numerical facts. After this, we selected elements and constructs of particular interest for an in-depth discussion.
Phase E	**XP workshop at VTEC.** Equipped with a theoretical understanding of XP based on previous research, together with experiences from an organization already using XP and a good understanding of the current development process at VTEC, we performed an XP workshop where all members of VTEC were invited to participate. Participation was on a voluntary basis, but we were happy to see that the interest in XP was not limited to our reference group. Aside from presenting XP and previous experience from XP use, we used most of the time for open discussion among the participants.
Phase F	**Analyzing results from the workshop.** After the workshop (Phase E), we met with the participants of the reference group individually for follow-up interviews, again guided by our review of XP together with our grid results from phase D and feedback from phase E. We concentrated on the following practices: user stories, pair-programming, testing, collective code ownership, and keeping the design simple. After having transcribed workshop and follow-up data, we reviewed the accumulated material from two perspectives: a theoretical perspective and a practical perspective. Although in this paper we report primarily on the theoretical implications found from this study, we touch on some key practical aspects in our discussion of the findings below.

4 DISCUSSION OF THE FINDINGS

In this section we present and discuss our findings. To categorize and compare the bricolage of process use at VTEC (in short, we will refer to this as a bricolage perspective), we rely on the key issues outlined recently by Nerur et al. (2005) when moving from a plan-driven software development to agile approaches (i.e., a plan-to-agile perspective). Furthermore, we expand the Nerur et al. work by incorporating the work by Mathiassen et al. (2002) into the comparison. As Mathiassen et al. focus on achieving agility within the traditional plan-driven development standards—primarily using CMM to drive their discussion—this represents an agile-in-plan perspective. Finally, based on our findings, we draw some initial conclusions regarding adoption of XP within a plan-driven software development process (at VTEC), using Paulk (1999, 2001) and the XP@Scrum adoption into CMM (Vriens 2003) to compare and relate our conclusions. This creates a fourth perspective for achieving a more agile approach to software development: the XP at VTEC perspective. In future research, we hope to expand the XP at VTEC perspective with studies of organizations incorporating XP with well-established plan-driven approaches. Naturally, this perspective may also be expanded by considering agile methods other than XP. In Table 3, we present an overview of these four perspectives on agile development. We then spend the remainder of this section discussing this overview. We strongly suggest that the reader refer to the table when reading the text (numbered references in brackets between the table summaries and the outlined text are provided to facilitiate this), as the table is tightly coupled to the four key issues of management and organizational, people, process, and technology, including the subset of issues defined by Nerur et al.

4.1 Management and Organizational

When planning to change processes within an organization, one needs to involve considerations of the impact upon the organizational culture (Nerur et al. 2005). Mathiassen et al. use the concept *diffusion* when describing how to put changes into practice, and suggest the employment of an implementation workshop to achieve lasting changes. While culture in a plan-driven organization tends to be process oriented, the culture using XP is more social and team oriented (van Loon 2004). At VTEC, the development process is partly traditional, according to a plan-driven process, and partly agile in the sense that documentation has a lower priority than delivered code and functionality.

> *From the start all that is prioritized is the functionality. Not until late in the project the does customer ask for documentation, for example when problems turn up. Maybe we are prioritizing the wrong things and agree to develop too much; we should perhaps tell the customer that we can develop half the scope and spend the other half on documentation....but on the other hand, the customers do value functionality!* (Respondent D)

Table 3. An Overview of the Four Identified Perspectives to Agile Development

Perspectives		Agile-in-plan	Plan-to-agile	Bricolage	XP@plan
Key references		Mathiassen et al. (2002)	Nerur et al. (2005) VTEC case	VTEC	VTEC, Paulk (1999, 2001), Vriens (2003)
Management & Organizational	*Organizational culture*	Diffusion through workshop.	Change of culture is difficult.	Culture is receptive to a well argued and communicated case.	Throw communicative workshops early in the change effort. Coordinate with business goals [1].
	Management Style	Effective management for SPI initiatives.	Relinquish authority when adapting agile.	Not a large step from the bricolage practiced.	Continuous risk for power struggles from the management need to relinquish authority [2].
	Organizational Form	A resolute organizational effort	Traditional approach is formalized while agile is flexible.	Suitable for an agile shift.	Satisfy the level of management involvement required by the standards [3].
	Management of Software Development Knowledge	Knowledge creation through state-of-the-art comparisons.	Power shift from management to team.	Tacit knowledge communicated through socialization (=agile).	Define areas where knowledge creation is of interest, and assign responsibility to an SPI effort [4].
	Reward Systems		Suitable design of reward system is required.	No real incitement to stimulate an agile approach.	Team efforts and sharing must be recognized and rewarded [5].
People	*Working effectively in a team*	Team focus in SPI.	Might be an overwhelming experience.	A positive attitude to team work, uncertainty about working	Create an atmosphere that facilitates the team to develop respect, confidence and integrity [6].
	High level of competence		A culture of elitism might be created.	Focused on advanced engineering, requires skilled developers.	An innovative environment attracts competence [7].
	Customer relationships: commitment, knowledge, proximity, trust and respect	Involving customers in joint-venture activities.	Dedicated and knowledgeable customers might be hard to find.	The customer does not participate enough, and early feedback is not possible.	Important to probe the customers' ability to participate in an agile project before it is launched [8].

Perspectives		Agile-in-plan	Plan-to-agile	Bricolage	XP@plan
Key references		Mathiassen et al. (2002)	Nerur et al. (2005) VTEC case	VTEC	VTEC, Paulk (1999, 2001), Vriens (2003)
Process	*Change from process-centric to feature-driven, people-centric approach*	SPI efforts must be in line with business goals.	Takes time to change.	Leaving control and quality assuring is the largest difficulty.	Coordinate change effort with business goals, and carefully interpret process attributes [9].
	Short, iterative, test-driven development that emphasize adaptability		One of the largest barriers. Involves major alterations.	Test environment for an embedded development project needs to be simulated.	Establish customer cooperation where responsiveness is a natural part [10].
	Managing large, scalable projects		Little data exists.	Involved only with small projects of 4-15 people.	Unsuitable for large projects [11].
	Selecting an appropriate agile method		Select with care.	Quality assurance and management control are crucial.	Combination of agile and plan-driven methods [12].
Technology	*Appropriateness of existing technology and tools*	Communication channels in a social system in order to perceive common understanding.	Mainframe technologies may find it difficult to assimilate agile methods compared to OO development techniques.	The tool ClearCase is used for version handling.	Must be assessed [13].
	New skill sets-refactoring, configuration management, JUnits		Tools play a critical role in successful implementation. People must also be trained to use these tools successfully.	Tools like "Safer C" to review the code and to find discrepancies against MISRA C. Coding style guidelines.	Education about practices, tools and modeling techniques [14].

Changes in this environment might prove to be difficult as the employees are used to doing things their own way (rather than in accordance to a prescribed way). Thus, the employees have already made the move away from the original plan-driven process toward what they feel is more fitting. Still, introducing requirements to meet common goals and working together according to XP (within the existing plan-driven environment) is likely to require some strong argumentation [1].

Managing an SPI effort is different from other organizational changes (Mathiassen et al. 2002). Because improving software processes will take a long time, perhaps years, it calls for effective and strong management. While working with plan-driven development processes where an authorized, coordinating project leader has control, the same role in an agile project resigns control of decisions to the team. Hence, changing from command-and-control management to leadership-and-collaboration will be noticeable in transforming from a plan-driven to an agile approach. "The biggest challenge here is to get the project management to relinquish the authority he/she previously enjoyed" (Nerur et al. 2005, p. 76). The management style at VTEC again consists of a bricolage-like mix between plan-driven and agile approaches without heavy control of every step in the entire process. Instead there are more experienced development leaders supporting the team members of the project that hold much trust from management as well as project coworkers. Therefore, there need not be any problems with relinquished authority at VTEC, but rather recognition of an approach already used. XP is oriented toward developers, while traditional development processes have more of a management orientation. As mentioned earlier, combining Scrum with XP (Vriens 2003) gain a set of management practices that can be used to produce a wrapper for the XP engineering principles. Nevertheless, there is a potential conflict (Vriens 2003) in management style between an agile approach and the requirements with a plan-driven approach [2], as becoming agile is becoming more self-organized, which is contradictory to the commitment to centralized leadership required to satisfy the standards (particularly in the higher levels of CMM and ISO/IEC 15504) [3].

The organization at VTEC is suitable to use agile approaches as they are rather more adaptive and knowledgeable than they are bureaucratic and formalized, which otherwise characterizes a plan-driven organization (Nerur et al. 2005).

When necessary we develop the requirements and later receive feedback upon them from the customer, and sometimes even add requirements ourselves. (Respondent D)

According to Mathiassen et al., SPI should emphasize knowledge creation and describe how the experience from software development practitioners is elicited into the SPI effort for comparison with current state-of-the-art theories, which are then fed back into the development work. The key factors for this are systematic evaluation and state-of-the-art knowledge. In traditional development, the knowledge is explicit in the form of documentation. Since agile approaches encourage lean thinking and little documentation, much of the knowledge stays tacit in the heads of the team members. Nerur et al. argue that this potentially can shift the power from the management to the development teams, and suggests that a decision is made on which knowledge should be codified and which may remain tacit. However, there also exist opinions among practitioners that since all code is collectively owned, no sole person possesses the knowledge about anything, and that this is power to management since individuals become replaceable. At VTEC, the priority is upon delivering working code before documentation. The knowledge is tacit and communicated among the team members through socialization (Nonaka 1994). This indicates that moving to agile will not be an obstacle when managing software development knowledge, but rather that some areas of particular interest should be selected for reporting of tacit knowledge in an SPI effort [4].

Adapting XP requires that management is attentive to other factors than individual technical competence when establishing the level of individual improvement with the staff, such as sharing competence and communicating. Nerur et al. suggest that a suitable design of reward systems is necessary to succeed with agile methodologies. For our case study, respondent C in particular highlights how people today (through the existing reward system) might be encouraged to withhold accomplished competence instead of sharing, thus creating more leverage negotiations with management on wages. To encourage communication and team efforts this must be rewarded to a greater extent than are individual accomplishments when moving to agile [5].

4.2 People

Working in an agile way means being member of a team, where communication and social interaction play an important role. Law and Charron (2005) describe that, in an integrated workforce, people act selflessly and contribute to the greater good which makes the team more than the sum of its parts. Descriptions of an ideal XP working area will describe a place were creative ideas are being exchanged between, and tested by, dedicated developers in a calm but stimulating environment. To reach this state there are many practices to embrace. According to Vriens (2003), and to Nerur et al., the ideas of shared learning, reflection workshops, pair-programming, and collaborative decision making might be overwhelming to programmers accustomed to solitary activities. At VTEC, there are strong-willed individuals, used to exchanging ideas and arguing for them. They also have a positive attitude to pair programming. However, adapting refactoring and collective code ownership must be introduced with care at VTEC.

I would like to receive an explanation if someone changed the code I had written! (Respondent C)

A bigger issue at VTEC is the habit of applying very flexible working hours. To practice pair programming, refactoring, and 40-hours weeks successfully, XP depends (possibly to a larger extent than a plan-driven organization) upon the presence of the team. Mathiassen et al. do not explicitly address the effectiveness of a team in their guidelines to a successful SPI effort, but do spend significant effort on describing the usefulness of workshops for project team members. Clearly the team is in high focus when working on changes to an organization and we foresee an even larger demand for the respect, confidence, and integrity of the team members [6].

An agile team depends to a higher extent on the competence of the team members than traditional development that strictly follows expert-reviewed documentation (Boehm 2002; Nerur at al. 2005). Cockburn and Highsmith (2001) express their belief that agile development teams focus on individual competency as a critical factor in project success. The experience and education level at VTEC is high. Vriens reports that the innovative nature of XP@Scrum development has also proven to be an effective way to attract highly qualified engineers to the organization and we foresee a similar pull by adapting XP at VTEC [7].

When an organization is working on improving its software operation, customers will be seriously affected. It is therefore important to involve the aspects of customers, or even better, to initiate joint activities aimed at improving the customer-supplier relationships (Mathiassen et al. 2002). Nerur et al. recognize that finding a highly dedicated and knowledgeable customer might be difficult. Among VTEC's customers, competence varies and they mostly have limited ways to become involved in the development process due to time constraints of their own. Probing and understanding the type of customer thus becomes very important [8].

4.3 Process

Agile methodologies rely on people and their creativity rather than on processes, and changing from a process-centric to a feature-driven people-centric approach is one of the largest barriers to cross (Nerur 2005). Leaving a plan-driven development model would result in several difficulties for VTEC as the vehicle industry has a long tradition in working according to standards and assuring quality through plan-driven development processes. To have the change effort coincide with business goals is, therefore, particularly crucial to VTEC [9], as this is recognized as an important success factor when changing existing processes (Mathiassen et al. 2002).

Vriens suggests implementing an independent quality assurance group for obtaining the requirements from the ISO 9000 and CMM standards. Further, he says that pair programming is effective in achieving a high level of assurance regarding conformance to standards, though it doesn't really give management (enough) visibility into non-conformance issues. ISO/IEC 15504 at capability level 3 states that "responsibilities and authorities for performing the process are assigned and communicated," while in XP there is an assigned customer and tester; all other responsibilities are assigned to the development team as a whole, and at any time different people can assume different responsibilities and authorities. This is not incompatible with ISO/IEC 15504 but highlights the need for an assessor to carefully interpret the process attributes of the standard.

One problem identified within the development process at VTEC is the lack of relevant feedback on releases. Customers require releases during a development project, but take too long to supply feedback for it to be relevant to the development.

The idea of short releases as XP means would not be easy to apply today as the customer does not really have the time to test and evaluate them. (Respondent D)

We believe, however, that the development process both at VTEC and other organizations that considers adapting to agile engineering principles could gain from more established cooperation with the customer where development of requirements and responsiveness to changes is a natural part [10]. Vriens (p. 2) states that "Both customers and programmers appreciate working iteratively, making small increments. The customer appreciates business value, and programmers value the learning by experience."

Agile methodologies differ in terms of team size. There is not much data collected upon the efficacy of agile approaches with regard to large projects since agility usually is targeted toward small- to medium-sized teams expected to be colocated, typically with less than 10 members. The current software development projects at VTEC consist of 4 to 15 developers, and there are currently no larger projects, so an agile approach would be feasible and even suitable in terms of size [11]. Paulk et al. (1995) express that as systems grow, some XP practices become more difficult to implement. XP is targeted toward small teams working on small- to medium-sized projects. As projects become larger, emphasizing a good architectural "philosophy" becomes increasingly critical to project success.

To VTEC, we feel that the main issues when selecting an agile method would be to keep the quality assurance level they have today along with the possibility to assess for ISO/IEC 15504. In his article, Vriens shows that using agile approaches for the software engineering and plan-driven approaches for management control is a way to go. Van Loon (2004) gives an overview of the relationships between XP practices and ISO/IEC 15504 processes, and concludes that XP is compatible with ISO up to level two before it needs additional management. There are many agile methods to select from when choosing the appropriate one, and while they all agree with the agile manifesto, they obviously are not the same in every aspect. Nerur et al. recognize that the methods differ in team sizes, mechanisms for rapid feedback and change, and that an organization must decide which is most suitable to its needs. Again, in VTEC, there are many indications that using an agile approach in combination with keeping some traditional plan-drive processes (although carefully selected) would be an attractive alternative [12].

4.4 Technology (Tools and Techniques)

Failing to understand the needs of the target user groups is a common mistake of the SPI effort. Mathiassen et al. (pp. 258) talk about communication channels in a social system in order to perceive this common understanding of the users needs, and argue that personal communication channels (as opposed to mass media channels) are generally most effective when it comes to convincing a target group of an innovation's value.

Nerur et al. express that an organization's existing technology can impact the efforts to migrate to agile methodologies. Companies that rely solely on mainframe technologies may find it difficult to assimilate agile methods compared to those that use object-oriented development techniques. The development language at VTEC is C and is not strictly object-oriented. There could be small difficulties at the beginning when adapting to an agile methodology. Regarding common code ownership, recall that respondent C wanted an explanation if the code were changed. However, none of the respondents thought this would be impossible for them to adopt, but rather argue that it be done with respect and communicated among the team.

Vriens notes a general high satisfaction applying XP, but thinks that XP does not give much help regarding documentation, modeling, and the use of UML and design patterns, and thus asks for further research on these areas. Tools do play a critical role in successful implementation of a software development methodology (Nerur 2005), meaning that the sharing of knowledge also applies to hands-on aspects for using XP and other agile methods. Organizations planning to adopt agile methodologies must look for, and invest in, tools that support and facilitate rapid iterative development, versioning and configuration management, and refactoring [13]. Employees must also be trained to use these tools successfully and committed to the fact that in XP, writing test cases first has everything to do with architecture and design (Vriens 2003) [14].

5   CONCLUSIONS

In this paper, we set out to expand the key issues identified by Nerur et al. (2005) as particularly relevant when an organization moves from a plan-driven to an agile software development process. In doing so, the case study at VTEC provided us with a picture of the bricolage of work practices that the organization and individual project members had drifted into using, rather than always following the prescribed development process. Triggered by a desire to become a licensed ISO/IEC 15504 developer, VTEC was particularly interested in, if possible, integrating XP into their high-level plan-driven (but updated) development process. By analyzing our data using the Nerur et al. key issues, and comparing this with the Mathiassen et al. (2002) exploration of how a plan-driven organization may become more agile (even without adopting any of the typical agile methodologies), we arrived at a set of characteristics for what would be necessary to have a combined XP and plan-driven approach. While we intend to continue to probe the feasibility and limitations of our characteristics by looking at other organizations (as well as continuing to study the VTEC case) that also share this interest, we would much welcome other researchers to report findings related to this study to the research community.

References

Abrahamsson, P., Warsta, J., Sipponen, M. T., and Ronkainen, J. "New Directions on Agile Methods: A Comparative Analysis," in L. Clarke, L. Dillon, and W. Tichy (eds.), *Proceedings of the 25th International Conference on Software Engineering*, Los Alamitos, CA: IEEE Computer Society Press, 2003, pp. 244-254.

Beck, K. "Embracing Change with Extreme Programming," *IEEE Computer* (32), 1999a, pp. 70-77.

Beck, K. "Extreme Programming Explained," Reading, MA: Addison-Wesley, 1999b.

Beck, K 2000. "Extreme programming explained: embrace change," *Addison-Wesley*, Reading MA.

Bell, R. C. "Analytic Issues in the Use of Repertory Grid Technique," *Advances in Personal Construct Psychology* (1), 1990, pp. 25-48.

Boehm, B. "Get Ready for Agile Methods, with Care," *Computer* (35:1), 2002, pp. 64-69.

Churchman, C. *The Design of Inquiring Systems—Basic Concepts of Systems and Organization*, New York: Basic Books Inc., 1971.

Ciborra, C. U., Braa, K., Cordella, A., Dahlbom, B., Failla, A., Hanseth, O., Hepsø, V., Ljungberg, J., Monteiro, E., and Simon, K. A. *From Control to Drift: The Dynamics of Corporate Information Infrastructures*, Oxford, England: Oxford University Press, 2000.

Cockburn, A., and Highsmith, J. "Agile Software Development: The People Factor," *IEEE Computer*, November 2001, pp. 131-133.

Daniels, K., de Chernatony, L., and Johnson, G. "Validating a Method for Mapping Managers Mental Models of Competitive Industry Structures," *Human Relations* (49:9), 1995, pp. 975-991.

Kelly, G. *The Psychology of Personal Constructs, Volumes 1 and 2*, London: Routledge, 1995.

Law, A., and Charron, R. "Effects of Agile Practices on Social Factors," in *Proceedings of 27th International Conference on Software Engineering: Workshop on Human and Social Factors of Software Engineering*, St. Louis, MO, May 15-21, 2005, pp. 1-5.

Mathiassen, L., Pries-Heje, J., and Ngwenyama, O. *Improving Software Organizations*, Boston: Addison-Wesley, 2002.

Moynihan, T. "An Inventory of Personal Constructs for Information Systems Project Risk Researchers," *Journal of Information Technology* (11), 1996, pp. 359-371.

Nerur, S., Mahapatra, R., and Mangalaraj, G. "Challenges of Migrating to Agile Methodologies," *Communications of the ACM* (48:5), May 2005, pp. 72-78.

Nonaka, I. "A Dynamic Theory of Organizational Knowledge Creation," *Organization Science* (5:1), 1994, pp. 14-37.

Orlikowski, W. J., and Gash, D. C. "Technological Frames: Making Sense of Information Technology in Organizations," *ACM Transactions on Information Systems* (12:2), April 1994, pp. 174-201.

Olsson, C. M., and Russo, N. "Applying Adaptive Structuration Theory to the Study of Context-Aware Applications," in B. Kaplan, D. P. Truex, D. Wastell, A. T. Wood-Harper, and J. I. DeGross (eds.), *Information Systems Research: Relevant Theory and Informed Practice*, Boston: Kluwer Academic Publishers, 2004, pp. 735-741.

Paulk, M. "Analyzing the Conceptual Relationship between ISO/IEC 15504 (Software Process Assessment) and the Capability Maturity Model for Software," *International Conference on Software Quality*, Cambridge, MA, 1999 (available online at http://www.telnet.com.tn/ Doc/ISO_15504_Maturity_Model_for_Software.pdf).

Paulk, M. "Extreme Programming from a CMM Perspective," *IEEE Software* (18:6), November-December 2001, pp. 19-26.

Paulk, M., Curtis, B., Chrissis, M. B., and Weber, C. V. *The Capability Maturity Model: Guidelines for Improving the Software Process*, Reading, MA: Addison-Wesley, 1995.

Schwaber, K., and Beedle, M. *Agile Software Development with Scrum*, Upper Saddle River, NJ: Prentice Hall, 2001.

Shaw, M. L. G., and Thomas, L. F. "FOCUS on Education: An Interactive Computer System for the Development and Analysis of Repertory Grids," *International Journal of Man-Machine Studies* (10), 1978, pp. 139-173.

Suchman, L. A. *Plans and Situated Actions: The Problem of Human-Machine Communication*, New York: Cambridge University Press, 1987.

Tan, F. B., and Hunter, M. G. "The Repertory Grid Technique: A Method for the Study of Cognition In Information Systems," *MIS Quarterly* (26:1), 2002, pp. 39-57.

Van Loon, H. *Process Assessment and ISO/IEC 15504*, Berlin: Springer, 2004.

Vriens, C. "Certifying for CMM Level 2 and ISO 9001 with XP@Scrum," in *Proceedings of the Agile Development Conference*, Salt Lake City, UT, June 25-28, 2003, pp. 120-124 (available online at http://www.agiledevelopmentconference.com/2003/files/R8Paper.pdf).

Weick, K. E., and Bougon, M. G. "Organizations as Cognitive Maps: Charting Ways to Success and Failure," in K. E. Weick (ed.), *Sensemaking in Organizations*, Beverly Hills, CA: Sage Publications, 2001, pp. 308-329.

Williams, L., and Cockburn, A. "Agile Software Development: Its about Feedback and Change," *IEEE Computer* (36:6), June 2003, pp. 39-43.

About the Authors

Helene Dahlberg received a bachelor's degree from the IT University of Gothenburg in 2005 and since graduating has been employed as development engineer at Volvo Technology Corporation AB (VTEC) at the department of Electronics and Software. She takes a special interest in achieving and improving processes for cost effective development of quality software. Helene can be reached at it2dahe@ituniv.se.

Francisco Solano Ruiz received a bachelor's degree from the IT University of Gothenburg in 2005 and since graduating has been employed as system developer at Elanders AB. One of his special interest lies in helping organizations to structure their information and developing cost effective web applications to store their information. He can be reached at francisco. solano@elanders.com.

Carl Magnus Olsson is a Ph.D. student at the University of Limerick, Ireland. He conducted the research reported here in collaboration with the IT University, Gothenburg, Sweden, and holds a guest researcher position at the Operations Management and Information Systems Department of Northern Illinois University, USA. He was a participant of the ICIS Doctoral Consortium in Seattle, 2003, and has published conference papers at IFIP WG 8.2, IFIP WG 8.6, and International Conference on Information Systems. He can be reached at cmo@ul.ie.

Appendix: Display of Repondent Grids with Ratings of Constructs Against Elements

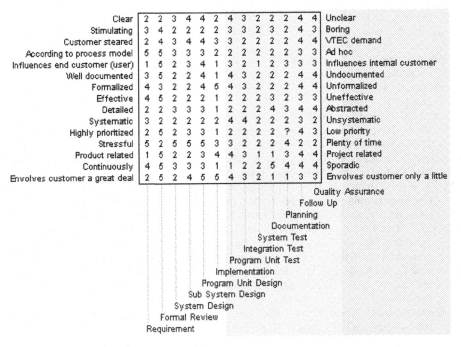

Left construct	Quality Assurance	Follow Up	Planning	Documentation	System Test	Integration Test	Program Unit Test	Implementation	Program Unit Design	Sub System Design	System Design	Formal Review	Requirement	Right construct
Clear	2	2	3	4	4	2	4	3	2	2	2	4	4	Unclear
Stimulating	3	4	2	2	2	2	3	3	2	3	2	4	3	Boring
Customer steered	2	4	3	4	4	3	3	2	2	2	2	4	4	VTEC demand
According to process model	5	5	3	3	3	2	2	2	2	2	2	3	3	Ad hoc
Influences end customer (user)	1	5	2	3	4	1	3	2	1	2	3	3	3	Influences internal customer
Well documented	3	5	2	2	4	1	4	3	2	2	2	4	4	Undocumented
Formalized	4	3	2	2	4	5	4	3	2	2	2	4	4	Unformalized
Effective	4	5	2	2	2	1	2	2	2	3	2	3	3	Uneffective
Detailed	2	2	3	3	3	1	2	2	2	4	3	4	4	Abstracted
Systematic	3	2	2	2	2	2	4	4	2	2	2	3	2	Unsystematic
Highly prioritized	2	5	2	3	3	1	2	2	2	2	?	4	3	Low priority
Stressful	5	2	5	5	5	3	3	2	2	2	4	2	2	Plenty of time
Product related	1	5	2	2	3	4	4	3	1	1	3	4	4	Project related
Continuously	4	5	3	3	3	1	1	2	2	5	4	4	4	Sporadic
Envolves customer a great deal	2	5	2	4	5	5	4	3	2	1	1	3	3	Envolves customer only a little

Grid from Respondent A

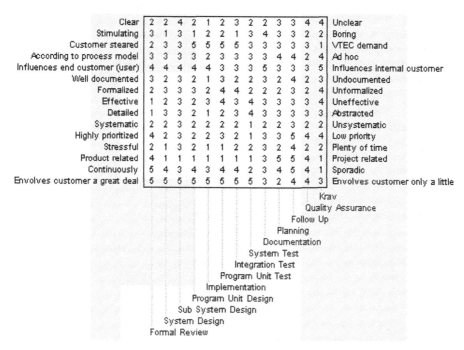

	Krav	Quality Assurance	Follow Up	Planning	Documentation	System Test	Integration Test	Program Unit Test	Implementation	Program Unit Design	Sub System Design	System Design	Formal Review	
Clear	2	2	4	2	1	2	3	2	2	3	3	4	4	Unclear
Stimulating	3	1	3	1	2	2	1	3	4	3	3	2	2	Boring
Customer steared	2	3	3	5	5	5	5	3	3	3	3	3	1	VTEC demand
According to process model	3	3	3	3	2	3	3	3	3	4	4	2	4	Ad hoc
Influences end customer (user)	4	4	4	4	4	3	3	3	5	3	3	3	5	Influences internal customer
Well documented	3	2	3	2	1	3	2	2	3	2	4	2	3	Undocumented
Formalized	2	3	3	3	2	4	4	2	2	2	3	2	4	Unformalized
Effective	1	2	3	2	3	4	3	4	3	3	3	3	4	Uneffective
Detailed	1	3	3	2	1	2	3	4	3	3	3	3	3	Abstracted
Systematic	2	2	3	2	2	2	2	1	2	2	3	2	2	Unsystematic
Highly prioritized	4	2	3	2	2	3	2	1	3	3	5	4	4	Low priority
Stressful	2	1	3	2	1	1	2	2	3	2	4	2	2	Plenty of time
Product related	4	1	1	1	1	1	1	1	3	5	5	4	1	Project related
Continuously	5	4	3	4	3	4	4	2	3	4	5	4	1	Sporadic
Envolves customer a great deal	5	5	5	5	5	5	5	5	3	2	4	4	3	Envolves customer only a little

Grid from Respondent B

	Follow Up	Planning	Documentation / Quality Assurance	System Test / Integration Test / Program Unit Test	Implementation	Program Unit Design	System Design / Sub System Design	Formal Review	Requirement	
Stimulating	3	1	2	3	1	2	5	4	3	Boring
Customer steared	3	4	4	3	5	3	3	4	3	VTEC demand
Influences end customer (user)	1	3	2	2	3	4	2	3	2	Influences internal customer
Highly prioritized	2	4	2	3	1	2	3	1	2	Low priority
Stressful	4	3	2	2	2	1	2	4	4	Plenty of time
Product related	3	2	2	2	2	2	3	5	5	Project related
Continuously	5	5	3	3	2	3	3	2	2	Sporadic
Envolves customer a great deal	3	5	3	4	4	3	2	2	1	Envolves customer only a little
Satisfactory	4	2	2	3	2	2	2	3	3	Unsatisfactory

Grid from Respondent C

Clear	3	4	4	2	1	3	2	4	4	Unclear
Stimulating	3	3	2	2	3	4	2	3	3	Boring
According to process model	5	1	5	5	2	2	4	4	4	Ad hoc
Influences end customer (user)	2	2	2	1	1	4	3	4	1	Influences internal customer
Well documented	3	1	3	4	2	3	2	4	4	Undocumented
Detailed	1	2	3	3	2	4	2	4	3	Abstracted
Stressful	2	3	3	2	2	3	2	3	2	Plenty of time
Product related	1	2	2	1	1	2	2	3	2	Project related
Envolves customer a great deal	2	5	5	4	4	4	2	5	2	Envolves customer only a little
Effective	3	3	3	2	5	4	3	4	3	Uneffective
Kundstyrt	1	5	4	3	3	2	1	3	3	VTEC krav
Formalized / Systematic	4	3	4	5	2	3	4	4	3	Unformalized / Unsystematic
High Priority / Continuously	2	5	5	1	2	3	2	5	3	Low Priority / Sporadic

Quality Assurance
Follow Up
Planning
Documentation
Test (System and Sub System)
Implementation
Design (System and Sub System)
Formal Review
Requirement

Grid from Respondent D

Part 8

Innovation Cases

21   UML: A Complex Technology Embedded in Complex Organizational Issues

Tor J. Larsen
Norwegian School of Management
Oslo, Norway

Fred Niederman
Saint Louis University
St. Louis, MO U.S.A.

Moez Limayem
Lausanne University
Lausanne, Switzerland

Joyce Chan
City University of Hong Kong
Hong Kong, China

Abstract   *Much computer science literature addresses the mechanics of UML and requirements modeling, but little research has addressed the role of UML in the broader organizational and project development context. This study uses a socio-technical approach to consider the interaction between UML as a technology embedded in a social environment. In this study, project developers were interviewed in detail about their use of UML along with influences on their decisions to use this tool and the results of using it. Data were analyzed using a causal mapping approach. Major findings included (1) the unanticipated observation that project success was only one of several distinct and important development outcomes; (2) a very large number of variables impacting project success were reported; (3) a number of important variables that exist in complex (nonlinear) relationships with project success; and (4) the majority of interviewees linked use of UML to project success.*

Keywords   Unified modeling language (UML), social environment, causal mapping approach

Please use the following format when citing this chapter:

Larsen, Tor, J., Niederman, Fred, Limayem, Moez, Chan, Joyce, 2006, in International Federation for Information Processing (IFIP), Volume 206, The Transfer and Diffusion of Information Technology for Organizational Resilience, eds. B. Donnellan, Larsen T., Levine L., DeGross J. (Boston: Springer), pp. 315-338.

1   INTRODUCTION

In the past few decades, advancements existed in different areas of computing, including hardware, networking, and software—only software development productivity seems to be progressing slowly, if at all (Cline and Guynes 2001; Chatzoglou 1997; Sauer 1999). To increase software development productivity, many efforts have sought methods for creating better documentation and requirements structuring. For example, data flow diagrams (De Marco 1978), data modeling (Chen 1976), and object-oriented modeling (Brown 2002) have all been added to the repertoire of system designers. The underlying concept is that visual representation, accuracy, and a fairly straightforward nomenclature in modeling system characteristics can serve to help bridge understanding between system users and developers. Such understandings should allow for reducing the number of systems that are technically valid but don't resolve business problems while also providing clarity for technical designers and coders to more efficiently translate requirements into artefacts.

This study is focused on one particular approach to system representation, the unified modeling language (UML). UML is a language for the specification, visualization, and documentation of software systems (Object Management Group 2004). It also supports business modeling, including structure and design (Booch et al. 1999; Jacobson et al. 1999; Rumbaugh et al. 1999). UML consists of a set of diagrams for representation of system models in diagrammatic notation. These diagrams fall into three categories: structural diagrams (including class diagram, object diagram, component diagram, and deployment diagram), behavior diagrams (including use case diagram, sequence diagram, activity diagram, collaboration diagram, and state chart diagram), and model management diagrams (including packages, subsystems, and models) (Object Management Group 2004). Although UML is relatively new, it is the most complete approach spanning from user-information processes to implementation concerns. It is also widely held to be the future approach to modeling information systems (Edwards 2003).

Research and practice reports on UML are diverse and scattered (Cho and Kim 2002; Johnson 2002; Sim and Wright 2001). We find documentation of negative as well as positive effects of UML deployment. Typically, a small subset of UML-related issues is addressed within a very narrow area of the project effort (such as Chabrol and Sarramia 2000; Rástocný et al. 2004; Saleh and El-Morr 2004). However, reflecting upon how UML is used in the organizational context, it quickly becomes apparent that decisions and implementation interacting at multiple levels must be involved. For example, managers may or may not purchase CASE tools supporting UML modeling or make them available to workers; workers may or may not be interested in using the tools or in using them faithfully to their initial design. Because personnel are likely to vary in their attitudes toward using CASE tools and UML and because tasks will vary in their requirements for documentation, not all projects can be expected to use the UML approach, unless the technique is mandatory in the organization.

To develop an understanding of the use of UML in context, this study considers influences on the use of UML and results from the use of UML at the organizational, project, group, and individual levels. We believe this is consistent with a socio-technical perspective where the UML and CASE tools that support it present a new "technology" and the various social contexts interact with it to produce its ultimate results (Mumford and Ward 1968). This is consistent with the discussion on principles of sociotechnical theory in viewing the domain as a set of human and technical subsystems that combine toward achieving overall goals of the whole system (Hirschheim et al. 1995; Lyytinen 1987).

In the remainder of this paper, we first review recent studies about UML and discuss where UML may fit into existing literature on MIS project success. Next, we discuss the research method based on extensive interviews and causal analysis of response. Then, we begin with a description of our observations regarding the nature of success, the dependent variables in development projects, and continue with a discussion of the results obtained through interviews and causal analysis regarding the research questions of this study. After that, we discuss implications of these findings for practice and for research. Finally, we conclude with observations about limits of the study and directions for future research.

2   LITERATURE REVIEW

A study of UML in the organizational context must take as its baseline that UML is a highly complex phenomenon (Siau and Cao 2001, 2003). This complexity shows itself in many ways. For example, content is important as well as formatting—elaborate and nice diagrams do not, in their own right, represent good design (Eichelberger 2003; Kim et al. 2000). On the other hand, without clear formatting, the content may not emerge accurately and clearly. When moving from the perspective of individuals to commonly expressed representation, such as UML, the end result may be colored by preferences among those making the representation as well as by observable aspects of business processes (Kjellman 2002). Moreover, UML having many rules governing each of several mapping techniques applied to different views of an application is generally not easy to learn (Sim and Wright 2001). In the spirit of requisite variety (Van de Ven 1986), a "technology" that has significant internal complexity, as we see from the computer science literature, should require some complex capabilities for assimilation in its organizational environment.

Because the use (or nonuse) of UML exists within a context of organizational transformation, change is looked upon as endemic to the practice of organizing (Iivari and Huisman 2001; Orlikowski 1996). UML in its totality might be looked upon as an information systems development (ISD) method and each of its maps as an example of an ISD technique (Iivari et al. 2004). Yet, relationships between organizational matters and ISD realities may coincide with or expand beyond well established views on ISD paradigms (Iivari et al. 1998, 2000-2001) or systematization of ISD issues into groupings such as organization, project, or supplier. The use of UML most likely involves a process of organizational change over time (Fichman and Kemerer 1997; Orlikowski 1993).

One purpose of this study, therefore, is to extend from the intricacies of UML rules and its role in technical development to additionally consider how its use or nonuse is manifested within the organizational environment. We further take the view that, from the perspective of the practitioner, such outcomes generally are not neutral in value. As a result, organizational research typically involves a search for factors that influence outcomes toward those which are preferred. Because the specific preferred outcomes will differ in light of differing goals, the umbrella term for preferred outcomes without regard to the particular outcome is labeled *success*. So, this research aims to understand how UML is manifested in organizations but more particularly how it may influence organizational success. It is also clear that the success of UML cannot be tested if UML is not used or available for use in a development environment. Therefore, in this research we also consider what organizational factors may affect the decision to make UML available for use and that may affect decisions regarding whether, when, and how to use it if it is available. To this end the following general research questions are posed:

RQ1: Within the organizational context, does the use of UML lead to project success, and if so, to which particular aspects of project success?

RQ2: What organizational factors influence the use of UML in system development?

3   METHOD

In order to address our research questions, a grounded theory approach was chosen. First proposed by Glaser and Strauss (1967), this paradigm line has been expanded and enriched by Information Systems researchers (such as Bryant 2002; Galal 2001; Hughes and Jones 2002; O'Connor et al. 2003). Although grounded theory and case study overlap in terms of data collection and analysis, they are reciprocal in the sequence of theory generation. In case study, data are collected for hypotheses testing, while in grounded theory, data serve as the foundation of theory building. In other words, grounded theory examines and describes empirical observations in the language of abstracted theoretical concepts. Moreover, it emphasizes the practical contribution of the theories generated by providing practitioners with a thorough understanding of the phenomena they encounter everyday (Glaser and Strauss 1967) and thus fits the interpretative orientation of this study. The intent is to get close to UML-related phenomena as the stakeholders themselves would perceive them but simultaneously hoping to avoid drowning in data (Nandhakumar and Jones 1997).

We conducted in-depth interviews with individuals involved with IT development who logically would be involved in the selection of development approaches and tools or users of these approaches and tools (see Appendix A for respondent demographics). This approach allowed targeting of the research to issues of interest as suggested by the literature without predetermining the content as viewed by the interviewees. The interview questions were generally semi-structured in that they provided a general topic of interest, but allowed interviewees to interpret the question in terms of their own experience and present responses that frequently varied from the specific topic area. An example of such a question is: Thinking back over the last 5 years or so, what are the most drastic changes with regard to how you work on projects? Research based on semi-structured interviews represents an intermediate level of engagement between researcher and research "subject" and is reportedly used in 8 percent of "positivist" research and 32 percent of "interpretive" research (Nandhakumar and Jones 1997).

Causal mapping serves as an analysis technique for observing relationships and providing insights into UML's role and its use in the organizational context (Larsen and Niederman 2005). Causal mapping provides a method for organization of qualitative data emphasizing the range of observations and the relationships among them. Our use of causal mapping can be understood in the context of the basic research method challenge of the personal pronouns of we, I, and you (Bohman 2000). "We" represents the objective approach to research—as in a deductive approach. "I" represents the individualized approach to research—as in an inductive approach. "You" represents the real world subjects and their views, attitudes or behaviors. Obviously, researchers using the voice of "we" or "I" attempt to express salient aspects of "you." Additionally, researchers employ a method within which aspects of "you" are studied and analyzed.

The particular concern in this research was that causal mapping strongly emphasizes a clear definition of the two elements of construct/variable and causal relationship between constructs (see Appendix B for this kind of statements extracted from interview transcriptions). Used in a straightforward and narrow manner, causal mapping represents the voice of "we"—a deductive and objective approach to research, as in Nelson et al. (2000). The present researchers argue that subjects—the "you" in research—may possess clear views of constructs/variables and causal relationships. However, the presumption, in Nelson et al.'s research is that these will be parsimonious on the individual level and across individual roles. The authors believe, however, that our domain of interest, UML within the organizational context, does not have the preexisting background of prior investigation to allow for identification of those constructs/variables and causal relationships before examining data; but rather the study accumulates data as the source for discovery of these.

Therefore, this data collection method was not intended to define a set of constructs/variables and causal relationships, as in Fahey and Narayanan (1989). Doing so would have the danger of leading respondents to fill in the suggested topics without considering whether the set of topics is complete. That is, since very many constructs/variables and relationships exist in the real world, directing subjects to talk about a preselected subset of these phenomena may lead to definitions that reflect the preselection rather than represent the real world. In this scenario, the outcome might appear clean, but actually hide the fact of missing elements (Kjellman 2002). Therefore, given the lack of prior research guidance, in this research subjects were encouraged to talk freely while guided toward the present research focus. Our approach should and must be closer to the spirit of having "you" talk as the "you" finds appropriate. Data collected in this manner would, hopefully, be a good source for defining constructs/variables and causal relationships with a high degree of validity.

Given the relatively larger numbers of identified variables affecting project success both directly and through linked chains of influence (e.g., OO design influencing scalability and scalability influencing project success), it became apparent that lessons could be learned about the organizational context of project success in addition to those regarding the role of UML per se. As an example, the final consolidated causal map for interview 3 is shown in Figure 1.

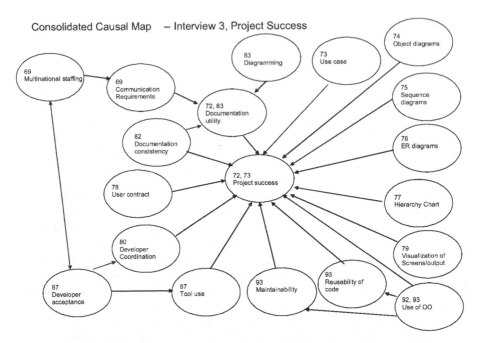

Figure 1. Consolidated Causal Map for Interview Number 3

We see from this sample consolidated causal map that even a single interview can yield a large number of variables that impact project success. Indirect relationships are also observed. For example, "Use of OO" to the right and bottom of Figure 1 impacts "Maintainability" and "Reusability of code," both of which have an impact on "Project success." The set of variables impacting project success and indirect relationships varied to a large degree among our 11 interviews. This is illustrated by contrasting the sample shown in Figure 1 with the consolidated causal map for interview number 8 in Figure 2.

Although some degree of similarity exists between these two sample consolidated causal maps, to be discussed in the results section, we conclude that our raw data clearly documents that the use and value of UML is a highly complex phenomenon. It can be observed that the range of variables is quite broad, that the nature of the relationships is not at all simple and straightforward, and that observation of particular variables seems to shift significantly with varied circumstances.

By contrasting the consolidated causal map with the interview transcripts and observation memos, checking and revision can be made. We consider the extent to which the wide range of variables may affect project success by first grouping them under a more abstract heading called *category* (Corbin and Strauss 1990). This grouping is done by developing a categorization of these variables (see Appendix C). As discussed in the next section, these variables are of different types and occur at different levels of analysis in the overall picture of project success.

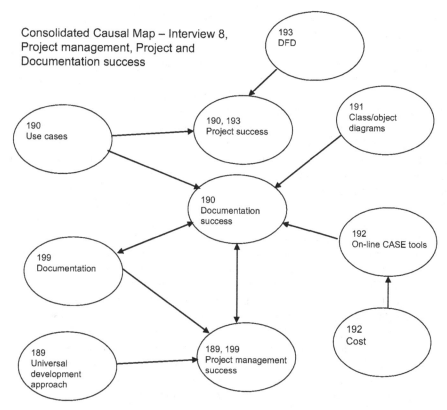

Figure 2. Consolidated Causal Map for Interview Number 8

4 RESULTS

RQ1: Within the organizational context, does the use of UML lead to project success, and if so, to which particular aspects of project success?

Most interviewees in the study clearly linked the use of UML with overall project success. Of the eleven interviewees, eight indicated a direct link of one sort or another. Commonly the source of that benefit was from providing a common understanding from which multiple staff members could work independently yet remain coordinated.

However, the interviewees also mentioned several variables linking UML with its influences and effects. These variables are presented by respondents in Appendix D. More than one respondent mentioned that UML could lead to documentation success independent of application or project success. They also mentioned UML having an impact on successful testing, and also on creation of more reusability. Each of these comments indicates more specifically how UML can be expected to influence overall project success. In some cases, however, the relationship between UML and application/project success was stated in negative terms—that the lack of use of UML resulted in poorer application and project results.

Emergent from the data were several potential outcomes of interest to participants that one might want to optimize or improve. Four distinct outcomes could be identified from the data. These can be categorized as project management success, project success, application success, and documentation success. Project management success refers to the approaches and the activities that an organization implements to improve the effectiveness of new development projects and, ultimately, of its IT portfolio. Project success refers to the outcomes generated for each project. Application success refers to the technical outcomes for a particular development project. Finally, documentation success refers to the outcomes for creating, storing, retrieving, and using the meta-knowledge pertaining to the requirements, design, and implementation of new systems. The views held on these issues are not singular or one-dimensional. Project stakeholders' evaluation of each success category (and how important each category is held to be) may vary considerably (Glass 2003; Klein and Jiang 2001).

It is worth focusing some additional attention on documentation success because it was discussed in various ways by the study respondents and it relates closely to the use of UML. The documentation success variables include documentation quality, consistency, utility, standardization, thoroughness, requirements/technical models linkage, and use of a document management tool. These variables describe aspects of successful project documentation in the sense that they are goals and measures for the documentation itself. Respondents mentioned quality of documentation as a cause of more successful projects, as an end in itself, and also observed that the lack of quality documentation can cause project failure or increase project cost or time to completion. Two comments illustrate the complexity of this variable.

> You know, you can document everything in the world and if you've got people that either (a) don't read it or (b) read it and don't care about it—it doesn't matter. You've just wasted a lot of time. So, you know, I've been on teams where they've spent a great deal of time doing everything by the book and being very formal about it. And doing a great job at it. It's not like they didn't do a good job at it but the problem was that the team didn't just follow it.

> Uh...yes, we had both of them [object and class diagrams]....those were very advantageous because you could clearly see, you know, at a glance, what all was involved with an object and what the procedures and methods were.

Documentation success, in its various aspects appears to be influential relative to project success, but probably not in a linear relationship at all levels for all projects. Granted that different projects will suggest different amounts of documentation, for a given project, too little documentation holds the potential to raise costs if there is need for rework or reorganization. However, as the creation of documentation has inherent costs, producing more than is needed or used will decrease project success by increasing costs that are not recoverable, particularly if those who could potentially profit from their use choose not to do so.

4.1 What Are the Relationships among the Four Different Types of Outcome Success?

As stated above, documentation success would generally influence application success. Application success should influence, though not determine, project success. Clearly an application that won't compile isn't going to be of much practical value; however, one that performs a task flawlessly that no one needs is not going to be viewed as highly valued either. The relationship between documentation, application, and project success is complicated by the potential for documentation success to influence not only application success but also to directly influence project success. Particularly as quality of information requirements documentation rises, effects should be felt on user acceptance as well as technical quality of the applications produced. All of these, however, focus on measures by application or project. Project management success, in contrast, considers portfolios of applications and approaches to development that can influence documentation, applications, and project success project by project. This presents a potential feedback loop in that project management success is rather hollow if individual projects are not successful. It is possible that an organization will have strong normative commitment to generally successful project management approaches, yet fail to implement or execute these methods in some or all particular projects. It is also possible that an organization applies appropriate methods skillfully on a project by project basis with little or no self-conscious project management organization. It would be expected that in most cases project success and project management success should move together, yet these scenarios show circumstances where they might move in opposing directions, therefore they require separate conceptualization and measurement.

> **RQ2**: What organizational factors influence the use of UML in system development?

Although most of the respondents noted the potential of UML to influence project success, a very large number of additional variables were also observed influencing project success and the other dependent variables. It would be simplistic to expect that UML alone without an alignment of positive values on these other measures would lead to positive outcomes. Thus, we cannot say that a specific culture carries influence on the use of UML or on project success (Iivari and Huisman 2001). Our data suggest that UML is partially used, at best. In our sample, consistency in managerial focus on development method issues is missing.

The wide range of variables and how they may affect success outcomes are addressed first by developing a categorization of these variables (see Appendix C). It will be noted in the discussion below that these variables are of different types and occur at different levels of analysis in the overall picture of antecedents to dependent variable values. The eight categories observed are environmental factors, organizational factors, staffing issues, coordination methods/process, OO and CASE tool use, specific modeling tools, and mixed direction factors (see Figure 3). After considering the range and nature of these variables and categories, we discuss the relationships among these factors influencing project success.

The **environment** category of variables includes package use/customization, user contract, physical arrangement, task complexity/project difficulty, and user characteristics. These variables share two distinctions from the perspective of the development project. First, these variables are relatively fixed from the perspective of the project. Ideally decisions such as whether or not to go with installation of a package or self-built system as well as negotiation regarding the user contract are initial elements of the project itself. Frequently, though, these elements are settled upon prior to the beginning of the development of the application. The task complexity or project difficulty may be extremely fixed given the nature of the desired functionality, or may be amenable to phasing, scope management, decomposition, or other tactics for managing complexity. Physical arrangement pertained to the actual working space of the developers which, in the example described, led to communication and coordination difficulties.

The **organizational factors** category of variables includes organizational culture, change management, leadership, and matrix organization. This category has fewer variables than we expected, but three of them would seem quite important in many circumstances and probably to be broad enough to include a variety of more detailed elements. Organizational culture and leadership (as suggested by Westerveld 2003) would seem both important and closely related, as expressed by one respondent,

> because the real issue is not technical, it's cultural. And what I keep…at least in our environment, I'm finding, it is a bottom-up trying to get this stuff in. And I'm becoming more and more convinced that bottom-up culture changes don't work. Unless you have a top-down commitment to doing it, the bottom-up…there [are] just too many people. People trying to advocate one way are actually adding to the chaos rather than actually producing a solution.

Change management was mentioned by four respondents, three times in the sense of managing behavioral change of developers and system users to take advantage of new capabilities, but it was also mentioned in terms of managing changes or revisions in the project requirements. The idea of a matrix organization was mentioned once by an individual in a larger company in the context of suggesting that IT managers need clout in dealing with business managers from some IT organization that cuts across various business departments and can, therefore, influence adherence to standards, even when they do not optimize development of individual projects.

The **staffing** variables include multinational teams, skills and knowledge, developer skills and staffing, staff learning curve, project staffing, staffing patterns, and internal/external staffing. Project success is viewed as negatively related to turnover and vendor turnover. The conjecture that staff issues should be related to project success is quite logical. Developing new systems must be the responsibility of employees (or consultants) and the quality of their work will clearly be reflected in the outcomes of the project. Of more interest are the variations on this theme expressed by the study respondents. Overall skills and knowledge was observed in the context of the degree to which UML methods and CASE tools could be implemented and in terms of the cost of training or learning to use these methods and tools for a particular project. Emphasis is placed on the extra communication requirements when project teams are blended from personnel of multiple countries and where there is a mixture of consultants, contractors, and full-time employees. Staffing patterns were viewed as important. Not only are the skills of the staff over the lifetime of the project important, but also the way that staff enter and exit from their portion of work on a project. Where turnover was mentioned, it was viewed as having a significant negative affect on the project in terms of requiring rework, venturing into new directions, and changing the culture of the group. Variables related to developers and developer teams were clustered together in this category. Skills and knowledge of the user was viewed as an environmental issue. Another respondent focused on the appropriate levels of technical and business-related skills of the project manager, which were viewed as critical for development team leadership and, ultimately, for project success.

The **coordination** variables are communication coordination and coordination between phases. Six of the respondents mentioned coordination and communication. Communication among developers and communication between developers and users were both mentioned. This particular element is similar to but slightly different from analysis-requirement specification-requirements gathering in that communication is a base for conducting those activities; communication also involves more open-ended exchange of ideas, which is a key to project success (Belout and Gauvreau 2004). In examining the flow of multiple causal statements, coordination seemed to moderate some of the environment, project management, and organizational factors as they in turn influenced UML and tool use as well as ultimate project success.

The **methods/process** category of variables includes OO project management, early testing, phased development, analysis requirements/specification requirements gathering, scope creep, task accounting, metrics, master scheduling, and quality assurance. These variables share the commonality of pertaining to the approach and methods used in project management that shaped the activities of the particular project. This category includes some specific activities, the inclusion of which contributed to project success. These are early testing, task accounting, metrics (as suggested by Avritzer and Weyuker 1999), master scheduling, and quality assurance. OO project management refers to the decision to move to UML for the documentation of the project and is closely related to the use of OO per se. Analysis, requirements specification, and requirements gathering are grouped into one factor as they all represent aspects of taking the time to document the desired functionality of the new application. These variables are derived from separate interviews, but each seems to be focused on taking the time to gather knowledge from eventual users/sponsors and to take the time to record this knowledge in a set of specifications. These variables would seem to relate in their instantiations to project success, but in general form to project management success. This topic area is a primary message of systems analysis courses since they have been offered, but, at the same time, remained a source of frustration as its absence or insufficient use of it is a cause of lack of project success according to our respondents.

The **OO and CASE tool use** variables include quality of use and standardization of use. The amount of use of either the OO approach, UML specifically, or CASE tools was not raised as an issue by the respondents. Rather how well the approach and tools were used was viewed as impacting ultimate project outcomes. The standardization of use might be viewed as a subset of quality of use, but we saw this as slightly different. Quality of use seemed to refer to how well the tools provided a mapping between user requirements and technical specification; standardization seemed to refer to how consistently the various development team members applied the tools. Logically, these are likely related; consistency might be a characteristic, among others, of quality across a group of developers, and higher quality users, if measured by other means, are likely to be more consistent. Several respondents mentioning the use of the OO approach noted that such an approach was only feasible with the appropriate use of CASE tools. Other respondents did not mention CASE tools and in some cases performed UML modeling with standard office tools such as MS-Word for describing use case scenarios and PowerPoint or Visio for graphically showing relationships. A number of respondents indicated that high market share CASE tools, particularly Rational Rose, can be expensive, particularly for distribution across the set of developers, and were not extensively used. Even when used, a number of issues with CASE tools were raised including difficulty with the size of documents relative to viewing screen size. On the other hand, multiple respondents indicated that significant benefits from the use of OO approach with CASE tools was largely due to improved communication allowing for smoother transition from analysis/design to coding and implementation. In the words of one respondent,

> It was beneficial because there were programmers, contract programmers, who had certain expectations. They expected to be given a specification from which to work, not, you know, go on figure out how to do this cart blanche. So there was "here's a use case," "here's a sequence diagram," "these are the classes/methods you need to implement." So creating a specification that can be given to someone is the benefit…in a format that they're going to familiar with.

Specific modeling tools included reference to tools in the OO/UML category, sequence diagrams, activity diagrams, use cases, and class/object diagrams as well as some more traditional tools including prototyping, entity-relationship diagraming, hierarchy charts, and data flow diagrams. None of the respondents cited all of these tools as helpful relative to their particular projects and a number of them pointed out that in some cases the use of a particular tool was not helpful for a particular project. However, each of these techniques in the right circumstances is held to be of value. The most frequently used technique recommended by the respondents is use cases. The two interviewees who referenced prototyping individual projects referred to this technique as highly influential in creating successful projects. In both cases, the prototyping was used to document specification and particularly to demonstrate both user interface appearance and characteristics.

The **mixed direction factors** represent something of a miscellaneous group of variables that were frequently mentioned, but where each contains some complexity. These variables include reusability/reuse, maintainability, simplicity, user satisfaction, production speed, scalability, and cost. This complexity derives from the fact that they can be measures of project success as well as inputs to it. For example, a successful project may be one where the code is more maintainable, simpler, produced more quickly and at lower cost. On the other hand, documentation techniques, project management approaches, and staffing activities that produce documentation that is more reusable, with tools that are cost effective, and which generate user satisfaction will lead to better project outcomes. Each of these variables appears in the text in multiple locations and represents a complex relationship with project success.

Upon examination of these findings, we believe in the range and potential power of the full list of variables; however, we hold out this categorization more tentatively. Our grouping of these variables tends to be influenced by consideration of variables in other MIS domains and traditional research that has proposed constructs influencing project success. It is quite conceivable that practitioners would have other bases for categorization, perhaps by cost, perhaps by clusters of variables that are found together in practice, or perhaps by the degree to which they have had control over the variables within their particular organizational history. Some of the variables clearly reside at the periphery of the categories to which they have been assigned. Physical arrangement, for example, could be housed in "environment" or "coordination." Whichever category one would place it, however, would not detract from the contention that under some circumstances each can influence project outcomes. The purpose of categorization, therefore, is to extract themes rather than to create solid constructs with categorical existence of which the variables serve as components.

4.2 Relationships among Variables and Categories

Among the elemental categories that we have provisionally populated with specific variables, we can identify some beginnings of logical relationships (see Figure 3). From the perspective of the project, the categories of environmental factors, organizational factors, staffing issues, and coordination were viewed as forming an outer ring. In many cases, the variables in these categories will be outside the direct and immediate influence of the project team participants. Much of the environment and organization may be relatively fixed for the duration of the particular project, yet the specific values of these variables may have significant effect on the ultimate project outcomes. These categories are likely to have direct effects on project success as well as effects moderated by the additional variables that are more likely to be under direct project control.

Methods, processes, and staffing variables are likely to share this characteristic of being outside the immediate and direct control of the project team, but perhaps to a lesser extent than the environmental and organizational variables. For example, the observed use of methods and processes by development team members in the actual circumstances of project work may have significant levels of choice by individual members—even though parameters of which, if any, tools are made available, and the degree to which such use is mandated may well relate to overall company policies and practices. Similarly, staffing decisions may be made solely outside of the project team in terms of organizational hiring and training and assignment to projects and teams. Decisions regarding the use of contract workers, consultants, and offshore outsourcing will rarely be part of the project team mission, although in some circumstances, teams or team members may influence these decisions. However, some staffing decisions, such as turnover, may be influenced by outside forces but also result from individual decisions and opportunities such as unexpected job offers, family crises, etc. In spite of these differences, for the most part these factors will be largely outside the control of the project team. Finally, coordination appeared to refer to a subset of the interaction

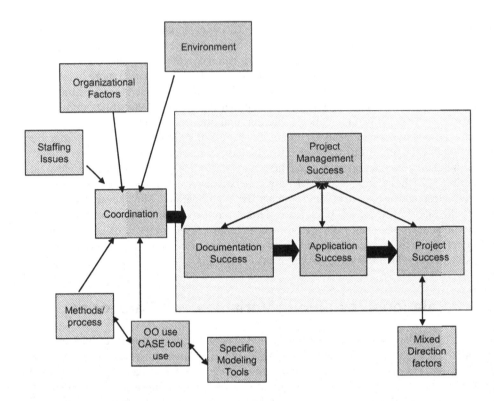

Figure 3. Combined Model of Project Success Precursors

of these other four elements—how well the organizational, environmental, process/ method approaches, and staffing blended together. It would appear that coordination was influenced by these other "outer ring" variables. We would suggest that these categories and the variables of which they are comprised are likely to have direct influences on dependent variables, but that in many cases, differing values of these variables will have counterbalanced effects given different actions and reactions by the project team members. Thus, we place these variables in something of an outer ring relative to the remaining categories.

The remaining categories, OO and CASE tool use and specific modeling tools, would seem generally in the hands of the project developers themselves based on our respondents' comments. At least we would see it this way among the array of CASE tools that are available at the time of the project. Truly it isn't likely that individual teams or team members are going to buy new CASE tools beyond those that are relatively inexpensive. But the quality, amount, and consistency of use of these tools would seem something that the team should be able to determine. We would see that the overall approach to OO/CASE tools, the selection of specific modeling approaches, and the approach to documentation are highly interrelated. We would expect the sum of these variables to be influenced by the "outer ring" variables; we would expect that for different teams working on different projects, the detailed quantity of impact on the variables comprising these categories would vary. By the same token, we would expect that these variables would act together in influencing project outcomes and that individual values of these variables may have additional influence on project success.

The final category, mixed direction factors, is included in the overall model for influences of dependent variables primarily as a reminder that these variables exist to the respondents and may be causes, results, or measures related to development activities. Our emergent model is shown in Figure 3.

5 CONCLUSION

This study has documented a number of observations about the role of UML, the object-oriented approach to analysis and design, and CASE tool availability and use as part of a more comprehensive look at factors influencing development project outcomes.

5.1 Implications for Research

Observations in this study suggest that project success is only one of four discernable outcomes of interest in the evaluation of development activities; application success, documentation success, and project management success are also key outcomes. The correlation among these should be strong, but at times there may be tradeoffs between them as well. This study provides a basis for differentiating different types of success. Future research would do well to quantify the strength of relationships among these different dependent variables as well as catalogue the contingencies in which each merits predominance in the business environment. Additionally, this study identified variables that are themselves complex. Most notably the variables clustered in the "mixed direction factors" category may be viewed in some ways as influencing project success while also being measures of success.

5.2 Implications for Practice

In this study, a multitude of variables were identified as relevant to development outcomes. Although, in general, the use of UML and CASE tools was viewed as influencing project success and other outcomes, practitioners will do well to consider the array of potential influences on project success before committing to using these tools. The authors have extrapolated from the overall interviews and specific observed relationships to suggest a clustering of reasonably similar variables, although it is not clear that these would move together from one project to another. The authors have suggested a model that would encompass meta-relationships among categories of variables at an overview level. In particular, our data suggests strongly that project size should be accounted for in decisions regarding use of UML simply because its employment in small projects is likely to result in overkill. We would also point out that in project settings where the use of UML appears relevant, its implementation and use requires the integration of policies as well as practices across organizational levels.

Finally, we suggest that practitioners keep firmly in mind that policies designed to optimize success at one level may have unintended implications on other important success indicators. For example, investment in tools to optimize application success will only contribute to greater project success if their costs are outweighed by resulting benefits. However, if these costs are distributed across projects, they may result in both project and project management success over time.

5.3 Future Research

These observations and extrapolations suggest an array of detailed research questions. For example, are there key combinations of variables that influence project success either constantly or across a usefully high probability of occasions? Are there environmental and organizational contingencies that define sets of relatively constant variable relationships? Are there rules of thumb leading to more precise measurement of the tradeoffs among dependent variables deriving from decisions on particular independent variables? For example, would some amount of use of UML signal a transition from more benefits (resulting from improved documentation quality) to less net benefits (resulting from higher levels of overall project cost)?

On the other hand, as this study was carried out in a Western country, it is not clear whether the result will be different in other cultural settings. The factors contributing to project success identified in this study include staffing factors such as multinational team and staffing patterns, as well as organizational factors such as organizational culture, leadership, and matrix organization. The contribution of a multinational team to project success comes from a combination of the merits of different cultures. Besides, people with different cultural background may have different leadership styles, which ultimately affect the level of system engineering project success. Therefore, a cross-cultural study on the use of UML could enrich these findings.

5.4 Study Limitations

This study aimed at considering the interaction of what turned out to be many variables. Such a study tends to be ambitious, and as such, cannot help having some limitations. This study is based on 11 interviews, which yielded a large volume of transcript and many elemental relationships. Nevertheless, it is possible that conducting additional interviews would have yielded even more variables and relationships and that some of those might have changed some of the subsequent categorization and projection of meta-relationships. Labeling and categorizing variables requires extrapolation from the words themselves, the context, and also the tone of the interviewee. It is possible that some measure of inferred meaning (or failure to recognize subtle nonverbal signals) from participation in the interview events influenced the ultimate labeling and categorization of underlying comments. To partly address this issue, all interviews were conducted by two individuals from two cultural contexts (one European, the other North American). Interviewers sought to clarify terms used within the interview setting; for example, interviewees discussing UML were often asked more specifically to which models they referred, or in discussing success, were often asked to clarify in what sense they were using the term. Nevertheless, some alternative meaning for common terms may have escaped the observation of interviewers. Along these lines, Nandhakumar and Jones (1997) point to the additional dangers in engaged research stemming from distorted accounts of behavior and deliberate misrepresentation. Although the researchers can never be certain that these behaviors did not occur, it was clear that interviews included a wide range of both critical and complementary commentary regarding organizational development policies and practices. However, the authors were careful not to predesignate labels or categories that could have led to preestablished conclusions.

5.5 Contribution

In the end, the observation of such a large array of variables, the interactions among multiple levels of organization, project, and individuals, and the multifaceted aspects of varied types of success indicators leads to the conclusion that UML is indeed a complex innovation that becomes embedded in complex organizational issues. It is our hope that presenting the structured observations of our interviewees helps initiate a process of ordering the complexity and diversity of influences in the relationship between social and technical influences in the development process.

References

Avritzer, A., and Weyuker, E. J. "Metrics to Assess the Likelihood of Project Success Based on Architecture Reviews," *Empirical Software Engineering* (4:3), September 1999, pp. 199-215.

Belout, A., and Gauvreau, C. "Factors Influencing Project Success: The Impact of Human Resource Management," *International Journal of Project Management* (22:1), January 2004, pp. 1-11.

Bohman, J. "The Importance of the Second Person: Interpretation, Practical Knowledge, and Normative Attitudes," in H. H. Kögler and K. R. Stueber (eds.), *Empathy and Agency: The Problem of Understanding in the Human Sciences*, Boulder, CO: Westview Press, 2000, pp. 222-242.

Booch, G., Rumbaugh, J., and Jacobson, I. *The Unified Modeling Language User Guide*, Boston: Addison-Wesley, 1999.

Brown, D. W. *An Introduction to Object-Oriented Analysis: Objects and UML in Plain English*, New York: John Wiley & Sons, 2002.

Bryant, A. "Re-grounding Grounded Theory," *Journal of Information Technology Theory and Application* (4:1), 2002, pp. 25-42.

Chabrol, M., and Sarramia, D. "Object Oriented Methodology Based on UML for Urban Traffic System Modeling," in *Proceedings of the Third International Conference on the Unified Modeling Language (UML 2000)*, York, UK, October 2-6, 2000, pp. 425-439.

Chatzoglou, P. D. "Factors Affecting Completion of the Requirements Capture Stage of Projects with Different Characteristics," *Information and Software Technology* (39:9), 1997, pp. 627-640.

Chen, P. P. S. "The Entity-Relationship Model—Toward a Unified View of Data," *ACM Transactions on Database Systems* (1:1), May 1976, pp. 9-36.

Cho, I., and Kim, Y.-G. "Critical Factors for Assimilation of Object-oriented Programming Languages," *Journal of Management Information Systems* (18:3), Winter 2002, pp. 125-156.

Cline, M. K., and Guynes, S. "The Impact of Information Technology Investment on Enterprise Performance: A Case Study," *Information Systems Management* (18:4), Fall 2001, pp. 70-76.

Corbin, J., and Strauss, A. "Grounded Theory Research: Procedures, Canons, and Evaluative Criteria," *Qualitative Sociology* (13:1), 1990, pp. 3-21.

De Marco, T. *Structured Analysis and System Specification*, New York: Yourdon Inc., 1978.

Edwards, C. "Modeling Standard Gets Ready for Second Round," *Electronic Systems and Software* (1:5), October-November 2003, , pp. 36-39.

Eichelberger, H. "Nice Class Diagrams Admit Good Design?," in *Proceedings of the 2003 ACM Symposium on Software Visualization*, San Diego, CA, June 11-13, 2003, pp. 159-216.

Fahey, L., and Narayanan, V. K. "Linking Changes in Revealed Causal Maps and Environment: An Empirical Study," *Journal of Management Studies* (16:4), 1989, pp. 361-378.

Fichman, R. G., and Kemerer, C. F. "The Assimilation of Software Process Innovations: An Organizational Learning Perspective," *Management Science* (43:10), October 1997, , pp. 1345-1363.

Galal, G. H. "From Contexts to Constructs: The Use of Grounded Theory in Operationalising Contingent Process Models," *European Journal of Information Systems* (10:1), March 2001, pp. 2-14.

Glaser, B. G., and Strauss, A. L. *The Discovery of Grounded Theory: Strategies for Qualitative Research*, New York: Aldine Publishing Company, 1967.

Glass, R. L. *Facts and Fallacies of Software Engineering*, Boston: Addison-Wesley, 2003.

Hirschheim, R., Klein, H. K, and Lyytinen, K. *Information Systems Development and Data Modeling: Conceptual and Philosophical Foundations*, Cambridge, England: Cambridge University Press, 1995.

Hughes, J., and Jones, S. "Reflections on the Use of Grounded Theory in Interpretive Information Systems Research," *Electronic Journal of Information Systems Evaluation* (6:1), 2002 (available online at http://www.ejise.com/volume-6/issue1-art2.htm).

Iivari. J., Hirschheim, R., and Klein, H. K. "A Dynamic Framework for Classifying Information Systems Development Methodologies and Approaches," *Journal of Management Information Systems* (17:3), Winter 2001-2002, Winter, pp. 179-218.

Iivari, J., Hirschheim, R., and Klein, H. K. "A Paradigmatic Analysis Contrasting Information Systems Development Approaches and Methodologies," *Information Systems Research* (9:2), June 1998, pp. 164-193.

Iivari, J., Hirschheim, R., and Klein, H. K. "Towards a Distinctive Body of Knowledge for Information Systems Experts: Coding ISD Process Knowledge in Two IS Journals," *Information Systems Journal* (14:4), October 2004, pp. 313-342.

Iivari, J, and Huisman, M. "The Relationship between Organizational Culture and the Deployment of Systems Development Methodologies," in K. R. Dittrich, A., Geppert, and M. C. Norrie (eds.), *Proceedings of the 13th International Conference of CAiSE 2001*, Berlin: Springer-Verlag, 2001, pp. 234-250.

Jacobson, I., Booch, G., and Rumbaugh, J. *The Unified Software Development Process*, Reading, MA: Addison Wesley, 1999.

Johnson, R. A. "Object-Oriented Analysis and Design: What Does the Research Say?" *Journal of Computer Information Systems* (42:3), Spring 2002, pp. 11-15.

Kim, J., Hahn, J., and Hahn, H. "How Do We Understand a System with (So) Many Diagrams? Cognitive Integration Processes in Diagrammatic Reasoning," *Information Systems Research* (11:3), September 2000, pp. 284-303.

Kjellman, A. "The Subject-Oriented Approach to Knowledge and the Role of Human Consciousness," *International Review of Sociology* (12:2), July 2002, pp. 223-247.

Klein, G., and Jiang, J. J. "Seeking Consonance in Information Systems," *The Journal of Systems and Software* (56:2), March 2001, pp. 195-202.

Larsen, T. J., and Niederman, F. "Causal Mapping for the Investigation of the Adoption of UML in Information Technology Project Development," in V. K. Narayanan and D. J. Armstrong (eds.), *Causal Mapping for Research in Information Technology*, Harrisburg, PA: Idea Group Publishing, 2005, pp. 233-262.

Lyytinen, K. "Different Perspectives on Information systems: Problems and Solutions," *ACM Computing Surveys* (19:1), March 1987, pp. 5-46.

Mumford, E., and Ward, T. B. *Computers: Planning for People*, London: B. T. Batsford Ltd., 1968.

Nandhakumar, J., and Jones, M. "Too Close For Comfort? Distance and Engagement in Interpretive Information Systems Research," *Information Systems Journal* (7:2), April 1997, pp. 109-131.

Nelson, K. M., Nadkarni, S., Narayanan, V. K., and Ghods, M. "Understanding Software Operations Support Expertise: A Revealed Causal Mapping Approach," *MIS Quarterly* (24:3), September 2000, pp. 192-222.

Object Management Group. "Introduction to OMG's Unified Modeling Language™ (UML®)," 2004 (available online at http://www.omg.org/gettingstarted/what_is_uml.htm).

O'Connor, G. C., Rice, M. P., Peters, L., and Veryzer, R. W. "Managing Interdisciplinary, Longitudinal Research Teams: Extending Grounded Theory-Building Methodologies," *Organization Science* (14:4), July-August 2003, pp. 353-373.

Orlikowski, W. J. "CASE Tools as Organizational Change: Investigating Incremental and Radical Changes in Systems Development," *MIS Quarterly* (17:3), September 1993, pp. 309-340.

Orlikowski, W. J. "Improvising Organizational Transformation Over Time: A Situated Change Perspective," *Information Systems Research* (7:1), March 1996, pp. 63-92.

Rástocný, K., Janota, A., and Zahradník, J. "The Use of UML for Development of a Railway Interlocking System," in H. Ehrig, W. Damm, J. Desel, M. Große-Rhode, W. Reif, E. Schnieder, and E. Westkämper (eds.), *Integration of Software Specification Techniques for Applications in Engineering, Priority Program SoftSpez of the German Research Foundation (DFG)*, Final Report, Volume 3147 of Lecture Notes in Computer Science, Heidelberg, Germany: Springer, 2004, pp.174-198.

Rumbaugh, J., Jacobson, I., and Booch, G. *The Unified Modeling Language Reference Manual*, Reading, MA: Addison Wesley, 1999.

Saleh, K., and El-Morr, C. "M-UML: An Extension to UML for the Modeling of Mobile Agent-Based Software Systems," *Information and Software Technology* (45:4), March 2004, pp. 219-227.

Sauer, C. "Deciding the Future for IS Failures: Not the Choice Your Might Think," in W. Currie and B. Galliers (eds.), *Rethinking Management Information Systems: An Interdisciplinary Perspective*, Oxford, England: Oxford University Press, 1999, pp. 279-309.

Siau, K., and Cao, Q. "How Complex is the Unified Modeling Language?," in K. Siau (ed.), *Advanced Topics in Database Research*, Hershey, PA: Idea Group Publishing, 2003, pp. 294-306.

Siau, K., and Cao, Q. "Unified Modeling Language (UML)—A Complexity Analysis," *Journal of Database Management* (12:1), January-March 2001, pp. 26-34.

Sim, E. R., and Wright, G. "The Difficulties of Learning Object-Oriented Analysis and Design: An Exploratory Study," *Journal of Computer Information Systems* (42:4), Winter 2001, pp. 95-100.

Van de Ven, A. "Central Problems in the Management of Innovation," *Management Science* (32:5), May 1986, pp. 590-607.

Westerveld, E. "The Project Excellence Model®: Linking Success Criteria and Critical Success Factors," *International Journal of Project Management* (21:6), August 2003, pp. 411-418.

About the Authors

Tor J. Larsen earned his Ph.D. in Management Information Systems from the University of Minnesota in 1989. Since then, he has worked as associate professor at the Norwegian School of Management, Department of Leadership and Organizational Management, and has acted as its Head of Department since 2003. During 2001-2002, he was a visiting professor at the John Cook School of Business, Saint Louis University . He has served as an associate editor for *MIS Quarterly* and is currently a member of the editorial board for *Information & Management*. Tor's publications include articles in *Information & Management, Journal of MIS,* and *Information Systems Journal*. In 1999, he coedited a book on innovation and diffusion theory for Idea Group Publishing. His professional memberships include AIS, IFIP WG8.2, and WG8.6. He is actively involved in the roles of reviewer and conference program chair. Tor's research interests are in the areas of innovation, diffusion, innovation outcome specification, MIS, and technology mediated learning. He can be reached at Tor.J.Larsen@BI.NO.

Fred Niederman serves as the Shaughnessy Endowed Professor of MIS at Saint Louis University. He received his Ph.D. from the University of Minnesota in 1990. His primary research areas pertain to using information technology to support teams and groups; global information technology; and information technology personnel. He has published more than 30 articles in refereed journal including *MIS Quarterly, Communications of the ACM,* and *Decision Sciences*; has presented papers at several major conferences; and serves as associate editor of the *Journal of Global Information Systems*. Fred can be reached at niederfa@slu.edu.

Moez Limayem is a professor at HEC Lausanne. Until recently he was a professor and the BBA Electronic Commerce program coordinator at the Information Systems department of the City University of Hong Kong. Before joining City University of HK, he was the chair of the Management Information Systems department at Laval University in Canada. He holds an MBA and a Ph.D. in MIS from the University of Minnesota. His current research interests include IT adoption and usage, CRM, knowledge management, and electronic commerce. He has had several articles published in journals such as *Management Science, Information Systems Research, Communications of the ACM, IEEE Transactions, Accounting, Management & Information Technologies, Group Decision and Negotiation,* and *Small Group Research*. He has been invited to present his research in many countries in North America, Europe, Africa, Asia, and in the Middle East. He won the best MIS paper award at the ASAC conference in 1998 and the ICIS conference in 2003. Moez also acts as a consultant for the UNESCO and several private and public companies. He can be reached at moez.limayem@unil.ch.

Joyce Chan earned a Master of Philosophy in Information System from the City University of Hong Kong in 2002. Her primary research areas include knowledge management, electronic business, and small- to medium-sized enterprises. She has presented papers at several major conferences including the Hawaii International Conference on System Sciences. She can be reached at isjoyce@cityu.edu.hk.

Appendix A. Respondent Demographics

R#	Employer	Background	Age	G	Management Responsibility	Title
1	Large accounting/ consulting firm Reports to senior manager or VP Organized by industry sectors	Bachelors in Engineering 1994, MBA96 With firm since 1998	29	M	In projects 2 ½ yrs Focus on success and risk, analyzing requirements	Project manager
2	Medium sized custom manufacturing Reports to IT director New role/division −IT not quite understood Reporting track −president is engineer −CFO −director of IS	BS Computer Science	40	F	Manages two teams of business consultants Supports sales and e-commerce Helpdesk since 09/2001	Business Integration Manager
3	Medium sized custom manufacturing Reports to IT director −president is engineer −CFO −director of IS	Bachelors in Information systems	40	F	Two years tenure Manages 13 developers	Application systems manager
4	Large accounting/ consulting firm	Bachelors in Philosophy Business certificate MBA Employed since 1999 in current role	31	M	Responsibility is in the middle of the hierarchy Last project, 8 people reporting directly, four more reporting in-directly	Development manager
5	Medium sized financial brokerage IT department Has 20-year-old IT in a transition process	Bachelor of Science in electrical engineering	47	F	Mentor for OO/JAVA (80%) Acts as liaison between IT department and business line IT users	Lead developer
6	Medium sized financial brokerage Not critically dependent upon IT, makes money! Outsource accounting (new) Move toward standard packages IT department MM level 0 but not formally measured Data management group	Bachelors in theology and philosophy Masters of divinity 12 years with firm	50	M	Soft supervision, no hiring, etc. Technical rather than management track, more consulting than directing	Senior technical data consultant

R#	Employer	Background	Age	G	Management Responsibility	Title
7	Medium sized health care facility Heavy into IT development Clinical team within IT department	Bachelors of science in nursing1999 MS nursing, emphasis in informatics, 2002	42	F	In charge of project implementation, but no reporting employees	Clinical business analyst
8	Small biotech firm IT department	College 1year, 1980, computer science Was employee; rehired as individual consultant	41	M	None	Contract programmer/ analyst
9	Small biotech firm IT department	BS, Computer Science, 1983 Worked in field since that time	41	M	In charge of project and one other employee	Software engineering manager
10	Large food product company Flattened out budgets IT department 1200 employees	Electrical engineering, 1968	50	M	None Technical consulting	Corporate level software architecture
11	Large food product company Management System Group–Organizational Technical Development	Master's in aerospace engineering	42	M	15 people recently, down to 10 today (08/2002	MIS consultant

Appendix B. An Example of the Analysis Table

Comment #	R	Page #	Statement	Cause	Effect
31	2	4	We're still trying to get people to understand the IS model and our roles because people look at us when we say we need to be part of their planning units and their teams and so far, they look at us "We're not ready for IT yet." We say, "No, no, you don't understand. We're a part of your team. We need to understand prior to when you think you need technology so that we can best help you. It also helps us in our planning." So we've got varying degrees of people understanding our role but it is starting to grasp on. People are starting to understand that role and I can't seem to have enough people to fulfil those roles.	Early involvement	User understanding
32	2	4	Also, recently, in the business integration team, we had taken on process mapping, which makes sense because if you don't understand the process, it's difficult to start mapping out a project and mapping out technology. So we are also facilitating and training process mapping so that's also new.	Process mapping	Project organization

Com-ment #	R	Page #	Statement	Cause	Effect
33	2	6	We had a team, a fairly large team, that pretty much encompassed a good portion of our IS department internally as well as we brought in external consultants because we didn't feel we had the expertise and knowledge in doing every-thing that we were going to be embarking upon.	Addition of consultants	Enhance knowledge base for project work
34	2	7	We had some knowledge but it wasn't practical. It was textbook knowledge and we wanted some practical experience so we hired, actually, multiple consultants. We didn't have one firm. We brought in multiple people. We project managed it but we had a project manager from the consulting firm work with us hand-in-hand.	Addition of consultants	Enhance knowledge base for project work
35	2	7	I thought I could because my background seems like I could do that but I very quickly learned that if I got caught too much in the technical details, I couldn't manage the overall scope of the project.	Focus on overview	Project management success
36	2	9	And we went out and personally trained all 100 distributors when we rolled out phase one. They liked that. They thought that was great.	Personaliza-tion of training	User satisfaction

Appendix C. Categories and Variables Observed in the Study

Category	Variables	
Environment	• Package use/customization • User contract • Physical arrangement	• Task complexity/project difficulty • User characteristics • Project size
Project Management	• OO project management • Early testing • Phased development • Analysis/requirements specification • Requirements gathering	• Scope creep • Task accounting • Metrics • Master scheduling • Quality assurance
Organization	• Organizational culture • Matrix organization	• Change management • Leadership
Staffing	• Multinational teams • Skills and knowledge • Turnover • Developer skills and staffing • Staff learning curve	• Project staffing • Vendor turnover • Staffing patterns • Internal/external staffing
Coordination	• Communication coordination	• Coordination between phases
Mixed Direction Factors	• Reusability/reuse • Maintainability • Simplicity • User satisfaction	• Production speed • Scalability • Cost
Documentation Success	• Documentation quality • Consistency • Utility • Standardization	• Thoroughness • Requirements/technical models linked • Document Management Tool

Category	Variables	
Specific Modeling Tools	*OO/UML* • Sequence diagrams • Activity diagrams • Use Case • Class/Object diagrams	*Traditional* • Prototyping • ER • Hierarchy Charts • DFD
UML/CASE Tool Use	• Quality of use	• Standardization of use

Appendix D. Direct Linkages between OO/UML with Influences and Effects

Respondent	Effect of UML/CASE tools	
1	• Project success • System consistency • Design quality • Use in testing • Extra overhead	• Project size • OO language • Developer preferences • Self-training • Rapid evolution
2	• Project success • Testing effectiveness	• Project size • Hardware capacity • Faith and trust • Training methods
3	• Project success • Reusability • Maintainability • Application success	• Developer acceptance • Hardware/software capacity • Training
4	• CASE tool use • Cost • Standardized use (leads to project success)	• CASE tool use • Cost • Staff skills and knowledge
5	• Project success	• Developer skills • Standardization • Task complexity • Training • Staff skills and knowledge
6	• Project success	• Organizational culture
7	(none observed)	(none observed)
8	• Project success • Documentation success • Skills • Sense of closure on project	• Cost
9	• Project success	• Reusability
10	• Project management success • Development across environments • Component oriented production environment	• Unified platform approach • Training
11	• Project success • Scalability • Reuse • Documentation success	

22 THE DIALECTICS OF RESILIENCE: A Multilevel Analysis of a Telehealth Innovation

Sunyoung Cho
Lars Mathiassen
Daniel Robey
Georgia State University
Atlanta, GA U.S.A.

Abstract   *Resilience is commonly portrayed as a positive capability that allows individuals and organizations to thrive in dynamic contexts. This paper questions this oversimplified view based on a dialectical analysis of a telehealth innovation. We analyze the major contradictions that characterize the adoption of the innovation. First, we analyze contradictions between individuals and groups within each adopting hospital. Second, we analyze contradictions between the adopting hospitals. This two-level analysis leads to a deeper understanding of resilience as a dialectical process. The analysis of the case shows that, although the participating individuals and organizations demonstrated apparent resilience in adopting the telehealth innovation, the innovation remained in a fragile state where it was unclear whether it would continue to diffuse, stabilize as-is, or slowly deteriorate. Hence, while organizational resilience facilitated swift and successful adoption, it also created tensions that endangered further diffusion and the long term sustainability of the telehealth innovation. We suggest that understanding the future success of the innovation would be facilitated to a large extent by a dialectical analysis of the involved contradictions.*

Keywords   Resilience, dialectics, telehealth innovation

1 INTRODUCTION

The use of information technology (IT) within healthcare is increasing because of the information-intensive nature of the industry (Anderson 1997; Dwivedi et al. 2001).

Please use the following format when citing this chapter:

Cho, Sunyoung, Mathiassen, Robey, Daniel, 2006, in International Federation for Information Processing (IFIP), Volume 206, The Transfer and Diffusion of Information Technology for Organizational Resilience, eds. B. Donnellan, Larsen T., Levine L., DeGross J. (Boston: Springer), pp. 339-357.

Investments in IT within healthcare have grown rapidly and were expected to reach $23.6 billion in 2003, rising at a rate of 9.3 percent from the $21.6 billion expended in 2002.[1] This growth is not surprising and will likely accelerate given that IT infrastructure and services in healthcare are estimated to be 10 to years behind other industries such as banking, airlines, and manufacturing (Raghupathi 1997). Since the late 1990s, telehealth innovations that include provision of health care services, clinical information, and education over distance using telecommunication technology have attracted special attention (Maheu et al. 2001).

The growing investment in IT within healthcare has led to increasing research interests in and experiments with healthcare and telehealth innovations (Chiasson and Davidson 2004). Many of these studies investigate the particular problems that are related to implementation and adoption of IT-based innovations within the healthcare industry (e.g., Aarts and Peel 1999; Berg 2001; Lorenzi and Riley 2003; Tanriverdi and Iacono 1998). Different types of explanations for implementation problems are provided, including knowledge barriers and management issues (e.g., Dwivedi et al. 2001; Tanriverdi and Iacono 1998), people and organizational issues (e.g., Aarts and Peel 1998; Berg 2001; Lorenzi and Riley 1997), social communication patterns (Davidson 2000), organizational structure and culture (Bangert and Doktor 2003), and enactments of different structures of reference by different stakeholder groups (Constantinides and Barrett 2006). These studies point to the importance of organizational processes in explaining the success and failure of telehealth innovations.

The purpose of this study is to continue this line of research by investigating the relationship between organizational resilience and adoption of telehealth innovations. According to the literature, resilience refers to the capability of individuals, groups, or organizations to adapt quickly to changes in their environments (Coutu 2002; Hamel and Valikangas 2003; Horne 1997; Horne and Orr 1998; Mallak 1998; Riolli and Savicki 2003; Starr et al. 2003). We base our analysis on an in-depth case study of a telehealth innovation adopted in a network of collaborating hospitals. The adopting organizations arguably demonstrated considerable resilience, resulting in successful implementation. However, many indicators suggest that the innovation reached a temporary and in some respects fragile acceptance, from which it might be unable to progress. To understand this outcome, we conduct a dialectical analysis (Bjerknes 1991; Israel 1979; Mathiassen 1998; Robey and Boudreau 1999; Robey et al. 2002) of the major contradictions that characterize this particular adoption initiative. We analyze contradictions at two levels of analysis: within each adopting hospital, and between the adopting organizations. This analysis is guided by the following research questions:

1. How is resilience manifest at the organizational and interorganizational levels of analysis in the adoption of a telehealth innovation?

2. How can the use of dialectics augment the analysis of resilience in the adoption of a telehealth innovation?

---

[1]News release, Sheldon I. Dorenfest & Associates, Ltd., http://www.dorenfest.com/pressrelease_feb2004.pdf.

We argue that the future of the innovation depends upon the development and resolution of the involved contradictions. This analysis leads us to an understanding of the dialectics of resilience in relation to adoption of IT-based innovations in organizational contexts.

The study makes three distinct contributions. First, it contributes to research on organizational resilience (Contu 2002; Horne 1997; Hamel and Valikangas 2003; Mallak 1998; Riolli and Savicki 2003; Weick 1993) by exploring the concept in relation to organizational adoption of IT-based innovations. We suggest that resilience in relation to adoption of innovations is an elusive concept inviting interpretations from multiple and often contradictory perspectives. Specifically, we argue that contemporary definitions of resilience raise interesting issues related to the dynamics of adoption behaviors and to interactions between different levels of analysis. Second, the study adds to our knowledge of dialectics, which is already established as a useful approach to IS research (Bjerknes 1991; Mathiassen 1998; Mathiassen and Nielsen 1989; Robey and Boureau 1999; Robey and Holmstrom 2001; Robey et al. 2002; Sabherwal and Newman 2003) and to organization studies in general (Das and Teng 2000; Ford and Ford 1994; Rond and Bouchikhi 2004). Building on this tradition, we demonstrate a detailed approach to conceptualizing, identifying, and analyzing contradictions to uncover the complex dynamics involved in adoption of IT-based innovations. Finally, the study adds to our understanding of the challenges involved in adopting and managing telehealth innovations in an interorganizational context.

The argument is structured as follows. The next section presents the theoretical foundation for the study by reviewing the literature on organizational resilience and on the use of dialectics in organization studies. After a discussion of the adopted research approach we continue with a dialectical analysis of resilience in relation to adoption of the telehealth innovation under examination. Finally, we discuss the contribution of this research and its implications for both research and practice.

2   THEORETICAL FOUNDATION

In this section, we review the two lines of research on which this study builds and to which it contributes: the literature on organizational resilience and the literature on the use of dialectics in organization studies.

2.1 Resilience

Resilience research has its origin in psychology (Coutu 2002; Reinmoeller and van Baardwijk 2005). It started with pioneering studies by Norman Garmezy of different responses and attitudes of children whose parents were schizophrenic. Garmezy concluded that a quality of resilience played a role in the mental health of those children. Since then, many studies have been carried out and theories abound about characteristics of resilience (Coutu 2002). The majority of these studies are at the individual level. Horne and Orr (1998) note that the term *resilience* began to be applied as an organizational quality in the early 1990s. More recently, the concept of the "resilient organization" has gained popularity as a quality that might help organizations survive and thrive in difficult or volatile environments (Riolli and Savicki 2003).

Most definitions of resilience as an organizational quality emphasize its relationship with effective adaptation. Mallak (1998) defines resilience as the ability of an individual or organization to expeditiously design and implement positive adaptive behaviors matched to the immediate situation, while enduring minimal stress. Mallak considers organizational resilience as closely related to individual employees' resilience. Hamel and Valikangas (2003) define resilience as the ability to dynamically reinvent business models and strategies as circumstances change. Starr et al. (2003) define *enterprise resilience* as the ability to withstand systemic discontinuities and adapt to new risk environments. Horne and Orr (1998) define resilience as "a fundamental quality of individuals, groups, organizations, and systems as a whole to respond productively to significant change that disrupts the expected pattern of events without engaging in an extended period of regressive behavior" (p. 31). In general, these definitions carry positive connotations. The underlying assumption is that resilient organizations thrive in dynamic environments.

For the sake of theoretical clarity, it would be better if the concept of resilience were decoupled from the concept of effective adaptation. Organizational resilience should be conceptually distinct from the outcomes with which it is associated. If it is not conceptually distinct, resilience becomes conflated and confounded with effective adaptation and its explanatory powers are removed. Reinmoeller and van Baardwijk (2005) offer from that point of view a more promising approach in which resilience is regarded as a *process capability*, instrumental in overcoming barriers to change and in developing multiple sources of competitive advantage. Three advantages to this approach seem apparent. First, resilience is related to the process of change, where specific capabilities may play roles in overcoming specific barriers to change. Second, resilience is multifaceted, not a single quality. Thus, organizations may possess some resilient capabilities and not others. Third, in a process perspective, resilience becomes a capability that may be related to both successful and unsuccessful adoption behaviors. For example, under conditions of external threat, an organization might quickly adopt an innovation without any certainty that it will be sustained in the long run. Indeed, resilient responses in the short run might neglect more fundamental organizational capabilities related to long-run performance.

The process perspective on resilience is consistent with the usage of the term in ordinary language. The *Oxford Advanced Learner's Dictionary of Current English* defines resilience as the "quality or property of quickly recovering the original shape or condition after being pulled, pressed, crushed, etc." (Hornby 1988). In the context of adoption of IT-based innovations, this definition allows for two different and quite opposite interpretations. On the one hand, this definition can imply that a resilient organization is able to adopt an innovation and quickly recover from the interruption and return to serving its mission. On the other hand, this definition can also imply that a resilient organization is able to absorb or reject an innovation without any significant change. The ordinary language definition is neutral, allowing quite opposite interpretations of how organizations manage innovation adoption challenges. In either case, however, the question remains: Is it in the long term interest of an organization to resiliently adopt (or abandon) the innovation in question?

When applied to the organizational adoption of IT-based innovations, the concept of resilience remains elusive and raises two specific issues of interpretation. First, there are interesting issues related to the dynamics of adoption of innovations, as when organizations successfully implement innovations and later return to traditional practices because the innovations were not sufficiently institutionalized. In such cases, there is potential benefit to interpreting resilience over time from a process point of view. Second, there are interesting issues related to human agency in adoption practices. Resilience is not an abstract organizational capability. It needs to be interpreted as specific and complex interactions between different levels of adoption behavior including individuals, groups, and organizational units. In other words, the analysis of resilience requires researchers to address levels-of-analysis issues (Klein et al. 1994). Resilience can be a single-level or a multilevel construct depending on the research context. As many IT-based innovations are networked and distributed, their adoption is enacted through complex social networks of multiple stakeholders. There is, therefore, a need to address issues related to level of analysis when applying resilience as a theoretical lens in this particular domain.

In summary, resilience is employed in this paper as a framework for studying adoption of IT-based innovations. We tentatively accept Reinmoeller and van Baardwijk's definition of resilience as process capabilities existing at multiple levels of analysis. However, we augment this definition with a consideration of dialectics and contradictions, as discussed next.

2.2 Dialectics

Organizational change has been the subject of extensive research in the fields of both management (Ford and Ford 1994; Van de Ven and Poole 1995) and information systems due to IT's role in organizational change (Mathiassen 1998; Robey and Sahay 1996). Dialectics has been adopted as one approach to understand and study social phenomena in general, and it has proven particularly useful as a framework to understand issues related to social change. Dialectics has been adopted in many organizational studies (e.g., Das and Teng 2000; Ford and Ford 1994; Rond and Bouchikhi 2004) as well as in many information systems studies (e.g., Bjerknes 1991; Chae and Bloodgood 2006; Mathiassen 1998; Mathiassen and Nielsen 1989; Robey and Boudreau 1999; Robey and Holmstrom 2001; Robey et al. 2002; Sabherwal and Newman 2003).

The core concept in dialectics is contradiction, for which a variety of definitions have been applied. According to Van de Ven and Poole (1995), dialectics assumes that organizations exist in a pluralistic world of colliding events, forces, or contradictory values that compete with each other for domination and control. The organizational consequences of IT can, therefore, be explained by reference to the relative strength of opposing forces, some promoting change and others opposing change (Robey and Boudreau (1999). Other researchers build on Mao Tse Tung's more elaborate notion of contradiction to analyze social processes (Bjerknes 1991; Israel 1979; Mathiassen 1998; Mathiassen and Nielsen 1989). Contradictions in these studies are seen as totalities that consist of two opposing elements. The opposites of a contradiction have two qualities:

the identity of and the struggle between opposing elements. The identity refers to the contradiction as a whole and explains the paradox in which opposing elements coexist. The struggle emphasizes the dynamics that drive change. In any given situation, the relationship between the two opposites is usually uneven so that one of the opposites exerts more influence. As time passes, the relationship between the opposing elements might change as a result of their mutual struggle. Also, there are typically several contradictions in any given situation, each with elements becoming more or less dominant as the situation evolves.

We see the different notions of contradictions discussed above as complementary. The main commonality underlying these understandings is their perspective that change is the outcome of contradictory forces. Put differently, the struggle between contradictions and between the opposites of each contradiction are the main forces driving change. In this study, we adopt dialectics to analyze a situation where a telehealth innovation has been adopted by multiple organizations. Following Rond and Bouchikhi (2004), our assumption is that dialectics will help reveal the contradictions involved and that this, in turn, can lead to an understanding of key forces involved in shaping the present situation and the future trajectory of the telehealth innovation.

To support a detailed analysis of relevant contradictions, we follow Bjerknes' (1991) suggestion for identifying and analyzing contradictions. This analytic process occurs in three steps: (1) define specific contradictions, (2) analyze each contradiction's identity and struggles involving the two opposing elements, and (3) synthesize by considering all contradictions involved in the situation. To identify contradictions in the situation under investigation, we combine two sources. First, Bjerknes proposes focusing on conflicts, or antagonistic contradictions, while putting less emphasis on contradictions in which potential conflicts are temporarily resolved. Second, Robey and his colleagues (Robey and Boudreau 1999; Robey et al. 2002) suggest that opposing forces may align with specific interest groups, or they can be conceived more abstractly (e.g., as cultural assumptions, institutionalized values, or organizational memory). However conceived, contradictions can be identified and analyzed between different levels of social analysis (Bacharach et al. 1996).

3   RESEARCH METHOD

3.1 Research Context

In March 2003, the department of neurology at a large university hospital (referred to as the hub hospital) in the state of Georgia in the United States launched a telehealth innovation named REACH (the Remote Evaluation for Acute Ischemic Stroke Program). This "telestroke" system allowed neurologists from the hub hospital to use telecommunication to participate in real-time stroke assessments for patients in rural hospitals. The innovation was first implemented in one rural hospital and gradually expanded to a number of hospitals, with initial technical problems being detected and resolved effectively. At the time of our study between December 2004 and February 2005, the innovation had been adopted by seven rural hospitals. Between March of 2003 and May of 2004, doctors had used REACH to evaluate 75 patients and to qualify 12 of them for treatment.

The need for the REACH system was justified by the critical lack of stroke specialist expertise in most rural areas as well as in many urban areas. This contributes to a higher rate of stroke deaths in rural and under served communities (Casper et al. 2003). For the case of non-bleeding, or ischemic, stroke, a blood-clot dissolving agent called tPA (tissue Plasminogen Activator) greatly reduces chances of severe disabilities if it is administered within 3 hours from the onset of stroke symptoms. However, it is estimated that only 2 percent of stroke patients receive its benefits, partly due to a lack of on-site stroke specialists. It is essential that a stroke specialist examine each stroke patient before tPA is administered. It is far from trivial to distinguish non-bleeding from bleeding cases, and administering tPA to a bleeding case will have immediate and most likely lethal consequences. Providing the services of stroke specialists over distances can therefore significantly increase the rate of tPA use, save many lives, and reduce chances of permanent disability.

The REACH system makes the hub hospital's stroke specialists available to examine patients at distant rural hospitals around the clock. It enables these neurologists to hear and see the patients in real time. A patient admitted to one of the participating rural hospitals gets a CT (computerized tomography) scan to help pinpoint the cause and location of the stroke, while the hub hospital is notified about the incident and the on-call neurologist is connected. The patient is then moved to a room where the telestroke cart is located, and an emergency room nurse enters the patient's information and lab results into the system. The hub hospital neurologist, now connected to the rural hospital through REACH, evaluates the patient on a standardized stroke scale through video-based interactions while seeing CT scan results and lab data on a screen. Voice communication between the neurologist and the clinicians and patient at the rural hospital is conducted over a land-line telephone. Decisions on tPA administration and possible patient transfer are then made by the neurologist.

The implementation and operation of the REACH system were financed by the hub hospital, with each rural hospital being responsible for its CT scanner and system infrastructure, including the fast network connection. The cost of building the telestroke cart with all necessary telecommunication, data processing, and video equipment for each rural hospital was paid by the hub hospital, and technical trouble-shooting was covered by the hub hospital's dedicated systems developer.

3.2 Case Study Design

A case study approach was adopted to study this telehealth innovation in the social context of the hub and rural hospitals. This choice is consistent with Yin's (2003) suggestion to consider three conditions to choose a proper research method: (1) the type of research questions posed, (2) the extent of control an investigator has over actual behavioral events, and (3) the degree of focus on contemporary as opposed to historical events. First, a case study has advantages over other research methods such as surveys and experiments in answering questions of *how* and *why*. Our research questions deal with explaining how and why a teleheath innovation is influenced by organizational processes traced over time. Second, our control over certain variables is not of concern in this study and we have no intention or need for manipulating the involved behaviors. Finally, we are interested in a contemporary phenomenon of a telehealth innovation within a real-life context as opposed to historical events. In addition, there is broad consensus among researchers that a case study approach is particularly well suited to study the development, implementation, and use of IT-based innovations in organizational contexts (Benbasat et al. 1987; Darke et al. 1998).

The research was designed as a single case study involving multiple sites. Thus, we define the case as the network of adopting hospitals. This definition allows us to examine relationships at different levels of analysis within the network and within individual hospitals. Despite some limitations, single cases allow researchers to investigate phenomena in depth to provide a rich understanding (Walsham 1995). Data sources included complete analysis of the telestroke encounter process, systems documentation, demonstration of REACH, site visits to the hub hospital and four rural hospitals, and stakeholder interviews. We interviewed 27 individuals in five hospitals including the hub and four rural hospitals: seven doctors, five administrative staff, three technical staff, nine nurses, one radiology technician, and two entrepreneurs. All interviews were semi-structured, lasted typically between 30 and 60 minutes, and were recorded on audio tape. Most of the interviews were individual except for four group interviews with either two or four participants. We generated field notes immediately after each interview to summarize the key content and to suggest possible interpretations. Two of the authors participated in the field interviews.

Based on the interview notes and all related documents, the two field researchers developed a comprehensive list of existing and potential contradictions related to resilience in the adoption of the telehealth innovation. This process was guided by the suggestions of Bjerknes (1991) and Robey and his colleagues (Robey and Boudreau 1999; Robey et al. 2002) with focus on contradictions among different stakeholder groups. This analysis revealed ten intra-organizational and five interorganizational contradictions. These two sets of contradictions related to adoption of the telehealth innovation were then grouped into more abstract categories of contradictions through rounds of discussions among all three authors. These iterations produced a set of six categories of contradictions covering all identified contradictions of relevance to the study. The following section presents our analysis of these contradictions.

4 RESULTS

In this section, we analyze the resilience of the project initiator group, the adopting organizations, and the adopting network as a whole in terms of the contradictions involved.

4.1 Resilient Adoption

REACH was conceived by two neurologists working at the hub hospital. They were aware that the blood-clot dissolving drug, tPA, was extremely underused in rural areas because of a lack of stroke specialists. Their medical vision was to demonstrate the possibility of administering tPA through the use of telehealth innovations. In 2001, they launched a systems development effort sponsored by the neurology department and the hub hospital. A core team was formed consisting of four stroke specialists and a dedicated systems developer to lead and conduct the innovation effort. All team members were patent owners of REACH, and they championed the innovation by visiting, persuading, and training clinicians and medical staff in the rural hospitals. The core team was also able to garner support for the project from the CEOs of some rural hospitals within a 2-hour driving distance from the hub hospital.

The individuals in the core team were very enthusiastic about REACH, its features, and its considerable potential for providing the neurological expertise required to administer tPA treatment to remote stroke incidents. They all shared the clinical and scientific vision that REACH could save stroke patients' lives and save many from permanent brain damage. They also realized the potential of telehealth services in other clinical practices and took pride in being pioneers in providing neurological services remotely. The members of the core team reacted swiftly to new technological opportunities in their environment; they formed a vision for telehealth innovation that could effectively extend available treatment opportunities (tPA) beyond current medical practices; and they created funding and formed a project that successfully realized that vision in collaboration between the hub and rural hospitals. In this way, the core group and the involved individuals demonstrated resilient adoption behavior.

The hub hospital also demonstrated resilience by proactively adopting telehealth innovations. The vice president of the hub hospital noted in an interview that "creation of a virtual delivery system is an ultimate goal and it is a win-win strategy in competition." According to him, the hub hospital had not sufficiently exploited its highly qualified medical staff because it served a rather small population base in competition with several other large hospitals. Forming alliances with rural hospitals and clinics seemed like a viable business model and growth strategy for the hub hospital. This would allow the hub hospital to provide clinical services to rural hospitals through systems like REACH and thereby effectively increase the number of patient referrals. Hence, the hub hospital recognized opportunities and threats in the environment, searched for new business models, and financially supported innovations like REACH, evidencing its resilience.

The network of participating rural hospitals also saw new opportunities related to this particular telehealth innovation. They were in many ways enthusiastic about REACH. According to one CFO at a rural hospital, about two-thirds of the rural hospitals were operating in the red and two of the four rural hospitals involved in REACH reported operational deficits in the previous fiscal year. It was common for regional hospitals to have severe shortages of specialists like neurologists, psychiatrists, and pediatricians. One nurse said that many rural hospitals were considered by local patrons as a "band-aid station," providing only temporary treatment. The rural hospitals saw opportunities to compensate for shortages of stroke specialists through REACH and to provide better clinical service and build their reputations through such telehealth innovations, even though they had no explicit revenue model for using the REACH system. In this sense, the rural hospitals demonstrated resilience by improving their practices and expanding their client base through adoption of the telehealth innovation.

Given these findings and the track record of 75 evaluated patients and 12 tPA treatments, it is fair to say that the individuals, groups, and organizations involved demonstrated the resilience required to successfully develop and adopt REACH, a radically new type of IT-based innovation that differed from previous practices both at the hub and the rural hospitals. But how sustainable was the innovation? Despite the project initiators' enthusiasm and support, the system subsequently faced problems of financing its continued expansion. The volume of usage remained low, generating problematic cost-benefit comparisons. Moreover, issues related to turning REACH into a fully institutionalized medical practice remained unresolved. To understand these issues more completely, we explored the demonstrated resilience from a process perspective by analyzing the contradictions involved in REACH. The major contradictions identified in REACH on both the intra- and interorganizational levels are summarized in Table 1.

4.2 Intra-Organizational Contradictions

We identified three major contradictions related to REACH within the hub hospital and the adopting rural hospitals.

Medical versus business agenda. Provision of high quality and state-of-the-art medical services is central to any healthcare organization. At the same time, however, the organization should have a sustainable business model to maintain its long-term existence. In that sense, the medical agenda and the business agenda are mutually dependent. This intrinsic relationship between two opposites constitutes the identity of this contradiction. In this case, we found these opposing elements to be in struggle. The medical agenda had driven the development of the innovation without being aligned with the business agenda of the hub hospital. REACH was first conceived as an academic pilot project, and the initiators did not explicitly consider the system's underlying business model. Thus, the medical agenda dominated the business agenda in the early development and adoption phases. Subsequently, when the system was actually being used at multiple sites, the struggle between the two opposites emerged as a conflict. One problem was that medical services provided from the hub hospital through the system were not properly reimbursed. In fact, the central neurologists provided free services over the system without any reimbursement. Also, the hub hospital only had vague estimates of the system's impact on referrals, and the rural hospitals expressed concerns about the low reimbursement for stroke patients from Medicare and Medicaid.

Emerging versus institutionalized work practices. Adoption of IT innovations does not occur in a vacuum. Innovations are introduced into the context of existing work practices, transforming them to some degree. The newly emerging and the existing work practices constitute in this way two opposites that eventually need to be reconciled in new, institutionalized work practices for the adoption to be successful. This intrinsic relationship between old and new work practices constitutes the identity of this contradiction. The struggle between the opposites was in this case expressed as differences between emerging and existing work practices at the rural hospitals. REACH required extensive interdepartmental and interorganizational communication

Table 1. Contradictions in Adopting REACH

Level	Contradiction	Identity	Struggle	Consequence
Intra-organizational	Medical versus business agenda	The long term survival of any healthcare organization depends on two opposites: provision of quality medical services and a sustainable business model.	The medical agenda of the initiators of the innovation were not aligned with the business agenda of the hub hospital.	Had more influence in development and early adoption stages.
	Emerging versus institutionalized work practices	IT innovations are contextualized against existing work practices, transforming them to some degree.	The emerging work practices around the telehealth innovation departed from the existing, institutionalized work practices.	Could be observed but had not yet emerged as significant.
	IT-based innovation versus established IT-infrastructures	IT innovations build on and require changes in an organization's IT infrastructure.	The telehealth innovation was not designed with the existing IT infrastructure and capabilities of the adopting organizations in mind.	Had been recognized during the adoption at each rural hospital and will continue to impact further adoption initiatives.
Interorganizational	Economic incentives of hub hospital versus rural hospitals	Urban hospitals and rural hospitals constitute different, but mutually dependent parts of the U.S. health-care system.	The telehealth innovation implied different economic incentives for the hub hospital and the rural hospitals.	Had been recognized but not addressed.
	Emerging medical practices versus institutionalized insurance practices	Institutionalized insurance practices provide primary support for medical services, but they also define the conditions under which such services must be provided.	The emerging medical practices resulting from the telehealth innovation were not aligned with current insurance regulations for reimbursement.	Had been recognized from early on but was emerging as an issue.
	Hub hospital interests versus commercial explorations	Any commercialization effort must be aligned with the interests of the initiating hub hospital.	Conflicts of interests between the hub hospital and commercialization explorations derailed the negotiation process.	The first commercialization initiative failed.

and coordination, a practice that was quite different from existing work practices in the involved rural emergency rooms (ERs). One interviewee at a rural hospital said that, before REACH, they had not experienced such intensive communication and coordination between the emergency medical service unit, the radiology department, and the ER staff. Training and education of staff was an essential mechanism to overcome the gap between old and new practices. Initial training of rural hospital staff was provided by the hub hospital, and many of the rural hospitals later conducted their own training as needed. However, the struggle was not effectively resolved. In one rural hospital the volume of system usage was extremely low, with only three cases over an 18 month period of system operation. One nurse expressed concerns about using REACH with such few encounters with the system. Overall, the struggle of the opposites had yet to become manifest as a serious conflict because of the recent adoption of REACH and the small number of adopting hospitals. The institutionalized work practices were, however, slow to change, due in part to limited use and to limited opportunities to learn new practices

IT-based innovation versus established IT-infrastructures. Like any other IT-based innovation, REACH built on and required changes in the rural hospitals' IT infrastructure. The mutual dependency between the telehealth innovation and the capabilities of the available IT infrastructures within each rural hospital constitutes the identity of this contradiction. The two opposites were in struggle as REACH was not designed with the existing IT infrastructure of the rural hospitals in mind. REACH required that certain IT capabilities and infrastructures be in place for its operation, for example, high speed Internet connections and digital CT scanners. However, some of the adopting rural hospitals lacked these capabilities. Also, most of the rural hospitals did not have full time IT employees. Those that did experienced high turnover of IT staff, making it difficult for the rural hospitals to maintain the needed IT capabilities. This struggle between the telehealth innovation and the IT infrastructure of the adopting hospitals was recognized from the early adoption stages.

4.3 Interorganizational Contradictions

We identified three major contradictions related to REACH across the adopting hospitals and the hub hospital.

Economic incentives of hub hospital versus rural hospitals. Urban hospitals and rural hospitals constitute different parts of the U.S. healthcare system. Rural hospitals serve smaller population bases and are geographically scattered around the nation, whereas urban hospitals serve larger populations with more resources and a more diverse portfolio of medical expertise. Urban hospitals support rural hospitals as well. Urban and rural hospitals are mutually dependent in that they cannot efficiently serve the entire population without each other. This interdependence between the economic incentives of the hub hospital and the rural hospitals to adopt telehealth innovations constitutes the identity of this contradiction. The introduction of REACH engaged the opposing incentives in struggle, as the innovation generated increased revenue for the hub hospital through stroke patient referrals. By the same token, REACH implied lost revenue for the rural hospitals. A CFO of one rural hospital expressed a deep concern of the revenue loss from using REACH. According to the CFO, the population base of stroke patients at many rural locations was mainly elderly and insured by Medicare and Medicaid. Because those institutions' reimbursement was below the incurred cost, rural hospitals lost money on these patients. The CFO added that the hospital would have reconsidered their adoption of the innovation if this problem had been understood in advance. Similar complaints were echoed by the other rural hospitals. This contradiction did not emerge as significant in the development and early adoption stages, since system installation and equipment were financed by the hub hospital with virtually no extra cost for the rural hospitals. However, it became an issue later as the innovation diffused.

Emerging medical practices versus institutionalized insurance practices. The U.S. healthcare system is currently sustained by insurance systems that reimburse providers of medical services. Medical practices and institutionalized insurance practices are mutually dependent and constitute an important identity in the U.S. healthcare system. These opposing elements are inherently in struggle. The emerging medical practices related to REACH were misaligned with insurance regulations for reimbursement. The reimbursement scheme requires telemedicine systems to be based on two-way video interaction, a requirement that REACH failed to meet. In addition, the neurologist on the hub side must, according to existing regulations, have a medical license in the state in which the patient incident occurs and must also be accredited by the rural hospital to participate (via telehealth services) in providing medical service for their patients. The struggle of these opposites surfaced as significant as the innovation was more frequently used.

Hub hospital interests versus commercial explorations. From the technology adoption life cycle and market development life cycle perspectives (Moore 1999, 2004), a successful innovation satisfies the interests of both the owners of the innovation and the stakeholders involved in commercialization efforts. By the same token, the interests of the hub hospital and any commercial exploration of REACH constitute an important identity in attempts to make the telehealth innovation commercially successful. Sponsored by state funds, two entrepreneurs were engaged to commercialize REACH. Rather late in the process of building a business plan for a commercial initiative, negotiations between the hub hospital and the entrepreneurs ended. The hub hospital and the involved entrepreneurs were unable to agree on a business plan that would satisfy the interests of both parties. Without explicating the details of these negotiations, the break-down was an expression of the struggle between the two opposites of this contradiction that eventually led to the failure of this attempt to radically change the underlying business proposition of the telehealth innovation.

4.4 Relationships Between Contradictions

In addition to the dynamics related to the struggle between the opposites within each contradiction, there are also important dynamics of interaction between contradictions in a given situation (Bjerknes 1991; Israel 1979; Mathiassen 1998). At any point in time, some contradictions may exercise more influence on the situation than others, and the relative salience of contradictions may change as the situation continues to unfold. We can therefore complement the analysis of individual contradictions by considering relationships between the contradictions involved in adoption of REACH. This analysis further helps us to understand the dialectics of resilience as it played out in this particular case of a telehealth adoption.

The contradiction between the medical and the business agenda dominated the adoption of REACH from its earliest development. The key stakeholders paid little attention to this contradiction as their promotion of the medical agenda shaped the initiative. The contradiction was never resolved and appeared to threaten the long-term success of REACH. This contradiction is also related to the contradiction between economic incentives of the hub hospital and the rural hospitals. While this contradiction remained latent because the hub hospital absorbed most of the costs for equipment and installation, no attempts had so far been made to develop business models that would benefit all involved hospitals. Also, the contradiction between emerging medical practices and institutionalized insurance practices surfaced as a principal contradiction both in the hub and the rural hospitals. This contradiction made hospital management more conscious of the business agenda for the telehealth innovation and led them to take a more conservative stance in financing the future of REACH. This in turn made the rural hospitals more attentive to the economic incentives for continued use of the innovation. While the contradiction between the economic incentives of the hub and the rural hospitals did not emerge as a major conflict, the business case for new rural hospitals to become involved remains weak as long as operational deficits continue and as long as the hub hospital expects the rural hospitals to share equipment and installation costs.

In the early adoption stage, the contradiction between the IT-based innovation and the established IT infrastructure emerged as a principal contradiction, as the project team had to deal with a variety of technological challenges in each adopting hospital. The impact of the contradiction was recognized by many stakeholders, but the fundamental contradiction was not resolved in time to avoid similar implementation issues as new rural hospitals became involved. The contradiction between the emerging and the institutionalized work practices and the contradiction between the hub hospital interests and commercialization explorations played minor roles in shaping the trajectory of REACH. However, there had so far not been any successful attempts to implement systematic training and education mechanisms for REACH. Also it had not so far been possible to involve new configurations of hub and rural hospitals as adopters of REACH because the contradiction between hub hospital interests and commercial exploitation remained unresolved.

5   DISCUSSION

We have presented a case study of the adoption of a telehealth innovation. Through the analysis above, we have shown that the initiating project group, the individual hospitals, and the entire network of adopting organizations exhibited considerable resilience in adopting the telehealth innovation. However, our analysis also shows that the telehealth innovation had arrived at a critical junction where it could either continue to be used and further diffused as a successful telehealth innovation, or it could be abandoned due to diminished financial support and sagging enthusiasm among key stakeholders. We argue that this crucial point in the innovation process arises because of the inherent contradictions within and across the network of adopting hospitals. The future of the innovation to a large extent depends on how these contradictions develop. From this perspective, resilience is best conceived as an ongoing process in which specific contradictions are confronted and resolved, at least temporarily. Given the interplay among multiple contradictions, each ebbing and flowing over time, resilience is not easily conceived as a general organizational quality. Rather, resilience emerges from an organization's involvement in change processes and its attempts to recognize and resolve the contradictions involved in such efforts.

Our research contributes in this way to understanding organizational resilience as an important process capability in the context of adoption of IT-based innovations. Our study suggests that levels-of-analysis issues should be addressed explicitly in considering organizational resilience. Resilience can be viewed as both a single-level and a multilevel construct depending on the research context. We agree with Klein et al. (1994) that describing the target that a researcher aims to explain has become more critical as modern organizations increasingly interact within complex business networks. When researchers deal with network-level phenomena like telehealth innovations, the levels issue should be carefully considered. As a consequence, our analysis of resilience included both the intra-organizational and interorganizational levels.

Another important consideration in understanding resilience is the notion of time. We have shown how resilience can be understood in relation to the adoption of IT-based innovations from a process point of view, and demonstrated that the resilience of an entity can change over time. In the presented case study, a network of hospitals demonstrated initially high resilience by quickly and successfully adopting a telehealth innovation that in some respects transformed current medical practices. However, the analysis also indicated that the resulting new practices were in some respects fragile and that the adopting hospitals faced emerging contradictions that would influence the future trajectory of the innovation.

Finally, we have demonstrated how the use of dialectics can augment a process perspective. The main assumption behind our analysis is that contradictions are major influences on organizational change. By analyzing the opposing elements of each contradiction, we may understand the paradoxical identity of a phenomenon as well as the dynamic struggle between opposing forces. Moreover, the analysis of the relationships between multiple contradictions allows us to appreciate the shifting requirements of technical innovation (Bjerknes 1991; Israel 1979; Mathiassen 1998). In this case, we identified six contradictions that shaped the adoption of a telehealth innovation, we analyzed the opposites involved in each contradiction, and we considered how the contradictions interacted during the adoption process. The relative importance of opposites and contradictions changed as the adoption process unfolded. In this way, we arrived at an understanding of the dialectics of resilience as it relates to adoption of this particular telehealth innovation.

This study has its limitations as well. The results section could have been substantiated with direct and detailed quotations of the interviewees. We also admit that there would be alternative perspectives to interpret resilience, for example, operational versus strategy level considerations of resilience. Within the limitations of the current study, all those issues worthy of consideration could not be covered.

6   CONCLUSION

This paper has addressed two questions: (1) How is resilience manifest at the organizational and interorganizational levels of analysis in the adoption of a telehealth innovation? (2) How can the use of dialectical analysis augment the analysis of resilience in the adoption of a telehealth innovation? We argue that resilience can be a useful perspective to understand and explain key issues related to adoption of telehealth innovations and IT-based innovations in general. However, resilience needs to be understood more broadly than is currently the case in the literature. Resilience applies across levels of analysis and it changes over time in the particular context of adoption of IT-based innovations. Resilience therefore lends itself well to a dialectical perspective in which the researcher uncovers the contradictions involved and explores how contradictions shape the adoption process. This approach leads to an understanding in which resilience facilitates swift and productive adoption of IT-based innovations while at the same time implicating tensions that endanger further diffusion and the long term sustainability of the innovation.

References

Aarts, J., and Peel, V. "Using a Descriptive Model of Change When Implementing Large Scale Clinical Information Systems to Identify Priorities for Further Research," *International Journal of Medical Informatics* (56), 1999, pp. 43-50.

Anderson, J. G. "Clearing the Way for Physicians' Use of Clinical Information Systems," *Communications of the ACM* (40:8), 1997, pp. 83-90.

Bangert, D., and Doktor, R. "The Role of Organizational Culture in the Management of Clinical e-Health Systems," in *Proceedings of the 36th Annual Hawaii International Conference on System Sciences*, 2003, pp. 163-171

Bacharach, S. B., Bamberger, P., and Sonnenstuhl, W. J. "The Organizational Transformation Process: The Micropolitics of Dissonance Reduction and the Alignment of Logics of Action," *Administrative Science Quarterly* (41:3), 1996, pp. 477-506.

Benbasat, I., Goldenstein, D. K., and Mead, M. "The Case Research Strategy in Studies of Information Systems," *MIS Quarterly* (11:3), 1987, pp. 369-386.

Berg, M. "Implementing Information Systems in Health Care Organizations: Myths and Challenges," *International Journal of Medical Informatics* (64:2-3), 2001, pp. 143-156.

Bjerknes, G. "Dialectical Reflection in Information Systems Development," *Scandinavian Journal of Information Systems* (3), 1991, pp. 55-77.

Casper, M. L., Barnett, E., Williams, G. I. J., Halverson, J. A., Braham, V. E., and Greenlund, K. J. "Atlas of Stroke Mortality: Racial, Ethnic, and Geographic Disparities in the United States," Centers for Disease Control and Prevention, January 2003 (available online through www.cdc.gov).

Chae, B., and Bloodgood, J. M. "The Paradoxes of Knowledge Management: An Eastern Philosophical Perspective," *Information and Organization* (16:1), 2006, pp. 1-26.

Chiasson, M. W., and Davidson, E. "Pushing the Contextual Envelope: Developing and Diffusing Is Theory for Health Information Systems Research," *Information and Organization* (14:3), 2004, pp. 155-188.

Constantinides, P., and Barrett, M. "Negotiating ICT Development and Use: The Case of a Telemedicine System in the Healthcare Region of Crete," *Information and Organization* (16:1), 2006, pp. 27-55.

Coutu, D. L. "How Resilience Works," *Harvard Business Review* (80:5), 2002, pp. 46-55.

Darke, P., Shanks, G., and Broadbent, M. "Successfully Completing Case Study Research: Combining Rigor, Relevance and Pragmatism," *Information Systems Journal* (8:4), 1998, pp. 273-289.

Das, T. K., and Teng, B.-S. "Instabilities of Strategic Alliances: An Internal Tensions Perspective," *Organization Science* (11:1), 2000, pp. 77-101.

Davidson, E. J. "Analyzing Genre of Organizational Communication in Clinical Information Systems," *Information, Technology, and People* (13:3), 2000, pp. 196-209.

Dwivedi, A., Bali, R. K., James, A. E., and Naguib, R. N. G. "Telehealth Systems: Considering Knowledge Management and ICT Issues," in *Proceedings of the 23rd Annual International Conference of the IEEE, Engineering in Medicine and Biology Society*, 2001, pp. 25-28.

Ford, J. D., and Ford, L. W. "Logics of Identity, Contradiction, and Attraction in Change," *The Academy of Management Review* (19:4), 1994, pp. 756-785.

Hamel, G., and Valikangas, L. "The Quest for Resilience," *Harvard Business Review* (81:9), 2003, pp. 52-63.

Hornby, A. S. *Oxford Advanced Learner's Dictionary of Current English*, Oxford, UK: Oxford University Press, 1988.

Horne III, J. F. "The Coming Age of Organizational Resilience," *Business Forum* (22:2/3/4), 1997, pp. 24-28.

Horne III, J. F., and Orr, J. E. "Assessing Behaviors That Create Resilient Organizations," *Employment Relations Today* (24:4), 1998, pp. 29-39.

Israel, J. *The Language of Dialectics and the Dialectics of Language*, Copenhagen: Munksgaard, 1979.

Klein, K. J., Dansereau, F., and Hall, R. J. "Levels Issues in Theory Development, Data Collection, and Analysis," *Academy of Management Review* (19:2), 1994, pp. 195-229.

Lorenzi, N. M., and Riley, R. T. "Organizational ISSUES=change," *International Journal of Medical Informatics* (69:2-3), 2003, pp. 197-203.

Maheu, M. M., Whitten, P., and Allen, A. *E-Health, Telehealth, and Telemedicine: A Guide to Start-up and Success*, San Francisco: Jossey-Bass, 2001.

Mallak, L. "Putting Organizational Resilience to Work," *Industrial Management* (40:6), 1998, pp. 8-13.

Mathiassen, L. "Reflective Systems Development," *Scandinavian Journal of Information Systems* (10:1&2), 1998, pp. 67-118.

Mathiassen, L., and Nielsen, P. A. "Soft Systems and Hard Contradictions: Approaching the Reality of Information Systems in Organizations," *Journal of Applied Systems Analysis*, (16), 1989.

Moore, G. A. "Darwin and the Demon: Innovating Within Established Enterprises," *Harvard Business Review* (82:7&8), 2004, pp. 86-92

Moore, G. A. *Inside the Tornado: Marketing Strategies from Silicon Valley's Cutting Edge*, New York: HarperBusiness, 1999.

Raghupathi, W. "Health Care Information Systems," *Communications of the ACM* (40:8), 1997, pp. 80-82.

Reinmoeller, P., and van Baardwijk, N. "The Link Between Diversity and Resilience," *MIT Sloan Management Review* (46:4), Summer 2005, pp. 61-65.

Riolli, L., and Savicki, V. "Information System Organizational Resilience," *Omega: The International Journal of Management Science* (31:3), 2003, pp. 227-233.

Robey, D., and Boudreau, M.-C. "Accounting for the Contradictory Organizational Consequences of Information Technology: Theoretical Directions and Methodological Implications," *Information Systems Research* (10:2), 1999, pp. 167-185.

Robey, D., and Holmstrom, J. "Transforming Municipal Governance in Global Context: A Case Study of the Dialectics of Social Change," *Journal of Global Information Technology Management* (4:4), 2001, pp. 19-31.

Robey, D., Ross, J. W., and Boudreau, M.-C. "Learning to Implement Enterprise Systems: An Exploratory Study of the Dialectics of Change," *Journal of Management Information Systems* (19:1), 2002, pp. 17-46.

Robey, D., and Sahay, S. "Transforming Work Through Information Technology: A Comparative Case Study of Georgraphic Information Systems in County Government," *Information Systems Research* (7:1), 1996, pp. 93-110.

Rond, M. D., and Bouchikhi, H. "On the Dialectics of Strategic Alliances," *Organization Science* (15:1), 2004, pp. 56-69.

Sabherwal, R., and Newman, M. "Persistence and Change in System Development: A Dialectical View," *Journal of Information Technology* (18:2), 2003, pp. 69-92.

Starr, R., Newfrock, J., and Delurey, M. "Enterprise Resilience: Managing Risk in the Networked Economy," *strategy+ business*, Spring 2003, pp. 1-10.

Tanriverdi, H., and Iacono, C. S. "Knowledge Barriers to Diffusion of Telemedicine," in *Proceedings of the 19th International Conference on Information Systems*, R. Hirschheim, M. Newman, and J. I. DeGross (eds.), Helsinki, Finland, 1998, pp. 39-50.

Van de Ven, A. H., and Poole, M. S. "Explaining Development and Change in Organizations," *Academy of Management Review* (20:3), 1995, pp. 510-540.

Walsham, G. "Interpretive Case Study in IS Research. Nature and Method," *European Journal of Information Systems* (4), 1995, pp. 74-81.

Weick, K. E. "The Collapse of Sensemaking in Organizations: The Mann Gulch Disaster," *Administrative Science Quarterly* (38:4), 1993, pp. 628-652.

Yin, R. K. *Case Study Research Design and Methods* (3rd ed.), Thousand Oaks, CA: Sage Publications, Inc., 2003.

About the Authors

Sunyoung Cho received her master's degree in computer information systems from Georgia State University in 2002 and is currently pursuing a Ph.D. at Georgia State University under the supervision of Lars Mathiassen. Sunyoung's main research area is information systems in the medical domain, especially telehealth systems. Her research interests cover adoption and diffusion factors and processes of IT-based innovations in the healthcare domain. Her current research is oriented toward a process perspective with research points of views from not only technological and organizational levels but also network and social levels. She can be reached by e-mail at sunyoung.cho@ceprin.gsu.edu..

Lars Mathiassen received his master's degree in computer science from Aarhus University, Denmark, in 1975, his Ph.D. in informatics from Oslo University, Norway, in 1981, and his Dr. Techn. degree in software engineering from Aalborg University, 1998. He is currently a professor of computer information systems at Georgia State University. His research interests are within information systems and software engineering with a particular emphasis on process innovation. He is a member of IEEE, ACM, and AIS, and coauthor of *Computers in Context* (Blackwell 1993), *Object Oriented Analysis & Design* (Marko Publishing, 2000), and *Improving Software Organizations* (Addison-Wesley, 2002). Lars can be contacted at the Center for Process Innovation, J. Mack Robinson College of Business, Georgia State University, PO Box 5029, Atlanta, GA 30302-5029, or by e-mail at lmathiassen@gsu.edu.

Daniel Robey is Professor and John B. Zellars Chair of Information Systems at Georgia State University, holding a joint appointment in the Departments of Computer Information Systems and Management. He teaches courses on qualitative research methods in information systems and information technology and organizational transformation. He earned his doctorate in Administrative Science in 1973 from Kent State University. Dan is editor-in-chief of *Information and Organization* and serves on the editorial boards of *Organization Science*,

Academy of Management Review, Information Technology & People, and the John Wiley series on Information Systems. Dan is the author of three books and numerous articles in such journals as *Management Science, Organization Science, Information Systems Research, MIS Quarterly, Human Relations, Journal of Management Information Systems, ACM Transactions on Information Systems, Information Systems Journal, Academy of Management Review, Academy of Management Journal, Information Technology & People,* and *Decision Sciences.* His current research includes empirical examinations of the effects of a wide range of technologies on organizational structure and patterns of work. It also includes the development of theoretical approaches to explaining the development and consequences of information technology in organizations. He can be reached by e-mail at drobey@gsu.edu.

Part 9

Keynotes

23 KEYNOTES

STRATEGIZING FOR AGILITY: CONFRONTING INFORMATION SYSTEMS INFLEXIBILITY IN DYNAMIC ENVIRONMENTS

Robert D. Galliers

Over the relatively short history of Information Systems planning and strategy, a major principle that has been taken as axiomatic in the mainstream literature relates to the concept of *alignment*. This often means that information and communication technology (ICT) systems should somehow align with an organization's business strategy. This is a self evident truth, surely? But when we come to examine this truth, we begin to uncover a number of problems and issues that need to be addressed. One such relates to the dynamic nature of an organization's business environment and the consequent need for flexible—or agile—IS. A second issue relates to our inability to foresee the future and the attendant—changing—business information requirements that will come with it. A third relates to the role that information can play in informing agile responses to changing circumstances and imperatives—a proactive, rather than reactive, role for IS, in other words.

Professor Galliers' keynote address aims to make a contribution to the conference by addressing these three issues, and by identifying what this means for agile IS strategy—or more appropriately, IS *strategizing*. His presentation will take an alternative perspective to the norm in that it will focus more on the *process* of IS strategizing rather than on the outcome of the process—the IS strategy itself. He will argue that benefit is to be gained from a more critical, inclusive, exploratory, postmodernist approach to the IS strategy process. This perspective can be contrasted with the common view, which is concerned more with exploiting the potential of ICT systems for business gain. An attempt at synthesizing the arguments arising from a consideration of the problems associated with the somewhat mechanistic treatment of alignment found in the mainstream literature will be attempted by utilizing concepts of architecture and infrastructure, of knowledge creation and sharing, and of ambidextrous organizations, with a view to refining an earlier sensemaking device of his: IS strategizing framework.

Professor Galliers joined Bentley College in the United States in July 2002 as Provost and Vice President for Academic Affairs. At Bentley, he has overseen new developments that include the introduction of Ph.D. programs in business and in

Please use the following format when citing this chapter:

Galliers, Robert, D., O'Connor, Rory, 2006, in International Federation for Information Processing (IFIP), Volume 206, The Transfer and Diffusion of Information Technology for Organizational Resilience, eds. B. Donnellan, Larsen T., Levine L., DeGross J. (Boston: Springer), pp. 361-363.

accountancy; internationalization of Bentley's programs by increasing the number of partnership agreements and expanding the international studies department; the creation of Bentley's Alliance for Ethics and Social Responsibility; the opportunity for business majors to take a second liberal studies major; the introduction of a joint MS + MBA degree, and a $16 million renovation of the library that includes expansion of Bentley's physical and electronic collections.

Previously Professor of Information Systems and Research Director in the Department of Information Systems at the London School of Economics, he retains his connection with the LSE as a Visiting Professor. Before joining LSE, Professor Galliers served as Lucas Professor of Business Management Systems and Dean of the Warwick Business School in the United Kingdom, and earlier as Foundation Professor and Head of the School of Information Systems at Curtin University in Australia

Professor Galliers holds an AB degree with honors in Economics from Harvard University, an MA with distinction in Management Systems from Lancaster University, and a Ph.D. in Information Systems from the London School of Economics. He was awarded an Honorary Doctor of Science degree by the Turku School of Economics and Business Administration in Finland in 1995 for his contributions to European Information Management research.

He is a Fellow of the Royal Society of Arts, the British Computer Society, and the Association for Information Systems, of which he was President in 1999. He has chaired previous ICIS and ECIS conferences, and has been a keynote speaker at ECIS and ACIS, among others. He is editor-in-chief of the *Journal of Strategic Information Systems* and on the editorial boards of a number of other major journals. He has authored over 60 journal articles and a number of books, the most recent being *Exploring Information Systems Research Approaches* (Routledge, 2006) with Lynne Markus and Sue Newell, the third edition of the best-selling *Strategic Information Management*(Butterworth-Heinemann, 2003) with Dorothy Leidner, and *Rethinking Management Information Systems* (Oxford University Press, 1999) with Wendy Currie.

BUSINESS RESILIENCE IN A GLOBAL ECONOMY

Rory O'Connor

Mr. O'Connor's presentation will cover four basic themes.

- Doing Business—Doing Business Globally. Mr. O'Connor will discuss the challenges of doing business in today's global economy. Following a quick look at the anatomy of any business, he will review some of the structural and implementation choices available to the global business player today.

- The Impact of Modern Information and Communications Technology. Mr. O'Connor will review the impact that modern information systems and communications technology is having on our ability to access, manage, and control information and what that means in terms of choice for business success.

- The Importance of the "Tribe." Mr. O'Connor will move on to look at the importance of identity to all of the stakeholders in business and how that influences strategic choices.

- Strategic Business Innovation—The MNC/Indigenous Challenge. "Keepin' on keepin' on"—finally, Mr. O'Connor will put forward some ideas on the need for new business models to resolve the cul-de-sac of "task-only" outsourced MNC activity. Using Ireland as an example, he will look at how we might forge new collaborative structures which will benefit not only the MNC but substantially transform indigenous industry.

Mr. O'Connor is Managing Director of Hewlett-Packard's European Software Centre. He is a 30-year veteran of the ICT sector, 15 of those years with the *Irish Times* where he played a leading role as IT manager in the delivery of the "new technology" in the 1970s. He joined Digital in 1986 as Ireland IS manager and moved to his first European role based in Galway in 1990. He was Worldwide Technology manager for Compaq's Software Manufacturing & Distribution business from 1995 to 2000 and was appointed Managing Director of the European Software Centre in 2001. The Galway operation has continued to develop its technology and business operations in HP. The center specializes in R&D in high performance technical computing, semantic Web technology and systems management tools and processes, software publishing services for the software industry, and software and Web management services for large multi-national enterprises.

Index of Contributors